Women in Ireland, 1800–1918

A Documentary History

MARIA LUDDY

CORK UNIVERSITY PRESS

First published in 1995 by
Cork University Press
University College
Cork
Ireland

© Maria Luddy 1995

Reprinted 1999, 2002, 2005, 2006

British Library Cataloguing in Publication Data
A CIP catalogue record for this book is available from the British Library

ISBN 1 85918 037 X hardback
1 85918 038 8 paperback

Typeset by Seton Music Graphics, Bantry, Co. Cork

Printed & bound by Antony Rowe Ltd, Eastbourne

for Rosemary Clarke

Contents

Motherhood

Women and Welfare

PART II   EDUCATION

INTRODUCTION 89

PART III   WORK

INTRODUCTION 157

PART IV   POLITICS

Formal Political Involvement

The Suffrage Issue

Local Franchises

THE EASTER RISING 1916

A Personal Experience of the Dublin Rebellion

A Woman Recounts her Experience in the Easter Rising

THE BRITISH ARMY AND WOMEN REBELS

CUMANN NA MBAN ADVISES VOTERS IN 1918

Other Political Movements

WOMEN AND SOCIALISM IN IRELAND

IRISH WOMEN OPPOSE HOME RULE

IRISH WOMEN AND THE CO-OPERATIVE MOVEMENT

Acknowledgements

This book has taken more than seven years to compile. Along the way I have incurred debts amongst friends and fellow scholars. My thanks goes to all those who suggested documents, and to those who supplied me with copies of material. I am grateful also for the help provided by archivists and librarians in our national repositories, the National Library and the National Archives, in Dublin, and the Public Record Office of Northern Ireland. David Sheehy of the Dublin Diocesan Archives has always proved the most accommodating and helpful of archivists. Renagh Lohan of the National Archives gave useful advice on sources. Though not all of the documents recommended to me made it into this collection I am sure that they will not remain unused. Cliona Murphy made a number of useful suggestions about sources in the early days of this project. Her advice was much appreciated. My particular thanks goes to Sr Mercedes of the Convent of Mercy, Baggot Street, Dublin for her assistance in locating photographs. Virginia Crossman, not only discovered and retrieved documents, but also offered numerous suggestions on how to improve the text.

I owe a debt of gratitude to a number of secretaries in the Institute of Education at Warwick. Heather Meldrum and Sue Bawden worked evenings and weekends on numerous, and I am sure they believed never ending, drafts with humour and wonderful competency. They were ably abetted in the last stages by Tracey Bale and Pam Charlton.

My thanks must also go to those who worked on this project at Cork University Press. My debt to Rosemary Clarke lies beyond words. This book is dedicated to her for the work done and that yet to happen.

Abbreviations

Illustrations

General Introduction

J ANE AUSTEN, THROUGH the words of the female protagonist in *Northanger Abbey*, passed this celebrated judgement on history texts:

History, real solemn history, I cannot be interested in . . . I read it a little as a duty, but it tells me nothing that does not either vex or weary me. The quarrels of popes and kings, with wars or pestilences, in every page; the men all so good for nothing, and hardly any women at all – it is very tiresome.[1]

Irish women have only begun to feature in our history textbooks in any significant way in the very recent past. For the historian, women's history presents an exciting challenge. For the interested reader, teacher and pupil of Irish history, a whole new area of historical study is unfolding. Irish women's history asks new questions of old sources, queries the very nature of historical study in this country and constitutes, arguably, the most important new field of Irish history to have emerged in the last fifty years.[2]

This collection is intended to act both as an introduction to Irish women's history for those coming to it for the first time, and as a source book for those already familiar with the subject. It will, I hope, be used in schools where women's history has, as yet, gained little ground. Introducing women into the history classroom is a stimulating experience for teachers and students of all age groups. The documents also provide material that can be utilised in women's studies classes. They raise many issues about women's lives and will, I hope, provoke awkward questions for students and teachers, questions which will reveal the complexity of people's lives in past times.

This volume is focused on women's own experiences; its aim is to outline the variety of thoughts, deeds and actions which made up women's lives in the period 1800–1918. As far as possible, women's own voices have been used, but women, like men, do not live in isolation in society and in a number of instances I have used the opinions and perceptions of men to throw light on the position of women in society.

Much of the material presented here was written by women such as Anna Haslam, Isabella Tod and Louie Bennett, who were well known in the nineteenth and early twentieth century, but who have now been almost com-

1 Jane Austen, *Northanger Abbey* (Harmondsworth, 1972), pp 123–4.
2 See the select bibliography at the end of this book for recent writings on Irish women's history.

pletely forgotten. One aim of this book is to remember these women who played such an active part in shaping modern Irish society. Although women's history is not about creating a hierarchy of 'worthy women', the inclusion and recognition of these women will, perhaps, raise questions in the readers' minds about how easy it is to 'forget' women. Many of the documents refer to the thousands of unknown and anonymous women who worked as agricultural labourers, domestic servants, within the home, in convents, hospitals, etc.; they too played a vital role in constructing society. They were active agents, shaping their own lives and the lives of their communities.

Although Irish women's history has developed quite strongly since the late 1970s, we are still at the stage of recovery. We have not yet identified the major trends and developments that have shaped the lives of Irish women from the earliest times, and this work does not intend to do that, rather it allows an exploration of various themes, subjects and forces that shaped women's existence.

There are four central themes: private life, education, work and politics. There are obvious omissions also. For example, it was originally intended to include a section on women who emigrated from Ireland in the nineteenth and twentieth centuries. However, the available material is so overwhelming that a short piece here would not have done the subject justice. There are other subjects which are touched on in this history, such as women and criminality, women in workhouses and various other institutions, and issues such as birth control and sexuality which deserve broader study. The extensive bibliography will act as a guide for those who wish to pursue particular topics in more detail and will, I hope, suggest new avenues of research.

Various types of documents have been used in order to provide as broad a range of sources as possible. I have included extracts from official parliamentary reports, political pamphlets, private and public letters, newspaper articles and advertisements, women's periodicals, diary entries, annual reports of various organisations, petitions to government, biographies and autobiographies. The selection of documents was made using a number of criteria: first of all the selection was focused on accounts that were representative of women's experiences and feelings. It was also intended, as far as possible, to take into account the experiences of women of different classes.

It is perhaps only in the personal diaries and letters of women that we find a true unmediated reflection of women about themselves, their own feelings and lives. Most of the documentary evidence reproduced here was published for public consumption in some form: as newspaper or journal articles, as evidence before various commissions, or as the reflections of observers on women's behaviour or work habits. In those instances the writing serves a particular function, either in propagating a cause, advocating a particular form of behaviour, or arousing public opinion to the rights or wrongs of particular issues or concerns. Those who had access to the print media tended to be well educated and from the middle and upper classes. It is very rare to have the unmediated voices of the poor, whether male or female, emerging in their own words in print. Even where poorer women were witnesses before commissions, they were not talking about themselves spontaneously, but replying to questions to which they might have a prepared answer. But that is not to say that we cannot see poorer women, or witness their lives through second-hand material. For example, James Greenwood, in his article on the 'wrens' of the Curragh (see document 51) allows us to understand, probably quite unintentionally, how these women organised their own lives and made their own choices about how they wished to live.

The collection is divided into four sections. In many ways these are artificial divisions since women's lives were not compartmentalised and separated out as they are in this book. The divisions do however serve a purpose in that they show the development of issues over a period of time. For example, the section on education shows a very clear difference in the opportunities available to women, particularly in relation to secondary and third-level education, in the twentieth century as opposed to the early nineteenth century. The sections on private and public reveal how little perceptions of women's function changed over the period. This is especially clear in relation to prescriptive literature.

Change, when it occurred, came about slowly. There were no watersheds that fundamentally altered the nature of women's place in society, or that radically changed their economic or social contributions to society. Even granting women the vote, seen by many suffragists as *the* tool for social change, did little to alter society or women's place in it. But it is clear from this collection that women of all classes shaped their own lives, made choices, however limited their circumstances, and were active agents of change within their own communities and within society at large. Middle-class women, in particular, became more vocal and articulate in their demands and concerns as the century progressed.

Women acted individually and collectively to bring about changes in their lives. They were instrumental in shaping Irish society and its values. This collection of documents ends in 1918 when Irish women acquired the vote, the culmination of many of the political activities that had engaged women's interests in the period. But in Ireland the winning of the vote did not mark the end of an era. The War of Independence, the creation of the Northern Irish state, the signing of the Treaty and the ensuing civil war created new Irelands, in which women found themselves operating in a different political climate, a climate which remained fundamentally hostile to them in their fight for recognition of their rights.

Part I

PUBLIC AND PRIVATE

Lady Morgan, Sydney Owenson (?1776–1859)
(National Library of Ireland)

INTRODUCTION

THE REV. JOHN Gregg, a Dublin cleric, in a sermon delivered in 1856, expressed views which were commonly held amongst clerics about women and their role in society. 'The *great* and *weighty* business of life', he stated, 'devolves on men, but important business belongs to *women*.' 'Women', he proclaimed, 'had the honourable employments of instructing childhood . . . their labour might be in the sickroom, the chambers of affliction, in the haunts of misery and amongst the struggling poor.'[1] The prevailing ideology, being supported here by Gregg, was that a woman existed for the benefit of her family. The perfect wife/mother was gentle, kind, patient, moral and spiritual. She tended to her duties within the domestic sphere while her husband, or the male members of her family, went forth into the harsh world of commerce and politics, the public world of work and money. This ideology of the separate spheres decreed a place for women in society based on the exercise of domestic duties, to which a woman was considered particularly suited because of her physical and mental abilities. Women's role in society was generally seen as one of submissive passivity.

The way women should behave in society and within their families had long been a concern of moralists, philosophers, clerics, scientists and doctors. Over the last two hundred years, at least, writers, both men and women, have been anxious to ensure that women conduct themselves with respectability and propriety in society. They have also advocated the importance of women's role in the home as wife and mother. Prescriptive literature, which relates how women should behave, flourished in nineteenth and early twentieth-century Ireland. Much of this literature was geared toward the better-off members of society, but poorer women were also expected to acquire those virtues of gentility, sobriety, passivity, and humility, which were deemed especially 'natural' and fitting to women. The models of perfection created and expected by these prescriptive writers had little relevance to the way women lived their lives. Indeed, the flourishing of such writing suggests an unease amongst commentators with the ways in which women were *actually* living their lives. Much prescriptive literature, often written by women

1 Rev. John Gregg, *Women: A Lecture Delivered by the Rev. John Gregg, 28th February 1856* (Dublin, 1856).

themselves, was created by the middle classes. Such literature attempted to suggest and idealise a way of life which accepted definitions of subordination as women's natural response to the world. Women were expected to remain in the domestic sphere looking after husband and children. They could extend their sphere by engaging in charitable work, which was essentially a continuation of their domestic functions within another setting. Such an expectation was made of all women, no matter what their class.

Historians of women have long been concerned with the divisions that arose between the private world of the home and the public world of work and politics, and there is an extensive literature on these debates.[1] The division, however, is to a great extent artificial. Individuals' private lives are rarely separated totally from the public world, reality is far more complex. Though activities may take place in the private or domestic sphere, they are written about and judged in the public world. Similarly, even individuals confined to the home have some degree of interaction with the 'public' world. Life was very different to that described in guide books, manuals, or 'improving' literature. There were many ways in which women escaped the confining restrictions of this type of ideology. Numerous women ignored the pre- scriptions completely. Others, from necessity, were forced into the 'public' world of work in order to maintain themselves or their families. Middle-class women found their way not only into the 'public' world of work but also, and with much opposition, into the 'public' world of politics. Life was difficult and harsh for poorer women, who had neither the time nor the inclination to abide by a code of femininity that bore no relevance to their lives. Whatever the prescriptive literature demanded of women, it is clear that, in the period covered by this study at least, Irish women were active agents of change, not only in their own households but also in the wider world.

MARRIAGE, MATERNITY AND SINGLEHOOD

While numerous Irish writers were concerned with idealising the role of women in society, women themselves were busy with the realities of living. Marriage was the 'lot' of the majority of Irish women who stayed in Ireland during the nineteenth and twentieth centuries. It is difficult to assess marriage in the early nineteenth century on any statistical basis since evidence such as that provided to the Poor Inquiry commissioners of the 1830s, and census data, give conflicting impressions. The evidence of the Poor Inquiry indicates that the 'lower classes' in Irish society tended to be 'imprudent' in their approach to marriage. They also appear to have

1 See for example, Barbara Welter, 'The cult of true womanhood, 1820–1860', *American Quarterly*, 18 (1966); Leonore Davidoff and Catherine Hall, *Family Fortunes* (London, 1987); Linda Kerber, 'Separate spheres, female worlds, women's place: the rhetoric of women's history', *Journal of American History*, 75, 1(1988), pp 9–39.

married earlier than better-off farmers. However, marriage for those above the level of subsistence farmer, cottier or labourer, was, according to one recent historian of marriage, a carefully negotiated bargain. Sean Connolly argues that the 'match' was an established feature of pre-famine marriage and its central element revolved around a bride-to-be providing a suitable dowry for her prospective in-laws.[1] Marriage for poorer women in pre-famine Ireland can be seen as an insurance against utter destitution. It was very difficult for single women to survive economically in a society that provided little in the way of suitable occupation. Poor women, as we will see later, played a vital role in the family economy. For the poor, marriage allowed the development of an interdependent unit whose members supported each other economically and emotionally.

Post-Famine Ireland is noted for its high levels of permanent celibacy. In 1871 43 per cent of all women aged 15 to 45 were married, but by 1911 this percentage had fallen to 36.[2] In 1841 the average age of marriage for an Irish woman was from 24 to 25 years, but by 1911 it was postponed to 28 years. For Irish men, the average age of marriage had risen to 33 years in 1911, from 28 years in 1841.[3] In the 1850s, Irish levels of permanent celibacy were roughly one in ten in the age group 45 to 54. On the eve of the First World War, about one-quarter of the adult Irish population was unmarried.[4] Historians are still debating the causes of the high celibacy levels and no definite conclusions have been reached. To account for the decline in marriage, it has been suggested that the process of farm consolidation which occurred after the Famine, and a move towards impartible inheritance, led to delayed or less frequent marriage. The inability to accumulate a dowry may also have delayed or postponed marriage. High levels of emigration may also have reduced opportunities for appropriate matches by reducing the pool of individuals from which partners could be chosen. A more recent view of the high levels of celibacy maintains that increasing economic security and the availability of marriage substitutes, such as nephews and nieces to provide emotional support, may have made marriage a less attractive option for numbers of individuals.[5] However, despite the high levels of celibacy, it is true that most people in post-Famine Ireland did marry.

Parents tended to exert a powerful control on the choice of marriage partners for their offspring. Matchmakers were used to assure social and economic compatibility. The families involved in the match would carefully evaluate the

1 Sean Connolly, 'Marriage in pre-famine Ireland', in Art Cosgrove, (ed.), *Marriage in Ireland* (Dublin, 1985), pp 78–93.

2 Mary Daly, *Social and Economic History of Ireland Since 1800* (Dublin, 1981), p 92.

3 Liam Kennedy and Leslie Clarkson, 'Birth, death and exile: Irish population history, 1700–1921', in B. J. Graham and L. J. Proudfoot, (eds.), *An Historical Geography of Ireland* (London, 1993), p 167.

4 Kennedy and Clarkson, 'Birth, death and exile', pp 158–84.

5 Timothy Guinnane, 'Migration marriage and household formation: the Irish at the turn of the century', (abstract of Ph. D thesis), *Irish Economic and Social History*, 25 (1988), pp 105–6.

economic benefits to be had from a particular marriage. The payment of the dowry, which went to the husband's family, generally went to ensuring the marriage of another female member of his family. Marriage was, particularly in post-Famine Ireland, a means of transmitting property. Affection or love were not major considerations, rather economic security and stability, and the family alliances formed, were the prime considerations. For a number of women, arranged marriages were not acceptable, and the opportunity to emigrate often allowed a woman the chance to remain single or to have greater personal choice in her marriage partner.

Emigration rates for Irish women were high in the nineteenth century. England and America were the favoured destinations of the majority of these women. There were significant levels of emigration from Ireland before the Famine with up to two million people leaving the country as seasonal or permanent migrants by 1845. In the post-Famine period from 1871 to 1911, 86,294 men emigrated while 89,407 women did so.[1] The pattern of migration for Irish women differed from the normal European pattern in that they tended to emigrate as single women rather than in family groups. There are numerous and complex reasons why people emigrate. For Irish women, especially in the post-Famine period, changing work patterns resulting from new landholding arrangements, the lack of employment opportunities in industrial work, the inferior status of daughters with regard to inheritance, and the lack of marriage opportunities may have made emigration an attractive option. While economic considerations were always important factors in the emigration decision, other less tangible considerations were also involved. The desire to control her own finances, to choose a marriage partner, and to achieve a certain level of independence may all have played a part in such decisions.

For those women who remained in Ireland and married, the production of children was the expected outcome. Motherhood conferred high status on married women and it dominated their lives. Post-Famine Ireland had one of the highest fertility rates in Europe. In 1911 the average family included up to seven children.[2] It is unclear what the level of infant mortality was for much of the nineteenth century. Kennedy and Clarkson state that in 1915 the rate was 69.9 per 1,000 births, apart from twenty-seven town districts where the rate was 134.4 per 1,000 births.[3] For families who could afford servants or 'help', the burden of motherhood and housework could be relieved. For many women, however, particularly those in poor health, pregnancy and birth could be a traumatic and dangerous experience. Women's involvement with their children was a source of power for them within the household, and was often a source of powerful emotion. While motherhood was the ideal for women who married, it could also impose a

1 Robert E. Kennedy, *The Irish: Emigration, Marriage and Fertility* (London, 1973), p 78.
2 Kennedy and Clarkson, 'Birth, death and exile', p 169.
3 Kennedy and Clarkson, 'Birth, death and exile', p 171.

financial and emotional burden, which women, or their partners, were unwilling to bear. It is clear that not all women, married or single, welcomed children into their lives. For an unmarried woman, an unwanted pregnancy could be disastrous. Illegitimate children were an economic burden. They caused scandal and loss of status and seriously damaged a woman's marriage prospects. A pregnancy outside marriage was often kept hidden from friends and family for fear of disgrace, or the loss of support either from the family or an employer. Not all mothers felt an attachment to their offspring and there were a number of ways women could rid themselves of unwanted children. The two most common methods were desertion and infanticide. Such incidents found their way into the public sphere through police notices and newspaper reports. There was, indeed, very little that was 'private' in Ireland, very little that was not discussed or written of in the public domain.

It is impossible to measure accurately the frequency of child abandonment and infanticide in Irish history. Trials for infanticide were infrequent, though a glance at any run of national and local newspapers in the nineteenth century reveals the frequent discovery of the bodies of infants. There were more cases of infanticide than ever came to light through the courts.[1] Some mothers obviously abandoned a child believing that someone, even if it was only a workhouse official, would take care of it. For other women, murder was the only solution and infanticide may indeed have been practised as a form of birth control in Ireland.

As previously noted, not all women could expect to marry in post-Famine Ireland. Table 1.1, below, outlines the numbers and percentages of women who were single, married or widowed in Ireland in the period from 1851 to 1901. Single and widowed women over the age of fifteen outnumbered married women at all times. Those who could not maintain themselves from their own resources, or who could not find adequate remunerative employment, were forced to rely on the generosity of relatives and friends, the charity of lay philanthropic institutions or the workhouse in order to survive. Women without husbands, particularly those who had children, were prone to poverty.

State provision for the poor consisted of an extensive dispensary system, and a state-supported hospital system which was well in place by the 1840s. The major institution for the relief of the poor was the workhouse. The Irish poor law, which was introduced in 1838, divided the country into 130 administrative divisions, designated unions, each of which constructed its own workhouse. From the 1850s women were to be found in greater numbers in workhouses than men. The entrance of women into workhouses tended to be seasonal, and coincided with fluctuations in employment, particularly agricultural employment. As the century progressed, the workhouses increasingly became medical centres used by the ill, young and infirm. Women

---

1 For some recent work on infanticide see James Kelly, 'Infanticide in eighteenth-century Ireland', *Irish Economic and Social History*, 19 (1992), pp 5–26.

also entered charitable institutions, such as homes for the elderly or sick, in greater numbers than men.[1] A combination of circumstances made women more vulnerable to economic hardship than men. Lack of employment opportunities, poor pay, lack of marketable skills, life crises such as desertion by a spouse, the incapacity or death of a spouse, pregnancy, ill health, the number of dependent children, age and family support systems, all influenced women's capacity to remain economically independent. While women found their way into state institutions of relief, they also made use of the myriad of charitable organisations established by men and women throughout this period.

Table 1.1: Women in Ireland: Single, Married and Widowed, 1851–1901

Year	Total number of females	Single < 15	Single >15	Married	Widowed
1851	3,361,755	1,335,033*	820,118^	867,973	338,631
%		39.71	24.39	25.82	10.07
1871	2,772,624	942,066	775,769	792,455	262,334
%		33.97	27.97	28.58	9.46
1901	2,258,735	665,710	791,087	590,907	211,031
%		29.47	35.02	26.16	9.34

Source: W. E. Vaughan and A. J. Fitzpatrick, *Irish Historical Statistics, Population 1821–1971* (Dublin,1978), pp 87–9.
* single, less than 17 years; ^ single, greater than 17 years.

For women who sought relief, charitable societies played a specific, functional role. Poor women used their facilities to tide them over lean periods and were adept at using whatever resources or facilities that presented themselves. Thus 'child-hawking' (doc.50), for example, can be seen as a strategy of survival. The 'wrens' of the Curragh (doc.51) can be viewed as a group of women who maintained their own support network in the face of social ostracism. Women who entered Magdalen asylums, or homes for 'fallen' women (doc.20) often used the facilities to 'retire' from their occupation, or at least to take respite.[2]

Many middle- and upper-class women established charitable societies throughout the nineteenth century to cater for the needs of the destitute, abandoned and orphaned. While women of all religious persuasions engaged in such enterprises, Catholic nuns organised, and managed, the most extensive network of charitable organisations and societies. Most charitable societies which had been organised by lay Catholics were eventually given over to the care of nuns. From mid-century, while lay Catholic women continued to engage in philanthropic activity on a personal basis, only a handful established

1 For further details on the extent of poverty amongst women, see Maria Luddy, *Women and Philanthropy in Nineteenth-Century Ireland* (Cambridge, 1995), pp 13–17.
2 See Maria Luddy, 'Prostitution and rescue work in nineteenth-century Ireland', in Maria Luddy and Cliona Murphy, (eds.), *Women Surviving: Studies in Irishwomen's History in the 19th and 20th Centuries* (Dublin, 1990), pp 51–84.

charitable institutions, none of which were to remain independent of church control.[1] Lay charitable initiative remained predominantly in the hands of women of denominations other than Catholicism. It can be argued that the takeover of charitable work by nuns neutralised lay Catholic women's instincts for social criticism or social change. Social activism through philanthropic endeavour was to lead many Protestant women to the cause of suffrage, and into those societies which sought legislative solutions for social problems. Catholic women are notable for their absence from these relatively radical organisations. It was however, religious communities which built the infra-structure of social welfare which bound the people to the church and the church to the people in nineteenth-century Ireland.

From the time of the Famine, there was growing concern amongst the middle classes about the idea of respectability, particularly the idea of sexual respectability. Throughout the nineteenth century, many charitable workers were concerned with the possible sexual corruption of young women and instituted refuges which offered young 'respectable' women shelter and train-ing for future employment. Those who were not considered 'respectable', prostitutes or unmarried mothers, found shelter in Magdalen asylums, peni-tent refuges or the workhouse. The first lay association to deal specifically with the plight of unmarried mothers was the Catholic Rotunda Girls' Aid Society which was established in 1880. In the following year a group of Protestant women organised the Dublin Hospital Girls' Aid Association. The justification for these societies lay in the belief that these unmarried mothers were not to blame for their situation and that help, provided at an early stage, would prevent their further degradation. The help provided was conditional and not all unmarried mothers were acceptable to the committees. Careful investigations had to be made regarding their circumstances to ensure that they could benefit from any aid provided. The societies put the babies out to nurse and the mothers were expected to pay for this service. If such payment was not forthcoming, the children were quickly placed in the workhouse. Charity was rarely provided gratuitously. Often its recipients had to prove their worthiness to receive aid, in this instance they had to take some respon-sibility for their children.

Three major religious denominations functioned in Ireland in the nineteenth-century: Catholicism, Anglicanism and Presbyterianism. The most reliable early figures for affiliation to a particular denomination come from the census of 1861, which showed that Catholics made up almost 78 per cent of the total population, members of the Church of Ireland (Anglicans) made up 12 per cent, and Presbyterians 9 per cent, the remainder being divided amongst non-believers, Methodists, Congregationalists, Unitarians, Baptists, Jews and Quakers, amongst others.[2] There is no doubt that religion played an

1 Luddy, *Women and Philanthropy, passim.*
2 Sean Connolly, *Religion and Society in Nineteenth-Century Ireland* (Dundalk, 1985), pp 3–6.

9

important role in the lives of women during this period. Religion not only defined and limited women's place in society, particularly the place of lay women, but it also, ironically, opened a door on the world of work for those women willing to form and join religious communities. In many instances lay women were enabled by the demands of 'Christian duty' to develop public lives and careers in philanthropy. For middle-class women, philanthropy became an acceptable means of conducting a moral mission in public, and such activity brought them very clearly into the public realm where they controlled finances, raised funds, ran institutions and catered for the needs of thousands of the poor and destitute.

Religion, an affair of conscience and privacy, also had a very public face in Ireland; in the rituals of the various churches and congregations, and in the setting up of Catholic female religious congregations. In 1800 there were 6 religious orders with 120 nuns inhabiting 11 houses in the country; by 1851 that number had increased to 1,500 nuns residing in 95 convents and to over 8,000 by 1901 with a total of 35 religious orders or congregations.[1] The establishment of convents allowed a freedom for women far beyond that which was available to lay women. Convent expansion provided a very large number of single women with the opportunity of engaging in socially useful work at a time when women generally were denied such opportunity. The work of nuns was innovative in many respects. They improved nursing skills in hospitals and they built up an extensive network of welfare organisations that catered for the poor. Nuns also ran schools, orphanages, reformatories and industrial schools, Magdalen asylums and homes for the elderly. There was no aspect of charitable endeavour in which nuns did not establish themselves as workers. Convents were also institutions of power. Within these walls women could, and did, create their own systems of labour and some had the opportunity of rising to positions of power and authority unmatched by lay women in secular society. The need for social compatibility allowed for the development of a class-based system of power within convents, which was most obvious in the distinctions that existed between choir and lay sisters. Choir nuns came from privileged backgrounds and engaged in the public work of the community. Lay nuns were generally less well educated and from much poorer backgrounds than choir nuns and they carried out the domestic tasks of the community. They had little say in the managerial structures of the community.[2] While nuns describe, and have described, their entries to religious communities as a 'vocation', this rhetoric should not blind us to the more realistic expectations that nuns, as women, might have had for convent life. From a social perspective, women's religious communities provided an esteemed alternative to marriage and motherhood. The extent of convent

1 Tony Fahey, 'Nuns and the Catholic church in Ireland in the nineteenth century', in Mary Cullen, (ed.), *Girls Don't Do Honours: Irish Women in Education in the 19th and 20th Centuries* (Dublin, 1987), p 7.

2 Caitríona Clear, *Nuns in Nineteenth-Century Ireland* (Dublin, 1987), *passim*.

networks allowed women to choose the type of convent, and hence the type of work, which best suited their interests, needs and abilities. It is hardly surprising that many women were attracted by convent life in this period. The active life of women who joined religious congregations was just one example of how women overcame the prescriptions of weakness and timidity attributed to them by their contemporaries.

PRESCRIPTIVE LITERATURE

The Story of Mary Murphy

Doc. 1.1: Mary Leadbeater, *Cottage Biography* (Dublin, 1822).

Mary Leadbeater (1758–1826) was a Quaker who lived in Ballitore, County Kildare. She married a small farmer in 1791 and became the postmistress of Ballitore. She is most famous for her work, The Annals of Ballitore, *which was first published in 1862. This recounts the lives of the people in her village between 1766 and 1824. She also wrote a number of moral tales. Her* Dialogues Among the Irish Peasantry *(Dublin, 1811) was an attempt to instruct the poorer members of society. Her* Cottage Biography *(Dublin, 1822) continues with tales of the people in her locality. Though not as overly moralistic as some of her other works, there is an obvious strand of moralising in this piece. Mary Murphy is hardworking and, though clearly very poor, manages to practise the best of habits. She is maternal, protective and teaches her children to 'practise' cleanliness and industry.*

Mary Murphy was the wife of a person whose livelihood depended on his pen, who was sometimes employed as a schoolmaster and sometimes as a clerk. He died, and left his Mary a young widow with one child, a son. The support of herself and her boy now depended on her own exertions. She took a nurse child, the daughter of a Dublin tradesman, for whom she was well paid for a year and a half, when the tradesman died, and left his wife in such distressed circumstances as not to be able to pay for her child. The nurse, who tenderly loved her little charge, and knew she could not be compelled to give her up till the debt was paid, was well enough pleased to have her left to her care. She reared her and her own boy together, and if any difference of affection is shewn, the young protegée has the greater share. She dresses her neatly, and likes to see her thus adorned. Both children are sent to school, when Mary is not employed out of doors; when she is, the adopted daughter stays within, and is taught, by example and precept, to practise cleanliness and industry. Poorly dressed as Mary is when at work, she keeps some decent clothes to wear occasionally. She plants and digs her potatoes in a little garden behind the house, and buys the remainder of what she uses. The pig she rears enables her to buy her rent, one guinea a year, and to provide other necessaries; an uncle lives with her, who is elderly, and rather weak of intellect, but works when he can get work, and gives his earnings to her; they are by no means adequate to his support, but his benevolent niece makes him kindly welcome. Her little girl is now about twelve years old; about a year ago she took her to see her mother, and to make a formal demand of what was due to her, without which she was told, that she could not insist upon keeping the child. The mother could barely support herself, and was therefore totally unable to discharge the arrears due for her

12

daughter. Yet she was desirous of having her and calling on her when her nurse was out, took her to walk and to buy a cake. When Mary returned and missed the little girl, she felt the alarm and anxiety of a mother, and ceased not in her search till she found where she was concealed, locked up in a room, from whence she replied to her nurse's voice, with screams of distress. The nurse had recourse to law to recover her, and the child joyfully returned to her protecting arms, and to her beloved home.

A Clergyman Tells Women What is Expected of Them

Doc. 1.2: Rev. John Gregg, *Women: A Lecture Delivered in Trinity Church . . .* (Dublin, 1856).

Leadbeater's story is particularly concerned with how poor women behave, and such writings continued to be a feature throughout the nineteenth and twentieth centuries. Writing in 1856, the Reverend John Gregg, a Church of Ireland cleric, focuses his attention on the better-off women in society. He uses the Bible to support his claims for women's subordinate role in the world. He sees men and women having distinct functions in society. He clearly supports the ideology of the separate spheres, believing this to be sanctioned by God.

. . . I do not address children today; I do not address mothers or daughters, as such; I do not address wives or young women, as such; all these have their own peculiar responsibilities and duties: my lecture is intended for *women*. There are *two* points especially to which I wish to direct the attention of you, women. There are two things which you ought to desire – which it is your duty to desire – which it is your interest to desire, and which it is for the good of society – for the everlasting benefit of yourselves and others – that you should desire, and these are, *excellence* and *usefulness*. Excellence has reference to yourselves – usefulness to others. Excellence has reference to your character, and is *internal*; and usefulness has reference to your conduct, and is *external*. There is a great difference between desiring excellence, and desiring to *excel*. I do not ask you to excel; I do not ask you to desire to excel, or to wish to excel, or to pray to excel; but I do ask you to think, to strive, to pray that you may attain to excellence. A desire to excel often proceeds from pride or vanity, but the desire of excellence always proceeds from virtue or grace. When we desire to excel, we are apt to envy those whom we do not surpass, and to be jealous of their superiority; and we are likely to use means to bring them down to our own level, when we cannot reach to their height. But this desire of excellence, in man or woman, is a virtuous passion, and may be a gracious one. I suppose I need not tell you that you are on a low level with us, as fallen creatures, and that you are our equals as redeemed sinners. You are capable, equally with us, of being restored to the divine favour, and of being possessed again of the divine image. *We* have features peculiar to us as men, and we have also our peculiar capabilities and responsibilities. The *great* and *weighty* business of life devolves on *men*, but important business belongs to *women*. The great dangers of life men are first and chiefly exposed to; but women have their dangers too. The larger portion of the labours of life – of public life – fall almost exclusively to the lot of men; but a most important portion of the duties of life, especially of private life, falls to the share of women. God has adapted our sex to the peculiar duties to which we are especially called, and for which you are not so well fitted; and He has adapted your sex to the peculiar duties to which you are called, and for which we are not at all fitted. Society does best when each sex performs the duties for which it is especially ordained.

Very little mention is made of women in the early history of the world. Compared with what is said of men, the information about women is very scanty. In the first six chapters of Genesis, in that small portion of Holy Writ, how very large a space do men occupy in the transactions of the world, and how little do you. They occupy much more than you in the history of the patriarchal times, and in the prophetical times also. According to profane history, women were, in heathen times and countries, as they are still in those countries, degraded. In eastern climes, though women are not so degraded *now*, perhaps, as they formerly were, yet woman is in a lower position far than God originally assigned her, and in a position far inferior to that to which, in later times, Christianity has raised her. I need not tell you who are acquainted with the present state of the world, that in nations more civilised, but not truly Christianised, woman – though not degraded, not in as low a condition as in Mahometan[1] or heathen countries – yet has not that weight and worth which properly belong to her, and as she has in countries that are both civilised and Christianised – in countries, I mean, that are blessed with the Christianity of the Bible. It is the Christianity of the Bible that has given you your proper elevation. I speak not to you, women in the congregation, who may be placed over families, households, and establishments, and who are at that period of life when Christian duties are devolved upon you of the most important and weighty kind. You, my friends, are more indebted to the religion of the Gospel than even we men are. You should feel almost a deeper interest in it than men. It has done more for you in this world than for them, and as much for you with respect to the world to come.

1 Followers of Islam.

The Nun of Kenmare on Woman's Work as Wife and Mother

Doc. 1.3: M. F. Cusack,[1] *Women's Work in Modern Society* (London, 1874).

Margaret Anna Cusack (1829–1899) was better known as the Nun of Kenmare. She was a wealthy convert from the Anglican church and had spent five years in a Protestant sisterhood before her conversion to Catholicism. She joined the Poor Clares in Newry in 1859, and when a branch convent was founded in Kenmare in 1861, she was one of the six nuns sent to form that community. Cusack was a prolific writer and her publications went some way to support the convent. During the 1880s Cusack had major disagreements with bishops and priests. She left the Kenmare convent and went to Knock where she succeeded in establishing a convent and a new community called the Sisters of Peace. Again, difficulties with the clergy forced her to leave Knock. She made her way to America and there founded more communities, but she was dogged by clerical and secular opposition. In 1888 she resigned as Mother-General of the Sisters of Peace and left the Catholic church in the same year. She returned to England and died in Leamington Spa in 1899. Cusack was very conscious of the class divisions that existed in society and she supported such distinctions. There were, however, in her eyes, expectations which could and should be made of all women. The importance of religion in women lives could not be overestimated: it was something to guide a woman's behaviour. The role of mother was one which was particularly important. Mothers were the 'regenerators of the world'.

. . . Every mother is forming the future generation, . . . every mother is affixing her stamp and seal to the society which will be when she perhaps has gone to her account.

It is an awful thing to think how far we can control and influence the destinies of an entire race, of a race preparing for its future life.

Mothers! arise in the greatness of your power, in the splendour of your strength, and be the regenerators of the world. You have in your hands the making or marring of immortal destinies; do not, I beg of you, be content with anything less. Use your God-given dignity; do not, I pray you, turn from it with the disdain of ignorance or the indolence of indifference. The evil one knows your power well, and lays his plans artfully to undermine it; if he even once persuades you that it is anything less great than it is, he has gained a point, he has taken a fortress. . .

It is scarcely necessary to say much of the influence of women in society. It is unquestionably great; and every woman, married or single, has a most sacred duty in this respect. How much sin may be prevented by the example of a good woman! How much virtue may be recommended by the life of a holy woman! But you will say, true; what then? we do not propose to be saints. But you must be saints, you must be holy, if you wish to enter heaven, I pray you, do not deceive yourself; what you are here,

---

1 M.F. refers to Mary Francis, Cusack's name in religion.

that you will be hereafter. The company you keep here, will be the company with which you will find yourself hereafter. To be holy is a question of salvation, for the unholy can never enter heaven.

You must act, speak, and live, and dress in society as a Christian woman. Is your life in society fashioned on the precepts of the gospel? Do you live in a round of fashionable amusements, and think little of God? Do you content yourself, or stifle your conscience, with going to a retreat once, perhaps twice, in the year, where you listen to exhortations not to love the world, and go back to it more than ever devoted to its service?

Do you go to God's house in the morning, dressed like a Christian woman, and to the opera in the evening, dressed like a shameless heathen? Is this the example you give to society? If so, we can scarcely wonder that Christianity is not thought of much account; that those men, who keep so sharp an eye on Catholic practices, and who know all too well what Catholic women should be, are scandalised or amused. Do you leave the support of God's church, and of works of charity, to the poor, who give liberally out of their poverty, while you give little and grudgingly out of your abundance?

Are you anxious to be thought well of by the world, to be esteemed for your liberal opinions? Believe me, you are only heartily despised for them. The world expects consistency, and if it does not practise religion, it expects you to practise it. What is your connection in society?

Is it known that you, at least, will not indulge in conversations about the least scandal, will not discuss before the other sex subjects which should not be mentioned even in private? You talk of converting others; but conversions are the fruit of martyrdom, and there are other martyrdoms besides the martyrdoms of blood. Do you martyr yourself? Do you die daily by a life of Christian piety, of Christian charity, and of Christian renunciation of the world? . . .

It needs scarcely to be mentioned how prominent the names of women are in the noble army of martyrs, how prompt they were to carry out their belief practically, even while such consistency was at the cost of life. And why, indeed, should it not be so, since they looked for another and a better city – a city whose builder and maker is God – a city of peace, a home of eternal beatitude.

Is this the metal of which the women of the nineteenth century are made? Are the women who will not sacrifice a little for God, likely to be the mothers of those who would sacrifice all? Is this eagerness to follow fashion even to its extremes, from a miserable fear that they should be considered as not being of the world, the way to win the kingdom of heaven? Is this – we had almost said contemptible – desire to win the approbation of those who are without, the way to bring honour to their religion? It deceives no one except those who deceive themselves, and it brings neither honour to those who are thus self-deceived, nor to the Church.

Even the most sceptical men of the day have, at least, some Pagan sense of honour, and some, at least, human respect for consistency. However heartily they may condemn the faith, they are, for the most part, respecters of those who are consistent in practising it. . . .

The Mother

Doc. 1.4: Nora Tynan O'Mahony, 'The mother', *The Irish Monthly*, 91 (1913).

Nora Tynan O'Mahony (1865–1954), poet and novelist, writing in the Catholic magazine The Irish Monthly, *deplores the emergence of the 'new woman' and advocates a return to 'traditional' social values.*

More and more, in these degenerate days of militant suffragettism[1] and similar foolishness if not actually wickedness, does the danger grow that the old-time honour and reverence due to and hitherto accorded to motherhood may become a thing of the past. Not that the menace lies so much in the disregard and irreverence of men, though assuredly the outrageous tactics of some of our modern militants is enough to bring the whole feminine half of humanity into general contempt and disrespect. It is rather in woman herself, and in the gradual distortion of her nature, slowly but surely being brought about by the hysterical shriekings of the suffragette sisterhood, that the real trouble may be found; and that in seeking for outside worldly power and influence she is losing her own greatest and most royal prerogative as undisputed mistress and queen of the home, and of her husband's and her children's hearts.

All this is so obvious, unfortunately, that the casual reader, setting it down at once as the merest truism, will in all probability pass on to the next column or page. One does not, however, need to be very old nowadays in order to remember a time when men regarded women of all ages and all classes with greater respect, and indeed homage, than is accorded even to the highest and most venerable amongst them today. Thoughtful men of an old fashioned school will shake their heads sorrowfully and tell you, 'Ah, these foolish creatures are lowering the respect due to women, they are trailing her honour and dignity in the dust'. And the regrettable lack of femininity, of sweet, gracious, dignified womanliness, not only in modern woman's manners but in her dress, all tend to bring her down to a lower level in masculine eyes than she ever sank to before. The mannish cut of the modern woman's scanty garments, the short skirts, the liberal display of ankle, the often bared throat and neck (even in the street), the jaunty set of her hat jammed down to one side, and completely covering her hair and her eyes – it may be convenient and comfortable, but it certainly is not womanly or dignified or nice.

Looking at the portraits of present-day fashionable ladies attending race-meetings and other outdoor functions as portrayed in the daily illustrated papers, one is struck at once not only by the mannish style of dress they wear, but by the entirely masculine and (in a woman) ugly stride and attitude adopted by them. One can hardly imagine a lady of this genre bending over

1 See below p 269–88.

the bed of sickness, or soothing a fretful child to sleep on her bosom; instead of being a 'ministering angel' of the house, her place, judging from her 'sporting' looks, at least, would seem rather out on the moors with the men and the guns, where, alas! we so often find her diffusing widespread death and devastation everywhere about her amongst the wild, innocent, defenceless things of the air and the earth.

This very desire on the part of modern women 'to go out and kill something', just like her husband or her brother, is surely a telling proof of her growing lack of femininity and of the tender, all-embracing love and pity for everything that lives and breathes that is one of the holy and beautiful attributes of motherhood. So soon as your true mother (for some there be who are not true mothers) first presses her newborn babe to her breast, and feels the caress of 'baby fingers, waxen touches' against her lips and cheek, so also does she begin to feel a kinship as of motherhood towards all helpless and suffering things in the world. What were formerly the unredeemed, unforgivable sins and failings of others, she now regards only with maternal pity and tender forbearance. For only a few years ago, she remembers, the poor wrongdoer was a babe at his mother's breast, a child at his mother's knee. God only knows what sin and folly might yet overtake this child of her own heart and body, and what could bring him comfort and forgiveness if not his mother's everlasting love and pity? . . .

The true mother has no thought of self: all her life, all her love, are given to her husband and children, and after them, and because of them, to all and everything that have next most need of her. With heart-aching anxiety and solicitude she watches by the bedside of her sick child while all the rest of the world is asleep; sick or well, indeed, she is watchful and wakeful, and there are few mothers whose thoughts and hopes and fears are not with their children in the silent watches of the night even more than in the day. The poor anxious mother may miss a great many of the careless pleasures of the childless woman of fashion; but she has that in her heart, in the loving possession of her children, in their care and nurture and instruction, and in their worshipping affection for her, that are more to her and far better than all the world besides . . .

In the Smart Set of modern society children are quite out of fashion; they are voted as expensive and troublesome little nuisances, necessitating the upkeep of a suite of nurseries and an increased staff of servants – and who would not prefer a motor car, when they could choose! In a few self-sacrificing households there may be one or two little ones; but the large families of other years are almost universally decreed as quite 'absurd' and 'impossible'. The gradual disappearance of home-life and the tendency of well-to-do folk to live at pleasure resorts and in hotels, where children would be objected to, in the modern selfish spirit, as being 'in everybody's way', are amongst the things that contribute to the dethronement of the mother and her babe, the Madonna and the Child, that should be the first and most sacred objects of every household, and about every hearthstone.

Will 'the vote', and the privilege of working and fighting side by side, and on equal terms, with their brothers in the great industrial and commercial or political marts of the world, ever make up to women for the loss to them of the love and reverence of men, the affection and the clinging trustful confidence of little children, who regard them as (what indeed God has made them in this world) a tender, loving, unfailing providence in every childish want and trouble? Women, who are wildly desirous of doing man's work in the world and to whom life in the home and the nursery spells but the deadliest dullness and dreariness, might well profit from the experience of many poor mothers forced from necessity to commit their children to other people's care, and who would almost give everything they owned in the world, save their children, to be able to give those bereft little ones a full and complete share of motherly love and attention.

A mother's influence, a mother's dignity, is very sacred and holy; hardly less so, one might say without irreverence, than that of the priesthood itself. . . . Who can measure her power and her influence for good in the world? The good wife and mother is the best guardian not only of the physical health and comfort of her husband and sons, but of their virtue and spiritual welfare as well. And this influence lasts not only through youth and early manhood, but through the long subsequent years of worldly struggle and trials during which they may wander far away from her; nay, it lasts far into the years beyond the day she is laid in her grave, saving her dear ones from many a temptation, helping them, if they should fall, to rise up as quickly again. . . .

WAYS TO MARRIAGE

A Case of Abduction

Doc. 2.1: Prisoners' Petitions and Cases 1828/3366, NA.

Abductions were a relatively common feature of eighteenth-century life but became less common by the early nineteenth century. An abduction involved the kidnapping of a woman, sometimes an heiress, leading to the loss of her reputation and often forcing her into marriage with her abductor. It seems likely that some abductions, at least, were consensual. It was one way of forcing parents to allow marriage to someone they considered unsuitable.

To the most noble the Marquis of Anglesea, Lieutenant General and General Governor of Ireland.

The humble pet[ition] of Catherine Owens and John Owens – her brother.

Herewith – that three men, Cremin, Stackpole, and Callaghan, were convicted at the last Cork assizes before the Rt. Hon., the Lord Chief Baron, for the abduction of the said Catherine Owens. He, the said Cremin, being the principal therein and the other two accessories – all sentenced to die on the 19th April.

That the prosecution approaches your Excellency with the greatest humiliation, earnestly entreating of your Excellency to commute the sentence under which the said three persons are now, as the chief object of peti[tioner] was that the said Cremin should marry prosecutix –

That peti[tioner] humbly submits to your Excellency her deplorable situation, and that the said Cremin's sentence may be commuted so as to enable peti[tioner] to get married to him and thereby to become an honest woman – as otherwise she will bear a name which will attach to her [for] posterity.

That peti[tioner] is much moved since the trial, least she might be mistaken in the person of Callaghan, under such frightful and sudden circumstances, and this doubt is confirmed by the excellent character which he got at the trial – as well as by other circumstances which has come to this peti[tioner's] knowledge since the trial and this peti[tioner] is informed that his counsel declined examining witness on his behalf so good an opinion had they of this Callaghan's case.

That peti[tioner] John Owens states to your Excellency that he identified the person of Stackpole whom he had never seen or known before, and who lives a considerable distance from peti[tioner] and peti[tioner] is since credibly informed that the said Stackpole has a large family of young children being himself an aged man, and most unlikely to join in such a transaction.

Under all those circumstances peti[tioners] approach your Excellency, humbly hoping your Excellency will extend to the culprits your usual clemency, and make such commutation with sentence or such other order with premises that will best tend to the future safety and happiness of peti[tioners] and as shall seem meet to your Excellency.

And peti[tioners] will pray -
her
CATHERINE X OWENS
mark
JOHN OWENS

An Engagement

Doc. 2.2: James H. Cousins and Margaret Cousins, *We Two Together* (Madras, 1950).

Margaret Gillespie (1878–1954) was born in County Roscommon. She completed a degree in music, and in 1908 helped form the Irish Women's Franchise League.[1] She also helped to establish the suffrage newspaper, The Irish Citizen, *published between 1912 and 1920. She married James H. Cousins (1873–1956), a poet. They went to live in India in 1913. There she became a founder*

1 See below p 273.

20

member of the Indian Women's Association, established in 1917. She also became the first woman magistrate in India.

. . . The six months previous to our marriage was a testing time for me. I had to leave Dublin and retire to the bosom of my family to be taught how to cook, to collect a trousseau, and learn household management. I was then the eldest of a dozen children. The three nearest me were away from home; but the home atmosphere had been for years one of continuous babies, growing parental friction, a queer mixture of autocracy, kindliness, love of music and beauty, an irrational kind of religious faith, a sense of congestion. One could see everywhere what a lottery marriage had been; how many blanks had been drawn. What was my guarantee for life-long happiness in such an inescapably close relationship? It had taken me half of our three years engagement to grow content with Fate's choice for me. The second half of the engagement had built up knowledge, respect, admiration and affection in me for a truly worthy man; and it had made us enjoy one another's companionship and dependence on little mutual services. In those first years I used to analyse my lack of emotional care whether he turned up or not as I continued my piano practice and he happened to be later than our time of appointment. And now, so near the fatal or heavenly day of marriage, I still had some region of indifference or coldness or uncertainty about the future in me which I was rather ashamed of as being unworthy of him, and not the fictional sort of emotionalism that a bride is expected to have. Imagine then the effect on me of the question of an old friend of my mother's: 'With all these youngsters around you, Gretta, are you not afraid to get married?' Actually I was not afraid; but I had a clear knowledge of the uncertainty of the circumstances, and how they could alter cases. In those engagement days we hinted at control of our future. Jim had once clearly promised, 'Anything about the coming of children will be entirely left to your choice.' I believed him. I knew nothing of the technique of sex, but I had utter trust in his knowledge, his will and his integrity. So the question of my mother's friend did not ruffle my feeling as much as it might. Even at that early date I had settled in my mind that every wife should have been so educated that she could earn her own living; so that economic helplessness should not tie her to marriage, and force her and her children to remain with a man or in conditions that were a hypocrisy, a degradation, or a bad influence on the children. Now that I had secured the unusual degree of Bachelor of Music I knew I could always earn my livelihood. But deeper than these Jim and I had realised that our surest unity was in our similar aspirations to build purity and beauty and harmony into our lives and into the world. . . .

A Daughter Asks her Father for Permission to Marry

Doc. 2.3: *Lady Morgan's Memoirs: Autobiography Diaries and Correspondence* (London, 1862).

The novelist Sidney Owenson (?1776–1859), later Lady Morgan, was very much attached to her father. Here she writes to ask his permission to marry. Though from this extract, she does not appear to be 'in love' with her future husband, that love certainly developed through the marriage (see document 15 below).

Baron's Court
August 20, 1811

My Dearest Dad,

I am . . . at a loss how to begin to tell you what I am going to ask you – which is your leave to marry Doctor Morgan, whom I will not marry if you do not wish it. I dare say you will be amazingly astonished; but not half as much as I am, for Lord and Lady Abercorn have hurried on the business in such a manner that I really don't know what I am about. They called me in last night and, more like parents than friends, begged me to be guided by them – that it was their wish not to lose sight of me, which, except I married a friend of theirs, they might, as they never would acknowledge a Dublin husband, but that if I accepted Morgan, the man upon earth they most esteemed and approved, they would be friends to both for life – that we should reside one year with them, after our marriage, or if they remained in Ireland, two years, so that we might lay up our income during that time to begin the world. He is also to continue [as] their physician.

He has now five hundred a year, independent of practice. I don't myself see the thing quite in the light they do; but they think him a man of such great abilities, such great worth and honour, that I am the most fortunate person in the world. He stands in the first class of physicians in London, having taken his doctor's degree at Cambridge; his connexions are excellent, &c., &c., &c., and in person very distinguished-looking. Now tell me what you wish, for I am still, as ever, all your own loving and dutiful child,

SYDNEY OWENSON

Arranging the Match and Marriage

Doc. 2.4: *Peig: The Autobiography of Peig Sayers of the Great Blasket Island* [Translated into English by Bryan MacMahon] (Dublin, 1973).

Peig Sayers (1873–1958), was born in Dunquin, County Kerry. Her family were poor and Peig herself spent many years 'in service'. Her marriage, as she describes below, was an arranged one and once married she moved to the Great Blasket Island. It is clear that Peig had practical expectations of marriage, seeing it as an opportunity to become her own mistress. Peig is perhaps best known as a story-teller and her autobiography, dictated to her son, was first published in 1936.

One Saturday in the beginning of Shrove,[1] Seán was in Dingle; when he came home he told me that he had news for me.

'What news?' I asked him.

'News of a match, my girl!'

'God above! Who's the man?'

'An Islandsman', he said. 'An even-tempered, honest boy and a good man as well, so I hope you'll take my advice. They'll be coming to visit us some night soon.'

The way matters then stood between my brother Seán and myself, if he ordered me to go and bail the ocean I'd obey him for no one in the world stood higher in my affections than did Seán.

Three nights after this, three men walked in the door. They got a hearty welcome. My father had no idea that they were coming but then he realised fully what had brought them. After a little while one of the men produced from his pocket a bottle with a long neck; bottle followed bottle until they had a fair share of drink taken and then we had no shortage of talk! I didn't open my mouth, but I was peering from under my eyelashes at the young men. I couldn't decide which of the three was asking for me because I knew none of them. I could neither choose one nor bar any. Each one of them was too good a man for me even if I were seven times a better woman than I was.

Oh dear, that match didn't take long to make! There was little more to it than 'Come along' and 'I'm satisfied'. My father came over to me.

'Raise up your head!' he said. 'Will you go to the Island?'

I considered for a while for I had two choices in the palm of my hand – to marry or go into service again. I was sick and tired of that same service and I thought it would be better for me to have a man to my back and someone to protect me, and to own a house too, where I could sit down at my ease whenever I'd be weary.

My father spoke again: 'What have you to say?' he asked.

'I know nothing at all about the Island people', I said, 'but you know them through and through. Whatever pleases you pleases me and I'll go whenever you tell me.'

'God be with you', my father said.

The bargain was made; Peats Guiheen and myself were to be married in a few days' time.

Saturday was the day appointed. There were neither motor-cars nor side-cars there at that time – it's a different story altogether nowadays. When we were ready that morning Seán tackled the horse and a crowd of us sat into the cart. When we got to Ballyferriter, the place was black with people for

1 Shrove or shrovetide was the week preceding Lent. Since marriages did not take place during Lent couples often married at shrovetide.

there were seven weddings there that day and there was a great throng of people present.

When we left the chapel there was right tip-of-the-reel and hullabaloo; the young people had music and dancing and the older people were singing and drinking. A good part of the day was spent like this; when Seán called for me it was time for everyone to be moving towards the house, so some other girls and myself went off home with him. It was customary at that time for every-one who attended the ceremony to go to the house for the wedding recep-tion. The men would arrive later in ones until at last we were all together. Then the revelry would begin.

But when we got home there was no good news to greet us but word that a fine big daughter of my brother Seán was at death's door. We never expected news like that for the fit had come on her all of a sudden. She died that same night.

So, according as each man arrived at the house he'd sit down quietly without speaking a word. Ever afterwards my brother had great affection for the island people because of the fine manner in which they had sympathised with him that night.

We had a wedding-feast and a wake[1] at one and the same time. That's the way my poor wedding went.

The Islanders had decided to go home on the following Tuesday. Seán tackled the horse; then two barrels of porter, a jar of whiskey and the eatables that hadn't been consumed because of the girl's death, were loaded onto the cart. Then we moved off down to Barra na hAille – the cliff top. My sister Máire was with me, as was Cáit, my brother's wife. When we reached the creek four currachs[2] were launched on the water and the barrels and other goods were loaded into one. There were four men to each currach. I sat in the stern of the currach in which my husband was and as this was my first time ever on the sea I was terrified out of my wits.

The evening was beautiful and the sea was calm and the men were rowing easily until at last we reached the island haven. I was amazed that evening as if I were entering the City of London. When we moved close to the island the place was black with people big and small all gathered there to welcome us. I made my way through the crowds as best I could and all the while I was turning over in my mind how I'd come to accept this kind of home without a relation or a friend near me. I didn't know one person among all those who were shaking hands with me and I kept asking myself if the day would ever dawn when I'd open my heart to these people or make as bold amongst them as I would among the people of Vicarstown. Oh, never, never, I told myself, could they be as kind as the people of Vicarstown. The blessing of God be with you, Cáit-Jim, I said in my own mind, you were the lucky one! Whatever

1 Keeping watch over a corpse before its burial. Assocatied in Ireland with lamentations and merry-making.
2 Boats.

happens, your feet will be planted on mainland clay. Not so with me! How lonely I am on this island in the ocean with nothing to be heard forever more but the thunder of the waves hurling themselves on the beach. But I have one consolation – a fine handsome man, and as I can gather from the whispering going on around me I'm not the first woman who cocked her cap at him! But he's mine now, and no thanks to them to do without him! I'll have friends aplenty on this island as long as God leaves him to me. And hasn't he a fine presentable appearance! And his knowledge of the ways of the sea! I thought I would never be in danger of drowning if he and I were in the same currach.

I stayed where I was until my husband came to me and then, side by side, we walked upwards to the house with a crowd of the village children following us. They were wild for sweets, the poor things, and their mouths were working at the thoughts of them.

The old people of the place had gathered into the house to welcome me. I was shy and backward because I knew none of them, but before long I pulled myself together. Then Old Mici Guiheen, my father-in-law, addressed me; he was a rough strong hardy man but age was catching up on him. 'Flint' was his nickname.

'Welcome a hundred thousand times, Peig', he said.

'That you live long in the whole of your health', I answered and my head was bent with a sort of shyness.

'Take your shawl and hang it up there, child', said Máire O'Sullivan, my mother-in-law. She was, as the saying goes, all about me! Then: 'Never mind! I'll do it myself as you're exhausted', she added.

I took off my shawl and she hung it on a little peg that was driven into the wall. You're a good mother-in-law and a gentle one too, I told myself, and it's a great blessing that I took the sound advice of my brother Seán. I knew well that Seán didn't want to tie me to a good-for-nothing, so I didn't go against him the night my match was being made.

Peats Flint was now bound to me by the Church; we belonged to each other and everything we owned we held in common. That was the way we promised it would be. Many a person promises and is sorry afterwards, but I wasn't sorry when I saw these fine people-in-law around me. They had the house very nicely and tastefully done up, the walls bright with whitewash, new furniture too, and gleaming sand spread on the hearth. A neat lamp hung by the side of the wall and the dresser was laden with lovely delph. A great grey cat with a gloss on its fur lay in the corner; there was also a small dog – the little fellow came to make friends with me and lay down beside me. My husband Peats and his brother, Micheal, were busy about the house putting things to rights, for the local people were due to arrive as soon as ever the lights were lighting, for the wedding celebrations had not yet ended.

Marriage Amongst the Poorer Classes

Doc. 2.5: *First Report from His Majesty's Commissioners for Inquiring into the Condition of the Poorer Classes in Ireland, Appendix A, HC 1835 (369), xxxii.*

The Poor Inquiry of the mid-1830s has left us with much contemporary evidence about the life of the poor in early nineteenth-century Ireland. For the poor, marriage was a strategy for survival. One witness noted 'if a man is very poor, he expects nothing but poverty with a wife, and his choice is soon made'.[1] At the least, marriage provided a companion who could share the subsistence burden. The desire for children was also, in some instances, an attempt to provide insurance for the future. Children were expected to look after their parents in old age. Another witness noted:

> *I think early marriages are most useful here; a man looks forward to being supported in age by his family . . . if a man marry at the age of 35, he will be broken down and unable to work before his children can be grown enough to support him, as a boy seldom gets more than half a man's hire 'till 18; but when a man marry young, his children will be able to support him before he is beyond his labour.[2]*

Evidence provided to the Inquiry came primarily from those in positions of authority, the clergy, police and magistrates, but the commissioners also sought information from 'ordinary' members of the community.

Parishes Chapel Russell and Kilcornan, Barony of Kenry, Co. Limerick.

The poorer classes marry earliest. It is a frequent practice for a man to elope with a farmer's daughter, and not to marry her until he forces her parents to give a larger fortune than their means would justify, in order to save her character. The labouring classes marry earliest. Marriages have often taken place when the parties had nothing more than a guinea to give the priest. They say they marry in order to have a place of their own, instead of working for another. . . .

Munster: Co. Tipperary.

Marriages are certainly contracted at a very early age among the peasantry; the usual period for men being at 21, and for women at 19; but both sexes frequently seek partners two or three years sooner. It has been observed that the most numerous families are to be found, first, with the lower order of farmers, and next with persons who are mere labourers.

Munster: Co. Clare.

. . . There are few farms over 12 acres, and the sons of a man holding a farm of that size will, by the division of it into small lots, become eventually nothing more than cottiers. All are poor, and all of them but too prone to premature matches, but decidedly the more prone in proportion to their destitution. As for the labourer, he seems to think he never can get married early enough. A farmer's son will wait 'till he gets a fortune, or 'till he settles

1 *Poor Inquiry, Appendix A*, 1835, p 364.
2 *Ibid.*, p 393.

his sisters; but with the labourer, an acquaintance began the night before at a wake or a dance is sometimes consolidated the next morning into matrimony. 'Not long ago', said he, (Mr Sheehy, Roman Catholic Rector of Kildysart) 'a girl of about 13 came down from the mountains with a young lad of 19 or 20, and wanted me to marry them, which I refused; and the very next night the mother of the girl came, and insisted upon being married to the same man who had proposed to be the bridegroom of her own daughter. I complied, and the mother said that either she or her daughter should have a husband, in order to have somebody to look after their acre of ground.'[1] Mr O'Grady observed: (Daniel O'Grady Esq.; an extensive gentleman farmer) that there was reason to think that the wish to have children, on whom they could depend in their old age, was an inducement to marry with some, but not so much with the young people, who do not often give themselves time to make such calculations as with those rather advanced in life.

He has heard it observed, when a destitute unmarried person has been seen begging, 'What a fool she was not to have got married, and she would have had children to keep her from that line of life.'

Marriage Customs in Rural Ireland

Doc. 2.6: Michael MacDonagh, 'Marriage customs in rural Ireland', *The Englishwoman*, 22 (April–June 1914).

Michael MacDonagh provides an outsider's view of the Irish marriage customs that prevailed in the first decade of the twentieth century. His article is concerned with the 'match' and the dowry, both important features of Irish marriage in post-Famine Ireland.

. . . Of all a man's affairs, his marriage is supposed to concern other people the least. In rural Ireland, it is the one personal matter that is most meddled with by other people. Indeed, the match is often an affair of bargaining between the parents of the 'boy' and the 'girl'. The parents think it as much part of their duty to provide their children in later life with husbands and wives as to afford them in early years shelter, food, clothing, and education, and the young couples are rarely allowed, and just as rarely expect, a voice in this disposition of their future lives. In many things the Irishman will not brook interference, or is impatient of control. Yet that being of fiery, disturbing, and upsetting vitality sinks at once to ashes when his father takes in hand the selection of a wife for him. In affairs of the heart, the Irishman yields to the authority of parentage, to the experience of age.

Wedlock being an indissoluble partnership, with the most serious responsibilities, material considerations, more than sentimental, decide the issue. The pecuniary circumstances of both bride and bridegroom are minutely

1 Recent work by historians suggests that this early marriage age is atypical. See, J.J. Lee, 'Marriage and population in pre-Famine Ireland', *Economic History Review*, xxi (1968), pp 283–95; Cormac Ó Gráda, *Ireland: A New Economic History 1780–1939* (Oxford, 1994), passim.

gone into by the respective parents, and in the end they agree that the boy shall receive so much land, if not the entire farm, on condition that so much money shall be forthcoming on the girl's side. But money is not everything. It is recognised that matrimony, to be successful, requires some more sterling and enduring factors. In the final result, character is the deciding quality. Therefore, the negotiations for the settlement of the pecuniary terms are not entered upon until the upbringing, habits, and qualities of the young man and woman are closely inquired into. Both sides think highly of 'pedigree'. The family of the boy (or the girl) must be 'dacent, respectable people', there must be no 'wake point'[1] in their history. But in this respect, also, the judges are not the young people themselves, but the parents.

The great marrying season in Ireland is Shrovetide, the week preceding Lent. During the forty days of that penitential season other people, in obedience to the ordinances of the Church, abstain from matrimony as well as from meat, eggs, butter and milk. As Shrovetide approaches, the parents of marriageable sons and daughters know that their children are possessed of a craving for connubial joys, and consequently set about getting suitable mates for them. In doing so, the old people are animated by parental caution and foresight in the interest of their offspring. They are most solicitous to see their children comfortably 'settled' – a word implying a permanent position in an established home, which has become consecrated by long use in connection with Irish matrimonial agreements.

When a farmer holding, say, thirty acres of land, at a moderate rent or purchase annuity, has a daughter of marriageable age, he conveys the intelligence in an indirect, off-hand manner to a neighbour possessed of a farm almost about the same size as his own and a son likely to make a good husband for his girl. Meeting his friend at a fair or market, he will say, with a laugh, 'Whisper here, Jim; I'm bringing up my little Maggie for your Johnnie.'

'Ah, now, Tom', the other replies, 'you do me a great honour entirely. But, mind you, my Johnnie is very particular, and has high notions altogether, wherever in the world he got them. What do you think the young rascal does be saying? What a big fortune he will be wanting with his wife, no less. Did you ever hear the like?'

'Fortune is it?' the father of the girl exclaims, 'Why, my Maggie is a fortune in herself. Still, for all that, I wouldn't mind giving a few pound, or maybe a milking-cow, or a couple of heifers and pigs, with a good stock of clothes, so that my girl shouldn't go empty-handed to your boy. But she can turn her hand to anything about a house an' farm, and it's many a one that would be glad to take her without a farthing's-worth of value.'

The subject, having thus been broached, is discussed by the parents whenever they meet, and often a long time elapses before the terms of this business arrangement are finally settled, and the young people get to know that they are to be partners for life.

1 Weak.

If the farmer who is looking out for a husband for his daughter finds that there is no boy in his own neighbourhood who possesses the necessary qualifications – moral and physical, of course, but financial especially – he makes enquiries elsewhere, generally of some person whose avocation takes him into other districts, and brings him into close touch with the people; and having, through one of these travellers, heard of the 'makings of a match' in another part of the county, he starts off on a Saturday morning for the market town usually frequented by the other farmer whose son he wishes to get for his daughter. In the afternoon, when the task of the day is over, the interesting subject is debated in the tap-room of a public-house, and 'wetted' – as they say – with a couple of glasses of whiskey or pints of stout.

'Tell me now', says the visiting farmer, 'how much land are you willing to give over to your boy if he got a good match of a girl for a wife?'

The other farmer, to avoid committing himself at once to a definite reply, will ask in return, 'How much fortune will you give your daughter?'

Though it is the intention of the first farmer to give one hundred pounds – which is usually the dowry of the daughter of a small farmer – he will begin by offering only fifty pounds, until he finds out how far the other is disposed to go in providing for his son. The second farmer will vow that he intends to treat his son decently. He will give the boy ten acres out of his farm, or, perhaps, four acres suitable for growing crops and the grazing of so many cows and calves, sheep and pigs, with the prospect of the whole farm passing to him ultimately. Then the first farmer will try to get still better terms for his girl's husband.

In many cases, the whole farm, or the succession to it, goes with the husband, when he is the eldest son. This may simply mean that the daughter-in-law joins the household as a help to the old mother – 'the crathur'[1] – and things go on otherwise as before, or, if the newly-married son has 'got the place', there may be an agreement by which the father and mother continue in their old home, superannuated; or are relegated, with an agreed allowance, to an adjacent cabin. But the farm, one way or the other, is the boy's share in the transaction. The chief difficulty is the fixing of the girl's dowry or 'fortune' as it is always called, as a set-off to the land. This, as we have seen, consists sometimes of money, and sometime partly of money and partly of live-stock or furniture. Indeed, the negotiations may be broken off because the girl's parents refuse to give another 'ten pound note', or a calf or pig, or even a kitchen table, or a feather bed. Occasionally the question is referred to some old and substantial farmer or publican who is held in esteem by both parties, and his advice is invariably to 'split the differ' – that is, to come to an agreement on half the amount of the additional sum of money, or half the value of the additional live-stock, or furniture in dispute. . . .

The bride's money is usually retained by the parents of the bridegroom for their own use and benefit. Probably it will be expended in providing a hus-

1 The creature.

29

band for a daughter of their own. More than that, the same sum of money may do a similar service in a surprising number of cases. Indeed, as many as a dozen nuptial knots have been known to be tied by means of one and the same £100. Tim O'Donoghue gets a fortune of £100, clear of marriage dues and wedding expenses, with his wife. The money is then handed over by his parents to Ned McCabe, who marries their daughter, Mary Kate. Ned McCabe passes on the £100 to his own sister, Julia, who thereby secures a mate in Terence McGrath; and Terence's sister, Agnes, by its agency, becomes Mrs Maurice Doogan. So this identical £100 passes on, marrying all the eligible girls in the townland, leaving joy, happiness, and contentment in its wake, just as if it were a beneficent fairy with a wand of enchantment.

It is a curious fact that the priest, to whom the Irish peasant flies for advice in all his other troubles, difficulties and crises, is rarely consulted in regard to a marriage. There is a superstition that a 'priest's match' leads to an unhappy union. But there is hardly a parish in rural Ireland that has not got its recognised lay 'go-between', or match-maker. The delicate service of bringing young people together with a view to matrimony is mostly undertaken by the match-maker for no other reason than to satisfy a friendly well-meaning desire to see united in wedlock a boy and girl who are enamoured of each other, but are not personally acquainted, or else are too bashful to settle matters themselves. In some instances, however, a fee is charged. There is the not uncommon case of a man who is eager for a wife, and has failed to find her. He consults the match-maker, tells him the kind of girl he would like, and gives him a few sovereigns as an inducement to keep a look-out for him.

A WIFE WRITES OF HER LOVE TO HER HUSBAND

Doc.3a: Maurice O'Connell, (ed.), *The Correspondence of Daniel O'Connell vol. 1, 1792--1814* (Dublin, 1973).

Mary O'Connell (1778–1836) and her husband Daniel O'Connell (1775–1847) maintained an extensive correspondence during the periods when O'Connell's work as a barrister and an MP necessitated their separation. Their mutual love and respect is clearly visible in that correspondence.

From Mary O'Connell to Daniel O'Connell.

6 March 1803

My darling love,
   . . . Never was there a husband and wife, I will venture to say, so completely blessed in each other's affections as my darling and his little woman . . .

Tralee, 25 March 1803

My dearest love,

. . . Believe me, darling, there is not a wife in existence more sincerely anxious to promote the happiness of a beloved husband than I am nor to deserve his love . . . I love you, my darling, so much and so sincerely that to see you look thoughtful or at all alter your manner towards me gives me the most sensible concern lest I may have unintentionally offended you . . . Will you take care of yourself? You know how apt you are to take cold . . .

Doc. 3b: Maurice O'Connell, (ed.), *The Correspondence of Daniel O'Connell, vol. 2, 1815–1823* (Dublin, 1973).

From Mary O'Connell to Daniel O'Connell.   14 July 1817
Clifton [near Bristol],

My own darling Dan,

Nothing amuses Ellen and Kate more than reporting your expressions of affection for their mother who indeed feels most grateful for the manner you, my own darling, write and speak of me to our dear children. I assure you, my darling, you are our continual subject. When a kind husband or father is spoken of, Ellen and Kate will exclaim, 'Mamma, sure he is not so good a husband or father as our father?' You may guess, darling, what my reply is. You know what you deserve and you are aware that, in existence, I don't think there is such a husband and father as you are and always have been. Indeed I think it is quite impossible there could, and if the truest and tenderest affection can repay you, believe me that I feel and bear *it* for you. In truth, my own Dan, I am always at a loss for words to convey to you how I love and dote of you. Many and many a time I exclaim to myself, 'What a happy creature I am! How grateful should I be to Providence for bestowing on me such a husband!' and so indeed I am. *We* will, love, shortly be married fifteen years and I can answer that I never had cause to regret it. I have, darling, experienced all the happiness of the married state without feeling any of *its* misery, thanks to a fond and indulgent husband . . .

Motherhood

BIRTH CONTROL

Doc. 4: Oedipus [Thomas J. Haslam], *The Marriage Problem* (Dublin, *c.*1868).

The production of birth control literature is not something we associate with Ireland. However, Thomas J. Haslam (1825–1917) published a birth control pamphlet around 1868. Thomas was the husband of Anna Haslam (1829–1922). Both were Quakers and suffragists. Thomas produced the first suffrage newspaper in Ireland, The Women's Advocate, *which ran to only three issues.[1] Anna formed the first suffrage society in Dublin in 1876, and she and Thomas campaigned vigorously on a number of issues concerning women's rights. In the following extract Haslam proposed the use of the 'safe period' as a method of birth control. Haslam may have been familiar with the work of George Drysdale (1825–1904), whose book* Physical, Sexual and Natural Religion, *published in London in 1854, advocated the use of the 'safe period'. The calculation that Haslam uses to describe the 'safe period' would be unlikely to work for the majority of women. It is evident from this piece that Haslam did not fully understand the information he was providing. It is unclear how widely distributed this pamphlet was. It was available, as a statement on the cover made clear, for 'gratuitous circulation amongst Adult Readers only'.*

One of the most urgent social problems of the present day, therefore, is the discovery or general diffusion of some effective expedient, by means of which mankind can secure the satisfactions of married life without exposure to the miseries resulting from an excessive number of offspring. Or – to express the same thing in more precise language – what is urgently required is some safe practical method by which married persons can regulate the number of their offspring in exact accordance with their wishes.

. . . There is undoubtedly one method of preventing the birth of off-spring which has long been known to medical men, and which has been largely put in practice in several countries of Europe, as well as in the United States of America. The introduction of a small piece of soft and elastic sponge into the vagina immediately before the act of copulation, and its withdrawal immediately afterwards, will prevent the entrance of the spermatic fluid into the uterus, and will thereby effectively prevent impregnation. There is, how-

1 See below p 269.

ever, one insuperable objection to the general adoption of this experiment. It is somewhat revolting to the feelings of highly-refined and conscientious women. Without entering into the debated question of the morality of adopting any artificial preventives, it may be sufficient to observe that large numbers of our most elevated women have an invisible repugnance to their employment. What is wanted, therefore, in the present case, is the discovery of some expedient which is so simple, so natural, so inoffensive in every way, that the most sensitive and pure-minded woman who has ever lived might avail herself of it without any feeling of impropriety or degradation.

Providence . . . has enabled them [scientists] to discover the law, or rather one of the most important of the laws, by which the conception and birth of offspring are regulated. This law is happily so simple that every one who possesses a reasoning faculty can comprehend it without difficulty. Its intelligent apprehension will enable every married couple throughout the world, with very rare exceptions, regulate the number of their offspring in exact accordance with their wishes. Its practical application involves nothing more difficult – nothing more offensive to the most exalted notions of pro-priety – than entire abstinence from sexual intercourse during a certain limited portion of every month. It has been established by ample evidence that women generally are not liable to impregnation for more than a limited number of days in every month; and that abstinence throughout that period will effectually prevent the conception and consequent birth of offspring. Here, then, we have an easy, inoffensive, and practical solution of one of the most urgent problems of the present generation. . . .

To sum up the practical result in a few words. Women generally are liable to impregnation for one or two days before the appearance of the menstrual flux, during the whole period of its continuance, and for about six or eight days subsequently to its cessation.[1] In the case of a small minority, their liability extends to a further period of three or four days. By careful observation, how-ever, every woman can determine for herself the duration of her own period of liability with sufficient accuracy for all practical purposes. If she does not wish for offspring, she has only to abstain altogether from sexual intercourse throughout that period. It is, doubtless, possible that the observance of this rule may necessitate the occupancy of separate beds by many married couples during the periods of abstinence. On the other hand, should they find it impossible, from whatever cause, to carry out this restriction, and should the production of offspring be altogether undesirable, they must then consider for themselves whether the emergency be such as to justify the adoption of some preventive expedient like that of the sponge, as the smaller and less objection-able of the two evils. Should any of my readers find themselves in this dilemma, I would strongly recommend them to discuss the matter unreservedly with their medical adviser.

1 Haslam is correct in highlighting the existence of a 'safe period', but is incorrect in his assertion of when the 'safe period' occurs.

It is surely not too much, however, to ask of any married couple who cannot afford to maintain a family in comfort and independence, or whose state of health would not permit them to have vigorous offspring, to observe the rule of strict abstinence during a period of about twelve or fourteen days out of every month; when that abstinence will be the means of saving themselves and their possible offspring from so much misery. There may be some difficulty in the practice of this abstinence during the first few months of their married life; and during this period separate beds may be absolutely indispensable; but when the ardour of youthful passion has been in some measure satiated, they ought to be able to restrain themselves to this extent without any superhuman sacrifice. When Providence endowed mankind with the noble gift of reason, it was in order that we might regulate our conduct in accordance with the dictates of prudence, and not allow ourselves to be carried away by the violence of our propensities to the injury, and not infrequent destruction, of our unfortunate children. The generation of offspring by parents who are not in a position to maintain them in health and happiness is one of the most brutal and selfish enormities which man or woman can commit.

A MOTHER RECORDS HER CHILD'S DEVELOPMENT

Doc. 5: MS Small notebook on Mary Margaret Murphy (after Cronin Coltsman) of Clifton, Co. Cork, giving date of birth, details of education, etc., 1857–1886. MS 19441, NLI.

The mother who kept the notebook, in which these details of her child's development were recorded, was clearly delighted with her baby. Nothing was too insignificant to be noted down.

Baby born 5th June 1857 at 20 minutes before 8 morning.

Christened on 7th by Father O'Sullivan.

Dedicated and laid on altar by Father John.

Baby's first word, said Dada on 13th February 1858, and Mama on 14th February.

Baby's first tooth May 7th, 2nd tooth May 28th 1858. She had four teeth in the middle of June, 6 in August.

Baby walked alone for the 1st time on 26th September 1858 and not again till the 12th October when she did so for good and began on that day to say bread and butty. We had a family party on this day and she sat at the top of the table after dinner with me and called out Dad Dad to John.

Baby's hair was cut 6th March 1860 by O'Leary first time. . . .

Baby first time knelt at the altar in St Vincent on 17th September, 1859. First time she was ever in a church.

Baby went to mass for the first time on 17th March 1860 – with me and
Mary Williams, she was very good, at St Mary's the quarter past 11
Mass said by Father Healy and then drive with me by herself for the
first time to Shanakiel . . .

The first week in July 1861 she knew all her large letters.

Baby knew first chapter in catechism in August 1861.

Wednesday 22nd October 1862

Marmary's first lesson from Miss Scotland in music, French and reading.

Monday 3rd November

Marmary's first children's party at Mrs June Joys, Montenotte – from 4 to
half 7.

Marmary had a great children's party on 7th July – 32 children.

9th July 1863

Marmary began breakfasting with us and attending morning prayers.

19th July 1863

Marmary first used a knife at dinner – her four front teeth all came.

Marmary cut 2 back lower jaw teeth February 1864.

She commenced hooping cough Xmas 1863.

Began Miss Hogan

January 1864

She began a 2nd time with Miss Scotland on 15th February 1864. Began
to learn writing February – also arithmetic and little history of England.

Marmary made her first confession on 1st May 1865 to Father McCabe at
St Vincents.

Began drawing with Miss Stopford 21st June 1866. 2 lessons in the week.

Tuesday evening 23rd October 1866:

Bought Shetland pony from Mr Dennon for £12, called her Little Mary.

Marmary's first ride on her about the place on 24th October and first on
road up to Murray on 25th October 1866.

Marmary's first concert – 27th October 1866.

Marmary went to confess first time to Father Keown 4th September 1867,
third time on 21st October.

Marmary made her first communion on 1st May (Friday) 1868 at the
convent – Sisters of Mercy – 2nd time on July 2nd at St Patrick's.

Marmary first went to London with us in May 1868 for 3 weeks.

Mad^elle returned from Paris on 4th July 1868 having been away 2 months.

Miss Hogan began teaching Marmary on 30th June Tuesday 1868. She is
to come Monday Tuesday and Friday of week at £6 a quarter.

Mr Stopford recommenced with Marmary on 9th July 1868.

Mad^elle Graffet left us and went to Mrs J. Lyons on Thursday 8th October
1868.

Marmary confirmed on 20 December 1868 at St Patrick's.

Marmary began with Miss Brennan October 16th; 2 hours a day at £3 a
month, not Saturdays.

Mary's last lesson with Stopford 20th February 1871.

Mary went to Rohampton in April 1871, left in end of June.

Mary entered Kensington in May 1872.

Mary returned from Kensington January 1873.

Miss Flynn began piano and weekly 13th February 1873.

Mad^{elle} de Chambourd came on.

Mr Stopford began again January 1873.

Mary's first ball at Shanabreit – 18th January 1876. She wore white silk, white tulle, white narcissus and silver flowers. She danced 20 dances and enjoyed herself very much. It was Mary of Richmond's second ball, 180 at Shanabreit.

H. F. C. proposed for Mary on 18th December, 1876.

T. D. Coltsman proposed and was accepted by Mary on Saturday 23rd November 1878.

Mary married on the 29th April 1879 at St Patrick's Church.

Mary's baby born 26th July 1884 at 5 o'clock evening.

Dan Francis Alphonsus born 19th August 1885 at 11 o'clock . . . he stood alone and walked 3 steps at end of December 1886.

ADVICE TO MOTHERS

Doc. 6: *Northern Whig*, 1 September 1886.

The advertisement below shows that commercial interests had developed 'cures' to deal with some of the problems of infants. Such remedies were affordable only by the better-off members of society.

Advice to mothers! – Are you broken in your rest by a sick child suffering from the pain of cutting teeth? Go at once to a chemist and get a bottle of Mrs Winslow's Soothing Syrup. It will relieve the poor suffering immediately. It is perfectly harmless, and pleasant to taste; it produces natural quiet sleep by relieving the child from pain, and the little cherub awakes 'as bright as a button'. It soothes the child, it softens the gums, allays all pain, relieves wind, regulates the bowels and is the best known remedy for dysentery and diarrhoea whether arising from teething or other causes. Mrs Winslow's Soothing Syrup is sold by medicine dealers everywhere at 1*s*, ½d.

Doc. 7: *First Report of His Majesty's Commissioners for Inquirying into the Condition of the Poorer Classes in Ireland*, Appendix A, HC 1835 (369), xxxii.

The Poor Inquiry of the 1830s provides us with some information about atti-tudes to illegitimacy in pre-Famine Ireland. What the extracts make clear is that for single women having children could plunge them into destitution. The witnesses who gave evidence to the inquiry on illegitimacy frequently invoke a moral tone. It is difficult to assess how the women themselves felt about these events.

Union of Templemichael and Ballymacormic. Barony of Ardagh.

. . . Women who have illegitimate children are, according to two witnesses [Mr Carbery, general merchant – Rev. Mr O'Donoghue, Roman Catholic clergyman], constantly compelled to resort to begging . . . The difficulty of supporting herself and the child leads rather to begging than prostitution. The refusal of the reputed father to maintain the child produces in most cases ill feeling between the parties, and sometimes is the cause of violence. The dif-ficulty of obtaining support is frequently injurious to the health of both mother and child.

Parish of Castlepollard. Barony of Halffoure, or Demifoure, Co. Westmeath.

. . . Girls who have had illegitimate children are looked on with great contempt both by men and women, and are seldom married, nor would a farmer give his daughter to a bastard except he was much richer.

Women have been known to bring actions against the reputed father for nursing, and recovered in the shape of wages. Women who have had bastards are sometimes driven to begging, and in some instances to prostitution, and with regard to the children the females are, in general, brought up very badly. The males sometimes get service . . .

Parish of Kildysart. Barony of Clonderalaw, Co. Clare.

. . . The mothers of bastards, in three cases out of four, are farmer's ser-vants, who are particularly exposed to danger from the promiscuous manner in which such servants, both male and female, are obliged, from want of other accommodation, to sleep together. Farmers' daughters, however, are rarely known to become pregnant from this cause. They are, from their possessing fortunes, more exposed to another danger, that of abduction; which has, however, become less common of late years . . .

Parish of Tracton. Barony of Kerrycurrihy, Co. Cork.

. . . Girls who have had illegitimate children find the greatest difficulty in procuring husbands; nor has it occurred in the parish that any of the poorer class have been induced to marry them by persons of higher station. Though such women may sometimes be associated with, yet, in general, they are very much looked down upon; they would not be hired as a servant in a respectable family.

Parish of Skull. Barony of West Carberry.

Mary Driscoll lived in the house with a miner after his wife died, and had a bye-child by him about three years ago. Mr Barry made them separate when the man would not marry her. She begs about the neighbourhood; people know her and are charitable to her. She was about 15 or 16 when she had the child; she is not more than 19 now; her health has not suffered in any way.

Nelly Scully, an old woman, had eight bastards, four of them died when young, three of them are daughters and one a son. One daughter married a servant boy, who is now a labourer; another is at service and a third has the bastard, and is living with the mother. The son is about 11 years old; the woman is a regular beggar, she gets no assistance from the married daughter . . .

Mary Carty is daughter of the former Nelly Scully; she lived as servant maid with a man whose wife had left him. She had a child by him about 3 years ago; she was not more than 15 then. He left her a trifle of money, and a cabin rent free, and went off to America. She lived with her mother since in the cabin.

Norah Driscoll had a bye-child about 7 or 8 years ago by a labourer; she was about 17; she was a servant-maid; the child died and she continued in service. About four years ago she had another by a man who promised to marry her. Mr Barry endeavoured to make him do so, but he would not; he gave her 10s. She has the child, and goes about the country spinning wool, and selling eggs, and jobbing in different ways. She has a great many friends who assist her; she does not beg.

Mary Sullivan was servant-maid to a gentleman, she had a bye-child by him about 3 years ago. She was about 20; he made some allowance for the first year; her mother has a house, and pays 15s. a year for it. She has one son at service, who gives her no assistance and another about 12 years, whom she supports at home. Mary is at service, and gives her what she can earn, but it set her to keep the clothes on herself. She has but small wages, 3s. or 4s. a quarter, perhaps.

MOTHERS DESERT THEIR CHILDREN

Doc. 8a: *The Police Gazette or Hue and Cry*, 20 December 1864.

Descriptions of women suspected of abandoning their children, as well as stories of actual abandonment, were reported regularly in the newspapers.

Description of Maria Morony, native of Clare, who stands charged with, having on the 9th December, 1864, at Sallybank, in the barony of Tulla Lower, parish of Killselly, deserted her infant, leaving it destitute, and exposed to danger:– 28 years of age, 5 feet high, stout make, sallow complexion, round face, brown eyes, crooked nose, dark hair; wore a green rockspun shawl, reddish cotton gown; ordinary looking and dravish [?] voice. Was discharged from the Limerick workhouse on the 8th instant; the name Maria Morony is supposed to be fictitious. . . .

Doc. 8b: *The Nationalist,*[1] 19 May 1900.

A Miss O'Brien, from Clonmel, came before the board [of guardians] with a delicate looking infant in her arms which, she said, was deserted. She asked the guardians to take it into the [work]house. In reply to questions she stated she could not say who it belonged to. A young woman left the child with her on Wednesday week and promised to give her a month's wages for its keep when she was settled in employment. The woman went to America, for she sent 2s 6d from Queenstown. Her name was McCarthy from Kerda. . . . The board refused to accept the child.

REPORTS OF INFANTICIDE

Every year, newspapers carried hundreds of reports of the discovery of the bodies of infants, and also some reports of the prosecution of women accused of infanticide. The following accounts are typical of the reports made in newspapers. Amongst other things, these reports show how well women were able to disguise their pregnancies.

Doc. 9a: *Belfast Newsletter,* 6 November 1882.

An inquest was held by Mr Thomas Lindsay, city coroner, in the boardroom of the Londonderry infirmary, on Saturday afternoon, on the body of a female infant found in a bucket in the institution during the morning. A jury having been sworn, and having viewed the body, witnesses were examined.

Mary Gray, a probationer nurse in the infirmary said she knew the woman Mary Jane McGarvey or McGillaway. She was a servant who had been employed in washing and scrubbing the floors and assisting the nurses generally. She had assisted that morning at eight o'clock in serving the breakfast, and left witness at a quarter past eight o'clock. Half an hour later witness saw her in the bathroom, and thought it necessary to call the matron. Mrs Maclean, the matron, said when called she met the woman McGillaway in the hall leading from the bathroom, and ordered her to her bed. She had a bucket in her hand which she laid down, and witness lifted a cloth which was in it, and under which she saw the body of a full grown

1 A county Tipperary newspaper.

female infant. The matron then called the house surgeon, Dr McNaught, and the matter was reported to the constabulary, and a constable was placed in charge of the apartment where the woman lay. Sir William Miller said that on his morning visit to the house he heard of the occurrence and saw the body of the infant and also the mother. He had since made a *post mortem* examination of the body, and found that the lungs did not present the appearance of ever having been filled with air, and from the colour of the blood in the pericardium he concluded that life had never been established. The body was full grown, the skull and brain were perfect, and there were no external marks to account for death. There was nothing to lead him to believe, if the woman had been seen and properly treated, the child might not have been born alive. With regard to the infant's body, there was nothing to show why it could not have been born alive. It was possible it might have gasped, but he believed that respiration had never been properly established.

The jury returned a verdict to the effect that there was no evidence to show them that the child, the subject of this inquiry, had been born alive.

Doc. 9b: *Belfast Newsletter*, 7 December 1883.

Yesterday, Constable George Beattie arrested a woman named Margaret Denny, alias Mary Burgess, in the hiring fair at Armagh, on the charge of infanticide. About a month ago the dead body of a female child, about one month old, was found in a stream of water at Ballinashonemore, near Armagh, and the coroner's jury returned a verdict of willful murder against some person or persons unknown. Since that time the police have been looking for the mother, but without success until yesterday, when the prisoner was arrested. An inquiry was held yesterday evening before Mr Thomas Hamilton RM,[1] and the prisoner was remanded for a week.

Doc. 9c: *The Nationalist*, 17 October 1900.

At the Dublin commission today a young woman named Hannah Kavanagh, 20 years of age, a native of Cloughjordan, Tipperary, domestic servant, was charged with infanticide on the 22nd September. Sergeant Dodd and Mr Campbell QC prosecuted, and Mr J. J. O'Mahoney, instructed by Mr J. H. Minton, defended. Evidence was given as to the birth of the child and its subsequent caring. Amongst the witnesses were Mrs Johnson, in whose employment the servant was. She deposed that Mr Johnson saw accused wringing her hands on the evening of 22nd. Patrick McKenna, Cloughjordan, in whose employment accused had formerly been, gave her an excellent character, and it also appeared from other evidence that there was a promise of marriage on the part of Burns, the father of the child, and that accused had cared well for

1 Resident Magistrate.

the child, paying for its nursing out. The body of the child was found drowned near Pigeon-House Fort, Dublin. Mr O'Mahoney said it was a sad and sordid story of a woman's undoing, only lighted by the generosity and charity of Mrs Johnson.

The jury found the prisoner guilty, with strong recommendations to mercy. Justice Gibson sentenced her to be hung on 16th November.[1]

A DAUGHTER WRITES OF HER MOTHER

Doc. 10: Diary of Lady Anne Jocelyn, MS 18430, NLI.

Lady Anne Jocelyn (1795–1822), was sixteen when she wrote the following piece about her relationship with her mother. There are other references to the relationship scattered throughout her diary.

1810, December 26.

. . . I hate to look back to this time last year. I felt so unhappy and miserable. I believe I love mama too much, she is not always as kind as I think she ought to be. Many and many a bitter moment and tear she has cost me, but God is just perhaps, I do wrong, myself, and am too high minded, but, I thank Him in my heart and feel grateful, she is altered, I think, though still sometimes bitter and harsh.

1812, August 2

. . . Mama and I had a most disagreeable conversation, she is so foolish and fanciful she quite provokes me, poor woman . . .

FRANCES POWER COBBE REMEMBERS HER CHILDHOOD

Doc. 11: *Life of Frances Power Cobbe By Herself* (London, 1894).[2]

Frances Power Cobbe (1822–1904) was born in Newbridge House, north of Dublin. She spent the first thirty-six years of her life in Ireland and then moved to England where she became a well-known journalist in the cause of women. She was involved in campaigns around issues relating to education, suffrage, and particularly women's status under the law. She was also

1 While the death penalty could be imposed for this crime, the Home Office had, in 1864, adopted a policy of advising the commutation of the death penalty for all cases in which a woman was convicted of killing her own infant under a year old. See Ellen Ross, *Love and Toil: Motherhood in Outcast London, 1870–1918* (Oxford, 1993).
2 For more on Cobbe's life see Barbara Caine, *Victorian Feminists* (Oxford, 1992).

very involved in the anti-vivisection movement. She remained unmarried and lived for over thirty years with her companion, Mary Lloyd.

. . . My childhood, though a singularly happy one, was an unusually lonely one. My dear mother very soon after I was born became lame from a trifling accident to her ankle (ill-treated, unhappily, by the doctors), and she was never once able in all her life to take a walk with me. Of course, I was brought to her continually; first to be nursed, – for she fulfilled that sacred duty of motherhood to all her children, believing that she could never be so sure of the healthfulness of any other woman's constitution as of her own. Later, I seem to my own memory to have been cuddled up close to her on her sofa, or learning my little lessons, mounted on my high chair beside her, or repeating the Lord's Prayer at her knee. All these memories are infinitely sweet to me. Her low, gentle voice, her smile, her soft breast and arms, the atmosphere of dignity which always surrounded her – the very odour of her clothes and lace, redolent of dried roses, comes back to me after all three score years with nothing to mar their sweetness. She never once spoke angrily or harshly to me in all her life, much less struck or punished me; – and I – it is a comfort to think of it – never, so far as I can recall disobeyed or seriously vexed her. She had regretted my birth, thinking that she could not live to see me grow to womanhood, and shrinking from a renewal of the cares of motherhood with the additional anxiety of a daughter's education. But I believe she soon reconciled herself to my existence, and made me, first her pet, and then her companion and even her counsellor. . . .

A GIRL WRITES TO HER PARENTS AND SISTER

Doc. 12: Letters to Kate D'Alton from her daughter, Catherine. D'Alton Papers, MS 20966, NLI.

Catherine D'Alton was a schoolgirl at the time of writing these letters to her parents. There is a certain formality attached to her letter to her mother, and those to her sister and father seem much freer.

Catherine D'Alton to her mother.   9th May 1841
[addressed to Summer Hill, Dublin,
franked Waterford]

My Dear Mamma,

I was delighted to hear from your letter that you were all so well and that the little ones have so happily gone through the awful process of inoculation. I hope they are getting on well, particularly Helen, as from the weakness of her constitution I would be more apprehensive for her than for Johanna. We

42

are now practising the devotions for the month; owing to the lateness of the hour at which they are said in the public chapel, we are not able to attend them, but every day at one o'clock Miss Tuam reads prayers for us in her own chapel which she has very tastefully decorated; afterward we sing the litany and the 'laudette' outside the chapel. We have received great encouragement as we were told the litany was not so well sung in the great church.

We went last week to visit the poor house; one hundred persons have already been admitted, they appear to be very well treated but I fear when they become more numerous it will be difficult to keep them in order. We went through all the rooms; the house is built in Elizabethan style and the room which is occupied by corridors would I think have been much better laid out if it were added to the dormitories; there, the beds are placed about a foot from each other so that when they are filled the closeness of the air will be very unwholesome. I will be much obliged by your sending me a mousselline de laine[1] and two white frocks as soon as possible as we will shortly begin to wear our summer dresses. When you see Charlotte Daly tell her I am very jealous with her for not answering my last letter as I expected she would be a more regular correspondent. Give my love to all and accept dearest Mamma your affectionate child.

CATHERINE M. J. D'ALTON

[Note on same letter]
Dearest Mrs D'Alton,

Kate just brought me this as the dinner bell rang which obliges me to content myself with saying that I consider Kate's disposition to be much improved. She seems full of earnest good resolution. A thousand regards dear Mrs D'Alton

from your sincerely obliged, M. TUAM

18 July 1841

Dearest Eliza,

You are I am sure too well acquainted with my various occupations to feel jealous at my not writing to you more frequently; I assure you nothing would give me greater pleasure than to keep up a constant correspondence with you, and as we expect to have vacation during the ensuing month I hope then to make amends for my silence. I suppose this election has created general excitement in Dublin. I was sorry to hear that the Conservatives were unsuccessful; they have all been returned in this city but in the country the Liberal members have triumphed; at their chairing which took place on Monday the members of the Temperance Society walked in procession, displaying their banner. They were followed by a file of the principal gentlemen of the town

1 Muslin-like fabric made with wool.

and county after which the chair appeared tastefully ornamented with flowers; it was enthusiastically received by the multitude with loud cheers while the numerous spectators who crowded the windows testified their approbation by the waving of handkerchiefs.

I suppose you do not go to many parties now as the city is generally very quiet during the summer months. How is dear Mamma's cough? I hope she is in every respect good. Tell Papa I hope he intends to comply with my request of visiting Waterford this summer and as you know from your experience how anxiously I desire to see him after so long an absence, you will I am sure induce him to come. When did you hear from Grandmamma? Do not forget when you write to give my most affectionate love to her and to Grandpapa. Give my love to Charlotte Daly and tell [her] I am expecting an answer to my last letter.

I must bid you farewell dearest Eliza and requesting you will write to me soon,

I remain with love to all.
Your affectionately attached sister,
CATHERINE D'ALTON

[On same sheet]

Miss Tuam and Miss Hannah desire me to request that you will assure Papa of their regret for the accident which he has met with as well as the pleasure which the[y] feel at his providential escape. I am sure it is scarcely necessary to beg you will spare Papa the pain of stooping and let us know how he is as soon as possible.

[Also on same sheet]

Dearest Papa,

Since I wrote to Eliza I have received your letter and am much grieved to hear of your accident. The good spirits in which you wrote lead me to hope that all danger is past and that my dearest Papa will soon be restored to perfect health as I cannot however but feel uneasy until assured of your perfect recovery. Will you request Eliza or some of the little ones to give this assurance as soon as possible? How happy I would be could I visit and attend you during the painful hours of illness – as this however is impossible I am sure my dear Papa will accept my desire of doing so. I regret I cannot write to you more at length but shall not fail to do so as soon as possible and with every assurance of affection I remain your fond child,

KATE D'ALTON

Single Women

OLD MAIDS

Doc. 13: Mrs Frank Pentrill, 'Everyday thoughts – old maids',
The Irish Monthly, 13 (August 1885).

*As we have noted, for many men and women in the post-Famine period,
marriage was not always a possibility. This extract from Mrs Frank Pentrill
(the pseudonym of Mrs Carew Rafferty) brings out some of the odium
attached to spinsters and old maids. There is, according to Pentrill, little
joy to be had in this state.*

. . . I am pleading for the old maid looked down upon, forgotten, thrust
aside, as if in all this great world there was no place for her. Men have entered
into an instinctive conspiracy to agree in saying that no one is so much to be
pitied as she who manages to be independent of them and women despise
her as a failure – a woman who somehow has missed her vocation. Yet has
she? God, it is true, has not called to her to that highest vocation; the mystic
union of his chosen spouse nor has he given her the sweet duties and pleasure
of wives and mothers. But shall we therefore say that the unmarried woman is
of no use in the world; that she is mere flotsam on the tide of life, to be
tossed aimlessly to and fro, till she falls to pieces, so that she is a kind of social
Mohammed's coffin, hanging between heaven and earth and tasting the
pleasures of neither.

Happy wives with children gathering at your knee, when you sit in the
light of your hearths, think of the lonely women who are standing outside in
the cold. I am not speaking of the homeless and moneyless, but of the
thousands whose life is one long dreary monotony. They, perhaps, devoted
their youth to the care of aged parents – of a sick brother or sister. They gave
up their youth, their hopes, their happiness, to some sense of duty; and when
those for whom they did it died then they were left utterly alone. They sit in
gloomy rooms and they wander through the world – alone; they will probably have to meet death – alone.

You, who are happier, extend to them a little of your bounty, genial
warmth, and, specially, welcome them at those times of the year which for
the unhappy are periods of increased loneliness and regret.

I have been pleading for the old maid, and now let me plead with her; particularly with her who is just entering that lonely path which is not, I own, very bright or brilliant, but where there are still flowers to be gathered and pleasant fruit to be eaten.

Just as white hair is beautiful and venerable, but the transition black and white stage ugly and unbecoming, so it is with old maids. They are both good and charming, when, recognising that spinsterhood is their lot, they set about making it as useful and agreeable as possible. . . .

THE JOYS OF BEING SINGLE

Doc. 14: *Life of Frances Power Cobbe By Herself* (London, 1894).

While many thought that being single was a burden rather than an advantage, Frances Power Cobbe recalled in her autobiography the freedom being single allowed her. She notes also the importance of financial independence to the single state.

My brothers were all older than I; the eldest eleven, the youngest five years older; and my mother, when I was born, was in her forty-seventh year; a circumstance which perhaps makes it remarkable that the physical energy and high animal spirits of which I have just made mention came to me in so large a share. My old friend Harriet St Leger . . . who knew us all well, said to me one day laughing: 'You know you are your father's son!' Had I been a man, and had possessed my brother's facilities for entering parliament or any profession, I have sometimes dreamed I could have made my mark and done some masculine service to my fellow creatures. But the woman's destiny which God allotted to me has been, I do not question, the best and happiest for me; nor have I ever seriously wished it had been otherwise, albeit I have gone through life without that interest which has been styled 'woman's whole existence'. Perhaps if this book [her autobiography] be found to have any value it will partly consist in the evidence it must afford of how pleasant and interesting, and withal, I hope, not altogether useless a life is open to a woman, though no man has ever desired to share it, nor has she seen the man she would have wished to ask her to do so. The days which many maidens, my contemporaries and acquaintances –

'Lost in wooing,
In watching and pursuing',

(or in being pursued, which comes to the same thing) were spent by me, free from all such distractions, in study and in the performance of happy and healthful filial and housewifely duties. . . . Destiny, too, was kind to me, likewise, by relieving me from care respecting the other great object of human anxiety – to wit, money. . . . Thus it has happened that in early womanhood and middle life I enjoyed a degree of real leisure of mind possessed by few; and to it, I think, must be chiefly attributed anything which in my doings may have worn the semblance of exceptional ability. I had good, sound working brains to start with, and much fewer hindrances than the majority of women in proving and employing them . . .

A WIFE MOURNS THE DEATH OF HER HUSBAND

Doc. 15: *Lady Morgan's Memoirs: Autobiography,*
Diaries and Correspondence (London, 1862).

Sydney Morgan had been married for thirty-one years before her husband's death in June 1843. She felt his loss very deeply.

Oh, my husband! I cannot endure this – I was quite unprepared for this. So ends my life.

November, 1843 . . .
The winter fire kindles alone for me now. The chair, the table, the lamp, the very books and the paper cutter, all *these* are here, this November – gloomy, wretched November!! How I used to long for November – social, home-girt November; now I spend it wandering through this deserted house . . .
[The next entry in her journal is many months later.]
April 1844:
Time applied to grief is a worldly common place – time has its due influence over invisible grief, that which is expressed by visible emotions – it softens sighs and dries tears! but *le fonds* remains the same! Time gives you back to the exercise of your faculties and your habits; but the loss of that which is, or *was*, part of yourself, remains for ever. This melancholy Sunday morning! April! The first word written in this one gay record of pleasant sensations!
[There is a long blank, and then the following entry, headed:]
'A period without date':
In the most awful moment of my life, I was not without aid and solace; my sister was with me, my brother-in-law, and my niece Sydney Jones and her husband came to see me immediately, and I was removed from my own home to lodgings, whilst all the wretched business that necessarily followed my most miserable loss was arranged. After that, I accompanied my sister to Brighton, where I was received by the dear, kind family of Horace Smith with affection and sympathy. My dearest sister being obliged to return to her family in Ireland (she has been with me since the death of her own dear child). . . .

THE UNHAPPY FATE OF WIDOWS

Doc. 16: *Reports of His Majesty's Commissioners for Inquiring into the Condition of the Poorer Classes in Ireland,* Appendix A, HC 1835 (369), xxxii.

Widows were, perhaps, the most vulnerable group of single women in Irish society. Because women's work opportunities were so limited, a widow's life was often a struggle for survival. The extent of that struggle was compounded by the number of children she was left to support. As can be seen from the following extracts, widows were viewed with pity by society. Some were supported by institutional charities; others were lucky to have a landlord look after them. Begging was often resorted to in order to make ends meet.

Town of Sligo. Barony of Carbery.

There are a great many widows with young children in this parish. Some are supported in the Mendicity,[1] and all are assisted in some way by charity, public or private, otherwise they could not subsist. They are in general very wretched, and their food is of the worst kind, and often insufficient.

There is very little employment of any kind open to them; they assist about the houses of the gentry and shopkeepers in the town and in the country; are engaged for a few weeks at the harvest. It is perfectly impossible that they could subsist without assistance from charity. There is no provision made for widows by the sessions; they are sometimes provided for by the owners of estates under whom their husbands lived, but very rarely on the properties of absentees.

Widows are very frequently driven to begging for subsistence, particularly when they have grown old and infirm. 'They are assisted by private charity, and thus become broken in, and ultimately beg publicly.'

Considering the earnings of a working man, it would be impossible for him to make any provision for his widow and family.

Co. Clare. Parish Killaloe. Barony of Tulla.

Assistant Commissioner visited some of the widows in this parish –

. . . The first was Mary Slattery. On asking for her at her own door, the decency of her appearance caused surprise, but her comfort was only apparent. 'I am', said she, 'the widow of a pensioner, and have not a simple person on this earth to look to. I can get no employment, and', pointing to the fire, 'I had not a halfpenny to buy a sod of turf to warm a drink for my sick child 'till a neighbour gave me what is in the grate. All I or my family had to eat today was four cold potatoes, and now I have nothing for my supper. I pay 1*s* a week rent for this cabin. I let that corner of it there to a woman and her four children for 1*s* 6*d*, a week; and though she pays me that, the rain comes down through the roof on her, and she never slept a wink last night, trying how she could [to] keep her bedclothes dry.' . . .

1 Alms house.

Parish Skull. Barony of West Carbery. Co. Cork.

1. Widow Collins: she and her husband did not agree; he left her about 12 years ago; she has two daughters; one is dumb, the other is a child. She does not beg regularly, but gets assistance from the neighbours. She pays £1 5s for her cabin; she traffics in fish, and gives lodging to beggars.

2. Widow Moore: her husband died of cholera about two years ago; he was a carrier. She has four children, the eldest only 12 years of age; she does not beg; she keeps a little huckster's shop, but she cannot stand it much longer. Whatever she had when her husband died must be almost gone by this time.

3. Widow Regan's husband is dead six years; she has two children, the eldest almost eight years, she tries to traffic a little in fish; she does not beg but gets assistance from the neighbours. She has no relatives to assist her; her cabin is on the ground where the old road stood; the neighbours built it for her, and gave her materials.

4. Widow Shaw's husband died two years ago of cholera; she has three children, the eldest about eight, she does not beg; her brother-in-law, a butcher, supports her; he is very poor himself.

5. Widow Jarman's husband is dead eight or nine years. A son that used to support her died in February of cholera. She has two unmarried daughters, not at service; she and the girls are going about among their friends; they live that way; they are much worse off than if they were begging.

6. Widow Driscoll's husband is dead five or six years; she has three daughters and one little boy; the children are little better than idiots. She does not beg, but she gets assistance from the neighbours.

7. Widow Whitley's husband is dead about two years; she has two little boys, the eldest about six. She lives with her father, a huckster, who is very poor himself.

8. Widow Daly's husband died two years ago of cholera, and left her three young children, the eldest about six. She has a little shop; she works at her needle. She is believed to support herself; she does not beg.

9. Widow Sullivan's husband is dead nine or ten years; she has one little boy about 10 years old, she lives entirely by begging; she has no house. James Mahoney [quarryman and labourer] says, 'she stops with me one week, with another a week, and so on'.

10. Widow Sullivan's husband died three months ago; she has three boys and three girls, all young children; her husband had some ground at £4 10s a year. She owes two years' rent. She will never be able to pay that; she must soon be out on the world.

11. Widow Sullivan's husband died years ago of cholera; she has two children, but they are unable to assist her, the eldest being only six; she traffics in fish and tobacco. She went out last season among the farmers for [a] handful of potatoes, and got them. . . .

Women and Welfare

WOMEN ORGANISE FAMINE RELIEF

The failure of the potato crop in Ireland, first observed in 1845, heralded the beginning of the Great Famine. Although there had been other famines in the earlier part of the nineteenth century, none matched the devastating misery that resulted from the Great Famine. The Famine lasted until 1851, and, by that year, it is estimated that up to one million people may have died from starvation and disease.[1] Various forms of relief were provided, through government aided schemes, religious bodies, and private individuals. The scale of distress and destitution made it difficult for such schemes to have any long-term effect.

A Lady Reacts to the Famine

Doc. 17.1: eds. Patricia Pelly and Andrew Tod, *The Highland Lady in Ireland, Elizabeth Grant of Rothiemurchus,* (Edinburgh, 1991).

Elizabeth Grant (1797–1885) was born in Scotland. She married John Smith in 1829 and they moved to his estate at Baltiboys in County Wicklow in 1830. Her attitude to the Irish poor was typical of her class. The following extract is taken from the journal which she kept while she lived in Ireland.

December 1846.

. . . The Poor Houses are full, therefore now I believe in the destitution cry. The people are starving I believe. Cold and nakedness and discomfort of every kind they are indifferent to, provided they can fill their stomacks [sic], stuff them rather with the lowest quality of food, its bulk is what they look for, for years the failure of the potato crop has been expected, yet no preparations were made to meet this coming evil. They have no forethought. If they get a shilling they must spend it. They can't make 11 *d* do and save the penny, they have no store for the rainy day, then when it comes they rail at all the rest of the world for not stepping forward to their relief instantly as if they

1 Mary E. Daly, *The Famine in Ireland* (Dublin, 1986), p 98. Daly argues that the numbers of deaths was underestimated due to the way data was collected.

deserved the quicker aid because they never helped themselves. There is no energy, no honesty, no industry among them. Already good effects have been produced. The Poor House will improve their habits, the dearness of provisions has driven many of the idle hangers-on at home out into the world to earn the food no longer to be had by grubbing for it. So we must live in hope that happen what may things can never again be so wretchedly bad as they have been.

12 January 1847.

Alas! the Famine progresses; here it is in frightful reality to be seen in every face. Idle, improvident, reckless, meanly dependent on the upper classes whom they so abuse, call the bulk of the Irish what we will, and no name is too hard almost for them, here they are starving round us, cold, naked, hungry, well nigh houseless. To rouse them from their natural apathy may well be the work of future years. To feed them must be our business this. Baltiboys is in comfort, few of our people in real distress, some in want of assistance and they get it, others in need of nothing. My habit of going constantly about among them keeps me pretty well acquainted with their condition, but lest I should miscalculate I am taking the whole estate regularly through at this time. Two days of visiting introduced me to no distress, only to two cases of *struggling* – that expressive word. I mean to make a *catalogue raisonné*[1] of our population to leave among our family archives as a curiosity for future squires and a guide to us now.

Hal has killed a beef for our poor and we make daily a large pot of good soup which is served gratis to 22 people at present. It is ready at one o'clock and I thought it quite a pretty sight yesterday in the kitchen all the workmen coming in for their portion, a quart with a slice of the beef; half of them get this one day for a dinner with a bit of their own bread; the other half get milk and the cheap rice we have provided for them. Next day they reverse the order. The Colonel is giving them firing too; so they are really comfortable; there are twelve of them and ten pensioners, old feeble men and women, or those with large families of children; some of them no longer living on our ground yet having been once connected with us we can't desert them.

So far well; but beyond our small circle what a waste of misery; how are we to relieve it? Such a dense population squatted here and there upon neglected properties, dying with want, wretched every year, but ruined this. At the relief committee yesterday it was resolved to institute soup kitchens at proper stations for general relief, to be supported by subscription, each subscriber to have a certain number of tickets. I think the gentlemen doing this, the ladies must combine for a clothing fund. The rags are scarcely coverings for decency; beds and bedding there are none, among the mob, I mean; such misery crushes hope, yet hope I will. . . .

1 The *catalogue raisonné* was a document compiled by Smith in early 1847 detailing all the people living and working in Baltiboys.

Relief Work in Dungarvan

Doc. 17.2: *Cork Examiner*, 1 January 1847.

This account of the relief work of some women in Dungarvan highlights prevailing beliefs about the true nature of women.

Dungarvan Dec. 27: The resolve of the ladies to establish these depots[1] is a noble one and their exertions to carry it out in the most useful and effective manner are decidedly unprecedented.

Woman, true to the instincts of her own beautiful – almost spiritual nature, saw that there was one great necessity, which male relief committees, or the desultory employment afforded by public works,[2] could not possibly remedy, and she immediately proceeds to supply it. She, by that more refined and subtle perception, that heart touching sensibility so peculiarly her own, felt, and truly felt, that there was many a hapless creature who, in this awful passage in our calamitous history, was forced, at whether through the pride which belonged to better days, or by reason of decrepitude or old age, to shrink away, forgotten by the world, into squalid and miserable domiciles, located in dark and filthy lanes, there to die, with hunger, and not one friendly hand to extend relief . . . many a poor widow and helpless female with no person to earn a shilling for her sustenation – with the poor house here full and she feeling this, put into execution, in these districts, a plan so comprehensive, that it will embrace, all the above cases of destitution within the sphere of its operation.

And what can be so delightful as to find these gentle beings leaving their drawing rooms, their perfumed chambers, their refined and elegant amusements, their lulling music, etc., to enter the house of poverty and wretchedness and rags and multiform misery, where every sight is almost loathsome, every scent pestiferous, every sound the moans of the creature stretched in a bedless dormitory, reduced to a skeleton by emaciating poverty and starvation, and bringing with them the nourishment afforded by these depots? To find them exploring these haunts of misery and hunger for the purpose of alleviating them is, indeed, a scene for angels to smile on – one performed by little less than themselves. There is in it a thousand times more of the heroine than in deeds which may sound far higher, but which could not affiliate with the wretched poor.

These benevolent ladies have thrown aside every distinction, which in ordinary times the conventionalities of society may, perhaps, act out from them. They feel fully the pressure of the times, the necessity for action, and since the formation of their plan, no exertion has been spared by them in carrying it out. Their only emulation is who can do the most good . . .

1 Refers to soup depots, or soup kitchens.
2 In late 1845 the government introduced a system of public works which provided employment for the poor. The wages earned were expected to be spent on food.

Already the ladies of Dungarvan have collected a sum exceeding £130 for their fund. The Marquis of Waterford has subscribed £20 to it, and Lady Waterford £10 . . .

The Abbeyside depot is in operation for the last week, the Dungarvan one will be soon on tomorrow. . . .

The Cork Ladies' Relief Society for the South of Ireland

Doc. 17.3: *Cork Constitution,* 30 January 1847.

This society was one of a number of relief organisations established by women in this period. Such organisations generally had landed women as patrons. Many aimed to provide aid to the female members of a family, in the expectation that such aid, by providing work, or the means to work, would benefit the whole family. The guiding principle in many organisations was that the poor should become self sufficient.

Patroness, the Countess of Bandon; Patronesses, the Marchioness of Thomond; Dowager Countess Mountcashel; the Countess Listowel; Dowager Lady Bernard; Lady H. Bernard; Lady A. Bernard; Lady H. Bernard (Cheltenham); Lady Jane Moore; Lady Mary Berehaven; Lady L. Aldworth; Lady Katherine Boyle; Hon. Mrs C. Bernard; Hon. Mrs White Hedges; Lady Beecher; Lady Chatterton; Mrs General Turner; Mrs Colonel Meade; Mrs Beamish; Mrs Newman (Deanery); Mrs D. Freeman (Castle Cor); Mrs Sarsfield; Mrs Penrose; Mrs R. B. Tooker; Mrs Ormsby; Mrs Lombard; Mrs St George; Mrs Herbert; Mrs Morgan (Tivoli); Mrs Captain Spread; Mrs Woodroffe; Miss Gibbings (Lapp's Island); Miss Crawford; Miss M. Crawford; Miss Warren; Mrs Beasley.

Committee of Management:
Mrs Sarsfield; Mrs Ormsby; Mrs Beasley; Mrs R. B. Tooker; Miss Crawford; Miss M. Crawford; Miss Warren; Miss Wheatley, secretary, 2 Albert Place, Cork; Miss A. M. Lee, treasurer, 3 Mount Verdon Terrace, Cork.

The treasurer looks forward to the Christian public to aid the infant and parochial schools in the city and county of Cork, by giving breakfasts to the most destitute children, and assisting their mothers to supply them with food. Also, to give relief to the widows and orphans, who have lost the men of their families by starvation. If funds admit, or are supplied by the sister country,[1] where the treasurer has applied for contributions, she hopes to add clothing, but for the urgent wants of nature, food to save the lives of thousands of children and poor families is absolutely necessary in the starving districts in the country parishes. The secretary will be happy to receive any contributions. . . .

1 England.

The following queries are to be answered by applicants soliciting relief from the Cork Ladies' Relief Society for the South of Ireland, and returned to the committee of management, addressed to the secretaries of the county associations:

I. Has a Ladies' Relief Association been formed in your parish or locality?

II. What is the name of the county, district, parish, and the nearest post town?

III. What is the extent of the district and the number of inhabitants?

IV. What is the state of the females, widows etc., as regards sickness, poverty, age and infirmity, and how many are unable to work for their own support?

V. Have subscriptions been entered into, and to what amount in your vicinity; or has relief been received from any other source?

VI. What schools are in the parish, infant or parochial, and how many children attend, and do the Ladies' Committee visit them?

VII. Have soup kitchens been opened throughout the district, and have the schools been supplied gratuitously with bread or soup, or if sold, at what rate?

VIII. Is there any public or private employment for the women, boys, or girls in the country farms, to assist the men by their industry?

IX. Have the poor in the country gardens – and do they require seed to encourage them to cultivate their ground?

X. Have you any objection that any of your statements be published or forwarded to the London Committee?

All letters from the country to be addressed to Miss Wheatley, secretary, No. 2 Albert Place, Cork.

Varieties of Charity

HOUSE OF REFUGE FOR WOMEN

Doc. 18: Leaflet, House of Refuge, Ash Street (Dublin, *c.*1809).

Throughout the nineteenth century, refuges were established to shelter women of 'respectable' character. The House of Refuge in Ash Street, Dublin, was founded in 1809 by a group of lay Catholic women. Its function, originally, was to offer shelter to female servants who were out of work. Like many Catholic charities which were handed over to the care of nuns, this refuge was given over to the Sisters of Charity on their foundation in 1815. Again, like many other charities, not every woman was taken in and references as to their good character had to be provided before they were admitted to the refuge. This document, printed c.1809, is a public request for funds to ensure the success of the enterprise.

A more interesting object cannot be presented to the commiseration of the charitable than a virtuous and unprotected female struggling with distress, and unable to extricate herself from it. Amongst the numerous victims comprehended in this extensive class of misery, a prominent place belongs to those destitute orphans, who had been saved by charity from early ruin, but who are afterwards, when depending for subsistence on their own industry, deprived of employment and consequently of support. The orphan charity receives the infant, from the embrace of her expiring parent, and watches over her with a patient's care, until it provides for her a situation in the world, from which she is likely, by her own exertions, to derive the most of future subsistence. Frequently, however, this orphan, either through the failure of her employer in business or some other unfortunate accident, is, at the most critical period of life, driven, without even a fault of her own, from the situation which afforded her bread: and whither then can she fly for shelter? The Orphan House, which had long been her only home, is closed against her: no sooner had she left it, than her place was occupied by some new victim of misery. Desirous to work, but unable to procure employment; ashamed to beg, or supposing it fruitless to extend for alms, the hand which is able to labour; assailed by hunger without any prospect of relief, no friend to succour, no home to shelter, no door but that of infamy open to receive her; Good God! over what precipice does she stand? Has she sunk under the calamities which burst open her infant years, she would at least have perished innocent – has she been preserved by charity, only to become the victim of vice?

To afford shelter to industrious and unprotected females, when reduced to distress, the House of Refuge has been opened in Ash Street. On producing unquestionable vouchers for the propriety of their conduct, they are received under its protection, and employed in washing, mangling,[1] plainwork,[2] and other branches of female industry, until suitable situations can be provided for them. In the mean time, much care is taken to enlighten their minds, and to impress the duties of religion more deeply on their hearts; so that, during their temporary residence in the House of Refuge, they are not only rescued from the hardships which they were suffering, and the dangers of vice to which they were exposed, but they are improved in those beliefs of virtue and industry, which will render them more certainly useful to those who shall hereafter employ them.

The governesses presume to express a hope, that, an institution this eminently calculated to relieve distress in its most alarming shape, to encourage industry, to preserve and to diffuse virtue, will have an irresistible claim on the bounty of the opulent. They beg leave however to state, that the subscriptions, and other pecuniary resources of the institution, are quite inadequate to the heavy expenditure, to which it is unavoidably subject; and they most earnestly solicit the generous aid of the public, to support and perfect an establishment which has already, even in its infant state, produced the most beneficial effect.

NIGHT ASYLUM FOR HOMELESS WOMEN AND CHILDREN

Doc. 19: Fanny Taylor, *Irish Homes and Irish Hearts* (London, 1867).

In 1861 the Catholic priest, John Spratt, opened the Night Asylum for homeless women and children in Brickfield Lane, Cork Street, Dublin. It was, as Taylor, noted, 'situated in the worst and most wretched part of Dublin, the Liberties, and therefore easily to be found by the miserable class of people for whom it is intended'.[3] The enterprise was eventually given over to the care of the Sisters of Mercy and by the end of the century it had two hundred beds and catered for over seven hundred people per week. Bread and cocoa were given to inmates in the evenings, and they were provided with tea and bread on Sunday mornings. In the following extract, Taylor describes conditions in the refuge, revealing how class distinctions operated even with regard to the homeless poor. Fanny Taylor (1832–1900), writer and novelist, was born in

1 Pressing clothes through a mangle.
2 Sewing.
3 Fanny Taylor, *Irish Homes and Irish Hearts* (London, 1867), p 104.

England and was a convert to Catholicism. She established the congregation of the Poor Servants of the Mother of God in London.

. . . The first floor of the refuge contains the very poorest class who apply for admission, the homeless and the starving, to whom a great charity is done; the beds consist simply of a mattrass [sic] and rug laid in a sort of open wooden box, one close beside the other. A greater charity to all our minds is given to the inmates of the second floor; here are iron bedsteads, not so close together, and a greater air of comfort is apparent; it is meant for the better-most poor who may be reduced to utter penury. I call it a greater charity, because the misery of this class, when brought to extremity, is greater than that of the very poor. The loss of shelter to them is shameful, as well as hard, and they are often driven into sin for want of it. The third floor is much smaller than those below, a sort of loft in fact. Here we find an altar and crucifix; here night and morning prayers are said, in which the inmates may join . . . Every night the inmates of the refuge receive a piece of dry bread, and in too many cases this is the only food they taste in the day . . . All the inmates must leave the refuge at eight in the morning, and the doors are often closed 'till five in the evening when the 'refugees' begin to flow in; the matron takes her place at a table, and inscribes in a book the name and occupation of each comer. It is left to her discernment who shall be sent to the upper dormitory. Persons in every kind of employment have sought refuge here. Governesses, dressmakers, seamstresses, domestic servants, some more, some less respectable, have implored shelter in these charitable walls . . . Weekly return of admission into St Joseph's Night Refuge, Brickfield Lane, Cork Street, Dublin, of homeless women, girls and children of good character, who there received nightly shelter and partial support for the week ending March 21, 1867: servants, 229; children, 68; children's maids, 28; cooks, 23; laundresses, 31; plain workers, 44;[1] shirtmakers, 24; dressmakers, 9; school teachers, 7; bootbinders, 10; petit dealers, 27; factory girls, 36; knitters, 42; travellers, 29; shopwomen, 7; scourers, 38 – total, 652 . . .

MAGDALEN ASYLUMS

Doc. 20: *Guide for the Religious Called Sisters of Mercy* (London, 1866).

Prostitution was a considerable problem in nineteenth-century Irish society.[2] At least twenty-three asylums or refuges were established to reclaim and rescue 'fallen women', the earliest dating from 1766, when the first

1 Women who engaged in sewing.
2 See Luddy, *Women and Philanthropy*, pp 97–148; *idem.*, 'Prostitution and rescue work in nineteenth-century Ireland', in Luddy and Murphy, *Women Surviving*, pp 51–84.

Magdalen asylum was established in Leeson Street in Dublin. The name was associated with Mary Magdalen, the penitent follower of Jesus. Most of the Magdalen asylums of the nineteenth century were managed by nuns. The following document details the procedures to be followed by the Sisters of Mercy in dealing with these women.

Necessity of seclusion

The more secluded and quiet the asylum is the better, as all means of intercourse between the penitents[1] and their former companions must be entirely cut off; even a glance at them through a window, or the sound of their voices through a gate, wall, etc., is sometimes sufficient to shake the resolutions of those whose conversion is still incomplete; therefore great vigilance is necessary to guard against the transmission of messages, except through the Sister in charge, as well as every sort of external intercourse. Few, if any, secular visitors should be admitted to the parts of the asylum where the penitents are engaged.

Principles on which to establish asylums

Establishing an asylum on the condition that the inmates should be confined in it for life, or else leave it destitute and unprovided for, prevents many from entering, who though they desire to withdraw from their sinful life, shrink from perpetual enclosure; it peoples Protestant asylums with Catholic unfortunates, because those hold out hopes of future character and situation. This may be seen in our cities where the Catholic asylums are all established on the above principle. Many who would not enter, or having entered, would not persevere at first without a hope of being restored to society at a future time, will, when grace has achieved the victory, choose to stay for life, in which they ought to be encouraged, but not constrained. Besides, providing for penitents leaves places for others to enter and receive the means of conversion; whereas many must be refused where all are expected to remain for life, unless the funds and accommodation are unlimited.

Future provision

We consider it best then, to endeavour to provide for those who have during their probation – which should be a fixed time, not less than three years – given proof of a real enduring conversion, by either restoring them to their families or getting them situations; while, at the same time, we would encourage those who choose the better part of remaining safe in the asylum for life.

In providing situations care must be taken not to clash with the House of Mercy.[2] Situations may be best procured through charitable friends at a distance. These good penitents often make valuable trustworthy servants, and excellent matrons when Providence so provides for them.

1 Title given to women who entered the Magdalen asylum.
2 The Sisters of Mercy had attached to a number of their convents institutions known as Houses of Mercy. Here young girls were taken in and trained primarily for service. These would have been provided with a situation on leaving the refuge.

Admission

Those who are admitted should come freely, without constraint; they should hear the rules read to them, and promise to observe them.

The applicants whose health is such as would probably prove injurious to others ought not to be admitted; it is better to send them to a hospital until cured.

Of cutting their hair

It is desirable to adhere to the rule, so generally established in asylums, of cutting closely the hair of each before admitting her amongst the other penitents.

1. As a means of bringing grace, which the willing sacrifice of their hair – on which they usually set such value – generally brings them.
2. As Magdalen began the evidence of her conversion by consecrating her hair to her Redeemer, so do they, and thus give reason to hope that they really intend to imitate her in her penance as they have done in her sins.
3. As a check to the wild sallies of passion and temptation; under these violent impulses, some, who would not yield to better motives, have been known to defer leaving the asylum until their hair should be sufficiently grown, in whom in the mean time grace grew and passion subsided, and they became good penitents. It is therefore, very advisable to encourage them from time to time, during their fits of fervour, to make a renewed offering of their hair to God in imitation of Magdalen. They should all be carefully prevented from oiling or greasing, or otherwise bestowing any unnecessary care on it, to which they are generally much inclined.
4. Cutting their hair is a test of their motive in entering, as too often wicked ones have entered, merely to draw out with them others who had been doing well.

Probation on entering

When penitents first enter, it is most desirable that they should be kept on probation for some weeks, in a part of the house separated from the rest of the penitents, except some of those really converted and reliable, who might be with them to aid in encouraging, stimulating and watching over them as true penitents give great help in winning the others to God; indeed, they are as angels of light or of darkness to each other – powerful for good or for evil amongst their companions.

When the penitents see their relatives

When the penitents are permitted to see the members of their immediate families – only those who are known to be such should they see – a vigilant, trustworthy person should be present, who will hear and see all that passes. This person must take care that no gift or message is given or received without the previous consent of the Sister in charge. Should she have reason to suspect the visitor is likely to prove injurious to the penitent, she should immediately inform the Sister.

Clothing
On entering, the penitent should be deprived of all that savours of vanity, or that could recall the sinful past. A list should be made in their presence of whatever they bring with them, and all be put by carefully in a place appropriated for such purpose and securely locked. They should be immediately clothed with the modest simple asylum uniform, which they should be required to wear in an orderly, neat manner, but without a display of vanity, which may be too often detected even in this attire of penance.

Food
Their food should be wholesome and sufficient, but plain and simple. It is a mistake to suppose that procuring them indulgences, beyond what are really necessary, will render them contented, and so tend to their perseverance; experience proves it has the contrary effect; it does but awaken their spirit of self indulgence, and urge them to satisfy it. It has happened that a small quantity of snuff brought into the penitents caused more evil than could be credited by those who have no experience of it. Snuff or tobacco should never be admitted, even though some should allege the privation as a cause for leaving. Had they *any* of the spirit of penitents, they would submit to privation. If they do not acquire this spirit, conversion is impossible.

Dormitory
A Sister's or matron's room should be so placed as to command a view of each dormitory; and it would be well that the beds of some real penitents should be placed amongst the rest. In some asylum dormitories a lamp burns all night before the statue of the Blessed Virgin. The dormitories should be locked when the penitents have retired to them, and the key be kept by the Sister: they should be prevented from having any access to them during the day. They should be required to rise and dress modestly and promptly when the signal is given.

Employment
The penitents should never be allowed to be idle; even on Sundays some suitable occupation should be provided, as devotions, religious instruction, learning to read etc.

Labour should form part of their penance; it should be proportioned to their strength and capacity. They will generally be found disposed to idleness. On the judicious employment of their time their conversion greatly depends, but they ought not to be over-worked or harassed, least it may deject them. Laundry-work is well suited to the generality of them. Should penitents be admitted very different from the ordinary class, it would be very desirable that they could be separated from these, and employed in a suitable manner; but constant occupation is necessary for all.

DUBLIN BIBLE WOMEN

Doc. 21: *Annual Report of the Dublin Bible Woman Mission, 1877 (Dublin, 1878).*

The Dublin Bible-Woman Mission was established in 1861. Its aim was 'to use women's work for the promotion of the spiritual and temporal welfare of the poor of Dublin'. To these ends, the committee ran mothers' meetings, employed trained nurses, organised district visiting and ran a temperance society.

The Dublin Bible-Woman Mission has every reason to look back with thankfulness, and forward with hope. Sixteen years ago its executive was represented by three ladies; its paid agency consisted of one Bible-woman; one Mother's Meeting was attended by about half-a-dozen poor women. The Mission now embraces no less than five branches, each having its own Mother's Meeting; more than fifty ladies are now labouring as District Visitors, otherwise in connection with its work; seven Bible-women and three nurses have been employed through its agency during the past year; and the number of poor ladies which now come within the range of its labours have been estimated by the fact, that at a tea, given in the Exhibition Palace, last October, by Lady Olivia Guinness, of all those who attended the several Mothers' Meetings during the year, no less than 450 poor women were present.

The object of the Mission is to bring the too-long neglected machinery of woman's work to bear upon the path of sorrow, suffering, and sin which in this, as in every large city, unhappily confronts us on every side. It is carried on in connection with the Church of Ireland, and its primary aim is to promote the temporal and spiritual welfare of the poorer members of that church in the city of Dublin. It does not, however, withhold its aid from the poor of any denomination that may be willing to avail themselves if it. While reserving to itself such due liberty of action as may be required for the accomplishment of its work, it seeks to act in harmony with the existing parochial arrangements of our Church, and to encourage feelings of good-will and respect towards the Ministers of that Church. Its object is not to supplant or interfere with the duties of the regular pastor, but rather to supplement and aid his labours – to fill up chinks and gather up fragments, so that nothing may be left undone and nothing lost. It includes, in its many agencies, the training and employment of Bible-women and district nurses, the management of Dorcas Funds,[1] Blanket Funds, Coal Funds, Lodgment Funds, etc.; the teaching (especially to the young) of needlework and other useful occupations; the establishment of Temperance Societies and Bands of Hope;[2] as well as an organised system of District Visiting by ladies among the poor. . . .

---

1 A fund to provide clothing to the poor.
2 Temperance societies for children.

WOMEN IN WORKHOUSES

From their establishment in 1838, workhouses were used particularly by women. Once within the workhouse women were expected to conform to certain standards of behaviour. The document which follows details the results of an investigation of the system of 'classification' used in workhouses in the 1850s. Such a system was intended to keep 'respectable' women and girls separated from the 'unrespectable'.

Evils of the Want of Moral Classification

Doc. 22.1: *Annual Report of the Commissioners for Administering the Laws for the Relief of the Poor in Ireland, HC 1854–5 (1945), xxiv.*

Generally speaking, there are few unions in which prostitutes do not mix freely with the other women, and at fifteen years of age every girl in school is transferred to the women's class, there to associate and intermix with them. The evils of this system were strongly urged by Dr Cuthbert, Physician to the North Dublin Union, in his evidence before the Select Committee of the House of Commons on the Dublin Hospitals this year; and some of the cases of corruption arising from this, which were reported to me in the different unions, were of the lamentable character. In the larger towns miscreants became inmates of the workhouses for the sole purpose of seducing young girls of tender years to leave the house and enter on a life of infamy; and, in many instances, they have been successful

In a foot note to this passage of Mr Kavanagh's report, it is stated that in the South Dublin Union, a wretched mother sold her own daughter of tender years, for the purpose of prostitution.

The following is an abstract of the reports received from the Poor Law inspectors, to whom this passage was forwarded for their observations:–

Mr Crawford, Inspector of South Dublin Union – A partial classification does exist in the workhouse, and all the young females drafted into the workhouse from the school are kept carefully separated from intermixing with those of known bad character, who are not permitted to associate with other females likely to be corrupted by them. There may be cases in which parties may have become inmates for the purpose of seducing girls to leave the workhouse for improper purposes, but no properly authenticated cases of this description have ever come under his observation, and cannot be of frequent occurrence. The master and matron state that no case of the kind alluded to in the foot note (a mother having sold her own daughter of tender years for the purpose of prostitution) has come to their knowledge.

Mr R. Bourke states that separate apartments have been for several years established in all the workhouses connected with considerable towns in his district – for example, in Sligo, Boyle, Ballina, and Castlerea, and likewise in other unions, as Swineford, though not contiguous to a large town. The inmates of these wards are completely separated from the rest of the persons occupying the workhouse, taking their meals in their own portion of the house as well as sleeping there. With regard to women of bad character who come in for hospital relief (by far the largest number), it is the uniform practice of the medical officers to set apart a ward for their separate treatment, and such ward is kept for them alone, except at periods when a pressure upon the hospital renders it necessary to admit others, a circumstance which rarely occurs except during epidemics. Has heard of instances where profligate women have enticed young girls from a workhouse, but none have come under his knowedge when a separate ward has been established, and in many houses the younger girls are placed together at night in dormitories apart from older women. Scarcely knows a single board of guardians where the subject has not been mentioned as an evil of probable occurrence and requiring to be carefully guarded against; and he is quite satisfied that the matrons and female officers in the district are not neglectful of the danger, nor remiss in providing against it.

Mr Phelan – The universal practice throughout the district is to separate prostitutes from the other female paupers in wards exclusively appropriated to them, with a superintending female pauper of advanced years, or occasionally visited for distribution of food, etc., by such person. Even when such a character enters with a child beyond two or three years old, the latter is carefully separated from her. When a woman enters with a bastard child, if she be not otherwise known as an immoral character, she is put into the general nursery, but when she come with a second bastard child, she is separated from the nursery and placed in the penitentiary.

Mr J. Burke – As far as can be done, females who live a life of open profligacy are separated, when in the infirmary, from females of good character – the medical officers being anxious to carry out such an arrangement. In Kilkenny Union, a separate apartment and yard are appropriated for prostitutes; in Carlow Union the guardians are about having a similar arrangement. In the other unions in the District, although there is no separate ward in the workhouse for prostitutes, the master and matron, who are aware of the importance of the matter, do all in their power to prevent prostitutes associat-ing with the other females. These unfortunate women, although ill-conducted outside, in general when they enter the workhouse conform to its rules, and do not exhibit, by their conduct, such depravity as might be expected from them. Has not been able to learn any case of a person becoming an inmate for the purpose of seducing young girls to leave the workhouse and enter on a life of infamy, except a recent one in Carlow, in which the attempt did not succeed, owing to the vigilance of the master. The only unions in the District in which prostitutes are found to any extent are Kilkenny and Carlow.

Women Move from Workhouse to Prison

Doc. 22.2: *Annual Report of the Commissioners for Administering the Laws for the Relief of the Poor in Ireland* HC 1861 (2803), xxviii.

Many contemporary commentators viewed with horror the life lived by young girls in the workhouse (see doc. 39). Many of these girls and young women had unstable life patterns and the following case studies reveal the behavioural problems which beset some of these young women and the rigid discipline that was often imposed in the workhouse.

South Dublin Union
Return of the time passed in the workhouse by the undermentioned women.

Name and Age	Date of each Admission	Date of each Discharge	Observations
MARY ANN MEEHAN	*1854*	*1856*	
Age on first	Jan 6	Dec 31	
admission - 13	*1857*	*1857*	
Orphan	Jan 3	Jan 8	
	Jan 9	Jan 28	
	March 3	March 12	
	April 8	April 18	
	April 20	May 14	Sent to prison for fourteen days – assault on wardmaster.
	May 27	June 4	Sent to prison one month for assault.
	July 1	July 2	Sentenced to four years' penal servitude for burning bed in workhouse.

Mary Anne Meehan was transferred from the school at proper age to a class of young women placed under Mrs Kennedy, the superintendent of children, where she remained till she went out to service. Mrs Kennedy states that while she remained with her she was well conducted. The school-mistress states that she was a well conducted girl in the school. It was not till after she left her service and returned to the workhouse that she became riotous and insubordinate.

Name and Age	Date of each Admission	Date of each Discharge	Observations
JANE O'NEILL	*1856*	*1856*	
Age on first	Oct 27	Oct 30	
admission – 16	Oct 30	Nov 5	
Single	Nov 7	Nov 22	
	Nov 24	Nov 26	
	Dec 8	Dec 27	
	Dec 29	*1857*	
	1857	Jan 27	
	Jan 22	Feb 7	
	Feb 9	Feb 26	
	Mar 26	April 9	One month imprisonment for cutting lines in laundry yard, and breaking forms.
	April 9	May 7	
	May 8	July 14	Three years' imprisonment and hard labour for setting fire to beds in refractory ward.

MARY KEELY Age on first admission – 15 Single, Servant	*1855* June 30 Sep 21	*1855* July 18 *1856* July 24	To prison for one month for throwing tins at wardmaster, and using abusive language to wardmistress Parvin.
	1856 Aug 21 Oct 22	Aug 27 Oct 28	Seven days' imprisonment for breaking window-shutters in refractory ward, and refractory conduct.
	Nov 3 Nov 24 Dec 18 *1857* Mar 11 Mar 21	Nov 19 Dec 17 *1857* Jan 2 Mar 20 Mar 30	Fourteen days' imprisonment for assaulting Wardmasters Brady and Cunningham.
	April 10 April 20 May 8 July 1	April 18 May 9 June 3 July 11	To prison for one year for setting fire to her bed in mill yard.
	1858 Dec 30	*1859* Jan 27	To prison; sentenced to four years' penal servitude for setting fire to her bed and breaking forty-two panes of glass.
MARY LYNAM Age on first admission – 17	*1856* Oct 20 Nov 3 *1857* Jan 12 June 8	*1856* Oct 28 Dec 6 *1857* May 14 July 2	Four years for burning beds in mill yard sheds.
ELLEN COLLINS Age on first admission – 5 Came in with parents	1846 Jan 10 *1855* Mar 12 *1856* Feb 9 May 25 June 2	*1846* Sep 3 *1855* Mar 31 *1856* May 12 May 31 Sep 6	Twenty-four hours' imprisonment for breaking glass.
	June 16 June 25 Aug 20 Aug 25 Sep 18 Sep 19 Nov 6 Dec 15 Dec 19 *1857* Jan 3 May 7	June 18 July 15 Aug 22 Sep 16 Sep 18 Sep 30 12 Dec 17 Dec *1857* Jan 2 May 6 July 14	Three years' imprisonment and hard labour for setting fire to bed.

It should be observed that although this girl was first admitted to the workhouse at five years of age, she left in less than eight months and did not return till she was about fourteen. She then only remained for three weeks, and did not return till she was over fifteen; consequently, between the ages of six and fifteen, she was only three weeks in the workhouse. She was for a short time in Mrs Kennedy's charge, who states that she was so wild she was removed to the mill yard.

JANE KANE	1852	1854	
Age on first	Jan 19	July 15	
admission – 14	1854	1855	
Deserted by	Sep 5	Jan 17	
mother	Mar 21	April 13	
	April 24	June 27	
	July 10	July 19	
	Aug 6	Aug 20	
	1856	1856	
	Jan 5	Feb 19	
	Feb 22	Mar 14	
	June 5	June 12	
	Aug 6	Aug 8	
	Aug 13	Aug 22	Three months in prison for assaulting a sentry and breaking glass.
	1857	1857	
	Jan 3	Feb 4	
	April 27	May 12	One months' imprisonment for breaking slates off from sheds.
	July 2	July 8	
	Sep 2	Oct 21	
	Oct 22	Nov 14	
	Nov 17	Dec 7	
	1858	Mar 24	Sent to prison.
	June 24	June 28	
	July 12	July 21	
	July 22	July 29	
	Aug 2	Aug 10	
	Aug 14	Aug 26	
	Aug 27	Sep 17	
	Oct 11	Oct 12	
	Oct 17	Nov 4	
	Nov 22	Dec 3	
	1859	1859	
	Jan 13	Jan 29	Sent to prison.

This girl's mother kept a brothel and the relieving officer states that he believes Jane Kane was in the habit of going to her mother's house when she was out of the workhouse. The frequency of such visits may be estimated by looking to the number of times she was discharged from the workhouse. Mrs Kennedy states that when she was with her she was always troublesome, and was hired from the workhouse.

MARY WAFER	1847	1853	
Age on first	Nov 25	July 22	
admission – 11	1854	1855	
Orphan	Dec 11	April 27	
	1855	1856	
	Aug 30	Feb 19	
	1856		
	July 18	July 25	
	July 28	Aug 16	To prison, three months, assault on sentry and breaking glass.
	Aug 18	Aug 26	
	Sep 18	Sep 20	To prison, forty-eight hours for breaking glass.
	Sep 22	Oct 14	To prison, fourteen days, assaulting wardmistress.
	Oct 27	Oct 29	
	Nov 6	Dec 6	
	Dec 8	1857	
		Jan 7	To prison, two months, assaulting wardmistress.

1857

Mar 3	Mar 30	To prison, fourteen days, assaulting two wardmasters.
April 10	June 7	To prison, one month, for riot and breaking glass.
July 1	July 2	To prison, four years' penal servitude, for burning bed.

When this girl was transferred from school she was placed in Mrs Kennedy's charge, who states that she was well conducted. She was hired out to service in 1853 and the Relieving Officer states that she conducted herself very well. He states that she sprained her ankle and was re-admitted to the workhouse. When she recovered she associated with others and became disorderly.

THE SISTERS OF CHARITY IN KILKENNY

Doc. 23: MS Annals of the Convent of Our Lady of Annunciation, Kilkenny, 1861. Archives of the Sisters of Charity, Generalate, Milltown, Dublin.

The Sisters of Charity were founded in Dublin in 1815 by Mary Aikenhead (1787–1858). A branch convent was established in Kilkenny in 1861, and the following document relates the sisters' experiences in the city. Religious communities keep a written record of their activities, and of notable events in the life of the community. One sister usually has charge of compiling the annals, which are then preserved within the convent. The Sisters of Charity also make a copy for the mother house in Dublin. The order is a centrally organised community governed from Dublin, in contrast to most other communities which are diocesan based and locally controlled.

On the 1st August 1861 four Sisters left the Novitiate House, Our Lady's Mount, Harold's Cross, Dublin (three of the Sisters were of the first class and one a domestic)[1] to found a branch of the order of the Pious Congregation of the Religious Sisters of Charity in Kilkenny. A small house was taken for their residence in James's Street, which, on their arrival, they found by no means suited to their convenience, but after the lapse of 14 months they took an adjoining house which was vacated by the priests of the parish. This added very much to their comfort as they then could have a refectory and community room. Shortly after the arrival of the Sisters a resolution was passed at the board of guardians that they should have free access to the Catholic inmates of the Kilkenny union. In the performance of the duties of their Mission as they went through the lanes and suburbs of the city they found a sad amount of ignorance and crime owing to the want of female schools and charitable institutions for the prevention of crime and reformation of youth. As the Sisters had no place in the convent in which they could give religious instruction they were obliged to meet the class for catechism in an old school room rented by the Rev. E. Walsh for the ragged children of his parish, as the

---

1 A lay Sister who carried out the domestic duties of the community.

Christian Brothers[1] at the time had no room for a junior class. The Sisters collected the boys from 8 to 12 years of age and who were in a sad state of ignorance, formed them into a class and besides the catechism taught them reading, writing and arithmetic. They were also prepared for their first confession and at the close of the year 1863 were received into the Christian Brothers' schools. The duties of the Mission are visiting, instructing and providing for the sick, poor and their families. The Sisters have a small dispensary in the convent which is under the patronage of St Martin where they give [out] good clothes and medicine.

Two classes of person attend for instruction each day; children of the respectable citizens at 11 o'clock, adults at one. The Sisters when on the Mission found the necessity of forming a class for grown persons who had never received the Sacraments of the Blessed Eucharist and Confirmation. Strange to say that in such a city as Kilkenny many of the Confirmation class attained the age of 60 or 70, instance, one old woman had to be carried in the arms of her daughter to attend morning class. The Sisters visit the workhouse twice each week and oftener if necessary from the number of inmates in the institution. It is the sole duty of the Sisters on those days [to visit] the hospital. In connection with it [the hospital?] is the Mission on Sundays and [they visit] through the week also if there are dying patients. A priest and a Sister of Charity alone could tell the state of this Mission, its ignorance and its crime. To what is it to be attributed? . . . To the neglect of founding schools for the children of mechanics and female poor. True there is a Presentation Convent school under the National Board[2] but this is not sufficient for the wants of Kilkenny and its extensive suburbs. We give the following instance of this sad neglect: a girl of two and twenty years of age living within view of her Parish church never made her first Confession and fell the victim of seduction. She merely knew there was a God and knew nothing of a future state, but on being instructed by the Sisters exclaimed in sentiments of deep contrition 'Oh! if I had known so much of God and my soul I never would have fallen.' Her brother, a boy of 14 years of age, was equally ignorant. [He] acquired a livelihood by begging and was always attired in female clothes until the Sisters induced him to put on the clothes becoming to his sex. He is now going to the Christian Brothers' school and is a fair way of becoming a useful member of society. Second instance: two sisters, the daughters of a widow, respectable in their rank of life until the evil eye of seduction fell upon them. The eldest, on being allowed a weekly support by the Protestants, apostatised. The younger felt sentiments of remorse and was brought by the clergyman of the parish to the Sisters for instruction. This gave them an opportunity for seeing and conversing with the elder. She was an intelligent young woman and reasoning with her on the state of her soul yielded to the

1 The Christian Brothers are a teaching order of religious men established by Ignatius Rice in 1802.
2 See pp. 94 below.

influence of Divine Grace and publicly in the Cathedral renounced her errors
and atoned for the scandal she had given.

The alms received and expended for the poor are as follows:–

1861	Received	£44 - 10 - 9
	Expended	32 - 5 - 4
1862	Received	£156 - 5 - 6
	Expended	148 - 17 - 6½
1863	Received	£162 - 5 - 8
	Expended	167 - 14 - 8

THE CARE OF UNMARRIED MOTHERS

Concern with the possible future corruption of young unmarried mothers led to the institution of homes for their care and the care of their babies. While such aid was considered charitable, there were, as can be seen in the following extracts, strict limits to the care provided.

Dublin Hospital Girls' Aid Association

Doc. 24.1: Anon., 'Dublin Hospital Girls' Aid Association', *Englishwoman's Review* (15 September 1881).

An association has just been organised at Dublin which supplies a want that is felt in every large town, although hitherto but little has been done to heed it – to help the young friendless women who have become mothers, when they leave the lying-in wards of hospitals and workhouses. Two ladies, Mrs W. J. Hancock, 23 Synott Place, and Mrs R. M. Purcell, 14 Richmond Place, have undertaken the work of Hon. Secretary and the Committee of Reference consists of Mrs Fleming, Mrs Fletcher, Mrs Gardiner, Mrs Acheton-Henderson, Mrs Marrable, and Lady Sinclair. There is also a Visiting Committee of Ladies, and a Consulting Committee of Gentlemen. Their programme simply and touchingly points out the need of such an institution. Those who have experience of the lying-in wards of hospitals soon learn the existence of a very painful and sad class of cases – that is to say, young unmarried girls who seek shelter when about to become mothers, some as young as fourteen years of age.

Many of those poor creatures owe their condition to the acts of others, over which they have no control, and often feel their condition so keenly that they fret themselves to death, thus swelling the mortality of such institutions, and having helpless babes cast on the world.

Those who recover and are discharged from the hospital find themselves at the gate without character, burdened with the support of a child, without a kind word or timely aid in their sore distress, and not knowing which way to turn. They are too apt to sink into a life vicious in itself, and ministering to vice in others, and after a few years of sin and shame are rescued as Magdalens. How much better it would be if they were rescued before entering upon such a career!

. . . The Dublin Hospital Girls' Aid Association has been started . . . the object being:

To enquire into the cases of all unmarried girls under the age of twenty-one, who are about to, or have recently become, mothers for the first time; if found hopeful, to aid them by kind sympathy and advice, to try and have them reconciled to their friends, or procure shelter for them in some of the existing institutions, and afterwards find honest employment for them, keeping records of cases investigated.

Magdalen asylums, penitentiaries, and homes do a vast amount of good, but in many cases Magdalens seek an asylum only when health destroyed by disease, and faded attractiveness precludes them continuing in a sinful life.

The Dublin Hospital Girls' Aid Association would tend to diminish their numbers; and to rescue them before entering on such a course is more hopeful than to attempt to rescue after several years passed in vice.

The Hon. Secretaries will put themselves in communication with the matron or head nurse of each hospital or ward where such cases arise. When a case comes in which is within the scope of the Association, an intimation could be sent to one of the Hon. Secretaries; then two ladies of the Committee could go to the girl as soon as she is in a condition to be seen, and the enquiry could then be commenced. . . .

Rotunda Girls' Aid Society

Doc. 24.2: *Annual Report of the Rotunda Girls' Aid Society,* 1887–8 (Dublin, 1888).

The good work of the 'Rotunda Girls' Aid Society' has been carried on with success for the year ending March, 1888.

We beg to submit the report of work done to our friends and subscribers. Before doing so, we feel bound to give expression to our sorrow for the sad death of our esteemed foundress and benefactress, the late Mrs Macan. To her was due the institution, and the successful working of the society, which has saved many from shame, sin, and sorrow. To Dr Macan we owe a great debt of gratitude, for kind and efficient help in the work of the year. Since the last general meeting of the Society, on the 10th of March, 1887, 56 cases have offered themselves, which proved on careful inquiry to be fit for its aid and sympathy.

Of the 56 cases, 35 are doing well in service; 4 emigrated to America, having been assisted to do so by the Society; 1 went to England, her child having been adopted by the wife of a Coastguard officer; 6 returned to their friends; 2 married; 3 are at present under medical treatment, in the Rotunda Hospital; 2 were so irregular in their payments that their children had to be returned to them; 2 went away without leaving any clue to their whereabouts, their children being admitted to the workhouse, and one died. Thus, of the 56 cases, only 4 can be looked on as unsatisfactory – 2 in which the girls went away.

The total expenditure of the Society, for the year ending March 10th, 1888, is £250 12s 7d, of this sum £95 5s 10d has been repaid by the girls themselves, leaving a balance of £155 11s 9d. This gives an average cost for each case, for 12 months, of £4 9s 6d.

We beg to ask our many friends and subscribers of the past to assist us in carrying out our work. We feel sure that they will not fail us, and we confidently hope to be able to say to them again next year that God's own work of mercy and compassion is still being done through the 'Rotunda Girls' Aid Society'.

Women and Religion

One of the most profound influences on women's lives in the nineteenth and for much of the twentieth century was religion. Religion affected women's behaviour in many complex ways. It formed a major part of their schooling, influenced and shaped their moral, and thence their social, responsibilities to themselves, their families and their communities. The Churches as institutions were also to affect women's perception of their role in life. Most religious doctrines espoused the view that woman was the helpmate of man, her duty lay in looking after her husband and children. Once those duties had been seen to, women could engage in charitable work which would benefit the poorer members of society. Religion also shaped women's perception of themselves as spiritual beings and led them to spiritual introspection about their lives.

A YOUNG WOMAN TRIES TO PLEASE GOD

Doc. 25: Diary of Lady Anne Jocelyn. MS 18430, NLI.

Lady Anne Jocelyn (1795–1822) was a member of an evangelical family. Her diary reveals an intense personal piety, filled with self-reproach and gloomy introspection.

1822.

July 3: Up late, horrible thoughts in the night, I trust rather a grief to me – reading bad I grieve to say, and prayers rather dead and cold. I tried a little to conquer my love of dress and please God will try more, but failed completely this morning. Having to try on a gown I was excessively ill-tempered in my heart, and showed it. At breakfast had some aspiring thoughts about pride, gave way to them, not talking to others good. I read a little after breakfast to myself in Mathew, I found I got a good deal more good that way and in prayers afterwards. . . . This whole evening I have felt melancholy and deserted and this whole day I have been so happy in being near the Lord . . . but Blessed be His name, He did shine a little on me since I have come to my room and has showed me a glimpse of my past vileness. Lord shew me more, but show me my dear Lord as a refuge from it all, of how He has striven with me. Oh Lord come now and make this heart wretched, as it is Thine faithfully for evermore . . . I exaggerated and spoke not quite true in several instances.

July 16: Up late, I had to write [an] exposition[1] for the servants and was filled with many thoughts of vanity and pride and omitted prayers, till after prayers [family] when I was short and very bad, had vain thoughts troubling me at prayers as to what they would think of my exposition; at breakfast I was self indulgent . . . I have given great way to idle animosity [anxiety?] lately. I must try to conquer it today in one or two instances – and am always copying people in manners, etc. Have not been striving against dress, but gave way to it dreadfully today, in one instance in particular. I missed my reading today, and my prayers shameful through the day. . . .

July 23: I have passed two unhappy days and all from not giving up all to the Lord. I have indeed been completely wretched. Oh, what a wretch I am! I fear all my religious and happy feeling was nothing when I cannot give Him up all, my dress has cost me a great deal. I must strive more against it, in the Lord's strength. I have been so far off from Him, and after enjoying such sweet Communion with Him it is dreadful. I feel as if there is a cloud between me and my Lord, I can't get at Him. I have had great times now and then, and then hypocritical, spoke to others, and felt I was acting so wrong myself, wasted my morning, wished for vain things, had some very envious thoughts. Lord help a poor wretch. I can't pray with any comfort, this is my state and my only happy moments are when I am crying over myself before the Lord. Oh what He has been to me in my trial, and that I should so grieve His Holy Spirit. . . .

Thurs 25: Had to write exposition which I had a great deal of pride about, and it was so bad and so long, this was sent to humble me. The Lord bless it and do so – did not read at all, the devil turned me from it by trifles . . .

A WOMAN WRITES OF HER RELIGIOUS FEELINGS AND WORK

Doc. 26: Diary and Correspondence of Sarah Jane Potts, 1870–1914. T. 1848, PRONI.

Sarah Jane Potts was inspired by religious feeling to keep a diary. She hoped, like many women who kept diaries, that the task of recording her ideas, feelings and occupations would help her to develop into a better person. She notes her failings, she records her training as a teacher, and her involvement in Bible classes and Sunday school.

6 Lower Fitzwilliam Street
Dublin

1879, Dec 31st: I have often thought of keeping a diary, indeed I have twice before commenced one and after a while destroyed them, almost without ever reading them once but as I am now so far away from home

1 A commentary on the Bible for the benefit of the servants.

(my parents living in Co. Armagh) I have again at the end of this year (1879) resolved to keep a diary in order that I may profit thereby, and earnestly hope and pray that I may do it faithfully. Tonight – in looking back over the past year I don't seem to be much nearer to Heaven than at the beginning, yet still I know that I really am a child of the Lord's though so unworthy and weak I can truthfully say 'There hath not failed one word of all his good promises'. After teaching for 5 years in Brookfield School, Co. Antrim (a Friend's or Quakers) I am now studying at the training school, Marlboro Street[1] . . . and stopping at the Governess's Home, where I am very comfortable. Mrs, Mr and Miss S— are so nice I do love them dearly. I have been here now 4 months and know this part of the city pretty well, have been to Christchurch – Patrick's Cathedrals also to Christchurch in Leeson Street. Am now past 20 years old (25th Nov.) how dreadful and yet I have never done anything scarcely in the way of supporting myself and fear I am not bringing glory to my King by my actions and 'By their deeds ye shall know them' saith Jesus.

1880, Jan. 6th: Have got a holiday today and as I have not written in this little book since the beginning of this year I shall be glad to come back to it again with all my joys and sorrows. On New Year's Day went to National Gallery with Miss Sloan in the morn, and had her company, looking at all the beautiful pictures, till 2 o'clock, we then went to the museum and I went all over that (Miss Sloan having left me) and spent two very happy hrs. admiring all the beautiful things there, both old and new. 'Twas then time to come home and after reading a little we had a beautiful dinner (5 p.m.) roast turkey and all were made very happy together. Next day went to school as usual in the holidays at 10 a.m. and stayed till 12, came home, nothing particular happened since, went to R. Robert's bible class as usual on Sunday. The house has been filled since New Year's day and I have been sleeping in Miss Sloan's room.

7th: Go back to my own room tonight, went to a bible class with Miss S— last night – and enjoyed it very much indeed, subject Gal 1, 11, 12, 13 . . . I have not been true to my cause today, nor have I fulfilled my duty as a Christian should do, I actually found myself once or twice saying what was not perfectly true, how weak I am and liable to do wrong at any time, oh! that I could always act – as becomes one of Christ's flock and thus bring glory to his name. Have been neglecting my music lately, indeed when I had no excuse, but mean to be more attentive in future and practice more regularly.

9th: Did practice today but find I have forgotten a great deal.

Drumnold [?] Nov. 15: What a time has elapsed since I last wrote in this and many changes have taken place. Am at home since June waiting on a situation and as yet have no prospect of any. How difficult it is to get settled for the first time. . . .

1 In Dublin.

74

Jan. 24th 1881: Still at home though I have tried so often to get something to do in my line; am intending now to try just whatever offers knowing that my Father knoweth all things and knows what is best for me. Have begun to teach the little ones about here scripture every Sunday evening and explain the meaning of certain verses to them. Like it very much and am glad have found something to do though ever so little for my dear Saviour. Have joined the Bible and Prayer union since beginning of New Year and have as yet continued to read the appointed chapter every day and ask the Lord's blessing on what I read.

24 Charles Sq. Hopton [?] London, April 22: I have been here now for some time, since Feb. 19 and am engaged in mission work. Visit our sick and poor every morn, read and pray with them. Have mother's meetings two afternoons in the week when I read and explain to the women out of the bible . . .

Brookfield 14 July [18]81: How changes do come! here I am back at Brookfield again as governess, feeling sure that it is just where the Lord wants me to be and I desire to do his will in all things. Am very happy in teaching the dear girls but I delight most in pointing them to the Saviour.

Sept 14: Still continue to like my work here, often meet with little discouragements and disappointments but am sure they are sent to keep and draw me closer to the Heavenly Father who sees and knows what is best for his children. Our little meetings with the children are not as free as I should wish. None of the girls take part in them when I am present, so I almost think it best to stay away for some time, at least to absent myself and at same time be engaged in prayers for the dear little ones.

Nov. 26th 1885: My 26th birthday. The girls have been rather disorderly lately, so we had school all day instead of the usual holiday . . .

METHODIST WOMEN

Doc. 27: C.H. Crookshank, *Memorable Women of Irish Methodism in the Last Century* (London, 1882).

Alice Cambridge (1762–1829) was one of the best-known women preachers in Ireland at the turn of the nineteenth century. There were other women preachers such as Anne Lutton (1791–1881), who preached primarily in Ulster, and the blind woman, Margaret Davidson, who drew large crowds to her meetings in Lurgan. Cambridge continued to preach even after the Methodist leadership decreed in 1802 that it was 'contrary both to scripture and to prudence that women should preach or should exhort in public'. On a tour to Ulster in 1815 it was noted that 'vast crowds flocked to hear her preach'. In Crookshank's History of Methodism *(London, 1885–8, 3 vols.), he records the lives of eighteen Irish women preachers and recounts many instances of women's activism in the cause of Methodism.*

Alice Cambridge was born at Bandon on January 1st, 1762. Her father belonged to the Established Church,[1] of which she ever considered herself a member; and her mother was a Presbyterian. Taken from school when very young, she had not the advantages of a liberal education; but subsequently endeavoured, as far as she could, by reading, to supply this serious lack. She acquired a taste for light literature, which could not tend to a healthy mental culture, until, in 1780, a severe trial, in the death of her mother, turned her attention to spiritual and eternal things.

Soon afterwards she began to attend the services in the Methodist preaching-house, and, under a sermon preached by the Rev. William Myles, was deeply convinced of sin. She then returned home to do what she had never done before – to pray – and continued for some time earnestly seeking the pardoning mercy of God, diligently using the means of grace, and greatly encouraged by the members of Society. At length, at a Band meeting, as one of those present related her religious experience, the Lord lifted on Miss Cambridge the light of His countenance, so that she was enabled through grace to magnify the Lord, and rejoice in the God of her salvation. From that hour, as she could affirm many years after, not only did she never once doubt that God had then and there blotted out her sins and accepted her as His child, but also she never thought or did anything which He gave her to know was wrong.

Entering upon her religious course in this spirit of complete submission to the will of God, Miss Cambridge could not fail to make rapid progress in holiness, becoming increasingly dead to the world and alive to God.

After Miss Cambridge had been for some years thus engaged in work for Christ, her sphere of usefulness was much enlarged, by commencing meetings in various parts of the town, at which she prayed and occasionally exhorted. These were so much owned of God, that she was invited to Kinsale, Youghal, Cappoquin, and other places, where similar meetings were held.

Many of the Methodists, and some of the Preachers, pronounced her public addresses irregular, and such as ought not to be tolerated in the Christian Church.

In appearance Miss Cambridge was remarkably neat and plain, resembling in this respect members of the Society of Friends. In social intercourse, she assumed none of that superiority to which her talents and usefulness might have entitled her, but was ever willing to sit at the feet of any, through whom she might obtain an increase of knowledge or grace. Her conversation was marked by cheerful gravity, and a strict observance of the apostolic precept: 'Let your speech be always with grace-seasoned with salt, that ye may know how ye ought to answer every man.' She abhorred that bane of social life, speaking evil of absent persons; while it was to her a source of special satisfaction to be able to reconcile those who had taken offence and become estranged.

1 The Church of Ireland.

She possessed some of the most essential requisites for public speaking. Her accent was pleasing, her enunciation clear and distinct, and her manner free from affectation and dogmatism.

Years rolled past, and Miss Cambridge continued faithfully and zealously to work for the Master. Thus, in the Summer of 1798, she held a meeting at Charles Fort, when nearly all the soldiers of the regiment quartered, there, with their wives and children, attended, and so powerfully did the Holy Spirit apply the Word that many of these veteran warriors were seen weeping like children, and some were led in penitence of spirit to the foot of the cross.

Notwithstanding the manifest success which attended the labours of this devoted woman, the hostility to female preaching continued to increase until it became so strong that, at the Conference of 1802, a resolution was passed, affirming that 'it is contrary both to Scripture and to prudence that women should preach or exhort in public', and directing that tickets be withheld from any who persisted in doing so. By this act Miss Cambridge was at once excluded from the Methodist Society, and deprived of the use of the chapels and other premises: but she did not on that account give up the work to which she believed God had called her. Conscious of the purity of her motives, she resolved to pursue the course marked by Providence, leaving her cause in the hands of Him Who Judgeth right; and she never had reason to regret her determination. Her sphere of usefulness gradually extended to almost every part of the kingdom; and while heartily sympathising with other Churches, Methodism continued to hold the foremost place in her affections to the end of life.

In 1809, Miss Cambridge left Dublin, and commenced business in Cork, where she not only held meetings at a stated time in a house fitted up for the purpose, but also occasionally visited and laboured in Mallow, Fermoy, Limerick, and other places, until 1813, when she relinquished all secular business, and gave herself entirely to the Lord's work. It is unnecessary to follow in detail her indefatigable labours, which extended over a further period of fifteen years, and included in their sphere almost every county in Ireland. It is not small tribute to her piety and Christian prudence than in many instances she overcame the strong prejudice against her proceedings, which had existed in the minds of some of the leading Methodists. Her greatest success was in Ulster. Towards the close of 1815, she for the first time visited this province. Vast crowds flocked to hear her preach; Methodist chapels, Presbyterian meeting-houses, and even an Episcopal church, were thrown open to her, and filled with earnest listeners; until at length she had to take her stand in the open air, no buildings being sufficient to afford accommodation for the immense numbers who collected, sometimes amounting to eight or ten thousand persons. Two years later, she again visited the north of Ireland, with the same general acceptance, and was accompanied with similar success, traces of which are to be found to the present day.

THE DRESS OF THE SISTERS OF MERCY

Doc. 28: *The Customs and Minor Regulations of the Religious Called Sisters of Mercy, in the Parent House, Baggot Street and its Branch Houses* (Dublin, 1882).

The Sisters of Mercy were founded in Dublin in 1828 by Catherine McAuley (1778–1841). The congregation took simple vows and did not observe the rule of enclosure. This meant that they could work in the wider community. Their work was extensive and involved aiding the destitute, instituting orphanages and schools, teaching and nursing. All religious communities followed 'rules' that had been specifically written for their particular community. Such rules and regulations governed all aspects of life within and outside the community.

1. The Habit worn in our Congregation is of black twilled woollen stuff, reaching from the throat to the feet, plaited round the waist, with a train, inner sleeves fitting close to the arm, and wide outer sleeves.

Width of Habit,	4 yards
Length of train,	16 inches
Length of outside sleeves finished,	32 "
Width of do.,	32 "
Depth of hem on do.,	6 "
Lay Sisters' outside sleeves, width	23 "

2. The cincture[1] is of black leather, 2 inches wide, fastened by being passed through a horn ring sewed at one end, and descending within one inch of the ground. Through this ring is also passed a Rosary of large black beads strung on a steel chain, to which an ebony cross inlaid with a smaller one of ivory is appended.

3. The Lay Sisters' Rosaries are strung on brass wire, and have a brass crucifix, instead of the ebony cross. The foundress would not allow any other beads to be worn visibly. It is become customary for the Professed Sisters[2] to wear a brass crucifix 4 inches in length in the cincture.

4. The veil of the Professed is of Nun's crape,[3] or light woollen material of the kind, bowed out from the face, of different lengths, to suit the stature of each Sister.

1st size (tallest Sister),	1 yard 12 in. finished
2nd " (ordinary height),	1 yard 8 "
3rd " (very low stature),	1 yard 5 "
Depth of hem,	2½ "

5. Lay Sisters' veil, 4 inches below the elbow; length when finished (ordinary height), 1 yard 7 inches. Two breadths are put in each veil; the width of material for the three sizes is:–

---

1 Girdle or belt.
2 Those who have taken their vows.
3 Crêpe.

1st size,	40 and 42 inches.
2nd "	38 inches.
3rd "	36 inches.

6. The Novice's veil is of clear, but not transparent, white muslin reaching 4 inches below the elbow, with a domino of white calico.

7. The domino of the Professed is made of black lustre, or Orleans cloth, and reaches 3 inches on either side of guimp, and long enough at the back to touch the chair when sitting.

8. The coif[1] is of Scotch Holland, or fine calico, closed round the face, but divided in front from the throat downwards, for 5 inches, with a hem 1½ inches deep, having a piece of French dimity[2] inserted after the manner of a frontal straight across the forehead.

9. The guimp is of the same material, descending in front from within about 2 inches of the cincture, with a lined hem 2½ inches wide.

10. The church cloak is of white serge, cut in a semicircle, within 3 inches of the ground, and only sloped sufficiently to fit the throat where it fastens under the guimp.

11. The Professed Sisters, both of the Choir and of the Lay Sisters, wear a silver ring, engraved with a pious motto, on the 3rd finger of the right hand; no other rings are worn.

12. The Postulant's[3] dress is of black stuff, made plainly in the secular manner, with a large cape of the same, reaching below the waist, a small cap of plain white net, and a black dotted net veil fastened over it.

13. The outdoor dress is a close bonnet of fine twilled woollen stuff, with a thick silk gauze veil tied on it; the strings of the bonnet and veil are of black ribbon, and no other trimming allowed but a curtain at the back and a plain band round the bonnet, of the same stuff.

14. A cloak of black twilled woollen stuff, or German cashmere, or of black broadcloth, according to the season, fastened up the front, sufficiently long to conceal the habit and underclothing. There are arm-holes, a deep falling collar, and a neckpiece (both lined) to the cloak, and the white collar of the coif is worn over it.

15. The summer cloak is lined all through with black glazed muslin. Black gloves, strong boots, loose hood of black cloth, are also worn, if the weather requires such protection.

16. When a Postulant wears the outdoor dress, a collar, resembling that of the coif, is pinned round her neck, over the collar of the cloak. A black silk neckerchief is allowed.

17. The religious habit, including veil, coif and guimp is not made out of the convent.

---

1 A close-fitting cap worn under the veil.
2 A light, strong cotton.
3 Those who were novices and had not professed their vows.

18. Check aprons and sleeves are added to the dress of the Sisters in the hospitals, but are not worn at Mass, Benediction, or Confession.
19. It is customary for the Sisters to wear a black stuff lined petticoat; blue check muslin pocket-hankerchiefs; and flannel vests during the winter months are allowed.
20. The Sisters do not leave off any part of the religious dress during the day, except the outer sleeves when engaged in the schools, hospitals, etc., and in manual work.
21. The Professed Sisters and Novices wear a night veil of white calico.
22. The Lay Sisters' habit has no train. They wear a white apron at the common exercises, and a check one when engaged in manual work.

LAY SISTERS

Doc. 29: *Guide for the Religious Called Sisters of Mercy* (London, 1866).[1]

Lay sisters carried out the domestic duties in the convents. They came from less wealthy backgrounds, and were less well educated than choir sisters. The following extract reveals what was expected of them as women and as nuns.

The judicious selection and careful instruction and training of Lay Sisters is the utmost importance. In the selection the qualifications described by the Rule should be considered essentials. Those admitted should be young, healthy, and active; and while, on the one hand, too high a degree of refinement would probably render them unfit for the duties of a Lay Sister, on the other, any remarkable rudeness, roughness of manner, or vulgarity of appearance would be still more objectionable, since the Rule requires that they '*should have manners and appearances suited to religious who must be seen in public*'.

Before admitting a Lay Postulant, her future duties and the nature of the state of a Lay Sister should be fully explained to her; for many pious young persons imagine that if they can but enter a convent, labour, care, contradiction, &c, will be at an end, and that they will be free to spend all the time they please in reading pious books and saying their prayers: they rarely realise to themselves that they embrace a life of labour and subjection by becoming Lay Sisters; this, therefore, should be strongly represented to them.

The '*plain education*' required by the Constitutions may be considered to comprise such a proficiency in religious instruction, reading, writing, and plain work, as is necessary for the discharge of their duties.

Occupation – 'though they shall be generally employed in domestic work, yet as circumstances may occur which would render their assistance in other situations necessary, they ought to be persons who could occasionally accompany the Choir

1 This *Guide*, though published in England, was used by the Mercy Congregation in Ireland.

Sisters, without there being any remarkable outward difference' . . . The ordinary occupation of the Lay Sister is the discharge of the domestic duties, as cooking, laundry-work and the like.

Whenever a Lay Sister is employed in the House of Mercy, on the visitation, or in any other duty with the Choir Sisters, she is always to consider herself under subjection to them in these duties, however junior to her they may be; and she should obey and act towards them with respectful deference. The Lay Sisters do not give instruction, or converse on the visitation, unless the Choir Sisters, whom they accompany, direct them to do so.

Dress – Their religious dress is the same as that of the Choir Sister, except that '*the Lay Sisters shall be distinguished by a white apron – which shall be blessed by the Bishop – along with the habit and veil, and shall be always considered an essential part of their religious dress. Their habit shall be without train'*. (Constitutions, chap, 9th, see. 2d) – Their habit is made only long enough to touch the ground; quite straight round the bottom, without any slope: the outside sleeves are about twenty-seven inches wide, and they descend to the middle joint of the finger. Their black veils are about nine inches narrower and nine inches shorter than those of the Choir Sisters. Attached to their chaplets[1] they wear a brass crucifix.

Diet – The diet of the Lay Sisters is the same as that of the Choir Sisters. When the bell rings for their meals, they should attend promptly, with their habits and sleeves down: they do not wear their coloured aprons at meals, or at any of the Community duties. They sit together according to seniority in the refectory. Their meals should be served hot and comfortable, like those of the Sisters who dine at the second table. When the Choir Sisters have recreation in the refectory, the Lay Sisters have it likewise.

Recreation – It is our custom that the Lay Sisters take recreation apart from the Choir Sisters, except when there is but one. When, however, the Mother Superior and the majority of the Vocals think it expedient to admit them to a portion of the Community recreation, it can be done with the approval of the Bishop; but in such case care should be taken to make them clearly understand, previous to profession, that this privilege is to be regarded as a concession, and not as a right; and that at any time when the Mother Superior thinks it necessary to deprive one or all of the privilege, she is at perfect liberty to do so, without consulting the Chapter, after having taken the advice of the Council thereon. Should it seem necessary, a Choir Sister may be appointed to preside at their recreation. The directions to be observed by the Choir Sisters at their recreations must be equally attended to by the Lay Sisters, who should most carefully abstain from all discussions on the respective merits, qualifications, &c. of the Choir Sisters, their connections, former rank, &c., and from all manifestation of preference or disapproval of any individual; in short, from all remarks and discussions which they would object to have mentioned to the Mother Superior.

1 A string of fifty-five beads.

Manner of addressing Sisters – In this country they address the Choir Professed as 'Mrs Mary N.'; to the Choir Novices as 'Miss Mary N.'; those in office as 'Mother Mary N.'; the Superior as 'Rev. Mother'; each other as 'Sister N.'; except while they are Postulants, when they are called by their Christian names without prefixing 'Sister'.

They have no vote – Lay Sisters have neither active nor passive vote,[1] however long professed.

Reason of these distinctions – When presenting their petition for reception or profession, they add, 'in quality of Lay Sister'. Such distinctions as these between Lay and Choir Sisters are not peculiar to our Congregation; they are common to all Orders that receive Lay Sisters: in some they are still more marked. The object of them is not to favour a worldly spirit of distinction or exclusiveness; the Vicar of Christ would not authorise by his approval and confirmation rules continuing such prescriptions, if they were intended to encourage such an unholy spirit. Distinctions like these are prescribed because experience proves their necessity and utility in preserving religious discipline and due subordination in the Lay Sisters, and in checking forwardness, presumption, and disrespect which a footing of complete equality with those whom Providence has placed in a higher rank might often produce in persons of limited education and scanty refinement; and because, by thus keeping them in humility and due subjection, they assist them to attain to the perfection of their holy and secure state. It is therefore considered expedient for the Community, and for the Lay Sisters themselves, that where the different grades of Lay and Choir Sisters are preserved, the distinctions between them should be well marked.

Manner of the Choir Sisters to the Lay Sisters – But though the Choir Sisters should refrain from undue familiarity with the Lay Sisters, they should treat them with cordial charity, and carefully abstain from speaking or acting towards them in a rude, sharp, inconsiderate, or mistress-like manner. They should practise towards them, as well as towards each other, all that is prescribed by our Rule on charity. They should never forget that the Lay Sisters are, equally with themselves, the spouses of Christ, and are very dear to Him, because they represent, in a particular manner, His state of humiliation when He came not to be served but to serve.

They should never find fault with them in presence of the inmates of the House of Mercy, Orphanage, &c., and should require these to obey and respect them.

They must not occupy the time of the Lay Sisters without permission or interfere with them in any way in the discharge of their respective duties farther than obedience warrants, since they have no more authority over them than over each other, except through obedience.

LIFE IN A RELIGIOUS COMMUNITY

Becoming a nun, or at least a choir sister, allowed women to partake in a variety of tasks which were not generally deemed suitable for lay women. Many who attempted to enter convent life found it a difficult and onerous option. They questioned their motives and suitability for a life which demanded a lot from them. Other women were made extremely happy by their entrance into communities.

A Request to Leave the Convent

Doc. 30.1: Cullen Papers, section 333/6/8, File 11: Sisters of Mercy, 1860. DDA.

Convent of Our Lady of Mercy
Baggot Street

My dear Archbishop,

As you expressed a wish on yesterday to Revnd. Mother that I should write and tell you my reasons for wishing to be dispensed from my vows, I now endeavour to do so as well as I can. I feel I have no vocation nor never had. I really think I came into the convent in a fit of fervour. I was only a few months from school and was to have returned there again only I came into the convent. I was really only a month thinking of it seriously and did not mention it to my confessor – Father Rorke, the Jesuit, till 3 weeks before I entered. The 1st time I spoke to him he told me to put it out of my head and to pray that the will of God might be done in my regard, but when I asked him again he gave me leave and so I entered immediately. He did not know me at all and I never was really candid with him, nor gave him my confidence. Ever since I was a child I have felt the greatest difficulty in going to confession and am afraid to tell my sins. Ever since I came into the convent I have staid [sic] away for a month from confessions and once as a novice I was three months away and as to Holy Communion, I have constantly staid away from it, even when making my vows I felt I was not in the state of grace as I had not made a good confession previously. Since then I made 2 or 3 general confessions and, after them, I got a little more faithful to my religious exercises etc., etc., but after a very short time I fell away again, from the moment I entered the novitiate up to the present day I have never known what it was to be faithful to my religious obligations. As to my external duties, I went through those often without a fault been [sic] found with me but of course without any merit . . . I did not do things for God, but often for creatures, one of my great faults is human respect, always thinking what people say or think of me. Besides I was very much attached to my superior which I fear was a great inducement to me to remain in religion. I thought I could never be happy away from her. I was under her care for the entire of my religious life with the exception of the last 2 years. I have never known what [it] was really to subdue myself 'till lately. I feel I never will be a good nun and that I have not expressed myself sufficiently in this note. Might I ask your Lordship to see Father Curtis. He was here today and [I] gave him full liberty to make known to you anything he knows of me through confession. I think I have really been candid with him and perhaps he could explain my reasons better than I could do in writing. I hope my Lord that I may expect to see you as you promised, after the retreat, as I can do nothing till I see you for I have made a promise to God not to do anything without your consent and blessing. If you chance to think of me during the retreat will you say a little prayer that God may direct me. Believe me to remain your much respectful and obedient child in JC,

SR MARY STANISCLAUS McCANN
Friday evening, July 6th '60.

P.S. Father Curtis told me that one of the greatest obstacles to my being in religion was the manner in which I approached the sacraments, but you can ask him anything you like about me that will [make] you a better judge about the matter.

Happiness in Convent Life

Doc. 30.2: Hamilton Papers, File 36/6/45 (Nuns, 1843), DDA.

St Mary's
May 12/'43

Revd. Dear Father,

Although you have not noticed any of the letters I have written to you since my entrance into St Mary's, I yet feel convinced your kind feelings in my regard have not ceased and that you did not wish to spend your precious time writing to me from the conviction that I was under the guidance of good superiors.

Now I come to the purpose of these hurried lines. They are to let you know that the day for my reception has been fixed for the 23rd of this month, and to beg a special intention in your masses and pious prayers for self and two lay Sisters who are to be received on the same day. Will you pray that I may never provoke God to take the Holy Habit from me, however, if I cannot serve God fruitfully in this dear community 'his holy will be done' but I have every hope from the wonderful mercy God has already shewn me that he will give me grace to persevere to the end. Will you above all pray that I may [be] humble and obedient, and the same graces for the lay sisters who are to be received with me and for all the noviceship. Before I conclude all I have to say is that I regret each day more and more that I have ever given an hour of my precious time to the world. Sr M. Josephine is expecting to be professed in little more than three months. I hope you will pray for her too. Mama and Papa are quite well. I sincerely hope you are the same. Ever believe me Revd. dear Father.

Yours sincerely, grateful child in JC.
LUCY MARY SHERLOCK

I go into retreat on tomorrow evening

A Sister of Mercy. Nuns from many orders were responsible for educating women over the years. (Mercy International Centre, Dublin)

Part II

EDUCATION

Women School principals in 1903, from the magazine, *Lady of the House*.
(National Library of Ireland)

INTRODUCTION

THE INTRODUCTION of the national school system in 1831 was to be a major event in Irish educational history. However, there was some provision for the education of Irish children before 1831. Hedge schools, or pay schools, offered education to boys and girls. Poor schools were operated by philanthropists and religious communities. Nano Nagle (1718–1784) and Teresa Mulally (1728–1803), for example, ran poor schools in Cork and Dublin from the late eighteenth century.[1] For those with money, education was provided privately either by a tutor or governesses, or, particularly for the wealthy, in schools in England and France. In 1831 the establishment of the Commissioners for National Education allowed grants to be made to local schools provided that children of all denominations would be taught, and that separate times were set aside for religious education. The national system which developed, however, took on a strong denominational character. Catholic and Protestant clerics were not in favour of non-denominational education and the majority of the schools under the national system were run by and for Catholics. The system entitled both poor girls and poor boys to an education. By 1900 there were 8,684 national schools in operation throughout the country. Lay voluntary groups, usually with a strong religious motive, continued to provide education for boys and girls, particularly those of the poor or destitute classes. Some of these groups operated 'ragged' schools in the cities of Belfast, Dublin, Cork and Limerick, throughout the century.

During the nineteenth century, girls of the poorer classes were offered the rudiments of education within the national system. The education provided was guided by their expected destination in life. Girls were unlikely to learn more than the most basic arithmetical skills, they were taught to read and write but since domestic service was the expected fate of most girls, great emphasis was placed on the learning of the domestic arts and sewing. A practical education for lives that would be spent in domestic labour. The range of the instruction provided to girls was narrower than that provided for boys. It was not until the Irish Education Act

---

1 For further information on these women see T. J. Walsh, *Nano Nagle and the Presentation Sisters* (Dublin, 1959) and Roland Burke Savage, *A Valiant Dublin Woman: The Story of George's Hill 1766–1940* (Dublin, 1940).

of 1892 that attendance was made compulsory and it was only from this period that girls attended the primary school to the same extent as boys.[1]

The restricted education offered to girls, at all social levels, reflected society's attitudes as to a woman's proper place. Women's role was in the domestic sphere, and the care of children and husbands, cooking and cleaning did not, it was thought, require vast educational knowledge. Women were considered naturally inferior to men, their intellectual abilities less capable of development. God had created men and women for different purposes, and therefore with different attributes. Physical and intellectual labour suited men, while women were considered weak in mind and body.

Primary state-supported education allowed equal access to education. Education beyond this level for girls was unusual. Secondary education for girls was generally confined to those from the middle classes whose parents could afford the fees involved, or who could spare the daughter from a need to find employment.

The most dramatic changes in girls' education in the nineteenth century came about in the secondary and third levels. The establishment of the Ladies' Collegiate school in Belfast (1859), the Queen's Institute (1861), and Alexandra College (1866), both in Dublin, heralded new directions in the education of middle-class women. These establishments attempted to provide vocational skills to their students and allow an education comparable to that received by male students at second level. It was the founders of these institutes, Anne Jellicoe, Margaret Byers and Isabella Tod, who initiated campaigns to improve educational provision for middle-class women at both second and third level. From the 1860s the question of the desirability of secondary and university education for women was vigorously debated, many of these debates reflecting those occurring in England at the same time. The passage of the Intermediate Act of 1878 was an important development in making higher education available to women.[2] The Act was passed in an attempt to improve school attendance and educational standards, as well as to provide a good basis for university education, and was originally aimed only at boys' education. A campaign led by Isabella Tod and Margaret Byers ensured that girls would also benefit from the Act. Under the Act a Board of Commissioners was formed, which organised examinations and awarded prizes based upon examination results. Fees were then paid to teachers on a 'results' basis, the government hoping that this would encourage more efficiency and

1 Mary E. Daly, 'The development of the national school system in Ireland 1831–40', in A. Cosgrove and D. McCartney, (eds.), *Studies in Irish History* (Dublin, 1979), pp 161–3.
2 Anne V. O'Connor, 'Influences affecting girls' secondary education in Ireland 1860–1910', *Archivium Hibernicum*, 41 (1986), pp 83–98; *idem.*, 'The revolution in girls' secondary education in Ireland, 1860–1910', in Cullen, *Girls Don't Do Honours*, pp 31–54. For a general overview on the elementary system, see Donald H. Akenson, *The Irish Education Experiment* (London, 1970). For the content of school readers, see J. M. Goldstrom, *The Social Content of Education 1808–1870* (Shannon, 1972).

dedication on the part of teachers. The most important aspect of the Act for girls was that it provided grants to male and female students on an equal basis. Public opinion in Ireland was originally opposed to examinations for girls. However, once the Intermediate examinations got under way, newspapers began to publish the results. Such reporting created competition between schools, particularly those of different religious persuasions.

Women who wanted to enter the male preserves of the universities attracted much criticism. Society was fearful that educated women would forsake their 'natural' sphere of action. Arguments were put forward by the medical profession which 'proved' that higher education would damage women's health irrevocably. Women's brains were too small to carry all that knowledge, their reproductive organs would atrophy, too much education, it was believed, would make them unable and unwilling to engage in marital or maternal responsibilities.[1]

In defiance of public opinion, a small number of middle-class women campaigned for access to university education. In 1879, the government, after years of debate regarding university education in Ireland, instituted the Royal University of Ireland. Under this new Act, the existing Queen's Colleges at Belfast, Cork and Galway remained in existence and the Royal University of Ireland was, in reality, an examination body. Since it was an examining body, students could prepare themselves in any way suited to them for exams. The degrees and scholarships of the RUI were open to men and women.[2] Colleges for girls were set up to allow them take advantage of this new system. The Dominican convent in Eccles Street, Dublin, was the first institution set up specifically to educate Catholic women. The nuns opened a college there in 1882 and candidates were prepared for the examinations of the Intermediate Board and the Royal University. It was not until 1904 that women gained access to Trinity College, Dublin, the last university to allow them take their degrees. Educational reform at second and third level were potentially of benefit to all classes in society. But one needed money in order to take advantage of the changes that had occurred. Table 2.1 shows the level of involvement in education by boys and girls in 1871 and 1911.

By the end of the nineteenth century, the educational provisions made for girls had altered considerably from those that existed at the beginning of the century. This change resulted to a considerable degree from the expansion of convent schools and the campaigns for reform organised by women activists. Though the provision of education clearly improved, the actual content of education for girls altered little. For most of the century girls were taught those skills, such as needlework, which were deemed particularly suited to

1 See Phyllis Stock, *Better than Rubies: A History of Women's Education* (London, 1978); Rosemary Deem, *Women and Schooling* (London, 1978).
2 Eibhlín Breathnach, 'Charting new waters: women's experience in higher education, 1879–1908', in Cullen, *Girls Don't Do Honours*, pp 55–78.

domestic life. In some convent schools, middle-class girls did receive a broader and more intellectual education, but even here the primary intention was to prepare them for a life of supposed 'ease' and accomplishment as wife and mother. Irish women did become increasingly literate over the nineteenth century but, for most, their education served to reinforce their role as wives and mothers in society.

Table 2.1: Educational Involvement in Ireland, 1871–1911

Years	Primary	Secondary	University
1871			
Male	316,300	12,000	2,900
Female	299,400	9,200	——
1911			
Male	325,500	27,500	3,100
Female	335,700	13,600	280

Source: *Census of Ireland, General Reports*, 1891 and 1911.

PRIMARY EDUCATION

Lady Shaw's School

Doc. 31.1: MS, Lady Shaw's Day School, Murray Papers, File 33/5
(Education, undated) DDA.

Many wealthy Protestant women lent their support financially and morally to educational establishments in the nineteenth century. Many of these schools were perceived by Catholics as being proselytising agencies, attempting to win Catholic children to the Protestant faith. Catholics tried, as far as possible, to keep a record of these schools and monitor their impact on the Catholic community. This report describing Lady Shaw's school was forwarded to Archbishop Murray in Dublin. It comes from the first half of the century.

. . . Lady Shaw's day school: I have deferred mentioning this school 'till the last on account of insinuations thrown out against it (by persons who never visited the school) to its disadvantage. This school has no connection whatever with any other establishment, it is entirely supported at Lady Shaw's expense – the children, about seventy in number, (amongst whom when I had visited this school there were two Protestants) are all fed twice a week and respectably clothed in winter – the most necessitous receiving breakfast four times a week – the scholars [who] are all females, [are] taught reading, writing and plainwork – the mistress is a Mrs Gregg, of course a Protestant – at this school I have met Lady Shaw – who enquired of me if her scholars attend the chapel on Sundays – adding in presence of the whole school that if I complained of any one neglecting this duty, that one should be expelled [from] the school. This declaration perfectly satisfied me, that no underhand work of proselytising was then or is now going forward in this school. I must add that many poor people will send their children here whether we like it or not, on acc[ount] of their receiving victuals and clothing.

But besides this school there is a Sunday School, which Lady Shaw's family attend – in this family there is a person who publicly declared himself no emancipator[1] – and I believe him – he introduced tracts – gets the testament read and part of it committed to memory . . . This gentleman acted in like manner formerly in a school established by Miss Arbrey, but which has been long since given up.

1 Referring to Catholic emancipation.

An Appeal by Some Ladies to Keep a School Open

Doc. 31.2: MS, Gloucester Place School, Letter to Archdeacon Hamilton, 5 December 1836. DDA.

Many lay women organised schools throughout the earlier part of the nineteenth century. For some women, it was an attempt to support themselves financially. For others, it was seen as a means of counteracting the proselytising efforts of either Catholic or Protestant schools. The National Board of Education was, as we have noted, established in 1831. Many bishops encouraged school patrons under their control to use the system in order to benefit from the financial advantages that went with it. Archbishop Murray of Dublin was in favour of using the system. The power exerted by clerics on schools and groups of lay women can be witnessed in the following document which shows a group of lay women attempting to keep their school operational in spite of the wishes of the archbishop to place their pupils in a near-by national school.

No 4 Lower Gloucester Place
December 5th 1836

Revd. Sir,

With feelings of pain and disappointment we have been informed by the mistress of the Gloucester Place school of your intention to discontinue it. We beg leave to submit to your consideration a few of the very important reasons which should, and we trust, will, influence you to relinquish so dreadful – so injurious a project.

The continuity of the great national school is it seems the ostensible cause alleged for the annihilation of the above establishment but tho' it has been opened for two months back, not a single child from the Gloucester Place school has gone to it, and you may rest assured, that if you persevere in the destruction of the latter, Lady Herbertson's Methodistical school so immediately in its vicinity will reap a plentiful harvest by your so doing – from her and Protestant schools, numbers of children have been constantly rescued, and well instructed at Gloucester Place in Roman Catholic principles – think for one moment not only of the horrible consequences likely to result to the 164 children which, it may be averaged, now receive a useful and religious education there, being let loose on the world, but to the rising and future generations of the very numerous and distressed population of that neighbourhood.

Mr Sweetman's having charitably given the house for the ground rent and nearly £100 having been lately expended to render it fit for education purposes, it is now quite unsuitable for a private residence and indeed never could be made so, as if the metal pillars were taken away it would fall, etc. – tho' the 'gentleman's committee' has pledged themselves to restore it in the same order as they received it, should the school ever be given up – Just figure

94

to yourself what a prodigal, nay unjustifiable, waste of the little funds of the establishment, if it were not to be discontinued, and at a period when it is completely furnished in every respect, even to a good supply of books for the children's improvement . . . The entire expenses of the school now amount to no more than from £50 to £60 a year . . . The £480 sent in by the Misses Field, for the original foundation of it, was collected not in these parishes – not for a merely ephemeral purpose, but that the institution should be permanent – would not £100 given towards the building of King's Inn Street school be a great injustice, if in return for such amalgamation Gloucester Place should not be supported and continued from the same funds as the former . . .

In addition to the school being at present so well furnished and fitted out for education . . . it enjoys the great advantage of the regular attendance of a clergyman . . . so that we earnestly implore you will be pleased to relinquish every idea of what you may term amalgamating it with that of Marlborough Street, but which in reality would be the total annihilation not only of the Gloucester Place school, but of all the advantages of a decidedly Roman Catholic education now enjoyed by the poor children of the vicinity for whom so many snares are laid by Lady Herbertson and her proselytising adherents – The favour of an answer is earnestly solicited and anxiously expected by Revd. Sir,

The undersigned
MARGARET GORDON
MARIAN AMELIA FIELD
MARY RONAN
E. O. FARRELL
M. A. MURRAY
ELIZA PALLES
M. A. LAMBERT

Estimate of the annual expenses of the school at present

Miss Begg's salary	£25 . 0
Miss Townly	20 . 0
House rent	20 . 0
	65 . 0
Allowance from Board of Education	15 . 0
	50 . 0

The children's pennies a week average above £10 a year which would meet their ticket money – and about ½ ton of coals each winter . . .

The Coombe Ragged School

Doc. 31.3: *Annual Report of the Coombe Ragged School, 1870* (Dublin, 1871).

The following document is an annual report describing the operation of the Coombe ragged school. Ragged schools were organised by Catholics and Protestants and were intended to cater for the very poorest and most destitute children. Most ragged schools provided food and, on occasion, clothing to their pupils. The Protestant ragged schools that operated in Dublin during the last century were, in a large number of cases, managed by women. Not only did these women, who were usually wealthy, manage the schools but they also wrote the annual reports which were presented to the public. They constructed these reports to gain the maximum financial support from their intended audience. The issue of proselytism made ragged schools controversial institutions from mid-century. The Coombe ragged school was established in 1853 in Dublin, and was run by a committee composed principally of Protestant women. One of the prime movers in the establishment of Protestant ragged schools in Dublin was Mrs Ellen Smyly (1815–1901).[1] Smyly had begun her work with children when she was nineteen. She married a medical doctor in 1844 and had eleven children, many of whom later helped her run her homes and schools.

Amongst all the means used for benefiting the poor, I do not think any have been more successful than the Mission Ragged schools. As the name 'ragged' implies, they are open to the very poorest of the poor, seeking to benefit them temporally, and raise them to a position of self-respect and industry. In their missionary character, their object is, by means of the children, to introduce into the homes of ignorance and crime the blessed truths contained in God's Holy Word. In this consists their superiority over all government schools, which cannot, of necessity, be of a missionary character.

For the past fifteen years the Coombe School has been exercising a wonderful influence in the neighbourhood. To it come daily about two hundred children – boys, girls and little ones so small, that the Infant School does not reach down far enough. There is even a 'Baby School', for the babies would hinder the studies of older brother and sister; so they are all put in a room together, and they learn such verses and hymns as are simple enough for them. They are, at least, out of harm's way, and thoroughly enjoy their school-life.

It would be impossible to calculate what may be the results of such long-continued missionary work. We are permitted to see examples of it here and there, quite enough to encourage us to persevere. Within the last few months we have been permitted to see much fruits, enough to throw all the difficulties and trials into the shade. Some of them must form part of our Report.

1 Vivienne Smyly, *The Early History of Mrs Smyly's Homes and Schools* (privately printed, Dublin[?], 1976).

96

The first is given by our Missionary to cabmen. Writing in November, he says: 'This day I went to see a cabman's wife that was very ill. They live in a small top-back-room in — street. While speaking to her on the 8th chapter of Romans, a young woman came in with a bowl of broth to the sick woman. Seeing me, she sat down, and seemed very attentive to all I said. When done, I put a few questions to her, thinking that she was Roman Catholic. When I gave her one of the bills for the meeting that evening, she said, "I think I could repeat the chapter you are after reading, and the most of the Hundred Texts." I asked her how she got to know so much of the Word of God? "I am a Protestant, thank God, but was a Roman Catholic when I was young. At that time we lived in — street. My father was dead, and my mother very poor. She had four of us to support. She sent me and my sister to the Coombe Mission School, so that we might get our breakfast there. I shall never forget the first day I went. I was taught a verse – John iii:16. I never forgot it, and I trust never will. I remained for four years at the school, and then my mother took us to my aunt's house, about six miles out of Dublin. There my Bible was taken from me, and they compelled me to go to Mass; but I knew about the Lord Jesus Christ, and prayed to God through Him, while in the Roman Catholic chapel; so, after some time, they got to know that I would never be a good Roman Catholic, as they called it; and I was sent to service in Dublin. And every Sunday evening, when I got out, I went to some Protestant place of worship. My mother died; but they would not allow me to see her, lest I might do her harm. I often prayed that the Lord would open her mind to the errors of the Church of Rome, and I do believe He has heard me. I often taught her some verses, which she could repeat. I am now married to a Protestant, and can go to church every Sunday; and at night we read God's blessed book. He has a good place with the — Company. I would like you to see him; and he will tell you what I have suffered for the truth." After leaving them, I went down to the North-wall, and asked to see him; and I must say, that I was fully satisfied that the lord, in His loving-kindness, joined those two Christians together. . . .'

Ever since the opening of the Coombe Schools, we have given a breakfast each morning to all who needed it; and there are many who come to whom it is the only certain meal. One day last winter, a lady, who came to visit the school, noticed the great poverty of the children, especially the infants. Her heart bled for them; and when she went home, she determined to do something for them. So she asked some friends, and they helped her so kindly, that she wrote, saying if Mrs P could take the trouble, she would provide money for a dinner every day for seventy of the poorest all the winter.

It was difficult to determine which were the poorest; so we have to settle to give the dinners in turn to half the infants one day; the other half the next. . . .

If any one doubts the necessity of giving food in our Ragged Schools, we would ask them to visit them, and ask the resident missionary to take them to see a few of the homes of the children. Such visits would do more than any words of ours to increase the numbers of our helpers, and to make the hearts of our friends glow with thankfulness, that thus, in the poorest parts of our city, the children are fed and taught, and trained to be useful servants and citizens. God grant that many of them may become servants of Christ, and citizens of that beautiful city whose building and maker is God!

School Textbooks

Doc. 31.4: Commissioners of National Education in Ireland, *Reading Book for the Use of Female Schools* (Dublin, 1846).

From the 1830s the Commissioners of National Education compiled readers for use in Irish primary schools. From 1846 reading books, which were supplementary to the main readers were also available to girls' schools. The books were in use throughout the century and were frequently revised. The extracts used in the readers were specifically 'intended for the instruction of females in household and domestic duties'. Topics covered included household management, attending the sick, motherhood, and the care of children. The following two extracts were typical of the type of material thought suitable for the girls' readers.

On Female Acquirements

Time is not unfrequently misspent in mere reading. The getting through a certain number of volumes is thought to be a meritorious exertion, and is looked back upon with complacency; though, perhaps, all this painstaking labour has been without benefit, and has done nothing towards enriching or strengthing the mind. Some read without recollecting; many more without thinking; and many again without applying what they read to any moral or practical purpose. For, after all, literature is a mere step to knowledge; and the error often lies in our identifying one with the other. Literature may, perhaps, make us vain; – true knowledge must render us humble.

We are all apt to imagine that what costs us trouble must be of value; yet there is much need of discretion, both in the choice and manner of our acquirements. In both, utility should always be a question – utility as it affects the mind. History, for instance, with all its accompanying branches, is in this view a suitable and most improving study.

Not unfrequently, too, are we wrong in our estimate of acquirements. We value them by their rarity; and are apt to neglect what is essential, because it is easy, for the sake of what is difficult because it is common.

It is very important, not only that the mind should be well informed, but that there should be a taste for knowledge; which should be appreciated for its own sake, not merely as a distinction. Slovenly attire, an ill-conducted household, and an ill-arranged table, are in the minds of many, identified with female acquirement. If the woman of mind bears with equanimity petty vexations, – if she lends a reluctant ear to family tales, – if she is not always expatiating on her economy, nor entertaining by a discussion of domestic annoyances; she is not the less capable of controlling her household, or of maintaining order in its several departments. Rather will she occupy her station with more dignity, and fulfil its duties with greater ease.

At the same time she should ever bear in mind, that knowledge is not to elevate her above her station, or to excuse her for the discharge of its most trifling duties. It is to correct vanity, and repress pretension. It is to teach her to know her place and her functions; to make her content with the one, and willing to fulfil the other. It is to render her more useful, more humble, and more happy.

Such a woman will be, of all other things, the best satisfied with her lot. She will not seek distinction, and therefore, will not meet with disappointment. She will not be dependent on the world, and thus she will avoid its vexations. She will be liable to neither restlessness nor *ennui* – but she will be happy in her own home, and by her own hearth, – in the fulfilment of religious and domestic duty, and in the profitable employment of her time.

Duties of a Cook

A cook should be healthy and strong, and particularly clean in her person. Her hands, though they may be rough from the nature of her employments, yet, should have a clean appearance. Her honesty and sobriety must be unquestionable.

The kitchen should be thoroughly cleaned twice during the week, and well swept each day; besides which, the broom and mop should always be at hand, to remove anything that may have fallen on the floor, while the business is going on. A dirty floor and fire-place, unpolished utensils, with basins, jugs, or other articles left lying about, are symptoms of a slovenly cook, and are sufficient to excite suspicions of her nicety in things of greater importance. The cleaning of the kitchen, pantry, passages, and kitchen stairs, should be over before breakfast, that it may not interfere with the usual business of the day.

After each day's cooking is over, the grate and hearth should be cleared, a small fire made up, and the boiler and kettle filled and set to boil. She should then proceed to wash her dishes, having previously prepared two tubs, one with clean hot water, and the other with cold; in which latter the plates and dishes should be well rinsed, before they are put on the rack to dry . . .

There are a few cooks who are not extravagant in coals. A good fire is essential while cooking is going on, which may perhaps, be the cause of the habit they acquire of keeping a large one at other times of the day. A cook should never suffer her fire to get very low; for she wastes both much coal and time by this negligence. A fire should be regularly supplied with coals, which would prevent it from ever being so smokey as to be unfit for use at a few minutes' notice; and it should be generally known that smoke is merely unconsumed coal; and if it get low, when anything is required to be prepared quickly, the cook has no resource, but to apply the bellows furiously; so that, before the fire burns properly, much must be wasted . . .

A good cook will always be careful that the spits are wiped clean while they are hot, and left ready for the next day's use. The jacks should be oiled and cleaned occasionally, or the dust will clog the wheels, prevent it going well, and will make it necessary to have it taken down and more throughly cleaned. It is bad management in a cook ever to be without hot water; especially if she lives in a family where there are young children, for whom it is in frequent, and sometimes immediate demand. The salt box and candle box should both be kept very clean. The former should be hung near the fire, as common salt attracts water from the air and dissolves; and the latter as far from the fire as can be, in a dry place.

Silver spoons should never be used in the kitchen, unless for preparing preserves: wooden and iron spoons are as cleanly, and may be used without fear of scratching or bending them.

Report on Convent Schools

Doc. 31.5: *Special Report of Convent Schools in Connection with the Board of National Education* HC 1864 (405), xlvi.

The National Board commissioned a special report on convent schools in 1860. In many of the schools run by nuns, the importance of the religious and moral aspects of education were fundamental issues in their teaching. Published by the government in 1864, the report was concerned with the standard of secular education imparted to the pupils. Writing in 1860, Head Inspector Sheridan noted that nuns had a 'limited acquaintance with those improved methods of teaching and school organisation which have received the sanction of experience'.[1] Nuns were not examined and classified as other teachers. Some of the information submitted to the inquiry was highly critical in tone. Inspector Andrew O'Callaghan's report of 1864, dealing with a convent school in Limerick, noted that the nuns 'have not succeeded in any marked manner in rescuing from total ignorance the children belonging to the more destitute classes'.[2] The government inspector did, however, recognise that if secular education was in some instances lacking, nuns certainly pro-vided a 'moral' education superior to that given in lay schools.

Mr Nixon, Tralee District, says, in reference to reading, including oral spelling and explanation:

In many schools the reading was unsatisfactory, owing principally to a bad accent and incorrect pronunciation; and I have constantly endeavoured, in the course of my inspection, to impress upon the teachers that the highest importance is attached to good reading, and that, therefore, they should give

---

1 'Head Inspector Sheridan's General Report, for the Year 1860', in *Special Report of Convent Schools in Connection with the Board of National Education*, HC 1864 (179), xlvi, p 11.
2 'District Inspector Andrew O'Callaghan's Report on Sexton Street Convent National School', in *ibid.*, p 158.

the reading their most careful attention. After finishing the reading lesson, the pupils of each class are exercised in oral spelling and in explanation of words. In oral spelling the answer is usually respectable, but in the meaning of words, great deficiency is frequently shown.

Penmanship – Writing is taught with much care in this part of the country, and with few exceptions, both teachers and pupils write well; in the convent schools particularly, the writing of the senior classes is excellent, both as regards execution and style. It would, in my opinion, be a very great improvement, and would also economise much time, if the copy books were so prepared as to have the precedent or copy line at the top of each page, and similar to those now in use in many respectable schools in large towns, but which are not in connection with the National Board.

Arithmetic – In too many cases this branch is not taught with that degree of care that the subject requires. It is made a dry exercise of the memory, and pupils are not infrequently found unable to account for the several steps of the process in some of the simplest questions in the compound rules and proportion, much less to give anything like the reason of the rule by which such questions are solved. It has always been my object, in examining upon this most necessary branch of knowledge, to see that the pupils are well grounded in the elementary principles, and are made to possess a correct notion of notation and numeration, as well as to have been made acquainted with the more useful tables; and this much once acquired, the study of arithmetic, under a judicious teacher, becomes to the youthful mind a profitable and a pleasing intellectual exercise. . . . .

Mr O'Loughlin, Mallow District, says, in reference to reading, including oral spelling and explanation:

Generally speaking, the reading is coarse, monotonous, and mechanical. Many of the teachers pronounce incorrectly – still more do the pupils. This, however, is only a secondary defect, though still an important one. What I mainly find fault with is, that the pupils repeat the words without understanding either the individual or collective sense of them. Hence, it is, that as reading is the source of most of their knowledge, the latter is the same half-understood thing as the former.

Penmanship – As writing is a purely mechanical operation, the main things essential to success in it are proper appliances, taste, and practice. The last is amply provided for by the every-day arrangements of the schools. Taste, in a matter where there is room for so little variety, is but another name for attention, and is, therefore, always at command; proper appliances are still, I regret to say, by no means so common in the schools as they ought to be. Paper is seldom superabundant; and notwithstanding the advantages offered by the Board, generally shows a large proportion of the rubbish purchased in the shops; the ink is invariably scarce, and so curdled and gritty as to be almost unfit for use; the pens are, in a word, abominable – mere rusty bits of iron, which, scraping, sticking, and spattering, make writing a physical impossibility. In order not to disfigure my note-book with them and the ink, I have always been obliged to carry about with me some for my own use . . .

Manual Instruction for Girls in Primary Schools

Doc. 31.6: *Commission on Manual and Practical Instruction in Primary Schools under the Board of National Education in Ireland, Final Report of the Commissioners*, HC 1898 [C. –8923], xliii.

Towards the end of the century there was an increased interest in the type of education which was being offered to girls in primary schools. In 1897–8, the government published the findings of its inquiry into the training of pupils in such schools. As ever, concern lay in ensuring that girls acquired the domestic skills necessary to manage their own homes, or to work as servants in the homes of others.

Cookery – We [the commissioners] regard cookery as a most important branch of practical instruction. It is of special importance in Ireland where the labouring and artizan classes are sadly ignorant of the art of cookery, their food in consequence being seldom prepared in as economical or nutritious a manner as it might be.

. . . According to the latest returns, viz., those for 1896, cookery was taught in 83 national schools in Ireland. 1,724 girls were examined in this branch, and 1,636 passed.

Before that year, the instruction in this subject had been carried on exclusively by members of the regular school staff, who either held certificates of competency or were regarded by the Commissioners of Education as sufficiently qualified. Owing to difficulties arising from cost of appliances, expense of materials, and want of suitable accommodation, the instruction made but little progress. It was taken up in very few of either the ordinary national schools or the model schools,[1] and may be said to have been confined to the convent national schools and to the practising schools of the training colleges for females.

In 1896 the Commissioners of National Education obtained from the government leave to engage some special itinerant teachers of cookery and laundry work. The sanction was given only as an experiment, and the number of teachers for whose employment provision was made, was limited to four. The teachers to be employed were persons who were trained in these branches under the Royal Irish Association for Promoting the Training and Employment of Women,[2] and who, at the close of their course of training, had undergone an examination, and obtained from the National Union for the Technical Education of Women diplomas of competency to teach.

1 Government training schools.
2 This is the organisation detailed in doc. 55, p 205.

These teachers travel throughout the country, remaining for a sufficient time at selected centres, and giving instruction in various national schools in the district, one or more lessons of two hours being given in each school each week. The course embraces twenty demonstration and practice lessons in household cookery suitable for national school pupils of classes IV, V, and VI. The necessary room for the purpose is provided by the manager of the school, who also arranges for the supply of materials, and for such appliances as the special teachers may find necessary in addition to what they bring with them.

. . . We are of [the] opinion that only plain cookery should be taught; and that the appliances should be simple and mainly such as the pupils will have in their own homes. This branch may be successfully taught in ordinary schoolrooms, when not otherwise occupied and with the simplest appliances.

. . . Needlework – From the foundation of National Education in Ireland, provision has been made for the instruction of girls in needlework; but the precise amount of time to be devoted to this branch was not fixed prior to 1890. In the year 1890, the Commissioners decided that the minimum time to be devoted to needlework, &c., should be one hour daily . . .

The ordinary course of needlework instruction extends from the second to the sixth class inclusive. In the lower class it comprises hemming and knitting, plain patching and darning, making pinafores, cutting pattern for plain shirt or of article of girls' underclothing, overalls, &c., and, in the sixth class, it requires proficiency in the different branches of plain sewing and knitting. . . .

MIDDLE–CLASS EDUCATION

Boarding Schools for Young Ladies

Doc. 32.1: MS Clonmel Boarding School for Girls, c.1800. Grubb Collection S.124, Society of Friends Archive, Dublin.

The Clonmel boarding school was established and run by Quaker women. Sarah Grubb, who founded the school originally in 1787, hoped it would bring about 'simplicity of manners and a religious improvement of the morals of the youth'.[1] Such aims were fulfilled by teaching the Quaker catechism and scriptures. The curriculum of the school was quite broad and reflected the backgrounds of the pupils. The school survived until 1845.

Clonmel Boarding School for Girls.
Originally established by the late Sarah Robert Grubb, is intended to be opened on the first of the seventh month, 1801, by Elizabeth Morris,

1 Cited in Michael Ahern, 'The Quaker schools in Clonmel', *Tipperary Historical Journal* (1990), p 131.

where it is proposed to teach reading, writing, English grammar, arithmetic, geography, with the use of the globes, and useful needle-work.

The terms for board and education, twenty-two guineas a year to be paid at entrance. Washing included, except gowns and frocks.

A teacher to be provided for such as incline to learn the French language, at half a guinea a quarter.

That the girls at the female boarding school at Clonmel cheerfully and duly attend to the sound of the bell for rising from and going to bed, meals, meeting, school and collect and arrange according to their sizes, solidly enter the dining rooms, when taking their seats, they pause under a grateful sense of the bounty they daily receive from the Father of Mercies and their own unworthiness thereof, then with becoming gratitude and no more conversation than is necessary eat their victuals and rise from those in like manner.

That they conduct themselves respectfully to all, and more especially to those who have the care of them, cherishing an affectionate esteem for these and every other branch of the family in their proper places, always ready to do any service required of them without reluctance or gloom.

That whenever they are spoken to, they give a respectful attention and looking at those who address them make the necessary reply without delay or hesitation, but always careful to speak consistent with their knowledge and to express themselves in as few comprehensive words as they are able . . .

That they do not cherish in themselves or others a disposition to follow any unbecoming fashion in their apparel or address which are inconsistent with their profession and consequently not to be allowed during their stay here, but that they encourage one another to simplicity of heart, conduct and appearance, always guarding against such a cringing civility as the intention of their hearts and feelings of their regard do not correspond with, yet standing disposed to the best of their ability effectively to serve those with whom they sojourn, but especially strangers and the sick . . . That they walk to and from meets in couples with a sobriety becoming the occasion, endeavouring to keep rank, and when at meets sit still, labour after composure of mind, guard against the wanderings of their imagination . . .

Miss Taylor's Seminary for Young Ladies

Doc. 32.2: *Catholic Directory* (Dublin, 1848).

The Catholic Directory, *from which the following advertisements come, was published annually between 1840 and 1868. From 1869 it was entitled the* Irish Catholic Directory. *The* Directory *provided information on important events in the Catholic calendar. It listed clerics and parishes, and convents and their attached institutions, and recorded news items considered to be of interest to the Catholic middle class. Convents advertised their boarding schools in the* Directory, *and aimed at encouraging parents to send their daughters for a useful 'feminine' education. Lay Catholic women also used the pages of the* Directory *to reach the right audience.*

MISS TAYLOR'S
SEMINARY FOR YOUNG LADIES
No 18 Wicklow Street, Near Grafton Street

The course of Education comprises the English, French, and Italian languages, which the children are taught to speak and write correctly and elegantly: compositions, history, geography, use of the globes and maps, astronomy, writing and arithmetic; music, dancing, drawing, and a variety of fancy works.

A professor of music; professor of dancing – Mr Garbois; writing master – an eminent teacher.

Miss T. feels pride and pleasure in being enabled to refer to young ladies of celebrity who have been educated in her seminary, and trusts, that by the due attention of herself, her sister, and eminent professors, to the improvement of her pupils, she will be honoured with a continuance of those favours hitherto so liberally extended to her establishment.

St Mary's Boarding School

Doc. 32.3: *Catholic Directory* (Dublin, 1848).

BOARDING SCHOOL
Under the Patronage of
HIS GRACE THE MOST REV. DOCTOR MURRAY
AT ST MARY'S CONVENT, CABRA,
DUBLIN

Young ladies are taught in this establishment the usual branches of English education, viz. grammar, history, geography, astronomy, the use of the globes, writing, and arithmetic, the French and Italian languages, and every species of plain and ornamental needle-work, for the sum of £30 per annum.

Each young lady, at entrance, is to bring two pair of sheets, two pillow-covers, four towels, four napkins, a knife, silver fork, and tea spoon – which will be returned on her leaving the school.

EXTRA CHARGES – Under Masters

Music	..	..	..	..	2 guineas per quarter
Singing	..	..	..	..	£2 per ditto
Drawing	..	..	..	..	£1 10*s*
Dancing	..	..	..	..	£2 per season

Under the Sisters

Music	..	..	..	..	£1 per quarter
Singing	..	..	..	..	£1 per ditto
Drawing	..	..	..	..	£1 per ditto

Payments to be made half-yearly in advance.

The dress is a uniform, which can be provided at the convent, if the parents wish. Previous to the removal of any pupil, a quarter's notice will be expected.

One vacation only is allowed, from the 23rd of July to the 23rd of August, and it will not be permitted to remove a child from the school, at any other season of the year.

Young Ladies at the Ursuline Convent, Cork

Doc. 32.4: *Terms of Admittance for Young Ladies, Boarders to the Ursuline Convent, Cork* (Cork, n.d.), leaflet.

The Ursuline order had its origins in France and was introduced to Ireland by Nano Nagle in 1771. Originally, the community was expected to take over the poor schools previously established by Nagle. However, the Ursuline rule of enclosure prevented them from operating four of the five schools. Within a few years, the Ursulines had begun to run exclusive schools for the wealthier members of the Catholic community. The prospectus below comes from the period prior to 1850.

Terms of admittance
for
YOUNG LADIES
to the
URSULINE CONVENT, CORK

	£	s	d
Pension, Thirty Guineas .. .. yearly			
Entrance, Three Guineas .. .. ”			
Offerings to the Chaplain, ... yearly	0	10	10
For hire of Drawer, Pens, Ink, Castile-Soap			
Tooth-Powder .. .. .. yearly	1	2	9
Washing .. .. yearly	3	0	0

The young ladies in addition to their other attainments, may also learn the following branches, on the following

TERMS

	£	s	d
Music .. .. yearly	11	7	6
Entrance	1	2	9

Dancing	..	..	..	..	..	..	4	11	0
Entrance	..	..	..	..	..	..	1	2	9
Drawing	..	..	..	..	..	..	13	13	0
Entrance	..	..	..	..	..	..	1	2	9
Training and hire of		..			..		1	2	9

Every young lady is to bring with her 2 pair of sheets, 6 napkins, 6 towels, a silver table and tea-spoon, a knife, fork, and goblet.

Books – An historical catechism, Butler's ditto, a practical ditto, a Prayer book, and Holy Week book, Farrell's English Grammar, Chambaud's French Grammar and Exercises, Telemachus in French and English, Goldsmith's Abridged Geography for Beginners, Walker's Geography for the more Advanced, Murray's Reader and Sequel, 2 vols Praval's Idioms, Entick's Dictionary, Turner's Arts and Sciences, and Voster's Arithmetic.

The several articles the young ladies bring with them to the convent shall on their leaving it be returned to their parents.

The parents who do not reside in Cork are requested to appoint a person there to whom the Superior may present her quarterly accounts, which are to be discharged at the end of the several quarters, and the pension advanced for the ensuing quarter; if any young lady should be obliged to leave the convent before the expiration of her last quarter, whatever remains of it overpaid shall be returned if her place there be relinquished. It is expected that three months notice will be given before the children are withdrawn, to leave time for apprizing those who may wait for a vacancy.

Every gentle and persuasive method shall be used to impress on the minds of the young ladies an elevated and habitual sense of decency and propriety, and to polish and refine their manners; if any should prove refractory, and persist in refusing compliance with the established rules and discipline of the convent, their removal must be requested to prevent the effects of bad example; which request, a painful discharge of duty, will, it is hoped, give no offence to their parents.

The young ladies' daily dress is an uniform of a dark callicoe; brown stuff for dress, or a silk of the same colour, (if the parents choose,) blue sashes and ribands; those who cannot take milk for breakfast are to be supplied by their parents with tea and sugar.

No child is permitted to sleep out of the convent except in case of illness, or to go out of it on Sundays except on extraordinary occasions; when on other days they get leave to visit abroad, they must return at 8 o'clock in the evening in winter, and at half an hour after 8 in summer, at latest.

St Catherine's Convent, Arthurstown, Co. Wexford

Doc. 32.5: *Irish Catholic Directory* (Dublin, 1880).

ST CATHERINE'S CONVENT
RAMSGRANGE, ARTHURSTOWN,
County Wexford
Boarding School for Young Ladies
Under the Patronage of
The Most Rev. Dr Warren, Lord Bishop of the Diocese of Ferns.

This School, conducted by the Sisters of St Louis of France, possesses many advantages deserving the attention of parents and guardians.

It is situated in a most healthy part of the country, in the middle of extensive pleasure grounds, from which there is a fine view of Waterford harbour and the surrounding scenery. The pupils can enjoy the benefit of sea-bathing without the inconvenience to them of a residence at a watering-place.

There is daily communication with Waterford by steamer, and thence by steamer or rail with all parts of the three kingdoms.

The deportment and manners of the pupils are scrupulously attended to; no efforts are spared to give the young ladies habits of order and neatness, that they may return to their families not only accomplished but helpful and intelligent in all the duties of woman's sphere.

Constant solicitude is given to the health and comfort of the pupils. The course of study comprises religious instruction, the ordinary branches of a solid English education, French, dancing, drawing, vocal and instrumental music, and particular care is given to all kinds of plain and fancy needlework.

Terms, &c., can be known on application to the convent.

ISABELLA TOD ARGUES FOR IMPROVEMENTS IN THE EDUCATION OF MIDDLE-CLASS GIRLS

Doc. 33: Isabella M. S. Tod, *On the Education of Girls of the Middle Classes* (London, 1874).

Isabella M. S. Tod (1836–1896) was a pioneering activist in the cause of women throughout the latter part of the nineteenth century. One of her interests lay in developing the educational opportunities available to the daughters of the middle classes. She was very critical of the existing sexual division of labour which condemned middle-class women to a decorative and useless role in society. Tod, who lived in Belfast, established the Ladies' Institute in 1867 to promote women's education. She campaigned vigorously to have Irish girls included in the Intermediate Education Act of 1878. She also wrote extensively on the education of girls. The following extract is taken from a pamphlet she wrote and published with the National Union for Improving the Education of Women. For Tod, as for many other activists, it was important that parents recognised that marriage was not inevitable for their daughters, and that an education was essential for a productive life.

. . . . Whilst urging the claims of girls to an education larger in its scope, and surer in its working, we are haunted by the recollection of one notion which we are aware is often present to the minds of parents, whether they give it expression or not. They look forward to *all* their daughters marrying, to *all* these marriages being satisfactory, and to the husbands being *always* able and willing to take the active management of everything; neither death, illness, nor untoward circumstances occurring to throw the wives on their own resources. When put before them they must acknowledge that such is not a true picture of life. We shall not stop to discuss whether such a state of things is even desirable. It is sufficient to point out that it does not and cannot exist. Yet they cling to it, and will not prepare their girls for anything else. To have such appearance, manners, and acquirements as will be pleasing to themselves in the meantime, and by attracting admiration may facilitate marriage, is the unavowed, though sole object, which too many seek for their girls. The girl knows it also, and acts upon it. . . . But the plain truth is, that *here lies the great obstacle* to the improvement of the education of women. Parents should remember that they cannot, with a wish, obtain for their daughters exactly the situation in life which they suppose to be desirable. It is, then, short-sighted to fit them for no other; nay, it is even cruel.

The one essential element, without which the reforms of teaching power, of methods, of subjects, of tests, and all else, can be of no avail, is that these young girls shall be looked upon as human beings with a great unknown part to play in life – as God's subjects, with the talents which He gave them, to be prepared for the work to which He may call them, *not* as colourless, characterless things, of no value, 'till placed in some relationship to others of their fellow creatures. . . .

It is indeed, in the first place, on the duty of enabling them to *be* whatever Heaven *meant them to be*, that we ground the claim of women to a full participation in the blessings of a liberal education. . . .

Why should those parents, who have the prospect of giving their girls what is counted a reasonable provision, suppose it a good thing that they should be incapable of doing anything to support themselves? Work is itself a valuable education, and the possession and management of property exercises and strengthens many qualities well worth a strenuous endeavour. But parents dread the loss of 'gentility'. If such a reputation is only to be had at such a price, is it worth the cost? Yet, good social position does not really depend upon uselessness. Here, as in many other cases, a reality is sacrificed to a name. . . . In truth, throughout the whole of the middle classes, it should be looked on as a matter of course that girls should be instructed in some business or profession, by which they could acquire a competency, and in which industry, forethought, and ability could obtain their due reward; so that it will be no longer impossible for a lady to earn ease and comfort, and the means of beneficence, for herself. . . .

The organisation of institutions for girls' education is the next point for consideration. But the very phrase goes to the root of one of the great difficulties of the matter. For girls of the lower classes, we have schools in each of the British islands, all more or less aided, inspected and directed by the State. The mistresses, as well as the masters, for these schools also undergo a regular training under government superintendence, and their status and abilities are measured by carefully bestowed certificates. So far the two sexes are alike; but on looking higher all is changed. While an elaborate network of important establishments for boys and young men, of varied forms, but all acting and re-acting on one another, cover the face of the country, we have only a few scattered and experimental attempts at anything of the sort for girls.

Some remedial agencies are already at work. Of these the most important are the middle-class examinations instituted by the universities. It would be difficult to overrate the good done by the extension of these examinations to girls and women. They have presented a methodical plan of study to conscientious parents and teachers, and have offered a standard to work up to, and a means of proving wherein lies strength or weakness. They also provide a test by which good schools and good teachers may be distinguished from bad.

. . . We are thus brought to the conclusion that the best preparation for the higher teaching which we desire is that future schoolmistresses and governesses shall receive their education in the same colleges in which girls of the higher and middle classes pursue their advanced studies, with the object of entering upon those liberal occupations which are opening their doors to them, or of cultivating those talents which will render home life more useful as well as more pleasing.

THE INTERMEDIATE ACT AND GIRLS' EDUCATION

Doc. 34: Anon., 'The Irish Intermediate Education Act', *Journal of the Women's Education Union*, 7 (1879).

The following document outlines the programme that had to be studied by girls taking the Intermediate examinations.

The programme for the first examinations to be held under this Act has been issued. The subjects are in seven divisions – Greek, Latin, English, modern languages (including Celtic), mathematics, natural science, music and drawing. These are divided into several sections, and each division and section has three grades – junior, middle and senior. The work has been arranged, and marks assigned with a view to be at once a useful test of attainment, but with the intention of raising the standard at no distant date. A number of rules have been drawn up by the Commissioners, in addition to those contained in the Act itself. Those relating to girls are as follows:–

Rule IX – Subject to the following modifications, the Act, and the rules in the schedule thereto, and these rules shall apply (and relate) to the education of girls.

1. The examinations of girls shall be held apart from those of boys, but on the same days.
2. Girls may present themselves for examination in two or more divisions; but one of these divisions must be the third, fourth or fifth.
3. Girls may pass in the Fifth Division by passing in arithmetic alone, and may pass with merit in such division by passing with merit in arithmetic alone.

Rule X – There shall not be any competition between girls and boys for prizes or exhibitions. The number of prizes and exhibitions to be awarded in each year to girls shall be determined by assigning one prize or exhibition, according to the respective years, or every ten girls in the aggregate who shall have passed in three divisions for each such year; and in the same way the number of prizes and exhibitions to be awarded to boys shall be determined by assigning one prize or exhibition, according to the respective years, for every ten boys in the aggregate who shall have passed in three divisions for such year.

The practical effect of these rules is to give girls equal advantage with boys, although there are some points which may, and probably will, be modified and improved. It is not to be expected that the number of girls who will be ready to present themselves for examination for the first year, or two, can be absolutely large. But so much hope and energy has already been diffused among teachers throughout the country by the expectation that the Act would give some real help to girls, that it is evident they will soon be in a position to reap the full benefit of it. The results are likely to be exceedingly valuable, in both widening the area, and improving the quality of middle-class education in Ireland.

A NUN WRITES OF THE INTERMEDIATE SYSTEM

Doc. 35: Unsigned note marked Sion Hill Convent, Blackrock. McCabe Papers, File 49/3–5 (Letters, nuns, undated *c.*1883), DDA.

In this letter, a teaching nun describes how her pupils were affected by the Intermediate examinations.

Sion Hill Convent, Blackrock, Dublin, 1883

Previous to the year 1880 our numbers in boarding school averaged 70. Since then they have been as follows; 1880–81: 106; 1881–82: 98. This September 1883 we begin with 85 but have a prospect of a large increase.

During these years about six of the parents objected to their daughters not going in for the Intermediate Examination but we only lost two pupils in consequence. On the other hand the great majority of parents express strong objections to the system, and many expressly stipulate that their girl shall not go in for the examination.

Referring to some of the strictures on convent schools that have appeared in the newspapers it may be well to add that (as in many other communities) several of our members have been educated in England and on the continent, that the foreign languages are generally taught by natives or those who have spent many years abroad, that our junior sisters spend their first years in study in which they are aided by lessons from secular professors, and that finally these secular teachers are employed in our schools when found necessary or useful.

With regard to the matter taught, we may state, that although not approving in every respect of the curriculum marked out by the Commissioners of Intermediate Education, we have judged it well, seeing that their standard has been accepted by all Ireland as the test of excellence, to allow our pupils to follow each year the course of study allotted to each grade according to age, and to answer the examination questions. They are thus conversant with the matters in which their brothers are interested and enjoy the best advantages of the system, such as they are, without its drawbacks.

THE ADVANTAGES OF INTERMEDIATE EDUCATION FOR GIRLS

Doc. 36: Isabella Mulvany, 'The Intermediate Act and the education of girls', *Irish Educational Review*, 1,1 (October 1907).

In the following document Isabella Mulvany[1] describes the advantages to girls of the Intermediate system and calls on parents to allow their daughters to undertake these examinations.

. . . Prior to the passing of the Act [Intermediate Act] the curriculum in the majority of girls' schools was limited to English, history and geography, French and elementary arithmetic with music and drawing. Instruction in classics and mathematics was available in certainly not more than half a dozen schools located in large centres of population, such as Dublin or Belfast, and working on the lines of the not long established English high schools for girls. Such were the sources from which were to come the first intermediate candidates. The requirements of the Board were at the outset wisely arranged to be of a moderate nature, their policy being to encourage scholars to come into the system freely. . . .

1 For information on Mulvany, see doc. 42.3 below.

What do we note has taken place? Marked increase not alone in the numbers taking the more solid educational subjects such as Latin, German, geometry, and algebra, but also in the percentage of successes all round. Further, in the subjects which formed the old curriculum for girls, the work is more thorough; for example, the percentage of passes in English rises from 53.8 to 91.1; in French from 69 to 81; in music, from 71 in theoretical work alone to 98.8 in practical and theoretical work combined; and in drawing from 40 to 96.

Is further proof of the potency and success of the Intermediate Education Act in uplifting the educational level for girls necessary? Yet, to judge from the comparative numbers of boys and girls entering, there must be larger numbers of girls remaining outside the scheme than of those taking part in it. In 1905, 7,018 boys entered, 2,659 girls, a disparity which can only take origin in either the indifference or prejudice of the parent or guardian. It is difficult to overcome prejudice . . . but can we not try to remove indifference?

The programme now introduced contains the essential subjects of study for a sound secondary education, and approaches more nearly to the satisfactory substructure for university work than any yet tried. Is this, then, not a fitting time for the parent to determine to get for his child the full benefit of any state measure of education, and also to co-operate with educationists in the effort to secure that the measure shall be adequate and stable. So long as the intermediate system is not backed up by the public support which should be accorded to it, so long will the secondary schools of Ireland be without adequate measure of state aid, aid which is now so liberally bestowed in the sister countries.

SCHOOL DAYS REMEMBERED

Katharine Tynan

Doc. 37.1: Katharine Tynan, *Twenty-Five Years: Reminiscences* (London, 1913).

Katherine Tynan (1861–1931) attended the Dominican convent boarding school in Drogheda from 1872 to 1874. She went on to become a well-known novelist and poet. Mary Colum (née Maguire) (1885–1957) attended the Sisters of St. Louis convent in Monaghan. She later became a writer and critic.

. . . Everything about the convent was very old-fashioned. The nuns entered the convent usually from the school-room . . . No newspapers were allowed to disturb the convent atmosphere, no magazines; nothing of what was happening outside in the world unless it came by word of mouth. The nuns talked, as doubtless they do to-day, of 'out in the world', as though it was the other side of the world. . . . The nuns were excellent musicians and linguists. They taught the ordinary subjects with ordinary success I imagine. But the progress of the world had stopped for them some ten or twenty or thirty or forty years before. Their books were old-fashioned. I well remember the intense indignation of the most capable of all the teachers, when, on her telling her class that the source of the Nile had never been discovered, Ten Years' Old, fresh from the newspapers of her vacation, cut in with: 'Oh yes, Dr Livingstone discovered its source in Lake Victoria Nyanza.' 'And pray who is Dr Livingstone?' Mother Alphonsus asked, shaking her veil and in contemptuous indignation moving on to something else.

A very simple curriculum indeed! But what was it they did teach that was better than much learning? What was it that brought the gentlest, tenderest, loveliest of their pupils flying back to that white peace of the convent from a rough and coarse world? What was it that made the most unworthy of their pupils, one with a keen eye for their simplicities, resolve that a girl of hers should go nowhere else but to a convent school?

It was the heavenliness of the convent atmosphere. I can find no other word.

I do not intend to convey that all the nuns were saints, although the very choice of the convent life carries with it, to my mind, a great measure of sanctity. One nun in my time, Mother Imelda, was such a saint I believe in the supernatural order as the Church loves to honour and set the seal of sainthood upon. Many of the nuns had their human defects, their weaknesses. Impossible to conceal them from the sharp eyes of school-girls. But if one laughs, one laughs tenderly. There were exquisite women among the nuns – beautiful women often. I used to think there never was such beauty as Sister Teresa's with her delicate classic profile, her face as finely moulded, as purely coloured as a Madonna lily, or Mother Joseph's with her opulent golden colouring, the magnificent intense blue of her eyes. Perhaps the white coif and habit and the black veil made the fittest frame for beauty. We might laugh at their simplicities, their innocencies. We might even discuss their little jealousies and preferences. But we left school in floods of tears: and doubtless a good many of those who left not to return found the change a hard one.

Many outsiders have remarked on the grace, the beauty, the refinement of Irish girls of the shop-keeping and farming classes, qualities not always shared by their brothers. Something of course is explained by the ups and downs of Irish history which have reduced the descendants of the old families to the cabins and placed the sons of the freebooters in the castles. But the convent schools afford the fullest explanation needed. Whatever of ladyhood is in a girl the convent school fosters and brings to perfection.

The convent school remains in my mind as a place of large and lofty rooms, snow-white, spotless, full of garden airs: of long corridors lit by deep windows, with little altars here and there – statues of Our Lord or the Blessed Virgin or the Saints, each with its flowers. A blue lamp burned at Our Lady's feet. The Sacred Heart had its twinkling red lamp. The corridors seem always

114

in my thoughts of them full of quietness. The rustling of the nun's habit as she came only added to the sense of quietness. . . .

At the convent school we slept in dormitories which contained long lines of little iron beds curtained in blue and white check. The curtains went completely round the beds, and when they were drawn at night there was a sense of isolation which had its charm for one of an overflowing family who could appreciate dimly how many ills come from not being sufficiently alone. . . .

There was only one looking-glass in the dormitory. Perhaps that fact began in me the habit of never looking in a glass, which was confirmed by sharing a bedroom with one sister or another, of a more determined will perhaps, or a more pressing vanity than I possessed. Of course the modesty of the convent was extreme. When we washed our feet we looped our curtains in such a way that no eye could be upon us.

We used to get up early in the morning – 6.30 in summer, 7 in winter, and hurry downstairs through the long kitchen corridor to the chapel for Mass. We always wore a black veil over our heads for Mass and a white veil for Communion days, so that we were like a little flock of nuns. We used to go down through one of the 'bows'. A section of the house was bow-shaped through its four stories. In each bow was the glass-screened and curtained door from floor to ceiling in which was the enclosure for the convent. The mystery of those doors which the world never passed had its irresistible appeal for me. Through the veils of the door you could see the shadowy figures of the nuns moving along the corridor beyond. That door shut off eternally the world from the cloister. . . .

I left school at the mature age of fourteen. I could have gone back if I liked, but no one troubled to make me go. Before I left I signed the convent pledge, which had nothing to do with strong drink. I do not mean that I signed a document, but all the nuns' pupils were willing to undertake that in the perilous world they would not dance 'fast dances'; they would not go to a theatre; they would not read novels. They did not ask a pledge against writing them.

The nuns added a counsel which was surely mediaeval. It was that we should not look male creatures in the face when we encountered them.

Mary Colum

Doc. 37.2: Mary Colum, *Life and the Dream* (London, 1947).

. . . A cubicle in a cold dormitory, a narrow iron bed with a white counterpane, a combination prie-dieu and wash-stand, a religious picture, a little space for prayer books and meditation books, a hook for a dressing gown, a mug for a toothbrush – this was my new domain. Each of about twenty little girls, all of the same age or nearly the same age, had its replica, for this was the juniors' dormitory. There were also a middle and a senior dormitory equipped in a like way. I arrived at school a month after the term opened and so was the last of the new girls. The first night, once in bed in the dark, the last prayer said, the impression of the music and the dancing and singing faded, and there rushed over me, not exactly a homesickness, for I was glad to be at school, but the sense of loneliness that comes over one in unaccustomed surroundings, and a dread of the new life and the strange faces. I have at no time been adaptable, have never found it easy to accustom myself to change of any kind – changes in people, or places, or things. So I cried myself to sleep, not only that first night but many nights. . . .

We rose early, at six or before in spring and summer; at half past six or seven in winter. Except in the depth of winter, when the morning light was dim and even dark, we started the day with study. But in winter we went straight down to the chapel after dressing, putting over our heads long black veils, thus obeying Saint Paul's instruction that female locks be covered in church. . . .

I spent most of the first day trying to familiarize myself with the rules. All the conventions and customs of a convent were both fascinating and difficult to get used to. Everything I did seemed to be wrong. I kept my seat when I should be standing up; I wore my house shoes when I should be wearing outdoor shoes; unwittingly I made myself audible so conspicuously during silences that for the rest of the year I hardly spoke at all. . . .

The unpacking of my trunk was another ordeal; it took place in the wardrobe room, where everybody had a locker with her number on it. On the first day there had been the humiliation of the bath-dress incident; now there came further humiliation. I was ashamed of my clothes, both inside and out, ashamed of what was called my school trousseau. I had been supervised by no woman, and some of it had been bought from an English mail-order house which advertised cheap school trousseaus. I had picked some garments out from pictures in the catalogue, and others made by a seamstress. I did not have new sheets, for it was decided that, from the piles of linen that were then usual in every house, enough could be found for my needs. Consequently, instead of the nice, smooth cotton sheets the Dublin girls had, I had brought hand-woven linen sheets that were enormously heavy and rural-looking. The hemming on my table napkins – which were not new either and which were larger than anybody else's – had a ripped stitch here and there, and they had to be handed over to the sewing sister to mend. My bath towels were too small and my face towels too large. My pillowcases were square instead of the oblong usual ones. . . .

Convents are really small, self-contained totalitarian states where life is lived according to a rigid schedule, with penalties for those who did not or could not keep to it. For me, however, the life became a happy, satisfying, if exacting one.

To try to act like everyone else became my constant preoccupation. We had everything in common. We rose, washed, and dressed on the same minute; said the same prayers in unison; wore the same uniform; did our hair in the prescribed way, plaited down out backs and tied with a black silk ribbon. 'Form ranks' or 'Get into ranks' – that was the order several times a day whenever we went anywhere in a body. We walked in step in ranks of two and two going to the refectory, going to the little chapel. We first genuflected in pairs before the altar, then we turned to our seats, the girls to the right entering the right seats and those to the left, the left seats, all with drilled and trained precision, for the procedure had been rehearsed many times. A couple of times a week we had actual military drill by a drill sergeant. Perhaps drilling and conformity and totalitarianism are not so alien to the ideals of the human race as we in democracies consider. The supervision was ceaseless; everything we did or even thought, it seemed to me, was known to the head of the school. Our letters were read coming and going, and the letters we sent out were thoroughly censored – not always, of course, for subject matter, but for style and manner. How to write a ladylike hand was the matter of a half hour's instruction from time to time. No criticism of the school in letters home, as I recall, was ever permitted, criticising the sisters being considered a very serious breach of conduct and manners. . . .

There were many punishments and penalties to be endured, though these were not excessive in spite of the rigidity of the discipline. Punishments were meted out if we did not know our lessons, if we were late for classes or meals or any ceremonial, if we broke the rule of silence or did not fold our chapel veils neatly and put them away in little lockers with our numbers on them. For we all had numbers and were often referred to by them instead of by our names. . . .

An Old World Training
But if we were well taught we were badly fed; almost no attention was paid to purely physical needs. As we walked in to breakfast from the little chapel, often exhausted before the day began through too early rising, we sat down to a meal composed of tea and bread and butter only. Dinner in the middle of the day was always insufficient and often so unpalatable that we envied Reverend Mother's niece who had the privilege of eating no dinner but instead had tea for a midday meal. In the afternoon we had tea or milk and inevitable bread and butter, and a similar meal in the evening. I do not think anybody, either nuns or pupils, thought much of the importance of food. We filled up on bread and butter. . . .

Yet, despite everything, the life at school was a happy one – despite the food, the cold in winter, the long hours of class and of study, the fearful efforts to grow in piety and to eradicate faults, the perpetual meditations on life after death. Education was regarded as a means for fitting our souls for God rather than as a preparation for life. Life itself was looked on as a preparation for eternity, and the tribulations of life as designed by God to perfect our spirits and enable our souls by suffering. There was an inclination to believe that the more we suffered, the more pleasing we were to God and the better were our

117

chances of eternal happiness. However, affection radiated on all sides. The nuns were affectionate; my school friends and I were very fond of one another. We had our intimate friendships, but these had to be in threes; the convent rule against what was called 'particular friendships' made all friendships triangular, as it were. This rule was perhaps designed to guard against those schoolgirl crushes that I may say from my own considerable experience of boarding schools were so very harmless. Trios on vacation would write long epistles to one another and exchange novels and books of poetry; the return to school after the holidays was the happiest of reunions . . .

Preparing for the Civil Service

Doc. 37.3: Siobhán Lankford, *The Hope and the Sadness: Personal Recollections of Troubled Times in Ireland* (Cork, 1980).

Siobhán Lankford (1894–1986), grew up on a farm in County Cork at the turn of this century. When she left school she travelled to Cork city each day to attend the Munster Civil Service College. Here she prepared for the civil service exams and in 1912 successfully passed an exam and took up a position in the Post Office. By the early years of the twentieth century professional posts within the civil service offered substantial work opportunities for young women.

The Munster Civil Service College was run by Philip Murphy, a northerner from near Enniskillen. He was an able and successful teacher, and he got his students to work really hard. Meticulous accuracy was the key to success in civil service exams, and so he had to eradicate any slip-shod methods students may have acquired as well as teaching them. . . . His school was co-educational,   . . . although we worked different hours to the boys . . . The school had a good cross section of students from all over Munster: farmer's sons and daughters from counties Cork, Kerry, Limerick and Tipperary, the sons and daughters of shopkeepers form all the towns of the county, and from Cork city itself, members of families of civil servants and the RIC[1] – the discipline and supervision of their fathers kept them close to their studies.

Fraulein Schuter, a German national taught French and German, and Harvey Dawson taught French too. . . . The students at the Civil Service College moved on quickly. The British service was well staffed by able Irish-men and women. It was said that during the days of promotion by exa-mination within the service itself, Irishmen were in complete control of this prestigious department. Examinations for service in the Post Office were open to the whole United Kingdom, and so I sat for a vacancy advertised for Mallow. A job in our home town would be very suitable, and my parents were very glad when I got this exam in March 1912.

---

1 Royal Irish Constabulary was the police force.

118

Training Monitresses

Doc. 38.1: *Special Report of the Convent Schools in Connection with the Board of National Education* HC 1864 (405), xlvi.

Monitresses were members of the teaching staff in primary schools and acted as assistants to teachers. School-rooms tended to be large, with a large number of pupils, and monitresses were employed to help out – each having a group of pupils to teach. These assistant teachers were recognised by the National Board which paid them a salary from 1862. The following document reveals the amounts paid to young women who acted either as pupil teachers or as junior or senior monitresses.

Ordered – That, in conformity with the terms of the Board's order of the 5th September 1862, the following appointments be made in the Baggot Street National School:

Mary Kelly .. .. }	To be paid as pupil teachers,
Margaret Dermody .. }	at the rate of £20 per annum from
Mary A. Madden .. }	15th September 1862.
Kate Bennett .. .. }	
Mary Lawler .. .. }	
Mary Kenna .. .. }	
Nannie Kelly .. .. }	To be paid as senior
Kate Byrne .. .. }	monitresses, at the rate of
M. A. Sharpe .. .. }	£5 per annum, from the
Agnes McDonagh .. }	15th September 1862.
Mary Ward .. .. }	
Mary Doran .. .. }	
Eliza Cox .... .. }	To be paid as junior
Eliza Hutton .. .. }	monitresses, at the rate of
Philomena Dermody .. }	£2 per annum, from the
M. A. Conlan .. .. }	15th September 1862.

Further ordered – That salary be withdrawn from A. M. Nevin, junior paid monitress, from the 15th September 1862, for non-proficiency.

Sisters of Mercy Training College

Doc. 38.2: *Irish Catholic Directory* (Dublin, 1880).

In 1838, the government opened the National Education Training school in Dublin. The Catholic hierarchy would not allow their priests to employ teachers trained in this institution, or in model (non-denominational) schools, so convent and Christian Brother schools, through the use of the monitorial system, became the training grounds for Catholic teachers. In 1872, the Sisters of Mercy in Baggot Street, Dublin, opened the first Catholic training college for women. The college was approved and given financial support by the government in 1883. The following document, dating from 1880, shows the requirements made of young women entering the Baggot Street training school.

AMDG
TERMS FOR THE ADMISSION OF PUPILS
TO THE
Sedes Sapientae[1] Training School
Under the care of the Sisters of Mercy,
Baggot Street, Dublin.

1. Young persons who desire to be apprentices as teachers in the above school must have completed their fourteenth year, and must produce unexceptionable testimonials.
2. They are required to live in the Sedes Sapientae, except during the usual school vacations. Their friends can only visit them on the second Sunday of each month.
3. It is desirable that candidates who wish to compete at the first examination should enter in August. Should they fail in passing the examination, or prove morally, intellectually or physically unfit for the duties of a teacher, they will be expected to return to their friends.
4. Candidates should be able to read and write well, to spell and to write correctly from dictation; to parse grammatically; to work sums in the four first rules, in money, weights and measures.
5. The terms are:

Pension, per annum	..	..	..		£15 0 0
Washing	..	..	..	..	£ 1 10 0

Payable half-yearly in advance.

CLOTHING
1 Black Stuff Dress (for Sundays)
1 Common Stuff
1 Black Hat (for Sundays)
1 Do do (for every day)
2 Dark Jackets
12 Collars
3 Chemises
3 Night Gowns and Petticoats
2 Pairs of sheets (2½ yds long, 1½ yds wide)
2 Pairs of Blankets
1 Quilt
4 Night Caps
3 Bedroom Towels, Soap, Tooth Brush, Nail Brush, Sponge and Bag
12 Pocket Handkerchiefs

1 Seat of wisdom.

2 Combs and Hair Brush

4 pairs of Stockings

1 Large Check Apron (with body and sleeves)

2 Black Aprons

1 Dressing Wrapper

1 Clothes Bag

2 pairs of Boots (strong)

2 pairs of House Boots

1 Umbrella

1 Clothes Brush, Blacking and Brushes

1 Large Cloak

2 pairs of Gloves

2 Neckties and Muffler

1 Knife and Fork (white handles)

1 Tea Spoon

TIN Boxes only allowed

Books and stationery to be procured at the Sedes Sapientiae.

One pound sterling will cover the requirements of the first year for books only.

Becoming a Governess

Doc. 38.3: Anon., *Seminary for Young Persons Designed to be Governesses* (Cork, n.d.).

Governessing was one of the few ways open to respectable middle-class women to earn their own living in the nineteenth century. It was generally badly paid and carried a peculiar status within the household. The governess was not considered to be part of the family, but neither was she acceptable to the servants as one of their number. Some convent schools provided governesses for Catholic families. In the earlier half of the century a small number of institutes were established to train governesses. The following document, undated, refers to a seminary established in Cork city. It was organised for young Protestant women. It was not until 1869 that the Association for Promoting the Higher Education of Ladies as Teachers, later known as the Governess Association of Ireland, was established.[1] The association wished to promote the education of women and also to improve the training of governesses. The association also aimed to improve the conditions of employment of governesses.

SEMINARY
for
YOUNG PERSONS DESIGNED TO BE GOVERNESSES

The parents or guardians of the young persons applying for admission to the above seminary, are requested to answer the following queries, and to assent to the subjoined regulations:

1 The Assocation was founded by Anne Jellicoe.

1st   Is it your desire that the young persons whose education you confide to the governess of this school, should be educated primarily for the glory of God, having their principles, habits and acquirement, solely regulated by the precepts of the Gospel?

2nd   Is it your decided wish and intention, that they should be educated for the express purpose of accepting any situation as governess for which the committee may consider them qualified?

3rd   Are you determined by precept and example at home, to further the instruction and advice they receive at school?

4th   Can you truly say you have not the means of fitting them for this situation of life, as we could not expect masters to give their gratuitous help to those who can afford to pay?

5th   It is expected that the greatest regularity shall be observed in bringing in the quarterly payments of five shillings each, on the 13th of January, 13th of April, 13th of July, and 13th of October, as no young person can be admitted without payment on those days. Five shillings also to be paid on admission.

6th   Are the young persons 14 years of age, as none can be taken in younger.

7th   What situation of life have their parents held, or do now hold?

8th   The young persons can only be admitted for three months on trial, at which time if not considered as giving a fair promise of their future competency to fill the situation of governesses, they cannot be continued at the school.

Lastly, – The committee request that the greatest care may be taken in answering the above queries and subscribing to the rules, as it must prove destructive to the very existence of the establishment to deviate from those regulations.

The committee take this opportunity of expressing their unanimous determination never to recommend any young persons into families, but those on whose moral deportment and religious principles they can place confidence. They therefore request, that none may embrace the advantage of this institution, but such as are anxious to adhere to its regulations, but above all who are desirous to walk by the doctrines and precepts of our most holy religion – ever remembering the motto of this school, taken from the Word of God, 'Them that honor me, I will honour, and those that despise me, shall be lightly esteemed.'

ST JOSEPH'S INDUSTRIAL INSTITUTE

Doc. 39: Anon., 'St Joseph's Industrial Institute and the workhouse orphans', *Irish Quarterly Review*, 9 (January 1859).

St Joseph's Industrial Institute was founded by Mrs Ellen Woodlock (1811–1884).[1] Woodlock, married and widowed when quite young, originally intended to join a religious community in France. Her novitiate was not successful and she returned to her native city of Cork to engage in philanthropic work. During the 1850s she lived in Dublin and established St Joseph's Institute there in 1855. The institute was founded to rescue the young workhouse girl from the misery which faced her in that institution. The institute does not appear to have survived for very long, although Woodlock continued in her philanthropic endeavours by organising Catholic visitors to the Dublin workhouses and helping to establish the Children's hospital in Temple Street in Dublin in 1873. Within St Joseph's, Woodlock hoped to train former workhouse girls for employment. She was totally opposed to keeping children in the workhouse. The following report outlines the difficulties she encountered in training these girls. The extract below records Woodlock's decision to take in twelve girls.

. . . Thus it appears that the average age of these twelve girls was 16½ years, and the average length of their detention in the workhouse 10½ years. They were chosen because they were so truly deserted – because not a moment was to be lost, if they were to be saved from the adult wards – and lastly, because knowing how to read and write, they could be made to give their whole attention to manual labour. There is reason to believe that these were above the average of workhouse girls in some respects; yet the evils of the system to which they had been subjected came out in very broad shadows as soon as they were brought into the strong light of everyday life; and what was only surmised beforehand soon came to be proved by facts, and confirmed by experience.

At first it had been contemplated to train them for domestic service; but a little experience showed that no more unsuitable destination could be devised for them. Girls of this class are stupid to the last degree, from the want of having their natural faculties called into exercise; and they are so totally devoid of knowledge of the common things of life, that they make the effect at first of being completely deprived of ordinary intelligence. Most of them have never seen the interior of a dwelling-house, have never handled a breakable article, or used a knife and fork; consequently they are so awkward, that they destroy a considerable amount of property, 'buying experience at famine prices', and often seriously injuring themselves; one can imagine it would take a considerable time to train a cook who never saw a pot put on the fire, or beheld a whole joint of meat in its integrity, or vegetables in their natural form; or a housemaid who could not go up or down stairs without falling; or a nursery maid who perhaps had never laid eyes on an infant in her life. It was soon dis-

1 Matthew Russell, 'Mrs Ellen Woodlock, an admirable Irishwoman of the last century', *The Irish Monthly*, 36 (1908), pp 171–6.

covered that a course of rudimental object-lessons should be gone through, before one of them could be trusted to execute the most trifling order or commission. What could be expected from a girl, who, never having seen a railway train in her life, could not contain her terror and surprise at being put into one? Or from another who had indeed seen snow on the roof and flagways of the Union Mansion, yet innocently asking on finding the whole country white after a fall, 'How will the dust be got off the trees?' or again from a third, who, accustomed only to the workhouse style of serving repast – the dry portion in nets, and the liquid in tin porringers,[1] being desired to bring up potatoes to the dining-room, made her appearance carrying saucepan and all?

Very difficult too it is to teach these girls the value of property. Naturally they know nothing of the use of money. As long as they can recollect, everything has been supplied to them, they know not how – food, clothing, and so on. The want of the half-penny, which want sharpens the wit of every scapegrace about the streets, never tempted or troubled them; consequently their utter indifference, no matter what amount of mischief they may achieve, is equally perplexing and tantalising to those in charge of them.

Their notion of dependence and independence are curiously awry. One of the most sensible of the set thought proper to boast one day of her brothers being well off in the world. It was remarked that if that were the case, it was a wonder they would leave their mother in the workhouse. 'Oh, indeed', said the girl, with the most conceited air imaginable, 'my mother would never go to them; she's a great deal too independent for that!'

Stupidity and awkwardness, confirmed into habit, are not peculiarities likely to be long endured by masters or mistresses even of the fairest temper; but the list of objections is not completed until violent passion and obstinate sulk are added. This, perhaps, is the most difficult thing to get over, and requires a particular study of individual character which many persons are not competent, or patient enough to exercise. Those who have experience of children are fully aware, that while boys may be governed *en masse*, influenced by a general appeal, and led on by the public opinion of the school-room, girls cannot be so taken. They require to be trained separately and singly; nature will have it so; and any attempt to ignore that law, stops the machinery at once. Now, in the workhouse, where girls, to the number of some hundreds, are shut up, with no higher order of influence brought to bear upon them than the strong hand of the salaried overseers, no gentler sway exercised than the scant word of approval now and then accorded to the least troublesome of the lot; where they are driven to the hall, or turned out to the yard, or ordered to this or that ward like a flock of sheep – it is plain assuredly, that whatever may have been the innate difference of temper and disposition, the outer character must inevitably tend to conform to a certain type, and that not of the best.

1 Small bowls.

The rule is so cut out that there is little choice left. The girl has only to choose whether she will obey orders at once without a word, or be made to do so with sharp pain and howling. She may let what gall she likes fester the inner life, under the pressure of what is dimly perceived to be injustice and tyranny; she may choke with despair when she would fain escape but finds no outlet. Sooner or later, that doggedness and darkness which distinguishes the class, over-crusts the whole character.

Coming thus before the mistress of a household, amidst the hurry and preoccupation of daily life, the girl can turn out no otherwise than incomprehensible and unmanageable. Coming into an institution, the business of which is to deal with difficult cases, and overcome with patience and hourly Christian influence the spirit of evil, the obstinate, surly creatures have a better chance. The only way is to believe firmly that the girl was born with a heart and feelings like other people; and seek out these buried treasures at any cost. One gets into deep soundings, but the search is seldom altogether in vain.

REFORMATORIES

Sparke's Lake Reformatory

Doc. 40.1: *Sparke's Lake Reformatory, Monaghan, Report for 1861* (Dublin, 1862).

The Sisters of St Louis, a French teaching congregation, arrived in Monaghan town in 1859. The Sisters opened their reform school in July of the same year. A juvenile sent to a reformatory could be detained for not less than one year and not more than five years. The parents, if living, had to support the child by contributing a sum not exceeding five shillings a week. The inmates of reformatories were expected to be educated and trained for occupations. They were, of course, also expected to be reformed.[1] The majority of reformatories were eventually managed by either female or male religious communities. The following extract is part of an annual report made by the nuns outlining their work.

. . . One child, M—, made her escape from the Reformatory, and was absent several hours. This girl at a very early age manifested a roving and unsettled disposition; she would frequently leave her uncomfortable home to go off with persons of bad character, . . . and at length earned the reputation . . . thief. Her parents sent her to good schools, and there . . . the short intervals between her adventures with pick pockets, cinder and bone gatherers, &c., she acquired a certain amount of book learning, but was pronounced by her teachers as utterly incorrigible in every sense of the word; she even stole the children's cloaks from one school which she attended. Her

---

1 Joseph Robins, *The Lost Children: A Study of Charity Children in Ireland, 1700–1900* (Dublin, 1980), pp 295–8.

worthy parents, deeply afflicted, tried severity and kindness alternately, and found all useless; the father then prosecuted his child, and entreated the magistrate to send her to a Reformatory, and he willingly and thankfully pays a portion of his earnings towards her maintenance there. She came to us in the month of December, and, as long as the intense cold lasted, went on well; but one bright morning in spring, M— disappeared during prayers. She was traced through field and meadows to a distance of eight or nine miles, and brought back in the evening weary and hungry. To all interrogations she invariably replied: 'I went looking for birds' nests and blue-bells.' Her large collection of wild flowers, and the grief she evinced when they were taken from her, proved the veracity of her statement; indeed, notwithstanding her other faults, we have never found her to tell a lie. This little event confirmed the opinion we had already formed, that each child must be treated differently, according to her individual disposition and propensities. . . .

The following is a statement of the disposition of time during each day:

6 o'clock		Rising, washing, arranging beds.
6 3/4	"	Public prayer.
7	"	Household duties { A special class take { lessons in needle-work, { marking, &c., &c.
9	"	Breakfast, refectory arrangements.
9 3/4	"	Recreation.
10	"	Sewing class { A certain number of girls to the laundry.
3	"	Dinner, refectory arrangements.
3 3/4	"	Out-door exercise, and gardening when the weather permits.
5	"	Occupied in school-room for three hours, learning catechism, sacred history, reading, writing, arithmetic, rudiments of geography, grammar, &c., &c.
8	"	Supper, refectory arrangements.
8 3/4	"	Public prayer.
9	"	Bed.

On Sundays, the intervals of public worship are devoted to outdoor exercise, and the study and explanation of that portion of the Holy Scriptures set apart for the day.

It will be seen by the foregoing table that we attach more importance to the religious and industrial training of these poor children than to mere book learning. This opinion has not been lightly formed: it has been handed down to us by persons of authority; eminent, not on account of the number, length, and success of their writings on the subject, but from having devoted all the faculties of head and heart and that during a whole lifetime devoted to the practical education of youth; this opinion has been confirmed by our own personal experience . . . Religious, moral and industrial training must be the basis of the education of the poor. The benevolent being who would procure for a little barefooted girl in Ireland the intelligent use of the implements of female industry – were it only of scissors, needle and thimble – would be a true benefactor to the country. A mere course of school tuition proves a real misfortune, in many cases a curse, to those girls, who are thrown on the 'battle of life', without being prepared for its duties and dangers. Many of our pauper children acquired, in the union school, as much book learning as falls to the share of a large portion of our shopkeepers' daughters; some indeed even inherited from an unfortunate mother, or a ruined father, a certain degree of refinement and gentility: what is their fate when love of liberty leads them to abandon the workhouse, the only home they have ever known? . . . We must seek the poor creatures in the Magdalen asylums of our large cities; among the incorrigibles of our reformatory schools; in the 'refractory cells' of our convict prisons; in the lanes and bye-ways of each town! With suitable training, those loved, though fallen ones, would have been the joy of the poor man's hearth; the pure and tender mother of his little ones; the faithful and careful steward of his *modique*[1] earnings; his guardian and solace in the daily temptations and afflictions of this sad pilgrimage.

With very many of these girls, great mischief is caused by *novel reading*; it was long before we could admit the possibility of this; it is, however, beyond doubt. Here then is one of the reasons why the transfer from the children's to the adults' ward in a workhouse is so fraught with danger. The education these poor children receive gives them a *vitiated* taste for reading – with certain dispositions it is a natural attendant on *désoeuvrement*[2] – this taste cannot be alimented in a lawful way; books of a healthy tone are not supplied, and it is not for religious, moral, historical, or scientific works that the inmate will brave the vigilance of an official; but novels, and those of the worst kind, are the books for the attaining of which ingenuity is taxed, and self-denial undergone, and it is to be feared that these may even sometimes be introduced from outside purposely to corrupt. The result of this reading varies with different dispositions, but in all cases, the mind becomes occupied with *ideal* notions of life . . .

1 Modest.
2 Idleness.

Reformatory Inmates

Doc.40.2: *Report of the Reformatories and Industrial Schools Commission*
HC 1884 (*c.* 3876) xlv.

The following document reveals the fate of a number of young girls who were transferred to Sparke's Lake reformatory from other reformatories for 'absconding or being incorrigible'.

Name	No.	Year of transfer	Cause of transfer	Ultimate disposal	Observations as to subsequent character
Catherine Carroll	- 18	1860	Absconding	Died 27th May 1862	——
Mary A. Reilly	- 30	1862	Incorrigible	Emigrated	When last heard of was doing well in America.
Mary A. Byrne	- 32	"	"	"	When last heard of in 1868 was doing well in America.
Eliza Barrett	- 33	"	"	"	When last heard of in 1869 her conduct was doubtful.
Cecilia Whaley	- 34	"	"	Died 31st March 1863	——
Catherine Norton	- 35	"	"	Emigrated	In a good situation when last heard of in 1870.
Catherine Connor	- 37	1863	"	"	In a good situation when last heard of in 1870.
Ruth Farrell	- 38	"	"	Returned to friends	Being so well conducted, was kept in school seven years after expiration of term as example to others; returned to friends 1872, and is doing well.

Name	No.				Remarks
Catherine Toole	- 39	"	"	Emigrated	Emigrated to America, and was doing well when last heard of in 1876.
Susan McAdams	- 40	"	"	"	Emigrated to America and joined a religious community in 1877.
Anne Dolan	- 41	"	"	"	Emigrated to America, and when last heard of was doing well.
Bridget McCabe	- 42	"	"	Returned to friends	Returned to friends, but did not go on well.
Catherine Broderick	- 43	"	"	Went to situation	When last heard of in 1870 was in a good situation.
Mary Ward	- 44	"	"	"	Emigrated to America, and wrote here for several years. Doing well.
May A. Kavanagh	- 45	"	Subject to Epilepsy	Returned to friends	When last heard of in 1870 was doing well.
Margaret Brady	- 46	"	Absconding	"	Got married and wrote here regularly for several years.
Julia Connolly	- 49	"	"	Emigrated	When last heard of was doing well in America.
Anne Kennedy	- 55	1864	"	Returned to friends	When last heard of in 1871 was doing well.
Teresa Darcy	- 56	"	"	"	When last heard of in 1873 was married and doing well in America.

Name		Year	Conduct	Disposal	Subsequent Career
Elizabeth Kelly	- 61	164	Had been in two Reformatories	Returned to friends	Her subsequent career doubtful.
Esther Merrigan At end	- 64 - 68	"			Being so well conducted, was kept in school 10 years after expiration of term.
Winifred McDonagh	- 69	1865	——	Went to situation	Her subsequent career doubtful.
Rose Malone	- 71	"	——	Emigrated	Doing well in America when last heard of in 1872.
Winifred McDonagh	- 72	"	Incorrigible	Returned to friends	When last heard of was doing well.
Nannie McCarthy	- 74	"	——	" "	Returned to friends, but soon joined her former bad associates.
Alicia Tobin	- 75	"	——	" "	Returned to friends, and last heard of in 1871 was doing well.
Eliza Bruce	- 76	"	Absconding	Went to situation	Was in a good situation in 1874 when last heard of.
Sarah Murphy	- 79	"	Refractory	Returned to friends	Emigrated to America; when last heard of in 1872 was doing well.
Agnes Clarke	- 83	"	Incorrigible	Emigrated	Emigrated to America, and wrote regularly here for several years.
Mary Delaney	- 93	1867	Attempt to burn Limerick Reformatory	Returned to friends	Her subsequent career very doubtful.

130

Margaret Mills	- 94	"	" "	" "	Returned home and supported her aged father for several years.
Esther Fox	- 105	1868	Bad Health	" "	Returned to friends, and died in Dublin.
Kate Johnson	- 107	"	To break up Association	Died 16th April 1870	——
Eliza Dwyer	- 111	1869	——	Sent to employment 26th February 1873	When last heard of in 1875 was in a good situation.
Eliza McDowel	- 112	"	——	Returned to friends 5th January 1873	When last heard of in 1875 was doing well.
Lizzie Hickey	130	1870	——	Returned to friends 31st December 1873	Subsequent career very doubtful.
Frances Walsh	142	1871	Subject to Epilepsy	Discharged 28th November 1873	Returned to her former bad associates.
Catherine Feen	145	"	——	Emigrated 1st June 1875	Emigrated to Toronto, married, and is doing well.
Catherine Sweeney	- 149	"	Bad conduct	Sent to employment 1872	When last heard of in 1875 was in a good situation.
Honora Feen	- 150	"	"	Emigrated	Emigrated to Toronto, and was doing well in 1880.
Mary C. Kavanagh	- 154	1872	"	Died 10th December 1874	——
Honora Sheehen	- 156	"	Incorrigible	Returned to friends 9th August 1875	Returned to friends, and was doing well in 1878.
Mary A. Murphy	- 164	"	——	Returned to friends 30th September 1874	Her subsequent career doubtful.

Mary Connor	- 239	1877	——	Returned to friends 22nd March 1882	When last heard of in 1882 was doing well.
Elizabeth Finegan	- 68	1864	Bad conduct and to break up associations	Returned to friends	Returned to friends and died.
Mary Keogh	- 218	1876	Absconding	" "	Was doing well in 1881.

INDUSTRIAL SCHOOLS

Girls in Industrial Schools

Doc. 41.1: *Report of the Reformatories and Industrial Schools Commission,* HC 1884 (c.3876) xlv.

Protestant reformatories and industrial schools were generally under lay management, while those run by Catholics were generally run by religious communities. The industrial schools were intended, not for criminal children who were bound for the reformatories, but for children who were exposed to crime. Children found begging, for example, and those whose parents were dead or imprisoned, could be taken up under the Industrial Schools Act of 1868. A child under twelve convicted of an offence could also be sent to an industrial school by a magistrate. The following extract is taken from the Aberdare Commission of 1884. The government appointed sixteen commissioners to report on 'the operation, management, control, inspection, financial arrangements and condition generally of certified reformatory and industrial schools'.[1] Glanmire school, which closed in 1890, was one of the few industrial schools to be managed by Protestants.

Miss Elizabeth Woodroffe examined.

13,706.   [CHAIRMAN] Are you corresponding manager of the Deaconesses Home, Glanmire, for Protestant girls? —Yes.

13,707.   How many voluntary inmates have you there? —About 12.

13,708.   How many ordinary inmates have you there? —Forty-one are now chargeable to the Treasury.

13,709.   Have you any under six years of age? —Two.

13,710.   Have you any suggestions to make to the Commission for the amendment of the Industrial Schools Act? —I should wish young girls on leaving the school to be 18 instead of 16 years of age.

13,711.   Will you give your reasons for that suggestion? —That they are too young at 16 to go out into the world; they are not prepared

1 Jane Barnes, *Irish Industrial Schools, 1868–1908* (Dublin, 1989).

to undertake the duties of many houses where we wish to send them to service. Ladies object to their being only 16; they say, 'Have you no one older?'

13,712. We have generally heard that the ladies in charge of those establishments have no practical difficulty in placing out children even at that age, that the children have had so many advantages in learning domestic work and acquiring knowledge which children in ordinary homes do not acquire, that there is no difficulty in placing them out. Is that your experience? —That is true in one way. We can place them out, but not so advantageously as we should do were they older. We cannot get them such good situations.

13,713. Of course the work of a child of 18 is generally more valuable than that of a child of 16, but the results of their training are very fairly good, are they not? —Yes, very fairly good, indeed.

13,714. And the children who leave those establishments generally turn out well? —They turn out well with very few exceptions.

13,715. Do you think that, with the fact before them, we should be listened to by the Treasury, who have the management of these things, if we were to ask them to continue payment for a couple of years longer? —We think we could do better if we had power to keep them till they are 18 or even 17 years of age. Some of them can go out at 16, or even younger, because some are more fitted than others; they are delicate perhaps when they are young, and small of size, dull, troublesome, and wayward in many ways, and it takes some years to put them into shape.

13,716. Are girls sometimes sent to you under the age of 14 years, so that you are only able to keep them for two years? —Just a few.

13,717. I suppose in those cases you have some difficulty in preparing them for a return to free life? —Yes; we should wish to have them longer.

13,718. Those are comparatively few cases, as a rule? —Comparatively few.

13,719. The greater part of the children come to you at what age? —12, 11, and 9.

13,720. Have you any children under the 13th section of the Act? —Not at present. We had one from the country.

13,721. Did that child give you any special trouble? —She did.

13,722. How old was she? —She was under 12 when we got her, now I think she is 19. She is now doing well and married, and she is comfortably off.

13,723. You were able to reform her? —Yes; she was put in for petty larceny . . .

A Visit to an Industrial School

Doc. 41.2: K. S. Knox, 'A visit to an industrial school', *The Irish Monthly*, 22 (1894).

The following document gives a good indication of the type of education which was considered suitable for girls within industrial schools.

For a long time I had been wishing to visit the industrial school, connected with the Convent of Mercy in Ennis, but what can be done any day is often left undone, and days grew into weeks, and weeks into months, without the visit being paid. But at last on a bright autumn day I went with a friend through the quiet streets . . . and turned down the narrow entrance leading to a large gate opening on the convent grounds. . . .

A bright-faced nun now entered and told us she would be our guide, and we followed up wide staircases and through long corridors to the schoolrooms. The first was devoted to the pension children as they are called, those boarders and day pupils who pay for the very excellent education they receive. Many Intermediate certificates, prizes, and exhibitions have been won by those girls, but for some reason the course, admirable as it is, has fallen out of favour in this school, and none of the pupils are to compete at the next annual examination.

We passed on to the National school, consisting of several rooms crowded with little occupants, in fact so crowded that the chapel is to be made into a school-room as soon as the new chapel, which is now building, is finished.

'This is the infant school', said Mother Philomena, smilingly glancing back at us as she opened another door, and we were in the midst of the tiny mites. They were sitting on low benches, or standing round their teachers, with grave little faces intent on book or slate, but they found time to glance at us, and dimple into smiles at a friendly look or word.

Many were not more than three or four years of age, still 'fresh from the hand of God', and I thought what a boon it must be to busy parents to have their little tots kept happy and safe for five hours a day.

Several of the 'over-grown infants', children backward for their age, were learning plain sewing and knitting, and not a few wielded their shining knitting pins with a skill which awoke my envy.

The kindergarten school delighted me. It was lovely to watch the absorbed faces of the tiny lads and lasses as they made trains and monument, or wove coloured straws into charming little baskets and boxes.

But time was passing, and the industrial school had yet to be seen. 'You must have three or four hundred children under your care', I said to our untiring guide. With a merry laugh she answered, 'There are nearly eight hundred when all are present, but some are now away.' Eight hundred children being prepared for the battle of life! It is a great work, carried on in a quiet, unpretentious, way, and the result is seen each day. The great majority of the girls turn out well, and while some join friends in the States or colonies, many find their life-work in their native country. The sisters are most anxious to train the children in habits of thrift and neatness and to fit them either for domestic service or to manage their own homes.

In the workroom we were shown beautifully made underclothing in knitting and crochet; and a little girl, who evidently felt the responsibility of her position, manipulated a knitting machine with considerable skill. This machine, which is rather a recent purchase, is found very useful, but the girls are not allowed to make their own stockings on it, the nuns wisely insisting on this work being done by hand. While a jersey was being 'set up', we passed through the bright, well-ventilated dormitories, so still and quiet after the busy hum heard through the rest of the house. 'I call this the Holy Innocents' dormitory', said our guide, as we stood to look at double rows of very tiny white beds, now smooth and unruffled. But we soon returned to the workroom to find a crimson jersey well under weigh [sic], which the youthful machinist told us she could finish in about three hours.

We were disappointed at not seeing any of the 'Clare embroidery', a new and very pretty work, a little in the style of Mountmellick, but done with coloured cottons . . . The nuns do not consider lace-making a very suitable employment for the girls, and but little of it is done in this convent. They think it unfits the children for what may be called ordinary every-day work. Unless exquisitely made, it is of but little value as a marketable commodity, and the very fine work is trying to the sight.

'We think a good deal of household duties', said Mother Philomena, as she opened the laundry door. The girls looked so very busy starching and ironing, that we did not linger long, and crossed over to the bakery where we saw delicious-looking loaves still in the oven. 'Indeed, we have to bake every day', said Mother Philomena. 'The children use a great deal of bread and milk. Some delicate, neglected little ones, when they come to us, are almost fed entirely on milk.'

The 'Industrial' girls are all trained in dairy work, the caring of poultry, and rearing of young cattle, and if they are not able to obtain permanent employment on leaving the shelter of the convent walls, I fear the blame must rest with themselves, for the nuns spare neither time nor trouble in teaching and training them.

A play-room is much needed, the only place now available being the lower corridors, which, though large and lofty, are not suitable for such a purpose, but as we are reminded, 'money is wanted for so many things'.

Somewhat reluctantly we turned to leave the industrial school, catching sight as we did so of a neatly dressed little flock in white pinafores running up to the workroom lessons, the national school being over for the day.

EDUCATIONAL PIONEERS

Miss Alice Oldham

Doc. 42.1: Anon., 'Obituary of Miss Alice Oldham, B.A.', *Englishwoman's Review*, 15 April 1907.

Alice Oldham (1850–1907) and Anne Jellicoe (1823–1880) were noted figures in the sphere of education in the latter half of the nineteenth century.

The educational world in Ireland has suffered a severe loss by the death of Miss Alice Oldham, BA. Her work as a teacher and lecturer was done in the Alexandra College, which she joined in 1886, and she was Secretary of the Association of Irish Schoolmistresses and Other Ladies Interested in Education. At the annual meeting of the association, held at Alexandra College, on February 5, the following resolution was proposed by Miss White, LLD:

'That the deep sympathy of this association be conveyed to the relatives of the late Miss Alice Oldham, BA, in the great loss which they have sustained by her unexpected death. It is a loss in which all cultivated Irish women share, but which is especially felt by the members of this association, of which, for nearly a quarter of a century, she was the mainspring. It was almost entirely due to her initiative, ability, and untiring zeal, that the Schoolmistresses' Association has accomplished the valuable work for women's education which it has done. We, therefore, wish to express our own deep sense of loss, our great appreciation of her work, and our sincere sympathy with her relatives.'

In seconding the resolution Mrs Haslam testified to the single-hearted devotion with which, throughout all the years, from 1882, when the society was formed, she laboured for the advancement of the higher education of women in Ireland, both in its intermediate and university spheres. 'No person outside of our committee can have any conception of the incessant uphill work which our movement has necessarily involved, or of the effective part which our vigilant Honorary Secretary has taken at every stage of our labours. The services which she rendered with her every-ready and practised pen have been invaluable, and many of the reforms which, from time to time, have been introduced into our Intermediate programmes have been largely due to her untiring exertions. The one consoling circumstance connected with her untimely removal is that she lived to see the fruition of her long-cherished hopes, in the throwing open of the lectures and degrees of Trinity College to women on substantially the same conditions as men, an achievement which, for the first time in our history, places our sex in a satisfactory educational position, and which no changes in the future are likely to nullify.'

Miss Oldham was laid to rest on January 1, in the beautiful burial ground at Dean's Grange. A fund is being raised to found a memorial in her honour.

Mrs Jellicoe

Doc. 42.2: Anon., 'The late Mrs Jellicoe', *Journal of the Women's Education Union*, 8 (1880).

Mrs Jellicoe was the apostle of employment as a means of salvation and elevation for women. Work with her was no imposed task; it was the act, the action, and the activity which made her give herself up to others, and, by so doing, enjoy the sweet and wholesome fruit of noble deeds. Nor was her work of any special kind, for it ministered to supply the deficiencies of heart, of mind, of soul. However, as the heart is reached through the mind, and as the soul had many to look after it, it came to pass that the mind grew into her particular charge. Too often did she behold in woman an instrument of evil through ignorance; too often did she see her a machine in the hands of others, although she never publicly advocated any of her rights save the right to be educated. . . .

During the years of her early married life in Clare she banded around the poor young girls in need of work, and taught them muslin embroidery. At this she employed more than a hundred, and she herself sent away the produce of their efforts, and saw that it was paid for. While working thus she was at the same time beautifying her home, dispensing social blessings, and shedding the lustre of her own clear conscience over her family circle, until a parting came which widowed all the days thenceforth but did not blunt her determination to labour for the good of others. On the contrary, grief whetted her purpose, and she found a solace in widening the sphere of her work. For the poor little children of the pestilential back streets of Dublin she started a school and partial home. Today it lives and thrives under the name of Cole Alley school. For the technical instruction and employment of women in such branches of art as scrivenery, telegraphy, porcelain painting, &c, she founded the Queen's Institute, which led to the creation of Alexandra College, for the purpose of affording the solid instruction, whose need had been made manifest in the working of the Institute. And Alexandra College became the special channel through which her full life was to flow out for the benefit of all, making, what was sixteen years ago an unspoken scheme enclosed within her own breast, an institution of world-wide fame today. Out of it arose the Governesses' Association, where teachers found work, and girls found means of becoming teachers; and from both sprang Alexandra school for training teachers and preparing students for the higher classes of college. In connection with all, there appeared literary societies, choral societies, and societies of many kinds for promoting advanced education amongst women, irrespective of class and creed. The series of Saturday lectures delivered every spring in Trinity College and open to the public proceeded from her exertions to give woman some at least of the educational advantages enjoyed by man. These are few of the visible work of her hand, her heart, her head, but none can say, save those who entered into the inner life, how many were the deeds which resulted from the sympathy, the love, and the charity absorbing her whole spirit. These are but feeble images of the real outcome of her energies; these are merely the mention of some of the fruit which she herself yielded. The yield of her yieldings has only begun; the seed which she sowed is only now showing above the ground which she reclaimed and ploughed. But as her disciples are many and wide-spread, the start and impulse given by her to education in Ireland will continue to make way, and her silent voice will teach for many future years that deedful lives and supreme dominion over head and heart come within woman's province. Her life was spent like the morning of a flower, which full of dew uncloses to the day, and takes its own share of sun and cloud to turn into fragrance and beauty before the night closes. And the night does not close on Mrs Jellicoe's life until the influence of her life passes away from amongst us.

Some Lady Principals of Irish Schools

Doc. 42.3: Anon., 'The education of the Irish girl: some lady principals of the Irish schools', *Lady of the House* (Christmas 1903).

The magazine Lady of the House, *published by Findlater's Department Store, was available to Dublin householders. It contained articles which were considered to be of interest to women. The following extracts relate the careers of a number of women principals in Irish schools.*

Miss Mulvany (Dublin)

Miss Isabella Mulvany, BA, Lady Principal of Alexandra College Preparatory School, is the elder daughter of the late Christopher Mulvany, Civil Engineer to the Grand Canal Company, and formerly of His Majesty's Board of Works Department.

Educated privately at first, Miss Mulvany entered Alexandra College – then presided over by its honoured foundress, Mrs Anne Jellicoe, the pioneer of the higher education of women in Ireland – in her fourteenth year, where her scholastic course was not only marked with success, but so revealed her now acknowledged powers and innate tact that, at its conclusion, the foundress appointed the appreciated pupil to the post of her private secretary – from 1875 until the close of Mrs Jellicoe's valuable life, in 1880, at which date Miss Mulvany was appointed to her present onerous position.

It was in 1884 that Miss Mulvany took her degree at the Royal University. She was one of the first group of lady candidates, nine in number, who presented themselves for that honour; and five of the other ladies, who all passed at the same examination, were her own assistants. Miss Mulvany made no prolonged preparation for this effort, then considered a mentally Herculean one; she had previously passed several other examinations for women in Dublin, taking a special First in Honours in Latin. . . .

Mrs Byers (Belfast)

Mrs Margaret Byers, the venerable foundress and sole proprietor of Victoria College, Belfast, is a County Down lady, widow of a missionary of the Presbyterian body, the vicissitudes of whose life she nobly shared. On her husband's death, Mrs Byers opened a Ladies' Collegiate School in Belfast with a view to providing for girls a wider education, such as has been at all times afforded to boys; this, as far back as the year 1859, may be regarded as pioneer work, and the proprietary 'College' of to-day, held in such high estimation throughout the north, testifies alone to that success which the innovator has achieved, and the soundness of her perception in adopting the wide system for female education which she so fully appreciated on witnessing its work and results in the United States of America.

Mrs Byers is an enthusiastic temperance worker, a field in which she follows the footsteps of her father, the late Mr Andrew Morrow . . .

Miss Deane (Derry)

Miss Margaret E. Deane, BA, received her early education at Strand House, Derry, the same, or at least the fundamental school of which she is now Lady Principal, which had been opened in 1860 by Miss Holmes, and subsequently took her undergraduate course at Magee College in the historic city, then went aboard to France and Germany for some years. In 1893 she entered at the Royal Holloway College, London, where she remained for two years, and afterwards graduated at the Royal University, Dublin, in October, 1895. For the past five years Miss Deane has been at the head of affairs at Strand House, where she entered as a pupil in her early childhood; and the published Honour List which she has forwarded to us in testimony of her arduous endeavours, ardently carried on under her heroic motto, 'The necessity for work is the highest moral opportunity we enjoy', carries conviction of her merited great success! On her field of action Miss Deane has just completed the building of new premises at Strand House, at a cost of several thousand pounds, and fitted with every modern convenience and hygienic arrangement, including electric lighting, heating by hot water, etc., and she is ably assisted in domestic matters.

WOMEN AND UNIVERSITY EDUCATION

Campaigns to Provide University Education for Women

Doc. 43.1: Isabella M. S. Tod, 'The education of women',
Journal of the Women's Education Union, 1 (1873).

*Isabella Tod was one of the first Irish women to campaign for higher
education for women. The following document is a report of a speech made
by her in Belfast in 1873 in favour of university education for women.*

In speaking of the proposals contained in the recent university bill,[1] Miss
Tod remarks:

Why should women be left out of account? Whatever the reasons may be,
all friends of education, all who care more for the education of the people
than for carrying out any particular theory as to the mode, should make a
united effort to obtain consideration of the claims of women now, while the
whole question is under discussion. If we neglect this opportunity, no other
may occur for fifty years to come. The indifferentism will get hardened in new
grooves, and we shall soon find ourselves worse off than English women,
who are claiming and getting some share of school endowments, if not of
college endowments. I am exceedingly thankful for the university examinations which have lately been instituted. They are the first really efficient help
that has been offered to women and, though only in their infancy, have
already done great good. But, after all, they only test teaching – they do
not give it. Considering that there are not, I suppose, above half-a-dozen
schools or institutions in the country that are capable of preparing girls
well, for the senior examinations at least, and that those who are working
privately with friends or tutors are at a disadvantage in many ways, my
wonder is that the average attainments of the candidates at these examinations has been so high. Of course, there have been exceptionally brilliant
candidates, but these would have done well under any system. We must draw
the attention of the government and the legislature to the facts of the case,
and claim from them that in arranging for the higher education of one half
of the nation they shall not shut out the other half from its advantages.
Having been only this moment asked to bring the matter before you, I
have no detailed scheme to suggest; but all the friends of education should
take it into immediate consideration, to see what is the most practicable
plan. No body in Ireland has a better right to take the lead in such a
movement than the Queen's Institute; and it would be well that those
who feel the importance of the subject should communicate with Miss
Corlett or the committee, and indicate their willingness to co-operate in
any feasible plan for opening at least some of the advantages of collegiate
education to women.

1 This bill was introduced by Gladstone and proposed amalgamating the two existing
Protestant universities in the country. These were Queen's University (which had three
constituent colleges at Belfast, Cork and Galway), and Trinity College, Dublin.

Ladies' Institute, Belfast

Doc. 43.2: Minute Book of the Ladies' Institute, Belfast. Victoria College, Belfast.

In 1879 the government introduced a university bill which created the Royal University of Ireland. When the bill was announced, Isabella Tod immediately formed a committee which sought to ensure women's inclusion in any benefits that would result from the bill's passage. The RUI was an examining body only, and, while its degrees and prizes were open to both men and women, the facilities available to women to prepare for examinations were not comparable to those available to men. Women were refused entry into Irish universities. In 1873, the Belfast Ladies' Institute had made an unsuccessful attempt to have women admitted to Queen's University, Belfast. Following the establishment of the RUI, and the successful matriculation of a number of girls, in 1882 the Belfast Ladies' Institute presented another memorial to the Queen's University, again asking that women be allowed to attend classes at the college. The council of the university agreed to the request. In 1886 women were admitted to classes at Queen's College, Cork, and to Galway in 1888.

Meeting held at 126 Albion Place, 29th September 1882.

Ladies present:

Lady McAlese	Mrs McElwain
Miss Bruce	Mrs Duffin
Miss Tod	Mrs Sinclair

Resolved that the following memorial should be sent to the President and Council of the Queen's College and that the secretary enquire from the President when it would be convenient for him to receive a deputation from the Ladies' Institute, to consult with him as to the mode in which the frame of the memorial may best be carried into effect.

2 Mount Charles, Belfast
29th September, 1882

To the President and Council of the Queen's College, Belfast.

Gentlemen,
Acknowledging the sympathy and help which we have always received from the authorities of the Queen's College, we beg leave to lay before you the earnest wishes of a class of ladies who seem to have a new and special claim upon your institution, in view of the altered circumstances of educational institutions in Ireland.

There are now a number of ladies who have passed the Matriculation Examination, of the Royal University, for whom instruction of the nature of that imparted in your Honours classes is in the highest degree desirable.

We therefore, very respectfully, beg you to take into your early consideration whether you might not be able to make arrangements by which these matriculated students might be admitted to the Honours classes of the Belfast Queen's College.

We remain gentlemen
fully yours

signed by LADY MCALESE, MISS BRUCE, MRS SINCLAIR, MRS DUFFIN, MRS MCELWAIN, MISS TOD, ISABELLA KELSO EWART.

Women and the University Question

Doc. 43.3: Lilian Daly, 'Women and the university question',
New Ireland Review, 17 (April 1902).

In 1901 the goverment appointed a Royal Commission to report on university education in Ireland. The commission (the Robertson Commission) issued its report in 1903. Lilian Daly, aware of the changes being proposed, argued that the true sphere of women lay in the home. The physique of women was weak, and study might, she argued, have harmful consequences for future generations. Ultimately, however, she argues, it is women who must decide the issue for themselves.

Since women form so large a proportion of the graduates of the Royal University of Ireland, it was deemed, by many, desirable that opportunity should be given them of expressing their views on the changes proposed in Irish University Education. With a view to this, a set of 'queries' has been drawn up and sent to as many women graduates as could be reached.
'1. Do you wish that in any changes which may be introduced in Irish University Education, all advantages in regard to (a) degrees, prizes, honours and examinations; and (b) in regard to facilities for receiving teaching, and the means of study, shall be given equally to men and women students without distinction, as laid down in the charter of the Royal University?'
Again, 'Should women be admitted to Senior Fellowships?'
Such are some of the queries put to women graduates. The space allotted for reply is so circumscribed as to indicate that only the shortest answer is solicited, but brevity does not always make for clearness: too brief an expression of opinion on points so fundamental may do more to cloud the issues of such questions than to assist the cause which they are intended to promote – ie., the Higher Education of Women.

For, while there can be no doubt that the education of women must be cared for no less than that of men, it in no way follows that the same means that make for the one are methods calculated to bring about the other. When demand is made that women should be given the same university advantages as men, either of two things may be meant. Such demand may mean that women should be admitted to every class, lecture, competition, and branch of learning open to men: and that men and women-students, without distinction, should be admitted to professional careers. Or the demand may mean that women no less than men claim the necessary means by which to accomplish the end of their creation; that no less care be taken to fit women to take their place in life as women than is taken to equip men for being men. But while brief consideration will make evident that the one demand is not the other: that to advocate the second is not to subscribe to the first: the further question as to how far, if at all, the latter claim essentially involves the former is a matter calling for more careful thought.

Human beings are more than 'brains'; and to cultivate brains disproportionately can be nothing but injurious to a complex nature. No medical evidence is needed to confirm the evidence of our senses that women-students, as a whole, are wanting in physique. What effect their occupation in the sphere of exhausting work may have on future generations is a matter calling for some thought.

Again, from another stand-point, it would seem that women, by competing with men, are tending to lower wages. To lower wages must of necessity lessen opportunities for 'home' life. Yet it is in home life that women specially are said to find their truest sphere.

Further, looking to home life itself, how far does 'women's rights' in the popular sense of that expression tend to that unity in the home, that it has ever been the care of moralists to uphold?

Is it for the welfare of our social life that women should strive to share those advantages in university and professional life, hitherto usually open only to men? But this question must not be confounded with the wholly different one: is the matter one which should be determined for women by the judgment and decision of men? Is it just that the decision to exclude women from the franchise, the professions, or from university or political careers, should be a decision emanating from, and pronounced by, the male sex alone?

That is the way in which the present exclusion of women from opportunities open to men is maintained. It is a decision arrived at by men and not shared in by women. And it must remain so as long as the male authorities, in whose hands rest the bestowal of collegiate and professional diplomas and qualifications, say, as they usually do, 'whatever a woman may wish in the matter, we won't leave her any choice, but shall ourselves exclude her from certain benefits as we see fit'.

Hence it may be quite consistent to urge the throwing open of all franchises, and professional and other avocations as freely to women as to men, without at all implying that it would be well for women to make use of such opportunity to the full. And while we hesitate to recognise that any strong case has been so far made, to justify women for abandoning to any large extent their special domestic sphere, we would say that the choice should be left in their own hands, and not in the hands of the other sex. This can be done only by throwing open many spheres now peremptorily closed to them.

Women and Trinity College, Dublin

Doc. 43.4: *Final Report of the Commissioners of the Royal Commission on Trinity College, Dublin, and the University of Dublin* HC 1907 (Cd. 3311), xli.

In 1892 Trinity College, Dublin, celebrated its tercentenary. At that time women were still not allowed to take degrees from the college. A number of female activists raised a petition, signed by 10,560 Irish women, requesting that women be allowed to take degrees. The request was refused. It was not until 1903 that women were granted full admission rights to TCD. The following document outlines the steps taken to accommodate women within the college.

Women Students

160. In pursuance of the resolutions of the Board of 21st March, 1903, and of the authority granted or confirmed by His Majesty's letter of December 1903, women are now admissible to all lectures, examinations, and degrees in arts and the Medical School, but not to fellowships or scholarships. The teaching of men and women in the college is in common, except that a separate anatomical department has been set apart for women in the Medical School. The resolutions . . . provided in certain cases for lectures being given to women in a separate building outside the college.

161. A lady has subsequently been appointed to a new office, that of registrar of women students, whose duty it is to give assistance to women students if any matter arises upon which they feel difficulty.

162. We think that for the success of the co-education of men and women in a great city like Dublin a watchful care is required, and we recommend –

i That the office of lady registrar of women students shall be made permanent, and that she shall be entitled as in right of her office to communicate with the Provost and the governing body.

ii That no woman student shall commence residence under the age of seventeen, nor unless she satisfies the registrar of women students that she is a person suitable for admission.

163. There is no doubt in our minds that there exist many parents in and about Dublin who prefer for their girls an education in colleges exclusively for women to co-education in mixed classes; and it is in our opinion of importance that the wishes of such parents should be consulted. We believe that without injury to its other means of usefulness, Trinity College can be made an organ for promoting the higher education in colleges of the former kind, and with this view we recommend that the governing body shall be invested with a power to recognise individual teachers in any public college for women in Dublin or within thirty miles of Trinity College, the attendance at the recognised courses of lectures by whom shall be accepted as equivalent

to attendance at lectures on the same or the like subject within the walls of the college: but so that no teacher shall be recognised unless it be proved to the satisfaction of the governing body that his or her lectures are of a university standard, and that he or she is furnished with all such books, appliances, and apparatus as may be necessary or proper for the instruction given. In case of the recognition of such lecturers, there should be a remission of part of the tutorial fees by the college.

164. We cannot but express our hope that, if such a power be given, it may, if possible, be exercised.

UNIVERSITY DAYS REMEMBERED

Kate O'Brien

Doc. 44.1: Kate O'Brien, 'As to university life', *University Review* (Autumn 1955).

The writer Kate O'Brien (1897–1974), was educated at University College, Dublin from 1916–19. In the following extract she reminisces about university life. In the second extract, Mary Colum (see doc. 37.2) relates her experiences of university life.

In my day at UCD . . . nobody cared very much . . . whether or not you got your degree; nobody cared if you had anything to eat or drink – and as for hot water! Well – ask my contemporaries how often we dabbled in it!

But we lived as students; our spirits were free. I came up to a Dublin still smoking from Easter Week.[1] The first European War was on, and all general conditions were sad and miserable. We were a hungry, untidy lot – we of 1918–19. But did we enjoy ourselves? Did we read, did we think, did we loaf, did we argue?

. . . So far as I recall few of my set cared much to slave at the programme they were to study – all was random, I seem to remember; and we were witty and wild, or so we thought. For our ages we were well read, and could floor each other magnificently with an inaccurate reference or a distorted quotation. We went in for what we were – students. And no quarter was allowed. You had to be up to it – your reading had to be wide, and you had to know something whereof you spoke.

That was a good condition for the young. There was little comfort in it, but there really was zestful and surprising life. And had you the brains, the wits, and some sensibility – you were growing every minute.

. . . Stephen's Green was very important in our student life. We used to follow W. B. Yeats[2] all around it, I remember. How proud, and to our

1 Refers to the Easter Rebellion of 1916.
2 William Butler Yeats (1865–1939), poet, awarded the Nobel prize for literature in 1923.

silly minds how ridiculous the great poet used to look – with his head in the air, and the ribbon flying from his *pince-nez*, and his immense fur coat! We used to track Maud Gonne[1] about, too, when she was out of jail. She was marvellous and tall, with her accompanying Irish wolfhounds. . . .

Mary Colum

Doc. 44.2: Mary Colum, *Life and the Dream* (London, 1947).

The summer that I was eighteen, after I had left boarding school, I got ready to go to Dublin to study for that university degree that was sup-posed to represent some security in life for me. 'If you have a university degree', it was argued, 'you can always earn a living.' As in an earlier day young women were trained in piano-playing, drawing, needlework, and a little French as an insurance against indigence, so in the first decade of the twentieth century the new-fangled higher education for women was con-sidered the appropriate thing for me. What female relatives I had were against the scheme and considered that a suitable arranged marriage would be better security for my future, but the men of the family, even my grand-father, were strongly for the four years' training in Dublin. . . .

Arrived at the residence house, I found a couple of my boarding-school companions. The girls, varying in age between seventeen and the early twenties, were from various well-known Irish schools; the older ones were studying for masters' degrees. The residence house was in the charge of nuns, though no nuns actually lived there; there were other residence houses in the city, some Catholic, some Protestant, some grander and more expensive than this one, but I had been told before I came that this one had a freer and more liberal atmosphere than the others. At the same time university education for women was not as usual as it is now, and we were far from being as unhampered in our movements as American college girls. On my arrival I was told the rules by a sort of chaperone who was domiciled in the residence house. No going out after supper – supper was tea and bread and butter – without express permission from the nuns . . . For the first year students, no going downtown at all without permission. But the heaviest blow to me, at first going off until I learned how rules could be circumvented, was the information that the first years could only go to such plays in English as were on the university course, and to such plays in other tongues as helped them with their language studies. . . . Myself and nearly all my fellow students among the girls were going in for the same sort of degree in modern languages and literatures. . . . There were some rivalries between the products of the different secondary schools, but actually we had all been educated in the same way, brought up in much the same

1 Maud Gonne [MacBride] (1866–1953), founded Inghinidhe na hÉireann (see doc. 89), spent time in prison for her nationalist activities.

manner and with pretty much the same attitude towards life. Mentally, morally, and intellectually we were well trained; I think practially any of us on leaving boarding school could have passed the B.A. exams of almost any American university that I know, but we were very ignorant of life and were more developed intellectually than we were in other directions. . . .

The university studies, on the whole, were simply an extension of our secondary school studies, but that, instead of going forward in chronology, we went backward; that is, our secondary education had brought us to the nineteenth century in the languages we studied, but now we started at the beginnings of languages and literatures and went step by step through their development down through the centuries. We were dosed with linguistics and early texts; at times it was all very far from being interesting, and I absorbed only the modicum that would enable me to pass the examinations. . . .

The vigorous intellectural life of the city was open to the students who wanted it, and even those who didn't could not have missed taking some of it in through the pores. If we learned about the past of literature in the classrooms, we learned about the present of literature, what literature was, outside from the men who were making it. Dublin was a small city, the suburbs stretched out to a distance, but the centre, the old part of the city, was circumscribed and bristled with movements of various kinds – dramatic, artistic, educational; there were movements for the restoration of the Irish language, for reviving native arts and crafts; for preserving ancient ruins, for resurrecting native costume, an array of political movements; here, too, were the theatres and the tearooms and pubs which corresponded to the café life of the Continental city. . . . Between Abbey street and College Green, a five minutes' walk, one could meet every person of importance in the life of the city at a certain time in the afternoon.

THE PAY AND POSITION OF TEACHERS

Doc. 45: Marianne Moffett, 'The pay and position of teachers', *Annual Report of the Association of Irish Schoolmistresses and Other Ladies Interested in Education* (Dublin, 1887).

By the last decades of the nineteenth century the status and pay of teachers had improved. Governesses, however, continued to be disadvantaged and much depended on the families with whom they were placed.

. . . . At the census of 1881 there were 12,846 women returned as teachers in Ireland; 7,440 were schoolmistresses, or assistant-mistresses – of which number over 5,500 belonged to the National Board. Of the remaining 2,000 some were mistresses in Church education and other primary schools; some in superior schools. It is with the payment of these last, and of the 5,500 returned as governesses and teachers, that we are concerned this evening. Within the last ten years, owing to the state of the country, the salaries of both resident and daily teachers have been greatly reduced. The country families, who formerly gave £75 to £100 a year to their governesses, can now only give £50 or £60, if even so much; those who gave £40 and £50 less in proportion; and so on to the poor nursery governess, worse paid often than the nursery maid whom she replaces.

The resident governess is less affected by the general depression than the daily teacher is. She suffers from it too; but there are other changes in the country which tell upon her position more painfully than they do upon her resident sister, who, on the whole, does not suffer to the same extent. The resident teacher in a school or family, though her salary may be lessened, is secure of food and lodging. Her mind, being free from anxiety on that point, is in a fitter state for teaching, and thus the life is less wearing.

The remuneration of first-class governesses now averages from £40 to £60 a year; some few get more. This sounds small, but add at least £35 cost of board, and you bring the salary up to £80, £90 and £100, as the case may be. I do not say that this class of teacher is paid as she ought to be; but I do say that to my mind in Ireland a first-class resident governess is the best off of any lady worker. A great deal is said and written about the trials and miseries of governesses in families, and I think an immensity of mischief has been done by the shoals of foolish novels and stories written on this subject. My experience has been that a great deal of the sorrows of governesses are of their own making; they do not accept their position. There is no business nor profession that has not got its own peculiar trials and worries. Sensible men and women recognise this fact, and make up their minds to it, taking the good and the bad as it comes, but not going out to meet the bad, as I fear many a governess does. If governesses would only realise the trial it is in a small household of moderate means to have a governess at all, I think they would bear more patiently the rubs of everyday life, and not be so ready to imagine grievances, and see slights that were never intended.

The resident governess who is most to be pitied is the so-called nursery governess. She is generally taken from that numerous class of ladies who, brought up in comfort, and even luxury, and often in ignorance of the real circumstances of the family, are suddenly, through some financial catastrophe, or through the death of the head of the house, left almost or absolutely penniless. Not half, not even quarter educated, there is nothing to be done but to go out as a governess, or mother's help; and with starvation, or semi-starvation, staring her in the face, any salary is taken; and knowing this, employers offer less than they would think of doing to a servant. . . . .

Last year I was asked to find a governess for a family in the north of Ireland. She was to teach young children, and as the gentleman was very much engaged, and often away from home, she was also to act as companion to his wife; so she was to be a perfect lady, cultivated, and refined, salary £20, and all found. And this gentleman held an important government appointment, and had, as I knew, good private means! I need not say I declined further corre-spondence. A lady I know a short time ago dismissed her nursery maid, and replaced her with a young lady, experienced, highly recommended, and nice in every way. She teaches the children, cuts out, and assists in making their clothes, also the dresses of the mother, takes entire charge in the absence of father and mother. For this she gets £20 – £6 or £8 more than her predecessor. . . .

Nursery governesses are expected to have the education, manners, and dress of ladies, to work harder on little better or the same wages as servants, and with none of the prerequisites or 'chances' which servants possess.

But there is a worse picture still – that of daily governess life. I suppose there is no one present who has not at some time had her sympathies roused by some tragic tale about the woes of some poor daily governess, and has not been asked to give some help to save her from starvation. Such things have come within my own ken; but never, till I had my attention specially drawn to the subject, had I the faintest idea of the misery, the wretchedness, the unutterable horrors of the struggle for bare existence of the larger portion of this class. At its very best it is an uncer-tain life. What is it at its worst? The supposed ordinary remuneration for a daily teacher is £1 per month for one hour a day, that is one shilling per hour, teaching only five days in the week. I say 'supposed remuneration', because, though some get more, a few a good deal more, and fewer still really good terms, the great bulk get less – an enormous number a great deal less. Three shillings per hour seems to be the acme of a first class teacher's ambi-tion. I have heard of five shillings, but that only in special cases. Now, what does this mean? A governess teaching six hours a day at one shilling per hour can earn at most £72 a year. But no daily governess works more than ten months in the year. Most would think themselves very lucky to get regular teaching for so long. £60 a year is the most they can or should earn. Should earn, I say, for I believe that no woman could teach with justice to her pupils for more than six hours a day. Teaching for six hours means work for much longer. Every conscientious teacher knows that the homework – preparation and correction – is generally the hardest and most trying part of her duties. Then there is the going backwards and forwards to her work, and from house to house, often long distances, which takes up so much time and strength. The National Board only requires four and a half hours from their teachers . . . An experienced Dublin teacher, a friend of my own, who for some years taught nearly the whole day, got measles. The attack, owing to the state of her health at the time, the result of overwork, was unusually severe. She told me that, exclusive of doctor's fees and other expenses, she lost at least £40. I do not think she ever properly regained her health. And she lived in a comfortable home. £60 a year for lodging, food, dress, books – this last no light part of a teacher's expenses. She could live on this sum; but what

149

about times of sickness, slack work, and that money which should be laid by for old age?

But you ask, do not numbers of teachers get more than one shilling per hour? Yes, I know they do; but, believe me, the number is very small, and is growing smaller every year. The registrar of one of the first class governess registry offices in Dublin told me the other day that the pay of daily teachers is not half what it was five or six years ago. Teachers who then earned easily £10 or £12 a month cannot earn £5 now. Two shillings, two shillings and sixpence, or even three shillings per hour is obtained, but only by very highly qualified teachers – generally for some speciality, such as good music, classics, or mathematics; and for short hours, or a short engagement. . . .

Now, as to the causes of all this evil. They are many, and of various kinds. The primary one is, I think, the low value which parents, either from ignorance or selfishness, place on education for their girls. Ignorance, because they have had little or no education themselves; selfishness, because it will cause them some trouble and self-sacrifice to procure and pay for good teaching for their daughters. They think, if they think at all about the matter, that something will turn up – marriage possibly; and if nothing does turn up, well, as to what will happen after their own deaths – they will know nothing about it. I wonder will they? This evil is, however, lessening every day. Fathers and mothers are beginning to see that it is better and cheaper in the long run to bring up their girls to do something for themselves; and in order to do so, they must now-a-days be educated. Another cause is the foolish idea that teaching is the only occupation a lady can follow. This idea is, I am thankful to say, dying out. It contained in itself the seeds of its own death. If teaching was the only occupation fit for ladies, then, of course, every woman who followed it must be a lady. Consequently, women who neither by birth nor refinement were ladies, raise themselves in the social scale. In doing so they did at least this good – they forced the ladies to look around for other work. But the mischief done was incalculable, and lasts and will last on long after the false idea that caused it is dead. Crowds of half-educated, and, in many cases, wholly uneducated ladies, seized on the only profession open to them, and profiting by the popular ignorance of what true education is, and to save themselves from starvation, undersold the really efficient teacher, till they too had to lower their terms, and to accept whatever they could get. Though, however, this evil is lessening, and ladies are learning every day to find fresh fields for labour, there is another cause, one which affects more especially the visiting teacher, and this is, strange to say, the spread of education in the country, especially through the Intermediate and primary schools. Girls, who some years ago only thought of going to service, to some trade, or at most becoming teachers in the primary schools, are now, encouraged by the good education they get at the expense of the country, either in the national schools or through the help of the Intermediate Board, either going in for Civil Service appointments, looking out for private tuitions, or for teaching in superior schools.

We all know how hard it is to get good domestic servants, and one often hears it said the spread of education among the lower order has ruined the servants. This is not true; but it is true that the spread of education, joined doubtless to the spirit of the times, has caused the class from which our best servants were drawn, to look down on that occupation, and to leave it to those whose education is so bad that they are fit for nothing else. . . .

IRISH SCHOOLMISTRESSES' ASSOCIATION

Doc. 46.1: Alice Oldham, 'A sketch of the work of the Association of Irish Schoolmistresses and Other Ladies Interested in Education, from its foundation in 1882 to the year 1890', *Annual Report of the Association of Irish Schoolmistresses and Other Ladies Interested in Education* (Dublin, 1890).

The Association of Irish Schoolmistresses and Other Ladies interested in Education was formed in 1881 to campaign for changes in girls' secondary and third-level educational opportunities. In 1880, the Ulster Head Schoolmistresses' association had been formed and that association affiliated to the ISA. These organisations helped develop the professional profile of (lay) women involved in Irish education. The following document recounts the history of the Association.

The association was formed at the end of the year 1881 by several ladies interested in education, amongst whom the most prominent, I think, were Mrs Jellett, our President, Miss La Touche, our Vice-President, and Mrs Haslam who has continuously been a member of our committee since the commencement of the association. It was a time when some very important changes had made an epoch in the education of women in Ireland. Up to that time the teaching of girls had been carried on entirely by private schools and teachers. No endowment, whatever, existed for the education of women, and no accredited tests of value of the teaching given could be obtained, except such as the Examinations for Women, established by the University of Dublin, and the Queen's University, afforded. The general education of girls throughout the country was lamentably poor and imperfect; higher education was only attempted by one or two institutions, such as the Alexandra College, Dublin, and the Ladies' Collegiate School, Belfast, while from university culture or degrees, women were entirely excluded. . . .

The association was inaugurated at a meeting held on the 28th of January 1882, at the Provost's House, Trinity College, under the presidency of Mrs Jellett, which was attended by about seventy school-mistresses and other ladies from different parts of Ireland.

The first work undertaken by the association, was the presenting to Her Majesty's Government of a memorial in conjunction with the Schoolmasters' Association, praying for an additional grant to facilitate the working of the

Intermediate Education Act. It was felt that the money grant given when the Act was passed was insufficient to accomplish all the good the scheme was capable of affording. This object which we have had in view for eight years, will, we hope be attained. The addition of a sum of £40,000 has been recently given by government to the Intermediate Board, and we hope will be made an annual endowment.

In the same year (1882), action was taken by the association in reference to a point on which we have had since to contend repeatedly with the Intermediate Board – the lowering of the standard, and narrowing the scope of their programme of studies for girls. Our principle on this point has always been that every subject should be left open to girls, as it is impossible to know what subjects will be most valuable or most easily pursued in the very various circumstances of the individual candidates, who are drawn from all parts of the country, and from different ranks and conditions of life. Also, that no attempt should be made to compel the study of certain studies, or discourage others, by giving an arbitrary value to any through the raising or lowering of the marks assigned to them, but that each study should be marked solely in proportion to its difficulty, and the time, ability, and study, required in its pursuit. Especially, we have always resisted the attempt to discourage the study of the higher and more solid subjects in the girls' programme. We have felt that thereby the great value of the examinations, in affording a high standard which must be attained if the monetary advantages are to be enjoyed, would be wholly done away with.

In 1882, the Board had excluded the subjects of mechanics and plane trigonometry from the programme for girls. A memorial was drawn up by the friends of the girls' education, protesting against any changes which would make the examinations unequal in value to girls as compared with boys, either in regard to their educational or their pecuniary importance. This memorial was signed by 3,000 persons throughout the country. The Committee drew up at the same time a special memorial, dealing with the subject in more detail. The two memorials were presented to the Board in December by a deputation from our own, and from the Ulster Association of Schoolmistresses. . . .

We are necessarily a small association, with small funds at our command. Not only is Ireland a poor country, but also, owing to the ladies who conduct the education of Roman Catholic girls being debarred from taking part in public action by their religious profession, our association is, we regret to say, limited to the Protestant section of the community, and, therefore, cannot become a large society. Hence many defects in our educational system which we feel keenly we cannot do much unaided to remedy. Such are the absence of any means for the systematic training of teachers in Ireland, and absence of a good educational library, the absence of any system of inspection of intermediate schools, or of any help and guidance in such schools from the universities, similar to the help given to schools in England by the great universities. In such large matters as these we look forward to getting much help from the new Irish branch of the Teachers' Guild. It will also help us much by bringing together teachers of all ranks and classes for the interchange of ideas, and the discussion of educational subjects.

Two women, one obviously more prosperous than the other, at work probably in the Waterford area c. 1820s. (Roch(e) Collection, Ulster Folk and Transport Museum)

Part III

WORK

Members of the Irish Women Workers' Union c.1914 with its co-founder, Delia Larkin (1878-1949), sitting centre, front row.
(National Library of Ireland)

INTRODUCTION

WOMEN'S WORK WAS concentrated in three broad areas in the period from 1800 to 1918: agricultural work, domestic service and textile work. All three were traditional areas of employment for women, and were to change quite dramatically over this period. It is only from the 1840s that facts and figures regarding women's employment are available on a regular basis, and for the pre-Famine period we must rely on contemporary reports of women's working lives. In many cases women's employment was an essential factor in the household economy. Mary E. Daly has noted that in those years women's earnings were used to pay the rent or other necessities, and that the employment opportunities of women, particularly in home industry, were a factor in allowing early marriage.[1] Mary Cullen has further detailed the importance of women's contribution to the family economy and the strategies used by women in times of distress, particularly that of begging, to secure the family's survival.[2]

The nature of women's work in this period was influenced and affected by a number of factors. Ireland was a predominantly rural society. Industrialisation occurred principally around the north-eastern sector of the country and to a lesser extent in the cities of Dublin, Cork, Waterford and Limerick. Most women workers found employment in agriculture, at harvest time, in milking and butter-making, and as indoor and outdoor servants. The wives and daughters of farmers also engaged in farm work, often without recompense and also without official recognition from the census enumerators. Census information does not reflect the true level of participation by women in agriculture. There was a dramatic change in the range of agricultural work available to women by the end of the century. Changing land-usage patterns, the shift from tillage to dairying, increased stock rearing which was less labour intensive, growing levels of mechanisation and the coming of the creameries,[3] which removed butter-making from the home, all took their toll on women's agricultural opportunities.

---

1 Mary E. Daly, 'Women in the Irish workforce from pre-industrial to modern times', *Saothar*, 7 (1981), pp 74–82.
2 Mary Cullen, 'Breadwinners and providers: women in the household economy of labouring families, 1835–6', in Luddy and Murphy, *Women Surviving*, pp 85–116.
3 See Joanna Bourke, *From Husbandry to Housewifery* (Oxford, 1993).

Many factors influenced the work opportunities available to women in Ireland. The rural or urban environment offered different prospects for women. Social class determined the necessity to work. There were also regional variations in the opportunities available to women. For example, women in Belfast or Derry had a greater chance of factory employment than women in less industrialised towns and cities around the country.

Employment in textiles offered an important supplement to the household economy in the pre-Famine period. The domestic textile industry employed up to half a million women in 1841.[1] The spread of the factory system and competition in the period from 1850 destroyed the domestic base of this industry. But even by 1900 textile production still remained a major form of employment. The linen industry became centred in Belfast and the shirt-making industry was concentrated in Derry and Donegal.[2] By 1902 up to 80,000 women were involved in this work, many working from their own homes on the outworking system, but with about 18,000 working from factories.[3] Homeworking, or outworking, was badly paid. The material was made up in the woman's own home, and paid for by the piece. Outworkers were isolated workers, who, driven by economic necessity, worked long hours, competing against each other for any available work. Wages for outworkers were always less than for those who worked in factories.

Despite its authoritative appearance, census information on occupations and status must, in relation to women at least, be treated with caution. Census enumerators used six categories to accommodate the occupations of the population. These categories appear self-explanatory but, to the modern eye, may seem inconsistent. The professional section included individuals who, for example, held government office, were teachers, students or members of religious communities. The domestic section included individuals who were domestic servants, charwomen, those engaged in service in hospitals or hotels. The third category, commercial, included merchants, commercial clerks, and coach makers. The agricultural section included farmers, graziers, agricultural labourers, and farm servants. The industrial category included those who owned lodging houses, cabinet-makers, millers, greengrocers, dressmakers, tailors, and general shop-keepers. The final category, titled 'indefinite and non-productive', included vagrants, schoolchildren, wives who were not engaged in paid employment and of course those who were wealthy enough not to need paid employment. The census figures for the period 1881–1911 show a decline in women's employment in the domestic, agricultural and industrial spheres, with a slight

1 Census, Ireland, 1841.
2 Daly, *Social and Economic History*, pp 76–7.
3 Department of Agriculture and Technical Instruction for Ireland, *Ireland, Industrial and Agricultural* (Dublin, 1902), pp 418–9; Eithne McLaughlin, 'Women and work in Derry city, a survey', *Saothar*, 14 (1989), pp 35–45.

rise in their commercial and professional opportunities. There is a significant growth amongst women in the 'indefinite and non-productive class'. The explanation for this increase lies partly in the way the census was compiled.

Table 3.1: Female Occupations in Ireland 1881–1911

Female Occupations in Ireland	1881	1891	1901	1911
Class I: Professional	62,195	75,272	32,674	37,531
% of female pop.	2.35	3.15	1.44	1.70
Class II: Domestic	392,093	220,654	193,331	144,918
% of female pop.	14.84	9.24	8.55	6.59
Class III: Commercial	1,494	2,161	5,026	9,747
% of female pop.	0.05	0.09	0.22	0.44
Class IV: Agricultural	95,946	91,068	85,587	59,198
% of female pop.	3.63	3.81	3.78	2.69
Class V: Industrial	262,931	252,255	233,256	178,698
% of female pop.	9.95	10.57	10.32	8.12
Class VI: Indefinite & Non-productive	1,826,900	1,744,387	1,708,861	1,768,079
% of female pop.	69.15	73.11	75.65	80.43

Sources: Census of Ireland, General Reports, [C 3365] HC 1882, lxxvi: [C 6780] HC 1892, xc: [Cd 1190] HC 1902, cxxix: [Cd 663] 1912-13, cxviii.

In 1871 the Irish commissioners were told to transfer wives who had previously been placed in the domestic class to the 'indefinite and non-productive class'. At the same time wives with specified occupations were to be removed from the relevant occupational class and placed in the domestic class. However, the English commissioners found this too complicated and abandoned the scheme, as did the Irish commissioners. But wives who shared an occupation with their husbands were placed in the 'domestic' class. In 1881 the daughters and granddaughters of farmers, who would previously have been counted as engaged in farming, were transferred to the 'indefinite and non-productive' class, though sons and grandsons were not. From the 1870s, more and more women, especially married women, were being placed in the 'indefinite and non-productive' class. This masks the real extent of women's contribution to the economic life of the country. By 1911 almost three-quarters of adult women were listed without occupation in the 'indefinite and non-productive' category. The proportion of women working fell from 29 per cent in 1861 to 19.5 per cent in 1911.[1]

Women also found employment in the domestic arena, as domestic servants, laundresses, and charwomen. For most of the nineteenth century, domestic service was the major employer of women's labour. In 1871 service accounted for almost 15 per cent of the female workforce. Domestic service masked a multitude of activities. Within a wealthy household women could

1 Census, Ireland, 1861, 1911.

work as lady's maids, cooks, housemaids, nursemaids, etc. As farm servants women could engage in house work and farm work. Conditions for servants varied and depended on the generosity of the employer. Long hours, poor pay and hard work were the general lot of servants but neither were servants completely powerless. They could, and frequently did, threaten to leave their places of employment for better positions. A good cook, for example, was valued by the household, and a mistress would be loath to let her leave. But whatever relationship was established between employer and servant, it was always an unequal one.[1]

There were few areas of employment which 'respectable' middle-class women could enter. Teaching and governessing were two of the mainstays for those forced to support themselves, but by the 1860s, Irish women had come to realise the necessity of educating and training women, particularly those of the middle classes, for employment. The area of 'professional' employment in nursing, teaching, etc., was one sphere where women's employment opportunities improved slightly by the early decades of the twentieth century.

Shop work was also an area that engaged a number of women. It was considered very respectable work for young women, but it was also difficult work. Shop assistants worked long hours, six days a week. Wages were not much better than that of factory workers, though shop assistants had to maintain a higher standard in appearance and dress. Office work also began to open up for women at the turn of the century. Women within offices had lower status than men and also became associated with the less well-paid areas of typing and bookkeeping.

Teaching and nursing were two careers that developed over the course of the nineteenth century. Before the 1850s nursing had very low status and was carried out by women who had no formal training in the area. The entrance of nuns into nursing, first as home visitors, and then as nurses in state hospitals, created a more respectable air around the profession. It was lay women, rather than nuns, who paved the way for the formal training of women as nurses and by the end of the nineteenth century nursing had become a respectable occupation, indeed a vocation, for many women.

Gender expectations placed limits on the type of work women could engage in. In those areas where they did find employment there were limitations placed on what they could do. In agricultural work, for example, it was men who came to use the new farm machinery, which women were thought incapable of understanding. Because of the expectations that women would marry and have children, they were further marginalised in the workforce and seen as temporary workers, where their labour was devalued and they were paid less than men, even for work of equal value. There was also the fear amongst male workers that women's labour would be used to undercut male wages. This caused tensions between male and female workers and also led to squabbles

1 Mona Hearn, *Below Stairs: Domestic Service Remembered in Dublin and Beyond, 1880–1922* (Dublin, 1993).

over what constituted men's work and what constituted women's work. Women tended to be confined to jobs that were low paid, casual, and 'unskilled'.

Women workers in the nineteenth and early twentieth centuries were difficult to organise into trade unions. The traditional areas of women's employment, domestic service and agriculture, for example, offered solitary or seasonal employment, and did not lend themselves to unionisation. Women did, on occasions, organise for better conditions. In Belfast, in 1874, for example, 40,000 millworkers went on strike for over a month.[1] Mary Galway organised the first trade union for women textile workers, the Textile Operatives' Society, in Belfast in 1893.[2] Other unions also represented women. From 1868 women national school teachers were represented in the Irish National Teachers' Organisation.[3] The Irish Women Workers' Union was established in 1911, in part organised against the prejudice faced by women from male trade unionists.[4] For women workers, joining unions became the most effective way to bring about change in their working conditions and in the perception of them as workers.

WOMEN AND AGRICULTURAL WORK

In 1801 the Dublin Society launched a project to publish statistical surveys of Irish counties. The information contained in the twenty-three surveys, which appeared between 1801 and 1832, gives a detailed picture of life in rural and urban areas. The surveys covered, amongst other things, living conditions, employment opportunities, agricultural information relating to crops and prices, and the level of education available in particular localities. The first extract below comes from a survey of County Armagh written by Sir Charles Coote.

The second extract comes from the First Report of the General Board of Health. *This report stemmed from government concern about the possibility of disease spreading throughout the country, and contained replies to queries sent to resident gentlemen, clerics, magistrates, and other 'respectable' individuals, regarding the state of the poor, their living conditions and general health. The information which was returned also provided information on the employment of women and children, and the conditions under which they laboured.*

1 Emily Boyle, 'The linen strike of 1872', *Saothar*, 2 (1976), pp 12–21.
2 *Missing Pieces: Women in Irish History* (Dublin, 1983), p 22.
3 T.J. O'Connell, *One Hundred Years of Progress: The Story of the INTO 1868–1968* (Dublin, 1968), p 14.
4 Mary Jones, *These Obstreperous Lassies: A History of the Irish Women Workers' Union* (Dublin, 1988).

Women's Earnings and Expenditure

Doc. 47.1: Sir Charles Coote, *Statistical Survey of the County of Armagh* (Dublin, 1804).

. . . Women's wear, of cotton, will amount to about £3 with cloak, petticoat, shoes, stockings, etc. If drugget is substituted for cotton, the cost will be about one-third less, and the article more durable. In general, the women are better clad than the men, and make a gayer appearance on holidays. Their earnings are generally spent on finery, as the man's labour procures them provisions . . .

The male servant of the farmer or manufacturer will receive about six guineas per annum, with board and lodging; the woman about £3. The general employment of the women is spinning . . .

Women's wages are about sixpence per day for [a] day's work; children's from threepence to sixpence. But, at some branches of the linen manufacture, if they had constant employment, they could earn tenpence per day.

> Average clothing of a man, per ann. 3 guineas.
> "   "   "   "   woman, "   "   2 guineas.
> "   "   "   "   child, "   "   15 shillings.

The wages having been stated, I shall state the average value of labour to the employer, or to the cottager, if he works on his own account.

> Of a man, per annum, £25.
> Of a woman, "   "   £12.
> Of a child, "   "   £7.

The average value of diet cannot be rated at less than £12 per man, £9 per woman, and £4 per child, per annum. For fuel, soap, candles, and house rent, the average may be six guineas.

Cr.	£	s	d	Dr.	£	s	d
Man's labour	25	0	0	Man's diet	12	0	0
Woman's	12	0	0	Woman's	9	0	0
Child's	7	0	0	Child's	4	0	0
	44	0	0				

	£	s	d
House-rent, fuel, soap and candles,	6	16	6
Man's clothing	3	8	5
Woman's	2	5	6
Child's	0	15	0
	£ 38	5	3
Balance	5	14	9
	£ 44	0	0

The balance is £5 14s 9d, which an industrious family will soon encrease [sic] to a sufficiency for stocking a small farm, or setting up looms for journeymen. There are no wages in husbandry, where so much money can be saved.

Munster Women and Farm Work c. 1818

Doc. 47.2: *First Report of the General Board of Health in the City of Dublin* (Dublin, 1822).

. . . . A want of employment for the poor exists at Dungarvan, Tramore, Tallow, and Anne's Town. At the latter place the wages of labour are reported to be a shilling a day for men, and eight pence for women; but this rate is almost nominal, as farmers now seldom employ any except their own families . . .

In the barony of Fermoy, and near Skibbereen, spinning wool and flax occupy the females, at which employment they may earn about two pence daily. In other parts of the county, as at Skibbereen, females are employed in manufacturing flax only, and are represented to contribute materially to the support of the family. In the neighbourhood of Mallow the females manufacture a considerable quantity of coarse woollen cloths, and it is hoped that the increasing cultivation of flax will give them additional occupation. In the neighbourhood of Macroom, during the time of planting potatoes, as also during that of hay-making and harvest, many females are employed; their wages threepence per day without victuals. Some few are employed by persons called haverlings, who distribute combed wool, which they get from the manufacturers. The wages earned by women, though occupied the whole day at such work, do not exceed from two to threepence. Some years ago large quantities of wool were spun in the parish of Clondrohid; but very little of this work is done at present. Our informant has seen females eight or nine years old, who could earn nearly as much as grown women by spinning. He considers this kind of employment to be salutary, as the spinners, when employed, are in constant motion. In other parts of the county, as in the vicinity of Millstreet, except the employment during the time of harvest at the rate of threepence per day, there exists scarcely any other. Some years ago the woollen manufacturers of Limerick used to send wool to this county to be spun by the women and children. A good spinner could earn sixpence per day at that work, and had constant employment; but since the adoption of the spinning machinery in England this occupation of the poor females has been discontinued, because the English manufacturers undersell them. Similar accounts are given from other parts of this county.

In the neighbourhood of Cove [Cobh], females are employed occasionally in spinning, particularly since the encouragement held out to the spinning-schools by the Linen Board. Many are engaged in agricultural occupations, some in making nets. They can earn about fourpence per day. All the works

163

in which the people are employed in that neighbourhood tend to the preservation of health. In Mallow females are but little and irregularly employed, and that in agricultural work. Flax is there manufactured in the small way for domestic purposes. In the city of Cork, females are employed as workwomen, mantua making, and straw bonnet making; as fruit-women, vegetable women, charwomen, and washer-women, at the rate of tenpence per day. A spinning-school, under the patronage of some ladies of distinction, has been lately established in Cork for the employment of young females.

In the county of Waterford the lighter labours of agriculture, and a little spinning, constitute the chief employment of the females. Many of the women in the neighbourhood of Cappoquin spin wool for sale, and worsted at a very small profit. The children are sent to bring in heath, leaves &c. or remain idle. The men cultivate half an acre of potato ground, for which they pay in work at a low rate per day, about sixpence the year round; but those not so employed depend upon an uncertain employment at tenpence per day, but are generally half their time unemployed. Country work is conducive to health, if there is sufficient food with it. The females near the sea coast manure the fields with sea weed, which they carry on their backs: this dangerous and laborious employment the reporter has never seen performed by men. In the evenings the females spin. The consequence of their laborious employment is premature old age. At Dungarvan those engaged in saving fish find sufficient employment. The lighter kinds of agriculture, with knitting, spinning, and in some places, as at Tallow, thread lace making, afford some employment. A few years ago females were pretty constantly employed in spinning combed wool, and could earn from threepence to fourpence per day, now they have little more than the usual business of the family, except at harvest and potato digging time. The lessened demand for agricultural labour has affected the females as well as the males. Field labourers are the most healthy. Sedentary tradesmen, merchants porters, salters &c. seem healthy in a degree next to the field labourer.

In the county of Tipperary field labour occasionally is the principal occupation of the females. Spinning will not requite the labour and loss of time, but serves to fill up the dead season, and to clothe the family. In the vicarage of Shanrahan they receive for spinning of wool or flax on an average fourpence per day, but there is no regular demand for such work. Where the food is sound and sufficient, and the habitations dry, the different kinds of employment at Templemore being rural, have uniformly a favourable effect upon the health. Disease seems chiefly to prevail amongst those not regularly employed. At Clonmel it is reported that there is no particular employment for females, yet they do not appear to suffer as much from want of employment as males. The families are in general idle, and the children brought up in the habits of pilfering and stealing. One of our informants at Cahir very judiciously enlarges on the evil consequences of want of employ-ment for females in the following terms: 'The females are totally unemployed, except during harvest and the potato season; but they are so ignorant that few know how to do anything, not even to work at their needle. Were they given habits of industry and cleanliness, it would add to the comfort of their families in every way, and they would bring up their children in habits of industry, instead of to theft and wickedness of every description. They are willing to work if they were taught and had the means, but they have not even materials of any kind to work with or upon.' At Roscrea some of the females are employed in the spring and harvest in agricultural labour; a few spin wool, of which stuff is manufactured there, but the majority of the females are idle, and inclined to be so; these sit over the fire most part of the day, or go about from house to house gossiping. If any person is taken ill in the neighbourhood, the cabin is instantly filled with them, and fever is extended in this way. They also frequent wakes; the children are neglected, or allowed to straggle about the roads half naked.

In the county of Limerick, barony of Clanwilliam, it is said that spinning wheels have been lately introduced, but the high price of flax causes a poor return for their labour. In the city of Limerick the washerwomen are in general healthy, as are any females who, from their particular avocations, are enabled to use much exercise; but the sempstress and knitter are in general subject to dyspepsia,[1] amenorrhoea,[2] and swellings of the lower extremities. The cultivation of flax extensively in the county of Limerick, for which the soil is said by this reporter to be better adapted than that of any other part of Ireland, would be of the greatest advantage to the health, morals, and comfort of the lower classes. Women can spin by the light of the fire. The want of fuel in winter stops industry, as the poor are obliged to go to bed to avoid cold.

In the county of Kerry circumstances are very similar; some females are occupied with domestic concerns, preparation of wool and flax for the wheel, and spinning; others in knitting stockings or gloves, or working the fields, or managing their dairies; but they are in general idle. In the barony of Magunihy they are in general totally unemployed, except in making butter, and this occupies but little of their time.

At Castle-Island a few of the females spin. The average quantity of flax which a good spinner would spin into coarse thread, fit for Bandle linen, is about one pound and a quarter per day. They are paid at the rate of four-pence per pound for spinning the coarse thread. They do not receive more than fivepence for converting a pound of flax into fine thread, although it takes twice the time. In the parishes of Ventry, barony of Corcaguinny, the female children, who were formerly a heavy burden on the poor, are now in a great measure become their riches; for, from the time they are six years old, they contribute their share to the dressing of flax, and after-wards, as they advance in years, they are able to spin it; so that there is scarcely a female in the nine parishes, which this reporter attends, idle; and

1 Indigestion.
2 Absence of menstruation.

what is more, they seldom work in the fields, they have so much to do about their flax and thread.

In the county of Clare females are employed much as in the last county. In some places there is little or no employment for females, as at New Market on Fergus, in other places they are occupied in dressing flax and wool, and in spinning. In some parts of the county the occupations of the field chiefly employ them. At Ennis they have little employment, except in the latter part of spring, in spreading potatoes, manure, and afterwards in weeding; during harvest time in binding corn and gathering potatoes. Of all employments the weaving of linen is most unwholesome, as the weaver thinks that the free admissions of air is injurious to the thread. In many places in this county the females are reported to be most deplorably idle during the greater part of the year . . .

The Labour of Women and Children

Doc. 47.3: *Report from His Majesty's Commissioners for Inquiring into the Condition of the Poorer Classes in Ireland, Appendix D HC 1836 (43), xxxi.*

A Royal Commission of Inquiry into the conditions of the poorer classes in Ireland was appointed in 1833. The commission gathered information by sending queries to important people in various localities, and also by taking oral evidence from witnesses. The following extracts are taken from the replies to queries relating to the earnings, and the financial contributions made to the family economy by the wives and children of labourers. The relevant questions are given first, followed by the names of the province, county, barony and parish to which the information refers, and the name of the individual who provided it.

Q6. Are women and children usually employed in labour, and at what rate of wages?

Q9. What in the whole might his wife and four children, all of an age to work (the eldest not more than 16 years of age) earn within the year, obtaining, as in the preceding case, an average amount of employment?

Munster
County Clare – Baronies Inchiquin, Islands
Dysart, pop. 1,666, Rev. C. Curtin P.P.[1]
6. Women are employed a little in the harvest, and usually get from 4*d* to 5*d* per day.
9. I think £22.10*s*.

1 Parish Priest.

Clondegad, pop. 4,650, Rev. Charles Fitzgerald

6. Women and children are employed in spring and harvest by a *few* of the farmers; women are paid 5*d* a day and children from 3*d* to 4*d*, according to their size.

9. About £20.

County Clare – Barony Tulla
Killaloe, pop. 8,614, Capt. Martin J.P.[1]

6. Women are occasionally employed at 4*d* per day; children scarcely ever.

9. About £7 per year.

Connaught

County Galway, Baronies Ballymoe (half) and Tuam
Templetoher and Buiounah, pop. 9,742, Rev. Wm. Bourke P.P.

6. Women and children are frequently at all kinds of work in the field, assisting their husbands and parents, or taking their place when with the *master* in England or in Leinster.

County Galway, Baronies Ballymoe, Tuam, Ballinahinch and Moycullen
Ballynakill, pop. about 7,183, Henry Blake Esq. J.P.

6. The women knit stockings, make flannel-yarn and help in manuring the farm, making nets, etc.

County Galway, Baronies Clonmacnoon, Clare, Kilconnel
Kilclocey and Creagh (Part of Ballinasbe) pop. 11,268, Rev. L. Dillon P.P.

6. Women are usually employed in harvest, saving hay, binding corn, and in winter, picking potatoes.

County Galway – Barony Longford
Clonfert, pop. 5,915, Hubert Moore Esq. J.P.

6. Women and girls are employed at farm work, and preparing turf for fuel; their wages are 4*d* per day.

9. From £6 to £8 per year.

Clonfert, Clontuskart and Kilmalinogue, pop. about 10,000, Rev. T. Strange
Bulson

6. Employed in hay-making, binding corn, weeding, picking and planting potatoes, footing turf, etc., women 6*d* per day; children, according to age, from 3*d* to 4*d*.

County Galway, Baronies Loughrea, Leitrim, Moycullen
Kilcummin, pop. 9,848, Rev. John Wilson

6. Women and children are seldom employed. In harvest the women get 6*d* a day for binding corn.

---

1 Justice of the Peace.

Union of Loughrea, pop. 7,797, Rev. Samuel Medlicott
6. Generally speaking, children have no employment, and women usually get half men's wages.

Counties Leitrim and Sligo – Baronies Carrigallen, Dromahaire, Tiraghrill, Rossclogher
Cashcarrigan, pop.—, Rev. John Maguire, P.P.
6. Little or no employment for women and children; when employed, glad to get their diet without wages.

County Leitrim – Baronies Leitrim, Mohill
Bornacoola, 2nd Division of Mohill, pop. about 8,000, Rev. James O'Ferrall, P.P.
6. Women and children are seldom employed, and when they are they get from 1*d* to 2*d* per day; but they are often employed in rearing their own turf and digging their potatoes, in the absence of their husbands, brothers and fathers, then earning wages elsewhere.

County Mayo – Baronies Burrishoole, Murrisk
Aughagower, pop. 11,693, Rev. Peter Ward, P.P.
6. They occasionally assist during the spring and harvest, there being no employment for them since the destruction of the linen trade. I have minutely inquired as to what a woman could earn at spinning linen or woollen, and find that the most an attentive spinster could earn would not exceed 4¼*d* per day; a female servant will, when so fortunate as to get service, obtain wages, sometimes 5*s* per quarter, sometimes 6*s*.

Munster
County Cork – Barony of Carberry West (East and West Division)
Moyross, pop. 3,459, Edward P. Thompson Esq.
6. But occasionally, at 3*d* per day: there has been a mine lately opened in this neighbourhood, which gave employment to a great many.

Sherkin, part of Tullagh and Cape Clear, pop. 2,083, Rev. David O'Keefe, R.C.C.[1]
6. Women are employed as servants for 20*s* a year; and children, when of an age to work, for 13*s* a year.
9. £1 for the wife and £1 10*s* for each of the children, when employed.

County Cork, Barony Carberry West
Durrus Kilcrohane, pop. 9,606, Rev. John Kelcher, R.C.C.
6. They are not employed at all, with the exception of a few young women, who may earn each year during what is called the season about 12*s* or perhaps £1, by making fishing nets, some young women, as servants, receive at most £1 each year; the young women assist the men in bringing the seaweed on their backs in baskets from the sea shore, and the turf from the mountain, but this is for their own families; generally speaking,

1 Roman Catholic Cleric.

the women and children are not employed at all, they know little or nothing of inside door work at all; there are in these parishes about 50, and at least that number of individuals who endeavour to make out a livelihood by buying eggs here and then taking them to Cork, where they are bought for the English Market; these individuals are generally young women of blameless morals and great industry; the distance they have to travel bare-footed with such a load as 300 eggs in a basket on their backs, is to many no less than 50 miles; some will take so many as 350 of these eggs, others not more than 200; they generally bring as heavy a load back from the city, and make ten or a dozen such journeys every year; the time devoted to such a journey is generally a week; their profits are inconsiderable, perhaps about £3 in the year.

County Cork, Baronies Duhallow, Kinnalea
Dromtariffe, pop. 5,926, Rev. Patrick Quinlan, P.P.
6. The labouring women and children are employed at the selling of potatoes, binding of corn, and picking potatoes; their usual hire with diet is from 3*d* to 4*d* per day.

County Cork, Baronies Muskerry East, Barretts
Donaghmore, pop. 6,794, Rev. Thomas Kenney
6. The wife and children are usually employed in cultivating the labourer's potatoes, in cooking, and in attending the labourer in collecting manure, in feeding a pig or more, in rearing fowls, in knitting stockings . . .

County Tipperary, Barony Iffa and Offa East
Clonmel (Town), pop. 15,134, David Malcomson
6. There are very few women or children employed in this town, except at a handweaving establishment, where there are 176 looms, which employ about 200 females in weaving calico.

Ulster
County Antrim, Barony Dunluce Lower
Billy, pop. 6,869, Rev. Hugh Hamill, P.M.[1]
6. Women are usually employed in harvest and receive the same wages as men during that time.

County Antrim, Barony Kilconway
Aghoghill, pop. 3,057, Rev. R. Alexander, Rev. G. Kilpatrick, Rev. G.
McClelland, P.M., J. O'Hara Esq. J.P., Alexander McManus Esq., J.P.
6. Yes at potato dropping, hay-making, turf-making and harvest, wages, 6*d* per day, without diet. The linen trade, which is carried on extensively in this parish, employs the women and children weaving, spinning, and winding for the weavers, boys commence at a very early age, perhaps about 12, or sooner, to weave, and in some instances the girls weave also.

1 Presbyterian Minister.

County Armagh, Baronies Armagh, Fews Lower
Keady, pop. 9,082, Rev. Joseph Jenkins

6. Women and girls are employed in weeding and flax work, at 6*d* a day,
    without diet, and occasionally in harvest reaping at 10*d* to 1*s* a day,
    there are two linen factories in the parish, which give employment to
    120 females daily, at from 10*d* to 4*d* a day.

County Cavan, Baronies Castleraghan, Loughtee Upper
Kildrumferton, pop. 9,687, Pierce Morton Esq. J.P.

6. Not usually for hire, but for the family about the farm; when hired they
    take half the wages of the men. The failure of the linen manufacture has
    almost destroyed the profitable employment of females in this part of
    Ireland: the profit which has been thus lost to the families of the poor is
    thus reckoned by the individual [a previous interviewee] before men-
    tioned – 'A poor man took conacre flax ground, say 10 perches – rent
    10*s*, price of a peck of seek 5*s*; horse to plant it 2*s* 6*d*, flax-dresser's fee 2*s*
    6*d*, total expense £1. The crop of this, by the labour of the wife and
    children, without taking up more than two days of the man's own time,
    produced 56lbs of rough flax, and this hackled by the flaxdresser, 42lbs of
    clean flax and 14lbs of tow. The clean flax spun into four hank-yarns, sold
    at 1*s* per hank, producing £8 8*s*, which, with 7*s* from the tow-yarn, at 6*d*
    per lb, makes a total of £8 15*s*. Here, then, was a profit of £7 15*s* on the
    labour of the wife and children, who are now, in most instances, a burden
    rather than an assistance.'

County Dublin, Baronies Kildare, Upper Cross, Rathdown Carberry (half)
Rathcoole and Calliaghstown, pop. 1,945, Rev. T. Hayden.

6. Women are employed in the hay season at 7*d* per day; the same for
    binding corn, or picking potatoes; children from 8 to 12 years of age
    get 4*d* per day for picking stones off laid-out lands to meadow, or
    gathering scutch grass roots, etc., and the same get about 2*s* 6*d* per
    week at McDonnell's paper mill, in Saggard.

[*The following extracts are taken from the composite report on the earnings of
women and children, compiled by the Commissioners, from the evidence
provided by the witnesses.*]

County Mayo, Barony of Murrisk

Women are hardly ever employed for hire in the barony; where labourers are
to be had 6*d* and less, no one wants women . . . There is no employment
for women but begging; in the harvest time a few women may be employed
in binding corn at 3*d* or 4*d* a day, but none of them are engaged for more
than 10 days in the year; I would not give 4*s* for the entire earnings of any of
them (Rev. Mr Dunge P.P). A good many cabins have fowls, but where eggs
are to be had at the rate of four a penny, and there is no corn to feed the
fowls on, it all having been sold for the rent in October, there can't be much

profit out of poultry . . . None of the witnesses estimate the earnings of a woman, by the rearing of fowls, higher than 3s a year.

The amount to be made by a pig depends on the length of time that the poor man can afford to keep it; at the present prices it is computed that a man may clear about 5s on a pig, kept for six months . . . a pound of flax costs 7½d, a woman spends two days in spinning it, and the two hanks fetch but 9d in the market, being three farthing a day for her labour. . . .

County Down, Barony Iveagh Upper

Some labourers' wives have employment in flax time, hay-time, and harvest in shearing corn, but there is little employment of this sort for women. Some of the farmers do not allow the labourers' wives to keep fowls for fear of injuring the corn in some places, however they have them. Mary McAlluden said 'My brother is a weaver, and has 3 acres of land; we keep 7 hens, and get 3½d or 4d a dozen for the eggs. Sometimes for a long time they do not lay any; we cannot afford to eat a single one of them; we are obliged to sell them to help out the rent which is very high.' Some women earn by spinning 3½d a day, if they are good spinners, and devote their whole time to it . . . When a woman has a family to take care of, she cannot earn more than 1d a day – she will not spin more than two or three hanks in the week . . . Mary McAllunden said 'that the yarn which she held in her hand cost in the market 1s 2d. She spun it in a week, she had five hanks, and would get 4½d a hank for it. A real good spinner will spin a hank a day.' Thus according to her statement, her week's wages amounted to 8½d.

But the labourers present all said that their wives did not earn by spinning more than 1d a day, and that the factory at Castlewellan had destroyed the spinning business for labourers' wives.

Barony Kilconnel

In harvest time there is some work for women, but in winter there is none (Capt. Davis). They are wanted in summer to assist in making turf and hay, and also in digging and picking potatoes. Ellen Deely says 'that she seldom got more than 3d a day in harvest; she has two sisters who would be glad enough to get work if they could; she is certain that not one of them ever earned 10s by labour in any one year; she is herself now in service with a shopkeeper in Kilconnel, where she gets but 10s a quarter with diet, and has to clothe herself; she would not be there if she could do better by working.'

The wives of labourers very generally keep fowls; they are not in the habit of keeping bees, there are hardly any in the barony. Martin Deely's wife states that 'her husband holds 3 acres and a half of land, at £1 1s 6d an acre; when the times are good she manages to keep four or five hens, and as many ducks, if she had to buy them they would cost her about 1s a piece; if she have good feeding for them, and can keep the cabin warm, they would give her about 2 eggs a day all the year round; she has never sold them better than three a penny. When her husband had but one acre she couldn't keep any fowls, and a person having but two acres could barely afford it either; as to rearing chickens, many a year she never reared any, and at most only about three couple, and if fowls were plenty she would not get more than 6*d* a couple for them . . .' Spinning is no longer followed as a source of profit; the present price of yarn does not remunerate. Whatever flax is spun is consumed by the woman and her family (Mr Fox). Mary Flatherty states that no woman could spin more than half a pound of flax in the day; flax costs 6*d* a pound, and she would not get more than 8*d* for the yarn, 'leaving, her, at most, 2*d* for her day's work, if she kept at it always'.

Life on a Farm

Doc. 47.4: Mary Carbery, *The Farm by Lough Gur* (London, 1937).

In 1937, Mary Carbery (1865–c.1945) published the story of the early life of Sissy Fogarty. Fogarty was born in 1858, the daughter of a substantial County Limerick dairy farmer. The following extract details the level of work carried out by women on the farm, all overseen by the mistress of the house.

Our farm was like a little colony, self-contained, where everyone worked hard and all were contented and happy. Besides the fields, the farmhouse and its good out-buildings, there was a quarry, a kiln for burning lime, a sandpit, a turf bog and the productive eel-weir. Eels were sent direct to Limerick market or taken by Meggy-the-Eels who came from Bruff to buy 'the take', which she peddled from house to house in the little town. Everything we ate and drank came from the farm except tea and coffee and J. J. (John Jameson's whisky), which was kept for visitors and for medicine. We lived by a strict routine, a necessity on a farm if it is to prosper, and all the indoor work took place in the two dairies and the large stone-paved kitchen which was about twenty-eight feet square and well-lighted by a large window overlooking the lake.

In the centre of the kitchen was a long oak table at which the plough-man and farmboys had their meals, sitting on forms.[1] For breakfast they had maizemeal stir-about with plenty of milk, sometimes potatoes; in later years home-made bread was added. Dinner was at 12.30, consisting of milk in 'piggins'[2] potatoes and 'dip' (a made-up gravy and bread); bacon was given twice a week, but later on every day. The men's tea was taken out to them at four o'clock, with bread and butter in great slices. The maids had the same food, but at a different time, and for supper at 7.30 bread and milk,

1 Wooden benches.
2 A round wooden vessel with a high wooden stave for a handle. It held one and a half pints.

hot or cold, or porridge with plenty of sweet milk. On this simple fare maids and men throve; they were all healthy, hearty and good tempered. . . .

This was the farm routine. All hands rose at 4.30 a.m., the fire was blown up until it blazed, turf and coke were piled on and an immense iron pot of water suspended from a crane was moved by a lever to hang directly over the flames to boil for the feeding of the calves. Outside, one of the boys lit a furnace in the yard over which was a boiler for more hot water. This was set close to the pump.

At seven, when the milking was over, my mother came from her room to receive the milk in the upper or lower dairy according to the season; the lower one, which was reached from the upper by stone steps, was cooler and used in summer. On the stone shelves were rows of flat earthen and glass pans; all was spotlessly clean and fragrant, in fact visitors who came to Lough Gur seldom left without visiting 'Mrs O'Brien's show dairy'. Here entered in a long file, the head dairywoman and her maids carrying milk pails on their heads; lowering them carefully, they poured the milk through strainers into huge lead cisterns, where the cream for butter-making was to rise, the remainder being strained into flat pans on the shelves. A lovely, homely sight: rich, ivory milk, golden cream – all to be hand skimmed – firm one-pound pats of perfectly made butter ready to be sent off to special customers in Dublin and London; other great pats for home consumption – we children did not spare it – and the bulk of the butter in firkins, each containing seventy pounds, set aside for the butter buyer to take to market.

At nine we had our breakfast: two boiled duck eggs every day for our father, a hen's egg for mother, for us children stir-about, home-made bread, and butter and milk. Breakfast for all was over by 9.30 when we children and Moll set off across the hills to school. The men had gone to the fields, the women dispersed – some to feeding numerous turkeys, geese, hens, ducks, others to wash the dairy and scrub and scald pails, pans, strainers and churns; one to do housework and another to prepare the men's mid-day meal and perhaps set a great batch of dough to rise in the warmth of the hearth while the brick oven was being heated by burning bundles of furze and sticks. Our dinner was at four o'clock. The evening milking was from five to seven. The morning routine of straining and scalding was repeated. Milking was some-thing of a mystery to us children, as our father forbade us to enter the byres, but from the outside we heard the rhythmical swish of milk falling into pails and the dairymaids singing or crooning, each to her cow. . . .

Women as Agricultural Labourers

Doc. 47.5: *Royal Commission on Labour. The Agricultural Labourer, Ireland* HC 1893 [C. 6849], xxi.

According to census returns, the number of women employed as agricultural workers fell markedly in the period 1881–1911. While census figures do not reflect the true participation of women in agricultural employment – many wives and daughters continued to work on family farms, often without financial recompense or recognition – the modernisation of Irish agriculture substantially reduced employment opportunities for women. The Royal Commission on Labour, which reported on the Irish agricultural labourer in 1893, provides some information on the role of wives and children within the economy of the labouring family.

Annual Earnings and Current Rate of Wages

Classes of Labourers:	Daily or weekly rate of wage		Annual earnings	Remarks
	Summer	Winter		
Westport Union, Co. Mayo				
Ordinary labourers on the staff of a farm	1s 6d to 1s 8d a day or 1s 3d with food	1s 2d to 1s 8d a day or 10d to 1s with food	£20 to £23 or about £15 with food	A few of Lord John Browne's best men earn up to £27 by taking piece work
Women	About 4s 6d a week	About 4s 6d a week	——	Women and girls are very seldom employed
Castlereagh Union, Cos. Roscommon and Mayo				
Ordinary labourers on the staff of a farm	1s 6d to 2s	1s 3d to 1s 6d	£20 to £23	On some estates whose wages are up to 12s men can earn £32
Women	1s a day Girls 8d to 1s a day	1s a day Girls 8d to 1s a day	——	Women and girls are very seldom employed

Helping at Harvest Time

Doc. 47.6: Siobhán Lankford, *The Hope and the Sadness: Personal Recollections of Troubled Times in Ireland* (Cork, 1980).

Siobhán Lankford (1894–1986) grew up on a farm in County Cork at the turn of this century. Here she recollects the use of the threshing machine and the role played by local girls in harvesting.

One threshing machine served the whole countryside in these days and its owner had a busy time. . . . The machine and all the gear was moved by the farmer who was next to thresh, so there was little delay, and the machine man himself spent the night with the farmer. He supervised the erection of the set so that an early start could be made the next morning. The set consisted of a big drum, and gear for harnessing four horses to large wooden planks which were connected with the drum. The horses, harnessed in pairs, walked sedately round and round in a circle all day and the drum gave out a loud boom as it was fed the corn.

It spewed out yellow straw, grain and the light fluffy chaff. A man in charge of each of these products whisked them away as they fell from the drum. The energy generated by these four horses in their leisured walk was incredible, and the threshing set was an enormous improvement on the flail.

The girl's job at the threshing was to open the sheaves. It was easy work. Bound with strips of the corn itself it was opened by pushing back the knot. A young man stood beside the machine man to hand up the opened sheaves. Only the owner could feed the threshing drum for careless feeders had had their hands mangled in its crushers. . . .

The threshing was the social event of the year. Groups of young men came to help . . . Besides the girls opening sheaves there were girls to help with the cooking. These had a busy time – huge chunks of corned beef, or bacon, or both had to be cooked, a large pot of cabbage white and crisp as it grew only on the open farm, a large pot of floury potatoes, innumerable cups of tea from constantly boiling big kettles, soft drinks and the indispensable tierce[1] or half tierce of porter . . .

Threshing finished about seven o'clock, and everybody came in for tea. The girls who had been working in the house had already milked the cows and got tea ready for all the men and girls in the haggard. They had worked very quickly so as to have time for the party which was the highlight of the harvest. Singing, dancing, telling stories, went on until well past midnight. . . .

1 A cask.

WOMEN IN INDUSTRIAL EMPLOYMENT

Female Industrial Work in the South at Mid-Century

Doc. 48.1: Anon., 'Female industrial employments in the south of Ireland', *Englishwoman's Journal* (November 1857).

This anonymous report tells of the schools and industries established or revitalised during the Famine years to provide employment for poor women. Middle- and upper-class women, who had acquired sewing skills as an accomplishment, put their knowledge to use by establishing sewing classes, in an attempt to enable poorer women to earn a livelihood.

Within the last ten years a vast change has taken place in the industrial employments of females in the south and west of Ireland. The Famine which, in the year 1847, desolated these parts of the island, apparently crushing all human energies, was in reality, its greatest boon; for from its ravishing hand sprung forth the germ of a healthy and vigorous life, amongst those of the population, who survived its devastations; just as from the decayed grain shoots forth the hardy blade, which in time yields fourfold fruit. When at length a lull took place in the pestilence, which raged for many months so hotly, people began to look around them and see how they were to remedy the utter destitution of the poor in their vicinity: and in remote country villages, as well as in towns and cities, there were not wanting ladies to form themselves into committees and associations, for the benefit of the female poor; many of whom were widows and orphans, deprived of house and home by the same stroke that took from them the husband and father, who had toiled for their daily bread.

The first means of enabling them to earn their livelihood by work was to *teach* them, for the greater part of both women and children were ignorant on this point, save of knitting stockings, and doing a little plain work, which was mostly confined to repairing the clothes of their families. But, with the natural quickness of the Irish in general, teaching was no difficult task, and 'ere long in many a country village sprung up a crochet school – that style of work being considered the most remunerative that at the time presented itself.

Girls of all ages quickly flocked into these schools, glad to earn even a few pence, and it was a pleasant sight to see their nimble fingers handling the crochet needle so expertly, while their poor wan faces lit up with pleasure, as the ladies, who kindly undertook the sale of their work, examined it and praised their industry. At first they were almost exclusively confined to making edgings; collars and sleeves, in crochet, not having come into fashion at the time. These did not, of course, pay them well, threepence per yard being about the highest price which could be obtained for them: and then an insurmountable obstacle arose, which was, that there was no known avail-

176

able market for their work, for the families in the vicinities of these crochet schools had purchased as much, and more, from them than they required; and having exhausted their English friends, who had given them a vast amount of help and large orders for edgings, could do no more; so that for a short time their industry seemed paralyied [sic], and they again relapsed into idleness which to say truth was not voluntary. Many a time, have we heard the regretful words – 'I'm idle for want of work', and felt how hard it seemed, to be unable to give them some.

But this state of things did not continue long, for, hearing that the sewed muslin embroidery was extending, and prospering in the north of Ireland, and giving to so many thousands there remunerative employment, some ladies (principally the wives of clergymen) entered into correspondence with some of the leading manufacturers in Belfast, as to the means of the females of the south sharing the benefits which their northern sisters enjoyed from embroidery work; to which enquiries they received a kind and speedy response, assuring them that every encouragement should be given them to form embroidery schools in their neighbourhoods. No time was therefore lost, no effort spared, to open schools for this purpose. In one instance, where no house could be obtained (this was in a small country town) and no suitable room was to be had, the large room in the court house was kindly given up for a time by the magistrates, until the committee of ladies, who were forming the working class, found a suitable place for the girls to assemble in. The plan adopted was this, the manufacturer sent a mistress from the north, who was fully competent to instruct in all the branches of sewed muslin embroidery work. The ladies' committee guaranteed to her the sum of one pound per week, for such time as it was necessary she should teach and superintend the work for the girls employed, and in some instances, the mistresses thus sent were about a year teaching in one school. The manufacturer sent the unbleached muslin stamped for working, also the cotton, so much being allowed for each strip, the calculation being generally exactly correct. The work completed, the muslin was returned to him, unwashed and just as it came from the workers' hands, the process of bleaching, finishing, and making up being performed in the north.

This commencement of sewed muslin embroidery in the south of Ireland was in the year 1850, and on looking back, it does seem strange that it took so many years to travel from Ulster to Munster, for it was first known in the former province in the year 1780; and in 1806 it was first introduced as a manufacture, in a small village in the County Down, but then, as now, the spinning of linen yarn being the staple manufacture of Ulster, the new style of work gained little favor, being confined to two or three small villages. The amount of wages received by the workers averaging annually no more than £5,000.

In consequence however of the adoption of machinery for the spinning of linen yarn, the hand-spinners were deprived of their accustomed employment, and the various articles of the recently-introduced manufacture becoming in increased favour and demand, not only at home but abroad, this style of work at once extended and developed in a manner almost incredible; spreading not alone through Ulster, but creeping also into other provinces. An important impetus and stimulus was also given to the work, by the mode of printing the patterns upon the muslin being changed; the lithographic press being employed, instead of the tedious and expensive mode of block printing, hitherto made use of for the purpose, which was in vogue until the year 1830.

At the present time the demand for sewed muslin embroidery – not alone in Great Britain, but in the United States, Canada, Australia, India, and indeed every country which opens its markets to British industry – is so great, that in Ireland alone it is estimated there are annually 200,000 females employed, and the yearly amount of wages received by those several parties connected with the work is £400,000, and upwards. So that this manufacture is of deep and vital importance to the females of Ireland, at least to those of the peasant class, who are generally the gainers by its fostering hand. Dependent, as this style of work is, on the caprice of fashion, it is nevertheless less dependent than other classes of fancy work for this reason, that changeful as certain descriptions of it may be, there are many articles connected with the trade, as free as most things of the kind can be, from the fluctuations of fashion in the article of female costume; whilst to meet the more vulnerable portions of it, the inventive power of the tasteful designer can be called forth, to create new articles to captivate the seeker after novelty, and to the restless enterprizer we look for the discovery of new markets, wherein to dispose of our industry. Therefore we look forward with hope to the future of this branch of female industrial employment throughout Ireland.

Hitherto we have spoken of it generally, now we shall come to individualize its working. The manufacturers are mostly connected with Glasgow, where all the work is finally sent by the various agents, who are scattered throughout the towns and cities of the south and west of Ireland. These agents take a house, or set of rooms, where assemble the females who apply to them for work. In some instances this is done on the premises, but in general the workers are permitted to take it to their own homes, which they much prefer, and which, for two reasons, is far preferable; – first, they are not penned up in close and, it may be, contaminating rooms, where bad air, and want of ventilation, may induce disease; and, secondly, they are by this means enabled to pursue their occupation in the bosom of their families, leaving it off when domestic duties require their attention, and resuming it at their own convenience, which makes the task far lighter, besides the beneficial effects on the health, of pausing now and then in their work, instead of bending over it continuously for hours at a time. The embroidery is divided into classes; the first class being generally some simple pattern in strips, either for trimming or insertion – or a very simple collar, for the working of which is paid about threepence. The fifth class is the highest, and has satin-stitch and rich embroidery introduced in it, and is well paid for – five and six shillings being given for a collar in this class of work. We have heard that in many instances it is sought for by, and given to, ladies of reduced means, who are happy by this means to add to their incomes, and avoid the publicity of other modes of employment; and here we may add, that in a large city in the south of Munster, we know of a depot opened mainly for embroidery, only the finest and best descriptions being received for disposal.

Having thus given a brief account of the present state of the sewed muslin embroidery work, we must turn to other branches of female industrial employments, and state that within the last few years a fresh impetus has been given to crochet work in this country, which has led to the establishment of various manufactories for its production. A firm in Cork, who possess a large drapers' establishment, have opened a school and factory for crochet work alone, in which hundreds of girls are employed, some working daily in the school, and others receiving materials to do the work in their own home. We have heard that they find a ready market for crochet of all descriptions, in every part of the world, but more particularly in America, where work of all kinds being very expensive, they are able to realise large profits; and ready sales are easily effected, which, for this kind of work, is essential, owing to the many changes of fashion in the shape of the collars and sleeves: although indeed, at present this fabric in every form is so much in vogue, that the market for its sale is seldom overstocked. How long it may continue to be in demand is, of course, very uncertain; and for this reason many persons object to its being taught and practised by the poorer classes, to the exclusion of plain work, which seems to them far more solid and useful as an acquirement than crochet and such fluctuating fancy works. But the argument against this theory is that at present, there is no remunerative field for plain workers. It is true that of late years into Ireland have penetrated those grinders of the poor – shirt-making manufactories, from which the needy workwomen, whom absolute want drives to their doors, receive the miserable wages which barely keep them from starvation, and which has called forth Hood's celebrated 'Song of the Shirt'.[1] But only those who can obtain no other livelihood would ever seek for this style of work; and many who have tried it, have declared that sooner than continue it, they would seek admittance to the parish workhouse, twopence being the amount they received for making a shirt in the class known as 'slop work', and which occupied them the best part of a day, and sixpence being the sum paid for a white shirt, highly finished, with several rows of the finest stitching on the fronts, collars, and sleeves, and which occupied them nearly two days in the making! Therefore, at present, they eagerly flock to the crochet schools, which enable them to earn as much as six and seven shillings a week, if they are clever workers, and

1 Thomas Hood's poem described the life of a seamstress and was very popular in Victorian England.

which is a style of work the girls seem infinitely to prefer to any other. It is, indeed, a pleasant sight, to see them sitting at their cottage doors in groups, singing and smiling, at their employment, comfortably clothed, by the fruits of their own industry, instead of being, as formerly, ragged, squalid, and idle, roaming about the streets and roads, getting into vice of every kind, and adding to the poverty of their families, instead of ameliorating it.

Attached to almost every convent is a work-school, to which the nuns devote a certain number of hours daily, for teaching and over-seeing the girls in their occupations: and from some of these convent schools is sent exquisite specimens of crochet work; the fine Guipure crochet and imitation of old point lace being frequently taught by nuns, who are themselves foreigners, or who, having lived on the continent, have learned the art in those countries where it is brought to the greatest perfection. But the sale for those refined and expensive sorts of work is limited, and they fear entering into it too deeply; the cheap and common kind of collars, sleeves, etc., finding by far a readier sale. Therefore, – unlike manufacturers, seeking for their own profit upon the work – the nuns' schools are most sought for by the workers, who there obtain higher prices than they receive at the manufacturers; where, we have heard, the profits to the proprietors are twenty per cent at least, crochet work of all kinds realising more in England and the colonies than it does in Ireland.

Another branch of female employment in this country we must not omit – we allude to the beautiful fabric known as Limerick lace, and which is now exported all over the civilized world. Indeed, no bride deems her trousseau complete without some article of this light and beautiful texture being contained in it, and very frequently are wedding dresses almost entirely composed of Limerick lace, its price enabling those who consider Honiton, or Brussel, beyond their means to obtain it instead. In the city of Limerick, where it is exclusively manufactured, there are about two thousand females employed in its workmanship; it is wrought in frames, several women embroidering at the same frame, if the article is of large size. The girls who are employed at the manufactories are apprenticed, generally for seven years, – at first only earning about two shillings a week, and when perfect at their trade, their wages not averaging more than from seven to ten shillings a week. Besides the workers, there are also designers employed, whose business it is to draw and invent patterns, which are tacked under the lace, and then traced accurately with the needle upon its surface. This style of needlework, however, we may consider altogether local, as we are not aware of its being carried on in any place but the city whose name it bears.

There is in the county of Waterford at a small town called Tallow, a school carried on by the nuns of the convent there, for the production of Maltese lace, in the manufacture of which they have arrived at great perfection. Some specimens we have seen, being not inferior to that brought from abroad, and highly creditable to the poor girls who make it, and who we believe are well paid for their work.

We are well aware that it is the fashion of the present day to decry the children of the poor being taught any of the above sorts of work; and the writers and speakers against it argue that it unfits them for the description of labour they may be required to practise in domestic life. One writer affirms that the generality of females who earn money in this way, seldom know how to spend it, that they can certainly adorn their clothes with tawdry finery, but would be unable to darn or mend them if torn. This is all very well to theorise about, but let him step into any of our cottage homes in the country, or lodgings for the poor in the city, and on questioning the mothers of those girls who are employed in any of these styles of work, he will find her acknowledge with gratitude that they are now kept from idleness and have consequently learnt domesticity, and that their earnings, small though they be, are of great value to her, and a comfort to themselves. These statements we know to be facts; – and those who would not teach a girl fancy work seem to forget that as the age progresses, we must progress with it. It was no doubt all very well in the days of our grandmothers to instruct their daughters in spinning, weaving, and knitting, but the loom has superseded the use of these employments in the present day; and, therefore, we can only weave now in romance, and spin in an old ballad.

Therefore do we wish good speed to all female industry, no matter of what class it be, only regretting that it is not better paid for, and feeling assured that in time females will show their capabilities for higher and more profitable pursuits, than they have yet attained to . . .

Dublin Factories in 1861

Doc. 48.2: Anne Jellicoe, 'Dublin factories', *Englishwoman's Journal* (October 1862).

Anne Jellicoe, whom we have already met through her work in education, investigated the conditions of Dublin factories in the early 1860s. She presented her report to the National Association for the Promotion of Social Science at an annual meeting held in Dublin in 1861. In the report, she outlines the various forms of factory employment open to women in the city, noting the pay and conditions of work which are applicable. She examines those crafts and trades which were undergoing increased mechanisation, and notes the attendant problems for women. Jellicoe also alludes to the moral implications of women's employment, particularly in regard to the performance of their domestic duties.

The influence of factory life on the social condition of the workwomen of Dublin is, doubtless, of small extent, if compared to its effects on the crowded population of the great manufacturing towns of England. Yet it will be found that a very considerable number of young women are engaged in manufactories in this city – a number likely to be increased as the industrial resources of the country become thoroughly developed.

. . . It is . . . important to inquire into the condition of those young women who must be regarded as the future wives and mothers of our humbler citizens, and to endeavour to ascertain what are the impediments that lie in the way of their progress.

Although factory life here is free from some of the deeper shadows which rest upon it in the sister island, it cannot be denied that there is large room for improvement and reform. In the absence of an accessible centre of information, an estimate of the numbers employed and the rate of wages paid has been carefully prepared from personal observation and inquiry.

The principal employments open to the humbler class of women may be divided into two sections – the trades which are guarded from general intrusion by the jealousies of 'craft', and those occupations to which the great army of 'toilers and spinsters' have free access. To the first division belong the winding of silk, the weaving of carriage lace; hat, cap and bonnet making, tailoring, bootclosing, brush and pin making, bookbinding, etc. In the second group are included the weaving of linen, cotton, and frieze, the making up of various articles of clothing, and the paper trade in most of its branches. In all of these employments, unless specially noticed, the wages average 6s per week of ten hours per day. The trade of 'silkwoman', which is on record as the earliest paid branch of female industry in England, affords employment to about one hundred women as winders and pickers of silk, in the peculiarly Irish art of poplin-weaving. The winders take apprentices of twelve years of age and upwards, and receive part of the payment for the work done by them. The men employed at the looms can earn £2 to £2 10s per week, but cannot be induced to make provision for a 'rainy day', and many families are now suffering severely from the depression of trade caused by the civil war in the United States. The weaving of carriage lace, fringe, etc., employs, in good time, from sixty to eighty young women. Over one hundred not very healthy-looking women are occupied in the finishing, etc., of hats. The apprentices give one year of their time without receiving wages.

Most of the employers in the above mentioned trades are interested in the moral instruction of the young women, who are a decent, orderly class. A knowledge of these callings is generally handed down from one family to another, and mental education is not so much needed as the handiness acquired by early acquaintance with the art.

In the cap-making there is a want of skilled industrious women, who may earn 6s to 8s per week. The sewing machine has been introduced in this branch of industry, but only for ornamental stitching, as the regular cap makers will not work at the machine. The making of straw bonnets afforded employment at one time to a very large number of women, but is now carried on merely in a private way.

Of the handicraft trades, bookbinding employs by far the largest number of girls, principally in stitching, folding, etc. Some employers see no objection to women taking a higher position in the art; and in one respectable house, a woman successfully manages a machine which was previously attended by a man. The wages range from 4s to 16s per week. The operatives take apprentices from the age of twelve, who must give one year or more of their time without wages, according to their need of instruction. Though not required to read or write while occupied in the lower departments, education greatly facilitates their rise in the trade. In one or two houses, girls are engaged at very low wages in routine work, which has the effect of afterwards lessening their value as intelligent artisans.

The women occupied in marine stores must not be passed without notice. Their trade of picking and sorting rags, though dirty and repulsive looking, is easy, and they are sometimes able to earn 8s a week. Large numbers are employed in this way; and, though generally illiterate, their employers give them a high character for honesty. These women must not be confused with the miserable creatures who frequent by-lanes, carrying baskets of rude toys and sweet stuff, which they barter with the street children for rags, in some instances torn from their already tattered garments.

The introduction of sewing machines has,[1] within the last two years, given rise to a new order of factories, which bring together in large work-rooms artisans whose callings had previously been carried on in their own dwellings. Of these occupations nearly 500 girls are employed in boot-closing in eight of the largest establishments in the city; they earn an average of 8s per week of nine hours per day, the cutters-out, machine-workers, etc., earning the largest proportion of wages.

Tailoring is another of the trades now in a state of transition from that of a handicraft to machine labour. English-made goods are coming over at a price only to be met by the use of machinery, yet an outcry has been raised against the sewing machine, on the ground that greater numbers of women and children can by its adoption be admitted to the trade. The making of waist-coats is a remunerative occupation for women; good workers can earn fully 10s per week by hand sewing. It is difficult to get clever workers in this as in many other trades, and they often object to the restraint of the work-room. The nature of the two last-named occupations, hitherto carried on day and night in stifling rooms, where fresh air was rarely permitted to enter, induced such habits amongst this class of tradespeople that many manufacturers have welcomed as a boon the use of machinery, by which punctuality, order, and industry are rendered compulsory.

There are three pin manufactories in the suburbs which give employment to a number of females both in the factories and in rooms in the city, in sorting, making up, etc., of pins; all the actual process of manufacture being now done by machinery. Those at work in the city can earn, 'even allowing them Monday', said one employer, 'seven or eight shillings per week'. Many of these women are of very low class, and there is great

---

1 From the 1850s, the American Singer sewing machine began apppearing in European homes.

difficulty in getting the work promptly executed. This idle habit of taking a holiday on Monday is not confined to the working classes, but prevails among children at infant and other schools.

Linen, cotton, and woollen factories afford the class of employment in which apprenticeship is not required. The older hands instruct beginners, and receive some payment out of the work of their pupils. About a thousand young women, principally the daughters of the poorer class of tradesmen, are occupied in these mills. A few are clean and tidy, but the majority, though quickwitted in many ways, are far inferior in appearance, manners, and habits, to what, with a little care, they might become.

The culture of the flax plant, a product so exactly suited to the climate of Ireland, is very little attempted, except in the province of Ulster: there it has taken such deep root, and attained so flourishing a growth, that in the county Antrim alone (independently of the preparing processes) over 660,000 spindles are at work, twisting its fibres into thread, whilst 4,000 power looms are occupied weaving it into linen. In the neighbourhood of Dublin we have one factory employing about 400 women and girls, who earn from 3s to 7s per week, according to their aptitude and industry. The girls are all above the age of thirteen in this as well as in most manufactories; so that schools are not demanded by law for their instruction. In one department a respectable woman acts as overseer, a plan which, if adopted in all work-rooms where girls are employed, would be attended with incalculable benefit, both in the moral training of the young women and as affording a healthy stimulus to their exertions to exert themselves, so as to be able to fill such situations. The manager of this factory is anxious to promote the welfare of the operatives, but finds that any improvement they gain is counteracted by the state of their dwellings and the habits they have acquired there. A considerable number of women of a similar class to those just mentioned are employed in paper mills, of which there are several near Dublin. The paper trade in its highest branches of cutting, stamping, edging, and making up of the paper into the numerous forms required for business purposes, affords a very suitable occupation for young women. The appearance of the girls so engaged presents a striking contrast to that of the great proportion employed in other manufacturing operations, these being tidy, intelligent-looking, and generally knowing how to read and write.

An employment which remains to be noticed is that of the needlewoman. In this department the sewing machine reigns supreme, and its busy whirr will soon be heard in every street. The females who are counted by hundreds in other trades may in this be reckoned by thousands, and, on account of the present dullness in the majority of manufacturing employments, fresh recruits of every age and grade – from the tradesman's daughter, anxious to earn a few shillings for the purchase of a dress, to the reduced gentlewoman, striving to eke out a meagre existence – are now pressing into this, the woman's great resource.

The exercise of a judicious and benevolent oversight is here more especially needed. In each of the large manufactories there are from fifty to two hundred women employed, who earn from 2s to 6s per week by working from nine a.m. till seven p.m., with an hour's interval. The preparing, finishing, etc., of the work for each machine occupies two, three, or five girls, according to the nature of the garment and the dexterity of the machine-worker, who can earn from 7s to 15s per week. . . . One, two, or three cutters-out are also employed in every work-room, as well as an overseer, whose business it is to keep the workers from idling. In a few houses girls are taught to sew and use the machine, and for this instruction they pay in either time or money. One of the workmasters said that he could find employment for double the number of hands but for the difficulty of managing the sewers, many of whom do not know how to hold a needle when they come to the factory, and often leave in disgust after a few days to seek some easier and more remunerative employment. Very many are quite satisfied with earning a few shillings a week, and will not exert themselves to obtain more wages. In most establishments trained hands only are engaged, as employers cannot afford to give time or room to the incapable, many of whom offer their services, and are refused, though skilful workers are in demand . . . In some houses the goods, partly sewed by the machine, are given out to women who can pay a deposit; some of these earn a subsistence by collecting their poorer neighbours to sew at low wages, or give out the work to those who have not courage (and too often not clothing) to go to business houses in search of it.

This last mentioned difficulty has been, in one instance, overcome by the efforts of a few ladies, who, having obtained an army contract for shirt-making, have established the Crimean Home, where the relatives of deceased soldiers can procure work to the extent of twelve shirts a week, for which they receive 6s. Machines are not used here, and the institution is self-supporting, paying salaries, rent, etc., and furnishing 170 poor women with the means of subsistence, besides giving them out of the profit of their own work a supply of blankets and coal for Christmas. . . .

Sweating in the Linen Industry

Doc. 48.3: James Haslam, 'Sweating in the Irish linen industry',
The Englishwoman (January–March 1911).

Textile manufacture was a traditional area of employment for Irish women. While most textile production declined in nineteenth-century Ireland, the manufacture of linen became an important industry, particularly in the north. By the early years of the twentieth century, Belfast had become the linen weaving capital of the country and women were the principal employees. Much of the sewing and embroidery work was carried on as outwork in women's homes. No one knew how many women engaged in outwork, but the number was thought to exceed the 22,000 women who worked in the making-up trades in factories and workshops. The following document is an account of the conditions under which women laboured as outworkers.

. . . I found myself in the midst of the women out-workers of Belfast. Their poverty was appalling. It cannot be said, truthfully, that they live in 'poverty, hunger and dirt' (to use the phrase of Tom Hood),[1] because, taking them on the whole, they make a heroic endeavour to keep themselves and their diminutive dwellings clean. As Dr Bailie, the Belfast Medical Superintendent Officer of Health, has said, 'Home work has no attractions for the indolent sloven, so that the homes of out-workers represent a fairly high average of cleanliness.' He confesses that there are regrettable exceptions – I saw linen goods sent from the best merchant houses in the country going to be made up in homes that were dark, damp, and stricken with disease, homes that were black with poverty, dens of filth and drink and profanity. These homes were in narrow, crooked streets, winding in and out of a labyrinth of slums, wherein women at night stood at the doors of candle-lighted cottages, and children flitted barefoot across the roads.

Taken, however, altogether, the Irish out-workers make a brave endeavour to form a bright contrast to their poverty by keeping themselves clean. That, perhaps, makes their struggle all the more pathetic. They work steadily and persistently for one penny per hour, and in *some cases less than one penny*! I was talking to an old Irish woman who was embroidering linen handkerchiefs at the rate of sevenpence per dozen; she could finish a dozen in one day. She had got up that day at five o'clock in the morning to do the housework. At periods of the day she attended to other domestic duties. Frequently she laboured on till ten, eleven, and twelve o'clock at night. This went on – this dreary, monotonous day – from week to week, month to month, year to year. And for what? For a mere sevenpence a day, or 3*s* 6*d* a week towards the upkeep of the family! Now this woman was not quite herself when I was speaking to her. Whilst one of her children – a girl aged eight years – had gone to the warehouse for more handkerchiefs, she had been scouring the fireirons. Her face and arms were besmeared with blacklead. But the room was tidy. The woman was kindly and well-spoken. She wept for a child that lay upstairs with a fatal disease upon it. All that she thought about, and all that she seemed to care about, was the welfare of her five children. The linen handkerchiefs she embroidered at the rate of sevenpence a day were selling in the highest-class houses in Belfast, London, Liverpool, Manchester, Birmingham, Glasgow, &c., at 8*s* 6*d* to 9*s* 6*d* per dozen.

'But why', I asked her, 'do you slave day after day for such a miserable pittance?'

'Well, sor', she said, 'it pays the rint; an' I want, sor, to see Jimmy serve his time to a dacent thrade.'

1 See note 1, p. 179.

And in order that Jimmy might have a chance, this woman was stitching herself into the grave. Two of the other children helped her in her embroidering work; and what they made in wages 'helped to pay the gas an' the coal'. The food was provided out of the husband's wage; he was a labourer, whose earnings did not average more than 12s per week.

I have given you this scene because it is typical of many others. I have given it to show two things: one is, that these out-workers are deserving of much better treatment from society; the other is, that they are worked under sweating conditions, not because they make articles sold at low prices in cheap shops – the articles they make up are sold in your best shops in the finest streets of the kingdom. There is no question about that among those, at least, who are acquainted with the trade. In the purchasing of linen goods, most of us unconsciously give support to one of the most outrageous forms of sweating in the United Kingdom. . . .

Sweating in the linen industry is so rampant, it is so complete a system of exploitation of human energy, it is such an imposition on an industrious class of workers, that one could hardly find words too harsh or bitter to condemn it. One day I took a friend with me to see some women out-workers in Belfast. It was a dreary night; the air was wet and chill with sleet. When I asked my friend what he thought about it all, he made use of a most profane expression. He was a man not accustomed to bad language, but evidently unable to express himself, at the time, in other words that would afford relief to his feelings.

All the victims of this abomination are women and children. There is nothing secret about the depth of degradation to which the system has been allowed to sink. Public meetings have been held in Belfast to protest against this disgraceful thing. Petitions have been sent to the Home Office for the institution of an open inquiry into the unjust and cheerless circumstances. But so far the government department has paid no heed to the cry. . . .

Miss Martindale[1] refers to conditions of out-workers in other trades besides that of linen, and to work in parts of Ireland outside Belfast, where the Truck Acts[2] are ignored, and where 'gombeening' is carried on by agents who give out linen articles to the home-workers, and compel them to take food for wages at their own price. I have taken from her special report the following figures:

1 Hilda Martindale was sent to Ireland in 1905 as the first resident factory inspector.

2 The Truck Acts were a series of Acts passed from the 1830s, against the 'truck system', whereby workers received their wages in the form of vouchers for goods redeemable only at a special shop, usually run by the employer. The Acts required wages to be paid in cash.

Handkerchiefs –

		s	d	
Handkerchiefs	..	0	7 a doz.	(1 doz. per day)
"		1	4 each	(1 handkerchief in 2 days)
Monogram	..	0	8 a doz.	(½ per day)
Initial	..	0	½ each	(10 handkerchiefs per day)
Four corners	..	0	1½	(3 handkerchiefs per day)

Fancy and
  Household Linens –

	s	d	
Muslin tray cloth	0	10	(2 days)
Muslin bedspread	4	0	(nearly 1 week)
Bedspread	7	0	(1½ weeks)
Cosy covers	0	3 each	(1½ per day)
Table cloth	3	0	(4 days)
" " (elaborate)	1	8	(3 days)
Side-board cloths	0	4	(1 day)
" " "	0	6	(1 day)
Ladies skirts	5	0	(9 days)
" "		3	6 (1 week)
D'Oyleys	3	0 a doz.	(1 doz. in 2 days)
(special order)			

Hand Knitting – This form of work is the worst paid. The length of time it takes to knit a pair of men's socks or gloves is too well known for the prices which I give below not to stand out as appallingly low, and I was not surprised to have the big houses pointed out to me belonging to the men who had become rich over this cheap labour.

	s	d		
Men's socks	1	6 a doz. pairs		
	2	0	" "	(Long)
	1	7½	" "	(Ribbed tops)
	4	0	" "	(Fine)

I have shown that the out-workers are shockingly remunerated for labour of a kind very trying indeed to their health; I have stated that the articles which come from the Irish sweating dens are sold in the best merchant houses in the country, and this is corroborated by Dr Bailie; it is common knowledge in Belfast; and I want next to emphasise the statement made by Miss Martindale that men have grown rich out of the abominable system. When I was in Belfast, I was not only told this, but I was introduced to one or two linen merchants and manufacturers, who in a few years have become immensely rich out of the sale of linen goods which have been passed through the wretched homes of the out-workers.

Let me return to the report issued by Dr Bailie. He mentions children's pinafores flounced and braided at 4½d per dozen; women's chemises at 7½d per dozen; women's aprons at 2½d per dozen; men's drawers and shirts at 10d per dozen; blouses and ladies' overalls at 9d per dozen. From these prices deductions are made which he says leave the earnings 'so extremely small as to make one wonder if they (the workers) are benefited by the work at all'. They are not benefited; they are cursed by it. The greatest wonder to me was that human beings could be found to do it. The effect is not to be lamented merely because it injures those who do the work, but because it is unjust to society. Dr Bailie remarks (and read carefully what he says): 'It cannot be too frequently or strenuously insisted that such underpaid labour must inevitably cripple and in great part nullify the good effects of any schemes of health reform. The underfed, over-wrought physique of the sweated worker, with its weakened stamina, and lack of resistance to the inroads of disease, is undoubtedly one of the main causes of a high death-rate. It is an obvious fact, too, that all sweated work is ultimately paid to the full by the State, when the prematurely incapacitated worker finds his or her inevitable place in the poor-house, hospital, or charitable institution. Any arrangement whereby the payment of the worker would be placed on a fair and firm basis should therefore be welcomed by all seeking for economy in administration, as well as the improvement of health of the people. The fact should not be lost sight of that the sweating evil injures more than those immediately concerned. Practically the whole of these underpaid workers are mothers, and the evil effects of their unremitting and ill-remunerated toil must be transmitted to the next generation. It is not possible to estimate the amount of the consumption prevailing that is due to sweating, but in it we certainly have a contributory cause.'

. . . Among a class of women anxious to work, and make money for urgent domestic use, I never witnessed such pictures of poverty, such examples of despair. I saw one woman, who had been working, on and off, for two days at a tea-cloth. This was the worst case I came across. For the work (embroidering) she received eight pence. When she learned that I might make use of the information, she begged of me not to mention her name to a living soul. 'Why, my good woman?' I asked. 'I might lose the work', was her quick reply.

Might lose the work! There is something sadly wrong with a woman's life when she will accept, and be compelled by circumstances to accept, an un-Christian contract that will bring her in eightpence by two days' labour! And what was the market value of the tea-cloths she was asked to embellish at the disgraceful price? They were sold at 15s to 20s each. The woman had a sick husband; she had two children employed in an adjoining linen mill; the rent of the dwelling was 2s 9d per week; comparatively speaking the back room was no bigger than a yard dog's kennel, and a workshop was not much larger: the walls were blue-washed and not papered. There were a few rickety chairs in the room, a broken fender, a small round table, and two boxes – sugar boxes – made to serve the purpose of clothes chests, covered with strips of linen. It was night, the room, dimly lighted by a small oil lamp on the mantelpiece, looked more like a prison cell than a family dwelling. And yet this woman was painfully agitated because she dreaded that I might 'give her away'. Scared by the demonstrations in Belfast to which I have alluded, the distributors of the sweated work had firmly warned these wretched women to keep their tongues still, and they had in some instances increased the rates of pay; yet the Home Office has neither had the courage, nor the conscience, nor the sympathy, to hold out a helping hand to the oppressed Irish out-workers, or to respond to the appeal for an investigation of their deplorable conditions. . . .

Inquiry into Making-Up Trades

Doc. 48.4: *Committee of Inquiry into the Conditions of Employment in the Linen and Other Making Up Trades of the North of Ireland* HC 1912–13 (Cd. 6509), xxxiv.

In his annual reports the Belfast medical officer, Dr Bailie, regularly complained about the health hazards suffered by women as a result of working from their own homes. In 1909, he emphasised that low rates of pay and long working hours not only led to ill health amongst women workers, but also led to the neglect of their home duties. Bailie's reports, and the efforts of individuals such as James Haslam (see above, doc. 48.3), focused government attention on the plight of outworkers. An official inquiry was instituted in 1912 to investigate the conditions under which women employed in the making up trades worked. The work consisted of producing linen and cotton household articles, handkerchiefs, and clothing. It also often involved embroidering these articles. A number of investigators visited the homes of the outworkers on behalf of the inquiry. Amongst these visitors was Mary Galway, the general secretary of the Women's Textile and Operatives' Association of Ireland. The extracts below reveal some of the findings of this inquiry and relate to outwork and factory work.

Evidence of Miss Jean Agnew.[1]

Q 8.   How many outworkers are there in Belfast and what proportion of them are employed in the making up of linen, cotton, etc.? Probably, having regard to the returns made under the Factory Act, about 4,000. Of these outworkers, approximately 485 are employed by various shops, 25 by ropeworks, 100 by clothing manufacturers, and 25 by hosiery manufacturers . . .

---

1 Had worked as a sanitary sub-officer for Belfast Corporation.

[*Miss Agnew provided examples of cases she had come across in her investigations.*]

Cases relating to drawn thread work.

Case 239. Firm QIA – Work: 'spidering' and 'blocking' handkerchiefs in four corners. Price: 'spidering' 1s per doz. and blocking 8d per doz., or 1s 8d in all per doz. handkerchiefs. Time: could not complete one handkerchief in two hours. Rate: less than 1d an hour.

Case 67. Firm J. A.: Work: drawn thread embroidery on cushion covers. Price: ¼d each. Time: can do over four in an hour. Rate: nearly 1¼d an hour.

Cases Relating to Embroidery (flowering).

Case 242. Firm H. A. – Work: embroidering dots on handkerchiefs. Price: 1½d per dozen. Dots were counted. She had to embroider 288 for 1½d.

Case 267. Firm H. A. – Work: embroidering blouse front. Price: 8d each. Time: had sat sewing from 7 p.m. to 11 p.m. the night before, and from 8.30 a.m. that morning till 3, stopping only to give the children their dinner. It was not quite finished. Rate: less than 1d per hour.

Case 19. Firm H. A. – Work: embroidering handkerchiefs with initial and spray in corner. Price: 5d per dozen. Time: could not do much more than one in an hour. Rate: about ½d per hour.

Q 85 Does this work constitute the chief part of the outworker's earnings? Do the women do any other work as well for pay? There are four classes of workers: widows and spinsters depending on the work for their livelihood; married women whose husbands are out of work; women whose husbands are labourers earning small pay; and there are a few workers in better circumstances who work for pocket money. The larger section do it to supplement small pay . . .

Evidence of Mrs John H. Baxter M.A.[1]
[*Mrs Baxter provided examples of cases she had come across in her investigations.*]

Case 2. Firm U. B. – Machine stitching pinafores and overalls: the adopted daughter of well-to-do trades people. She had worked at the trade for 11 years; preferred it to factory work, as it enabled her to look after the shop during meal hours. The pinafores were made throughout, elaborately tucked and braided, similar in design to

1 Acted as an investigator for the Committee of Belfast Residents.

. . . Firm insisted on perfect workmanship, and parts in which stitches were slipped must be ripped out and re-done. Price 10*d* to 1*s* per dozen, according to the size and amount of work; one dozen the very most she could do in a day and made between 10*d* and 1*s* a day. Thread and oil supplied by worker; no estimate could be given for oil; but for thread she paid 1*s* 3*d* to 1*s* 4*d* per fortnight. Considered herself an expert worker. Her sewing machine was paid up, so no deduction had to be made for hire of machine. I was informed that she had worked out two machines costing £11 and £7 10*s* respectively, and was now at her third, which cost £9.

Q 337.   It is commonly said that these home workers do not always give their whole time to the work. But is it not a fact that no woman inside a factory would give all her time to the work? The inside worker cooks her breakfast, sends the children off to school, goes into the factory and works, comes back at 6 o'clock in the evening, gets the supper, makes the beds, and does the housework. The outside worker probably does no more housework than that, but does it in the middle of the day, and works until 9 or 10, or 11 o'clock in the evening to make up for it.

Evidence of Miss H. Martindale:

[*Miss Martindale provided examples of cases she had come across in her investigations into factories.*]

Q 1125   Declarations regarding deductions:
Dated 1 October 1910: 'My name is M N M —. I reside at — and am employed in the factory of X and Co situated at —. I was — years of age on the — day of — 19—. I state that I am employed in stitching handkerchiefs in the above factory. I am a learner and have been employed in the factory for about three months. On September 17 (Saturday) I was fined 8*d* for bad sewing; my wages were 5*s* 6*d* for the six days ending on the previous Thursday, I received 4*s* 10*d*. During this week I was shown two handkerchiefs which were badly sewn. My cousin — repaired them and they were passed, but the forewoman said I should be fined. When I received my money, on the small pay envelope was marked '2 dozen badly sewn' and I was fined 8*d*. I received 9*d* for stitching 8 dozen of these handkerchiefs. X said I could have the two dozen handkerchiefs at cost price, 5*s* or 5*s* 6*d*. This is the fifth time I have been fined, but each time before it was 4*d*. Particulars of the fine are either entered in our books or on the envelope. I have earned as much as 10*s* a week. I told — I was in the union and he has not fined me since.'

Mrs D. (outworker) examined.

1419   (Mrs Deane-Streatfield) Have you brought some work with you? I have brought a very small sample. I have at times a great deal more, but just now I have not a great store of work in the place. (The witness produced some work.)

1420   Is this a tea-table cloth? Yes, I finished that today.

1421   (Mr Cohen) Is that thread-drawing? Yes.

1422   The Walls of Troy pattern, I understand? Yes.

1423   (Mrs Deane-Streatfield) Is it thread-drawing that you mostly do? Yes.

1424   Do you do fancy sewing as well? No; I just thread draw.

1425   It must be more difficult to draw these little pieces with a cut at each end than to draw a long piece? Yes, the scissors are never out of your hand. A very small hole you see there has to be cut two different ways with the scissors before you can draw it at all. It means cutting all the time.

1426   If you cut it wrong what happens? Then you have to pay for it; and many a time the pattern is not marked out for you properly.

1427   Is this a printed pattern first before you cut it? Yes. There is a pencil mark or an ink mark on it.

1428   How much do you get for doing this? When it has 10 stamped on it is $1s\,6d$ a dozen, and when it has 7 it is only $1s\,3d$.

1429   This thread drawing in bits is more troublesome than drawing a long shire? Yes, then there is another thing. There are advantages and disadvantages. A light piece of linen and a heavy piece of linen are different.

1430   How long would it take you to do one, of the 10 lot? I could not do one, no matter how hard I worked, in an hour.

1431   And that is $1s\,6d$ a dozen? $1s\,3d$, $1s\,6d$ and $1s\,10d$.

1432   It works out at between $1d$ and $2d$ an hour? It would not reach $2d$, barring it was an odd lot of work with extra good stuff in it.

1433   How long have you been at this work? For 10 or 11 years.

1434   Have you always worked for the same firm? No. I have worked for one firm for the last eight or nine years, back and forwards. At one place I could not stand the winding stairs. Plenty of people have got trouble through carrying burdens of work up.

1435   Do you take it in every day? Yes, and many times twice. If they give you a special lot of work in the morning and tell you to get it finished at night and if you do not do it, maybe when you go again, you will get no work at all.

1436   How long do you work generally? I have not made a special thing of it this last few months. I have had to give it up through the scarceness of the work and the long hours the children would be kept when they went for the work.

1437	Do the children help you? Yes, those that are not working out.
1438	When do you begin – in the afternoon? In the morning, after the children have gone to school.
1439	Do you have to get the dinner for your husband? Yes, at a quarter past one. I work from 3 to 5, and after tea.
1440	Do the children do their own work or just help you? I cut it and they do the rest. I have nearly stopped it altogether; it was injurious to my health – a sort of crush on me, if you understand.
1441	What do you reckon to make week in and week out? Many and many is the time we have only had 6s to 7s and 8s, four of us working all the spare time we had.
1442	Do you get any docket with this? Yes.
1443	Do you know before you begin what the price will be? Yes.
1444	Do you depend on this work? No, not this last few years since the children were able to go out.
1445	How many children have you at work? 3.
1446	It has not been so bad since then? No. My husband earns 24s a week, but he gives me 22s.
1447	Are different prices paid for the same kind of work by different firms? Yes; some firms pay better than others.
1448	Perhaps they do not give the same sort of work out? The stuff may be better at times.
1449	If you make mistakes do you have anything stopped; if you cut a hole, for instance? If you make a very bad mistake in your work the firm gives you the cloth back. You pay the price of the stuff and you lose the value of your work.
1450	(Mr Cohen) Is the work lower paid than it used to be? No, but the stuff is so middling that you cannot get the work done as quickly. It takes you far longer working on bad cloth.
1451	The stuff is more difficult to work? Yes.
1452	(Mrs Deane-Streatfield) Is it more adulterated – more cotton it? [sic]. More union and dressing – four times more.
1453	It is more difficult to draw when it is not pure linen? Yes, I have bits in the house, and fairly and truly it would not be worth losing your time at it.
1454	It is not worth working, because the cloth is so bad? It is not worth working but if they give it to you and you do not do it, you get no more work.
1455	Have you ever worked inside? No.
1456	Do you ever give work to your neighbours or do they ever give work to you? No.
1457	Have you a book? Yes, in the wareroom they keep a book. Some warerooms give out an outside book, but I have not that with my firm.

1458	Have you ever done any clipping? With regard to clipping I would not depend on it for a day, even if I had to go without. Those only do it who are in the greatest poverty.
1459	Do you know whether people who do stitching of all kinds sometimes bring it home from the factory? Yes, people bring their work that they do in the wareroom in the daytime home to finish it at night.
1460	(Mr Cohen) Thread drawing is not done inside the factory is it? There is a little, but those in the factory who do it get the advantage of the better work. If there is hard work to do it is given outside.

Varieties of Occupations

A WET NURSE REQUESTS THE RETURN OF HER CHARGES

Doc. 49: Letter with attachment, from M. Finlay to the Right Honourable
Lord Gower, August 22, 1829. Registered Papers, 1829/2033, NA.

*Wet-nursing, whereby newborn babies and children were given out to nurse,
was a common practice in institutions such as the foundling hospitals. It is
unclear how this business developed over the nineteenth century, but many
orphanages, and, by the end of the century, workhouses, were adopting a
'boarding-out system' for their charges. Under this system, women were paid not
only to breastfeed children, but also, in many instances, to rear them. Wet-
nursing provided another source of income for poor women. The woman who
presented this petition in 1829 obviously took in a number of children. Her
petition suggests that financial interests did not preclude emotional attachment
to the children reared.*

Foundling Hospital
August 22nd 1829

My Lord,

In response to your Lordship's letter of 20inst enclosing the memorial
of Sarah O'Reilly respecting the children that she was deprived of on the
29 July last. I have the honour to state for the information of his Grace,
the Lord Lieutenant, that the children were summoned from the nurse,
agreeable to the regulations of the hospital and not for the reasons stated
in the within memorial.

I have the honour to be my Lord
your most thankful
humble servant,

M FINLAY Esq.
The Right Hon. Lord F. L. Gower.

D. F. L. Gower

To his Excellency the Lord Lieutenant of Ireland and Grand Duke of Northumberland.

The humble and pitiful petition of Sarah O'Reilly of Mount Melick Chapel Lane. Your Exellrs most humble petitioner most humbly sheweth.

That petitioner nursed these thirteen years for that honourable and charitable institution the foundling hospital for the support and preservation of the infantage of this nation.

Your Excellency's humble petitioner was deprived of three children on the 27th of last month (July) by a false letter, without a name, on account of petitioner's husband being a Roman Catholic, your petitioner is a Protestant and all petitioner's ancestors who valiantly fought under our present king and his royal father and his ancestors, petitioner went to church regularly and brought her children there without any hindrance from her husband as can be proved by respectable witnesses.

Your Excellency's most humble petitioner has this reliance on your Excellency that you will be graciously pleased to order these three children, Anne Marky aged ten years, Peter Potter aged 7 years and Catherine Judge aged 4 years. [Petitioner] wet nursed the last named child – wet nursed another of the name of Peter Potter now in the house aged 13 years of age always got the bounty and they were a credit to peti[tioner] in leaving and cleanliness, as the paymaster Mr Finly [sic] can testify.

Your Excellency's petitioner has got no trial but stripped me of my children for which reason petitioner's heart is breaking and will be the means of shortening petitioner's days, if they were left until taken into the foundling hospital petitioner would not grieve but sent to other nurses without any thought only a false letter without a name. Your Excellency's petitioner with the greatest humility most humbly hopes you will let pet[itioner] have an answer and say whether pet[itioner] will have a fair hearing from the House for her children.

Your Excellency will have the prayers of petitioner and children while the[y] breathe on this earth if your Excellency returns pet[itioner] her children until they are of age to be taken into the house.

And as in duty bound petitioner shall for ever pray,

SARAH O'REILY [sic]

NB If it pleases your Excellency to return me one or two lines in answer to this letter direct to Sarah O'Reily, Chapel Lane, Porttown Mount Melick, Queens County.

WOMEN ACCUSED OF CHILD HAWKING

Doc. 50: *The Constitution or Cork Advertiser*, 27 February 1847.

The poor had many strategies for survival. Abandoning children whom they could not support was one such strategy, while 'child-hawking' was another. The following reports relate to this phenomenon, particularly where women hired out their children to beggars. At the time this report appeared, the Great Famine was devastating the country and the account reveals a fear on the part of the authorities that, if left unchecked, the poor might abuse public and private charity, and would also spread disease.

Several women carry children in their arms for the purpose of exciting compassion. When they meet anyone, especially a lady, supposed to be of a sensitive disposition, their cloaks are thrown open and those children thrust into their face. Some of them are wretched looking creatures, starved purposefully to make them appear the greater objects – indeed their inhuman mothers (if they *are* their mothers) seem to have studied how to reduce their 'allowance' to the smallest possible pittance compatible with the continuance of life. It is a process of *slow murder*, for it must end in death. This, however, may not be the worst, for to the poor infants release from the cruelty of such heartless wretches would be mercy; but many of them, we understand, are infected with small pox, and thus this deadly disease is carried through the city, and perhaps imparted to the families of persons whose humanity induces them to open their purses for their relief, and sometimes to admit the undeserving imposters into their houses while providing them with food.

In the foregoing we have intimated a doubt whether the persons who hawk those children are their mothers. Since it was written, we have lighted on the following passages in the report of the proceedings of the North Dublin Union on Wednesday. We quote from *Saunders*:[1]

Mr Arkins said that there was room in the workhouse for at least 800 additional paupers. It was a notorious fact that starving children were hired by beggars, and hawked about the streets. It was equally true that children in that workhouse were better fed and treated than were the children of tradesmen at present, the times were so bad.

Mr Espy begged leave to relate an anecdote. A friend of his heard one beggar woman ask another, who carried an infant, 'how much she paid for the child'; to which the interrogated mendicant replied, 'sixpence a day'. 'You fool', rejoined the other, 'I have an elegant one for half that, and it bawls all day.'

Captain Lindsay, would, with the permission of the board, relate another anecdote:

Two beggar women being engaged in conversation, one of them observed 'that the poor law was a fine law for the rich'. The other mendicant enquired how that was. 'Because it saves their souls', said the first, who being called on for a further explanation of her meaning, added, 'for before we got the poor house

1 *Saunder's Newsletter*, a Dublin newspaper.

the rich folk use to send us to the d . . . l,[1] but now they onl
poor house.'

Several guardians expressed their conviction that the pra
giving in the street was greatly more productive of harm than ɡ

EARNING A LIVING THROUGH PROSTITUTION: THE 'WRENS' OF THE CURRAGH

Doc. 51: James Greenwood, *The Wren of the Curragh* (London, 1867).

Prostitution was a sizable problem in nineteenth-century Ireland. In a society that offered few employment opportunities to women, prostitution was resorted to by women both out of necessity, and because it provided adequate returns for relatively little effort. Concern about prostitution was voiced by clerics, philanthropists, medical men and 'respectable' individuals in society. Prostitutes were generally ostracised from the community. One group of women who removed themselves from 'respectable' society were the 'wrens' of the Curragh. The women who made up the 'wrens', so-called because 'they live[d] in holes in the banks [ditches],[2] actually lived in makeshift huts along the perimeter of the Curragh army camp in County Kildare. The numbers of women living under these conditions varied, but, up to sixty women were reported to live there at any one time. It appears that the 'wrens' were living in the Curragh from the 1840s until at least the 1880s. In 1867, James Greenwood, a journalist from the British newspaper, the Pall Mall Gazette, *came to investigate how the 'wrens' lived. Much of his account is sensationalist, but through it we can glimpse the extraordinary circumstances of these women's lives.*

. . . To be particular, the nests have an interior space of about nine feet long by seven feet broad; and the roof is not more than four and a half feet from the ground. You crouch into them, as beasts crouch into cover; and there is no standing upright 'till you crawl out again. They are rough, misshapen domes of furze – like big, rude birds' nests compacted of harsh branches, and turned topsy-turvy upon the ground. The walls are some twenty inches thick, and they do get pretty well compacted – much more than would be imagined. There is no chimney – not even a hole in the roof, which generally slopes forward. The smoke of the turf fire which burns on the floor of the hut has to pass out at the door when the wind is favourable, and to reek slowly through the crannied walls when it is not. The door is a narrow opening nearly the height of the structure – a slit in it, kept open by two rude posts, which also serve to support the roof. To keep it down, and secure from the winds that drive over the Curragh so

1 Devil.
2 James Greenwood, *The Wren of the Curragh* (London, 1867).

199

riously, sods of earth are placed on top, here and there, with a piece of corrugated iron (much used in the camp, apparently – I saw many old and waste pieces lying about) as an additional protection from rain. Sometimes a piece of this iron is placed in the longitudinal slit aforesaid; and then you have a door as well as a doorway. Flooring there is none of any kind whatever, nor any attempt to make the den snugger by burrowing down into the bosom of the earth. The process of construction seems to be to clear the turf from the surface of the plain to the required space, to cut down some bushes for building material, and to call in a friendly soldier or two to rear the walls by the simple process of piling and trampling. When the nest is newly made, as that one was which I first examined, and if you happen to view it on a hot day, no doubt it seems [a] tolerably snug shelter. A sportsman might lie there for a summer night or two without detriment to his health or his moral nature. But all the nests are not newly made; and if the sun shines on the Curragh, bitter winds drive across it, with swamping rains for days and weeks together; and miles of snow-covered plain sometimes lie between this wretched colony of abandoned women and the nearest town . . .

A community like that which I am attempting to describe naturally falls into some regular system, and provides for itself certain rules and regulations. Fifty or sixty people, separated from the rest of the world and existing in and by rebellion against society, naturally form some links of association; and when the means of life are the same, and shameful and precarious; when those who so live by them are poor as well as outcast; and when, also, they are all women, we may assure ourselves that a sort of socialistic or family bond will soon be formed. It is so amongst the wrens of the Curragh. The ruling principle there evidently is to share each others' fortunes and misfortunes, and in happy-go-lucky style. Thus the colony is open to any poor wretch who imagines that she can find comfort in it, or another desperate chance of existence. Come she whence she may, she has only to present herself to be admitted into one nest or another, nor is it necessary that she bring a penny to recommend her. Girls who have followed soldiers to the camp from distant towns and villages – some from actual love and hope, some from necessity or desperation – form a considerable number of those who go into the bush; and I also learn that the colony sometimes receives some harvester tired of roaming for field work, to whom the free loose life there has, one must suppose, attractions superior to those of the virtuous hovel at home. She walks in and is welcome: welcome are far less eligible immigrants too. Suppose a woman with child who has followed her lover to the camp and loses him there, or is admonished with blows to leave him alone; or suppose a young wife in the same condition is bidden by her martial lord to go away and 'do as other women do' (which seems to be the formula in such cases); they are made as welcome amongst the wrens as if they did not bring with them certain trouble and an inevitable increase to the common poverty. I am not

200

speaking what I believe they would do, but what they have done. It is not long since that a child was born in one of these nests; and wrens had made for baby what little provision it was blessed with; wrens smiled upon its birth (it was a girl); and wrens alone tended mother and child for days before it was born, and for a month afterwards: – then the unfortunate pair went into the workhouse . . .

Although the birth of an infant is a novel event in the annals of the Curragh, the appearance of a mother with her baby in her arms is by no means rare; and though a child is certainly as much an 'incumbrance' there as it can be anywhere, no objection is ever made to it. In fact, a baby is obviously regarded as conferring a certain respectability upon the nest it belongs to, and is treated, like other possessions, as common property. At the present time there are four children in the bush . . . In sickness the wrens administer to themselves or each other such remedies as they happen to believe in, or are able to procure; and when these fail, and the case seems hopeless, application is made at the police barracks at the camp, and the half-dying wretch is carried to Naas Hospital, nine miles off. The medical officers in the camp are, of course, kept too busy amongst the men who are the wrens' friends to have any time to spare for the wrens themselves.

The communistic principle governs each nest, and in hard times one family readily helps another, or several help one; the deeps are not deaf to the voice of the lower deeps. None of the women have any money of their own. What each company get is thrown into a common purse, and the nest is provisioned out of it. What they get is little indeed; a few halfpence turned out of one pocket and another when the clean starched frocks are thrown off at night make up a daily income just enough to keep body and soul together. How that feat is accomplished at all in winter – in such winters as the last one – which was talked of only three weeks ago as a dreadful thing of to-morrow – is past my comprehension. It is an understanding that they take it in turns to do the marketing, and to keep house when the rest go wandering at night; though the girl whose dress is freshest generally performs the one duty, and the woman whose youth is not the freshest, whose good looks are quite gone, the other. And there are several wrens who have been eight or nine years on the Curragh – one or two who have been there as long as the camp itself. . . .

Whisky forms, no doubt, a very important part of these poor wretches' sustenance. Whisky kills in the end, or it swiftly destroys all that is comely or healthy in woman or man; but it can scarcely be doubted that without it the wren could hardly live at all. She would tell you existence would be impossible without it; and unfortunately it would be of little use to answer that 'enough' may be good for food, but 'too much' is poison. They get it easily; they get it from the soldiers when they can get nothing else; and hunger and cold and wet dispose them too readily to go home with their hands full of drink though their pockets are empty. Then at any rate they are warm; the appetite for food is drowned; they are drunk, and being drunk 'don't care';

201

and how not to care cannot always be an undesirable end when your lot is cast amongst the Curragh bushes. . . . Of course I wanted to know how my wretched companion in this lonely, windy, comfortless hovel came from being a woman to be turned into a wren. The story began with 'no father nor mother', an aunt who kept a whisky-store in Cork, an artilleryman who came to the whisky-store, and saw and seduced the girl. By-and-by his regiment was ordered to the Curragh. The girl followed him, being then with child. 'He blamed me for following him', said she. 'He'd have nothing to do with me. He told me to come here and do like other women did. And what could I do? My child was born here, in this very place, and glad I was of the shelter, and glad I was when the child died – thank the blessed Mary. What could I do with a child? His father was sent away from here, and a good riddance. He used me very bad.'

A FARM WORKER EXPLOITED

Doc. 52: *The Waterford Mail*, 7 September 1868.

Young girls and women were often exploited by their employers. Mary Dobbin, who requested entrance to the Carrick-on-Suir workhouse in 1868, was quizzed by the board of guardians regarding her circumstances. She claimed to have been sexually abused by one of her employers.

Amongst the applications for admission to the house on the books of Mr Jas. Lawrence R.O.[1] was that of Mary Dobbin, a young girl, who stated that she was only 13 years of age. She was taken out of the house by a farmer, living at Blackboy, on the 20th June last, and while in his employment he violated her person on several occasions, and threatened her if she told his wife he would do something to her. She left him three weeks ago and went about the country to look for service. She was with her mother, who is employed by a farmer living in the next parish, but she did not tell her of the occurrence. She was cross examined by the board as to what she did, and where she stopped during the three weeks, and seemed to give a fair account of her doings. She gave the names of several of the farmers at whose houses she stopped. She said that a child in the house where she was at service burnt its finger, and her mistress ordered her away, telling her if she went into the house again she would be hung or transported. She did so the following day, but did not tell the mistress anything that had occurred. Dr O'Ryan was requested to examine the girl, and having done so, stated that the evidence of her person did not sustain her statement that cohabitation had taken place. The board considered that in justice to all parties the matter should be thoroughly

1 Relieving Officer.

investigated, and made an order requesting Mr Hanna R.M.[1] to proceed with it. The girl was meantime admitted to the house . . .

DUPED WORKERS

Doc. 53: *Cork Constitution*, 11 January 1876.

Women migrated to towns in large numbers in the nineteenth century. The following document relates how a number of women, hoping to improve their opportunities, unfortunately found themselves in a worse position.

Yesterday in the northern police court, Dublin, before Mr O'Donnell a number of young women applied for advice. They said that about two weeks ago they and some others had been brought from Limerick by a tailor in Dublin, who told them that they would be able to earn 12/- or 14/- per week in his employment. They since had not earned 4/- a piece and one of them stated that she had last week only received [a] little over 2/-. Lodgings were taken for them but they had to find their own food. When in Limerick some of them earned 18/- a week and none less than 7/-. They first met the tailor who was in Limerick in a hotel and there made the arrangement. A man stated that he met the girls the other day going to Glasnevin Cemetery. They asked the way, and he at once saw from their accent, that they were from Limerick, from which place he was also a native. They then bitterly complained of the tailor, who, they said, had even refused to give them regular employment for a few weeks until they could find another place. His worship said that he was afraid that he could not promise them success, but would grant them free summonses against the tailor for next Wednesday. He thought the utmost he could do was ask him to send them back.

LOOKING FOR A REFERENCE

Doc. 54: Letter to the Rev. T. Dawson. MS 18518. NLI.

Women often sought advice about employment opportunities from their local priests. Clerics had extensive contacts among parishioners and with convents in Ireland and England. They also enjoyed a high status in Irish society: a recommendation from a cleric was almost a guarantee of a position. The following letter shows how this network system could operate. It also reveals the difficulty women faced in procuring a 'respectable' occupation. Employment

1 Resident Magistrate.

203

agencies in England and Ireland were available to women from the 1860s. In return for a small fee, such agencies attempted to secure positions for their clients as servants, lady's companions and governesses. By the turn of the century, a number of philanthropic and religious bodies had also developed their own employment agencies. The Girls' Friendly Society, for example, offered such a service to its members.

Newtown
Ballyglunin
January 23rd 1885

Revd. and dear Father,

I feel greatly flattered with your kind letter which I received this morning, and I thank you for it very much. I will certainly make every enquiry I can think of and if I am successful in hearing of anything likely to suit, I will let you know. My sister who is Mother Vicaress in a Franciscan convent near London might possibly know of something; I think she knows a good many people. The great difficulty seems to be the dear little boy; it would be difficult to get an engagement as companion with a little child. If the dear lady could teach, I should think she might get an appointment in a school, where the little boy could have lessons. Another thing one might try would be an engagement as mother's help; which would not be at all a disagreeable post. Or to accompany a lady going abroad. I have the greatest possible faith in the agency where I got my situation, I have known several ladies who have been benefited by means of it, and I can strongly recommend it. I will enclose you the address. Mdlle Christine Della, 264 Regent Street, London. Mdlle Della is highly recommended by many influential priests, and is a good Catholic. I should think if the lady wrote to her, stating her capabilities, age, and the sort of engagement she would like to obtain; and also state that she is anxious to get some occupation immediately; and enclose 12 stamps, it is my belief that she would soon get something suitable. In writing to an agent it is always advisable to make the very best of oneself; and to mention every talent that one possibly can for instance if one is clever at needlework; it is also essential to state if one has good health. Mddle Della is so well known that she has a very large connection and I think her thoroughly reliable. I wish from my heart I could give any information that might be of some use to the lady; to my mind the agency is the most practical way of getting an engagement; and it is also quite a private method of hearing of something. I will gladly mention the case to everyone I think at all likely and I sincerely trust that Mrs — may soon be as successful as I was, in getting a very comfortable engagement.

With very best regards, believe me dear Revd. Fr.
Yours very respectfully,
J. SIMONS

IRISH SOCIETY FOR PROMOTING THE EMPLOYMENT OF WOMEN

Doc. 55: *Irish Association for Promoting the Employment of Women in Ireland* (Dublin, *c.* 1861).

The Society for Promoting the Employment of Women was established in London in 1860. The Society developed from the feminist Englishwoman's *Journal. An Irish branch of the society was formed in Dublin in 1861. The Society was concerned primarily with advancing the employment opportunities of middle-class women. The organisers established classes to provide women with the skills necessary for clerical and technical work, and actively sought out employers who would hire such women.*

. . . A meeting of ladies for the purpose of promoting the employment of women was held on Monday, August 19th 1861, in the Solicitors' Room Four Courts, under the auspices of the national Association for the Promotion of Social Science, at which Miss B. R. Parkes[1] and Miss Faithfull[2] entered into the details of the working of the Society for Promoting the Employment of Women, some time since established in London. . . . A committee was subsequently formed . . . and a society established, duly affiliated to the National Association, and in constant communications with the London Society.

The committee believe the circumstances of the two countries, though requiring freedom of action in fitting the work to the special conditions of each, are precisely similar in regard to the deficiency of business-training hitherto provided for women; and with a view to assist those already in a position to earn their own bread, as well as such as are desirous of entering upon a course of independent exertion, a class for book-keeping, writing, and arithmetic, has been formed, which it is hoped, will enable the pupils to fit themselves for higher salaries, and render them more valuable to their employers. This class has been lately placed under a first class teacher, and appears to be popular, a number of names having been registered for it. The sewing machine class is in full operation, and several pupils drafted into it. This will return immediate profit to working women, and a knowledge of the machine will be useful to matrons in public institutions and overseers in workrooms. Arrangements are in progress with the hospitals for receiving women from the Society to be trained as nurses for the sick, and as ward-mistresses. The committee hope the law-copying and writing, the arts classes – such as lithographing, etching on copper, drawing on wood, and wood engraving, – will progress favourably, the present and

1 Bessie Rayner Parkes (1829–1925), was a convert to Catholicism and active in the women's movement in England.
2 Emily Faithfull (1835–1895), an English feminist, who started the Victoria Printing Press in 1859.

approaching requirements of trade promising fair openings in these branches of industry for women. Those who join the classes will be expected to work up to sufficient excellence to enable the Society to grant them certificates.

The new branches of industry the Society seeks to open are those for which the schools of designs were mainly intended to afford education, but which have not been successfully established, owing to the want of direct assistance beyond the functions of government institutions; and which, moreover, in the case of women, cannot be secured without the co-operation which a society thus constituted may afford in addition to the careful training required for success in the labour market.

Feeling the responsibility which rests upon them, the committee, while anxious to secure new openings for women, and to lessen the pressure on the branches of industry filled by governesses and needlewomen, will carefully limit the trade operations to employments fitted for the physical strength, and suited to the general powers of women, and so adapted to existing needs that they shall supply a want, instead of creating a surplus of labour.

Looking to future openings for working women, the committee have to suggest the desirability of finding an outlet for the emigration of a class of educated women, in combination with the similar arrangements of the London Society. The committee also recommend that the attention of the Society should be directed to securing the employment of women in such light and suitable occupations as engraving cyphers and crests on silver and ivory, coloring photographs, hair-dressing, and as far as possible in every trade by which the requirements of ladies are supplied. The committee purpose to confine the registry to occupations for which no other channel of communication exists.

The committee are enabled to say that they have succeeded far beyond their anticipations in enlisting public opinion in favour of the cause they advocate; and this, it appears to them, is no small matter. They hope, by this instrumentality, to arouse parents to provide for their daughters, as they provide for their sons, training in some useful trade or art, and means of profitable employment by the agency of business arrangements, when not secured by fortune from want. It is on public opinion that these matters mainly rest, for it is the public and not the Society that must find employment for women. All that can be done by a society is to act as a pioneer – to make experiments – to inaugurate efforts. The rest remains to be accomplished by what constitutes the real impetus of the movement, namely, its necessity, its justice, and its expediency, acting through the ordinary economic laws, without which mere benevolent interference is temporary and futile . . .

A DISCUSSION OF WOMEN'S RIGHT TO WORK

Doc. 56: Anon., 'Women and work', *Dublin University Magazine*, 80 (December 1872).

This anonymous contribution to the Dublin University Magazine *discusses the importance of employment for women, and argues for the right to equal pay for equal work.*

If we wish for an index of the civilisation of any country, we have only to ascertain the condition of its women. . . . In considering the question of woman's sphere, it may be well to glance at some of the different views which have been held concerning her. There have been those who have thought her just good enough to bear to man children, but not to have any control over them; to cook his food, but not to eat it with him; to carry his burdens, but not to share his comforts; in short, to be his slave and his football, she getting all the kicks and he all the coppers.

Others have enshrined her as an earthly divinity – a glimpse of whom, at the lattice-window of the antique turret, have nerved their hearts to war and their hands to fight; whose scarf they have worn as a puissant, talisman, and one of whose tresses has proved a perpetual inspiration. But what, then, were these divinities, of such potent influence to keep their knights in perpetual turmoil with one another and with all mankind? Alas! they were the merest nonentities – fit for nothing under the sun but to embroider tapestry and scarfs. . . . It is as impolitic as false to deny that there is a broad difference between the sexes. But that woman is unlike man, and that her sphere usually lies in a different direction, is no indication of her inferiority, as is not unfrequently claimed. For the distinction between them being not one of degree but quality, lays the foundation for a closer unity. The harmony of diversity or contrast is far greater and richer than that of resemblance . . .

However suitable it may be for women to look to their husbands for support, what shall be done in the case of those who have no husbands? And when the number of women exceeds that of men, how can it be that some will not, of necessity, be husbandless, except they migrate to Utah? Now, what shall such women do?

This leads to the questions of wages. For the same kind and quantity of work equally well done, shall she receive less compensations simply because she is a woman? Grave charges are reiterated against society for its injustice in this respect. To its plea that woman needs less remuneration than a man, it may be replied that the question of wages is primarily one of equity, and not of sex.

Is it the habit of employers to regulate their rates of payment according to the necessities of those whom they employ? Does the trade-value of any fabric in the market turn upon the question [of] whether it was made by male or female hands? In some departments, the very question reveals its absurdity. What would have been thought of a publisher who should have offered only half the usual copyright for 'Uncle Tom's Cabin', because it was written by Mrs rather than by Professor Stowe? or for 'Aurora Leigh', because Mrs Browning, and not her husband, was the author? . . .

In regard to the general principle of compensation, two things are evident: one, that it is the intent of society by the remuneration of labour, to provide for the increase of its members; the other, that man, as the natural representative of the family, on whom wife and children are understood to depend for support, receives higher wages than woman, who is supposed to have no such responsibility. But the wife may work at home as hard as the husband abroad, and thus earn the money as really as he.

Then, too, the tables may be turned. The husband, from inefficiency or vice, or other reason, may fail to discharge his duty, and the burden fall on the wife. In England, nearly all the women who have applied for divorce under the new bill, have proved that their families depended on them for subsistence; it being a part of their grievance that, with the support of themselves and children, they were burdened with that of their husbands also. And out of six millions of British women who are over twenty-one, one-half belong to the industrial class, while more than two millions are self-supporting. So that the old notion, that all women depend on men for a livelihood, is a mere figment.

Now, it is evident that the women who do men's work in the support of their own families, or of parents, brothers, or sisters, have need of far more remuneration than the men who may have neither families nor dependent relatives. But for such cases the laws of work and wages do not provide. Society is a cold-blooded impersonality, governed by certain inexorable rules, and never stepping out of its way to look after the unfortunates. Inexorable, I say, for I never heard of society displaying any weak tendencies to mercy. . . . In woman's pressing need of employment, she cannot stop to insist on her claims, whether real or fancied, but is glad to take what she can get. The trouble with multitudes is to find work at any price. In the case of man, if one vocation is not sufficiently remunerative, there are many others which he can enter; but to women, comparatively few avenues are fairly open, and where the supply is so much greater than the demand, the compensation will be proportionately small.

The question is farther complicated by the fact that, as a general thing, women who have families cannot devote themselves to any one employment. In the odds and ends of time not required by domestic duties, they may wash, bind shoes, braid straw, seat chairs, or do other things to eke out the household means. In these circumstances, it is sometimes a matter of accommodation to get work, even at very low prices. There is still another way in which women are indirectly cramped. However doubtful the expediency of strikes as a method of increasing wages, the knowledge that they are in the power of their operatives tends to check the cupidity of employers. But they have little fear of women resorting to such measures. . . .

208

Looking into still other departments, we find that in the manufacture of cotton, woollen, and silk goods, the most unwholesome and disagreeable parts of the work are given to woman. In the pin-factories, beginning at the age of five, the girls used to work from ten to sixteen hours; and this in civilised, Christian lands where man boasts his gallantry and protecting care! . . .

That a woman should aspire to do work on her own responsibility – it is this that is deemed so reprehensible, so utterly impracticable. Is there, then, nothing for her but marriage, starvation, or dishonour!

She seeks to win her way, but is met with strange menaces – that if she aspires to do certain things which she ventures to think she can do, and which some have testified she has done, and done well, why, then, forsooth, she must also do those disagreeable and dangerous things which she neither asks nor wishes to do. If you will be a clerk, Miss Aspiring, you shall be a black-smith; if you will be a doctor, you shall be a butcher. And so, because God has given some woman the genius to chisel statues, she must perforce cut out tumours. . . .

After all, however, the remedy lies mainly in the hands of woman herself. Let every girl, in the higher as well as lower classes, be trained to the idea of some object or vocation by which she can make herself useful and gain an honourable support. And while the foundations are laid broad and strong, let there be full play for individual development. The law of variety which runs though nature should not be overlooked in the education of women.

GOVERNMENT REPORT ON THE EMPLOYMENT OF WOMEN IN IRELAND

Doc. 57: *Royal Commission on Labour* HC 1893-4 [C. 6893], xxxvii.

Eliza Orme and May Abraham acted as assistant commissioners to the Royal Commission on Labour, which was set up in 1891. May Abraham (1869–1946), who was born in Dublin, became the first woman factory inspector in England, and was an active trade unionist, becoming treasurer to the Women's Trade Union League. Orme's and Abraham's report provides a wealth of detail about the employment of women in urban areas in the 1890s. Earning a living as a shop assistant was considered a very respectable occupation, but the conditions of employment, as can be seen in the following extract, could often be very harsh. The extract also recounts the conditions endured by women involved in the sewing trades. Embroidering handkerchiefs and linen was a major source of employment for rural women in County Donegal, where there was an extensive outworking system. The report of the assistant commissioners also provides one of the first objective accounts of industrial activities in convents. Convents were large employers of female labour in both sewing and laundry work. The conditions within these establishments appear to have been particularly good for the workers.

Shop Assistants

In some of the houses visited the female assistants received lower salaries than the men (e.g. No. 625, one of the largest Belfast houses). In others (e.g. No. 571, a large Dublin draper) no difference is made between men and women. The lowest yearly salary we met with was £10 (with partial board and lodging). The highest was £200 (with board and lodging), paid to the head of a department.

The commissions earned on the sale of damaged goods or on job lots are very uncertain, and are not considered in the above statement. In some cases they are said to amount to £20 per annum (No. 576). In some houses no commissions are allowed, but a bonus is given to the principal hands half-yearly (No. 571). In other houses (e.g. No. 573) no commissions are allowed and no bonuses paid, and the assistants receive nothing beyond the fixed salary.

In some cases (e.g. Nos. 571, 581, 587) no apprentices are taken. The more general custom is to take apprentices for a term varying from 18 months to three years, and to charge a large fee if they live in. In one case (No. 574) £84 is charged for a term of two years. In a few cases no fees are charged, and the apprentices live at home. In many houses apprentices receive some payment after the first year, and they are always supposed to have the same chance as ordinary shop assistants of earning commissions on sales. Sometimes these commissions are entered in a book, and set off against fines for unpunctuality and mistakes, and the balance, if any, paid at the end of the term. In these cases the girls affirm that there is seldom found to be any balance at all. In most houses places are found in the shop for apprentices who have served their full time.

At No. 571, shop assistants are reprimanded twice for mistakes, and are then fined 1*s*. In many shops (e.g. Nos. 572, 579, 582) the fine for a mistake is 6*d*. At one house (No. 573) the fines for different kinds of mistakes vary from 3*d* to 2*s* 6*d*. At No. 576, the fines for speaking and for mistakes vary from 6*d* to 2*s* 6*d*. For lateness in the morning 3*d* is charged (No. 577). In one shop in Dublin (No. 583) the assistants complain of the numerous and heavy fines. For failing to sell an article, they say the fine is 2*s* 6*d*, with the option of buying it themselves. For speaking to one another the fine is 2*s* 6*d*. This is a house where apprentices have their commissions reserved for payment of fines in the manner already described. The employers (Nos. 1,088, 1,101) refused any information about fines. As a rule, we did not find unfair fines charged in the drapers' shops in any towns in Ireland, and they are not a subject of general complaint among the shop assistants.

The following table gives the hours worked in shops visited, exclusive of meal times:

Table showing the number of hours per week (not including meal times) during which shop assistants are on duty in 26 drapers' shops in the largest towns in Ireland.

	Shops
Exceeding 35 hours, not exceeding 40 hours	3
" 40 " " 50 "	11
" 50 " " 60 "	5
" 60 " " 70 "	3
" 70 " —	2

The worst cases met with are the following. At No. 582, the hours for shop assistants are from 9 a.m. to 8 p.m. on ordinary days, and to 10 p.m. on Saturdays. This includes about 50 minutes on ordinary days, and one hour 20 minutes on Saturdays for meals. The employer (No. 1,098) has tried closing at 7 p.m., but found he was losing his trade, as two shops in his street remained open until the later hour. He considers that a simultaneous movement for early hours would be an advantage to shopkeepers, as gas or electric light would be saved. He favours legislative limitation of shop hours, and suggests 9 a.m. to 7 p.m., and to 4 p.m. on Mondays.

At No. 583, the hours are from 8 a.m. to 8 p.m. on ordinary days, and to 10 p.m. on Saturdays. The assistants state that the meals are uncomfortable, and at no fixed times. Except in slack times they only get 10 or 15 minutes to sit down for a meal. They are frequently kept in through Saturday night 'going over stock,' and outdoor assistants, some having several miles to walk, leave for home at 1 o'clock on Sunday morning. At No. 584, the hours are from 8 a.m. to 8 p.m. on ordinary days, and to 10 p.m. on Saturdays; but the assistants are free shortly after closing, and the meals are comfortably served. Twenty minutes each are allowed for breakfast and dinner, and 10 minutes for tea. At No. 585, the hours are from 9 a.m. to 8 p.m. on ordinary days, and to 10 p.m. on Saturdays. In busy times the shop may be open till 10 p.m. on ordinary days and till midnight on Saturdays, but the assistants 'make up stock' during the day, and leave directly the shop closes. Plenty of time is allowed for meals. The employer (No. 1,107) would like shorter hours, and thinks legislative limitation would not injure the trade. At No. 587, the hours are from 9 a.m. to 8 p.m. on ordinary days, and to 10 p.m. on Saturdays. In busy times the work continues until 10 p.m. on ordinary days, and 1 a.m. on Sunday mornings. The employer (No. 1,110) has discussed the question of legislative limitation of shop hours with several shopkeepers, and they agree with him in not objecting to it. He cannot shorten his hours while other shops remain open. The meals in this shop are breakfast, dinner, and tea. Supper is not laid, but assistants can have bread and butter. At No. 589, the hours are from 9.30 a.m. to 8 p.m. on ordinary days, and from 9 a.m. to 10 p.m. on Saturdays. Breakfast is at 8.45 a.m., dinner at 2 p.m., tea at 6 p.m. and supper at 9 p.m. This makes a deduction of about 45 minutes on ordinary days, and an hour and a quarter on Saturdays, leaving 60 hours per week.

Although there is no general rule of early closing in Ireland, many of the better class shops close at 4 p.m. on Saturday or Monday, and in these the assistants are free at the hour of closing.

As a general rule, shop assistants have the bank holidays and a fortnight in the summer. There are also several religious festivals which many of the employers observe, and in the south of Ireland this fact was always quoted as an explanation of low wages. At No. 578, no summer holiday is allowed, and deductions are made from the salary for bank holidays. The usual custom is to pay the salary during holidays after a certain time served in the shop, one or two years generally. At No. 581, they are allowed to be absent one month, and after five years' service get a week's salary. After 10 years service they get a fortnight's salary.

In very few cases are seats provided behind the counters in drapers' shops, but more often there are some in the showrooms, and assistants are allowed to use them when business is slack. The girls in No. 585 said no seats were provided, and they would like to have them. The want of seats is not a matter of general complaint. The sitting rooms and bedrooms and the meals are considered by shop assistants as matters of much greater importance.

The houses occupied by shop assistants in Ireland are often untidy and furnished in a very slovenly manner, but the essentials of comfort are not disregarded, and the size of the rooms, the light, warmth, and ventilation, the amount and variety of food, and the social management compare not at all unfavourably with those seen in England and Wales. A library and a piano supplied by the firm are not uncommon in large houses. In some case the assistants club together for a piano. The bedrooms are airy, though sometimes poorly furnished. Two girls in each room is very common. In a few cases some or all the assistants live out, but the general rule, as in England, is for them to board and lodge on the premises. Very frequently the women have a separate sitting room, with a good fire, on winter evenings. Sometimes it is used for 'trying on' during the day, and is then carpeted more warmly than rooms furnished for shop assistants only.

Tea with bread and butter is the usual breakfast. At No. 585 heads of departments have meat or eggs. At No. 572 eggs and cold meat are supplied to all. At No. 590 all have eggs and bacon. For dinner in the larger houses two joints are served sometimes, one cold and one hot. There is generally more than one vegetable, and in many cases tea, less often tea or milk, and in a few cases milk or beer is allowed. Frequently eggs and tea or fish and tea are given on Friday. At tea time milk is sometimes offered, but the rule is to have tea and bread and butter. In many houses supper is given to apprentices only, the assistants providing [for] themselves. In fine weather very few are at home for this meal. In some houses bread and butter are placed on a sideboard for those who wish to take any. In the best managed houses a comfortable supper is laid with bread, butter, and cheese and a choice of milk or eggs. Many employers refuse to supply stout, even to male assistants, unless a doctor's certificate is produced. The following cases of unusual discomfort were met with. At No. 583 the assistants say the food is so bad they frequently cannot eat it. No tumblers are provided, and they drink out of old jam pots or anything they can get. The meals are taken in a damp, uncarpeted cellar. The bedrooms are damp, cold and dirty. The employers Nos. 1,088 and 1,101 refused to show the premises. At No. 585 the food is not complained of, but the dining room is in the basement and very cold. There is no carpet. The bedrooms are crowded and comfortless.

Many of the shop assistants, especially in the south of Ireland, are the daughters of tenant farmers, and send nearly all their money home. For this reason the practice of buying food in addition to what is supplied at the employer's table is far less common in Ireland than in England. Witness No. 1,295 receives £30 a year as shop assistant in the south of Ireland, and is paid more than those receiving board and lodgings as she lives with an aunt. Her relatives said that for 10 years she had sent the whole of her money to her parents, with the exception of a few shillings spent on necessary material for clothing. She makes her own clothes entirely, and pays nothing to her aunt for board and lodging. Two apprentices, cousins of No. 1,295, are living in the same house and expect to spend their salaries in the same manner. As they live with their aunt, they have been apprenticed without fee.

Dressmakers, Milliners, and Mantlemakers

The payment (without board and lodging) received by dressmakers in Ireland is very low. That of milliners and mantlemakers in good houses is somewhat better. The wages paid by the employers we visited are given in the tables of reference. They were ascertained by examining the wages books or by receiving oral evidence from employers and employed.

The apprentices live out and take their meals at home, and the premiums paid for their apprenticeship are from £5 to £10, and in many cases no premium is charged at all. Sometimes when nothing is paid they are used as messengers (No. 579). The term served varies from one to three years, and something is paid after a year, or even six months, by the best employers if the girl is clever. In some houses all the capable girls are kept on, receiving 2s or 2s 6d a week as improvers.

Parents (e.g. No. 1,292) complained that during apprenticeship girls are kept running messages, holding pins and irons, and doing other unskilled work. They only begin to learn when they become improvers. On the other hand, employers (e.g. No. 1,034) say the girls know nothing when they leave school, and have to learn everything from the beginning. No. 1,309 said she taught her apprentices not only plain needlework, but cleanliness, manners, smartness, accuracy, and the qualities necessary in any business. It was only when these were acquired that she could hope to teach them dressmaking.

No. 1,034, with 20 years' experience as a dressmaker in the south of Ireland, said the only girls who came to her able to do plain needlework with tolerable neatness were from convent schools. She was herself a Scotch Presbyterian, and employed a Scotch forewoman.

In many workrooms no fines are charged at all. In some (Nos. 572, 573, 574, 576, 577, 580, 581, 583, 584, 590) 2*d*, 3*d* or 6*d* is charged for late attendance. At No. 578 they have never imposed fines, but intend to do so for late attendance. At No. 579 the door is locked at the hour for starting, and no latecomers are admitted. At No. 625 the doors are closed for a quarter or a half day against a latercomer. Fines for mistakes in work are very unusual. At No. 573 there are several, varying from 3*d* to 2*s* 6*d*. The ordinary amount in this workroom is 6*d*. At No. 584 they charge 6*d* for mistakes.

The general rule in Dublin and the north is to pay for overtime at a higher rate than ordinary work. At Nos. 571, 584 and 579 the hours are from 9 a.m. to 7 p.m., stopping at 4 p.m. on Monday for dressmakers. Three hours overtime (7 p.m. till 10 p.m.) is paid for as half a day, and tea provided . . . The wages of the ordinary workers in this shop (No. 574) range from 2*s* 6*d* to 15*s* a week. The employers object to overtime, thinking it makes too long a day. At No. 577 the hours and rules for overtime are exactly the same as above, wages of ordinary hands being from 2*s* 6*d* to 14*s*, with an average of 8*s* a week, except that if the worker is earning not more than 4*s* a week she only gets 6*d* and her tea. One shilling with tea is given for three hours overtime at No. 578, the wages of ordinary hands ranging from 2*s* 6*d* to 11*s*, and the ordinary hours being from 9 a.m. to 7 p.m. At No. 589, a large shop in Dublin, the girls sometimes remain till 8 p.m., the ordinary hours being 9.30 a.m. to 7 p.m. They receive no extra pay for this hour. In the south of Ireland there are constant complaints of girls being kept in without any payment or even food provided. Witnesses Nos. 1,304, 1,305 and 1,306, all employed for some years in millinery and dressmaking, declared that they were always kept at least an hour in the busy season, and once a month or oftener were kept till midnight in the dressmakers' workrooms. No. 1,306 was kept until 4 a.m. two nights running. On the first night the girls clubbed together and bought themselves food. On the second night the dressmaker provided bread and butter and tea. No. 1,306 had never seen an inspector in any workshop she had ever worked in. Witness No. 1,292, in the same town, said that her two girls (Nos. 1,293 and 1,294) were constantly kept by the dressmakers who employed them until 8 p.m. and even 10 p.m. One of these girls had been kept till midnight, and no food or even a cup of tea provided. When she complained she was told that a girl had been dismissed for grumbling a few months before. None of these witnesses had ever heard of pay for overtime in the workshops in their town. Witness No. 1,309, an employer of long experience in the town, said that as the girls expected their wages in slack times and often got a holiday on saints' days, they must expect unpaid overtime when business pressed. At a first-class dressmakers (No. 686) and a large linen drapers (No. 705) in the south of Ireland all overtime is paid for at the ordinary rate. Most of the employers in the south say they do not require overtime, as trade is slack and has been so for some years.

The sanitary accommodation is generally sufficient and conveniently arranged for the workers. Many of the workrooms were overheated, and in some the ventilation was bad. At No. 625 the rooms are heated by steam and well ventilated. One large room is divided into workrooms by partitions about five feet high, allowing a free passage of air. Some of the workrooms are tolerably ventilated, but very much overcrowded . . .

Shirt, Collar and Handkerchief Manufacture
Beginners sometimes receive as little as 2s a week. The highest wages paid in any of the places visited in any part of Ireland is 16s. In many of these factories there are laundries which are used for getting up the articles for sale, and sometimes in shirt factories they are also used for regular washing for old customers. The women employed in the laundries are entirely separate from the sewers in the workrooms, and are paid according to the usual rates in laundries. Some of the ironing rooms visited were hot and ill ventilated. At No. 691 the arrangements were exceedingly good under a Scotch forewoman.

In some factories in the north, payment is very irregular. At No. 639 it is sometimes delayed for three weeks.

Hemstitching and finishing is sometimes done in the handkerchief factory, but 'sprigging' is largely a home industry, and finishing is often done by machines in the cottages. Some firms sell machines to the cottagers at cost price and carriage (No. 647).

At one shirtmakers' shop in the south, the proprietress, an intelligent Scotch woman, said the girls are extremely ignorant when they begin, and are so anxious to get wages at once, that employers have to repay themselves by paying less than is really earned in later years.

In the places visited the hours ranged from 50 to 60 per week. The most usual hours are from 8 a.m. to about 6 p.m. with about an hour off for dinner and one half holiday in the week. In the south numerous holidays are taken in connexion with religious festivals. At No. 691, a large shirtmaker's shop in a town in the south, 2½ days are given twice a year at the time of the local horse races. At No. 629, a large firm in the north, the hours were formerly 8 a.m. to 7 p.m., but the firm could not by fines or other means obtain punctual attendance, as most of the women had to get breakfast at that time for those of the family who worked in the weaving factories. They then decided to start work at 9 o'clock instead of 8 o'clock. The pay list immediately went up an amount varying from £4 to £6 a fortnight, and this increase has been maintained. The firm find that together with the benefit to them of increased production, there is the saving in coal and gas in the winter months.

In these industries, overtime is not generally excessive. At No. 638 in the north, girls work at certain seasons three days in the week until 10 p.m. At No. 617, also in the north, the girls work till 10 p.m., only those on day wages receiving extra pay. The normal hours here are from 8.30 a.m. to 7 p.m. At No. 637 in Dublin one hour overtime is not paid for. In most cases the pay for overtime is at the usual rate.

The worst cases met with in sanitary accommodation are the following: at No. 637, in Dublin, there is no ventilation except through the windows, and these can seldom be open because the dust blows in upon the linen. The girls suffer from severe headaches; a good deal of gas is burned in the rooms. The lavatories for men and women are side by side in a dark cellar, and the girls object to the arrangement. At No. 641 in the north, the ventilation is bad, but as the rooms are lit by electricity the effects are not so bad as at No. 637. In several other places the rooms were overcrowded. At Nos. 682 and 691, shirtmakers in a southern town, the workrooms were light, airy, and well ventilated, and business was too slack to induce overcrowding.

Woollen Manufacture

In the counties of Dublin and Meath, the wages of the witnesses examined were as follows:–

Pickers, 5s to 8s
Weavers, 5s to 18s
Burlers, 8s to 14s
Spinners, twisters, carders, and winders, 5s to 14s
Darners, 8s to 10s 6d
Warpers, 8s to 12s 6d

In one case (No. 656) beginners receive 4s a week for the first six months.

In the county of Cork, where several large tweed factories are now established, the wages are as follows:

Unskilled workers, women, 6s to 7s
Unskilled workers, men, 12s
Darners, 9s to 15s
Menders, 10s to 15s
Twisters, 6s to 8s
Carders, 7s to 8s 6d
Scotch yarn spinners, 8s to 10s
Mending and sorting, 6s 6d to 8s
Finishers (piece work), 10s
Weavers, 10s to 22s
Winders, 13s

At No. 652 the weavers are fined 1d and 2d for late attendance, but 10 minutes grace is allowed. The damages to cloth are fined from 1s to 2s. At Nos. 653 and 656, if workers are late they are sent home for a quarter of a day.

At No. 654 the only fine is 1*d* and 2*d* for late attendance, while at No. 655 there are no fines. If, however, workers are late at starting time, they are compelled to remain during the dinner-hour in spite of the illegality of this practice.

There is a fine of 1*d* for late attendance at No. 657, and workers are sent home for part of the day. The damages to cloth are fined from 1*s* to 1*s* 6*d*.

Shuttle guards are not in general use, and are not considered necessary as the looms are slow.

In Nos. 652 and 655 the sanitary arrangements are fair, in Nos. 653, 654, 656, and 657 they are good . . .

Bacon Curing

The chief centres of this industry are Waterford and Limerick. Wages are from 6*s* to 12*s* a week, the work being to a great extent unskilled. At No. 710 the women are paid the ordinary rate for overtime, and regretted there was so little of it.

Fines are not general. In some places a quarter of a day is lost for late attendance, and at No. 661, 1*d* is charged instead.

The hours are very short in general. At No. 661, they are from 7 a.m. to 4 p.m. and on Saturday to 2 p.m. Overtime is only occasionally asked for.

The places in which the bacon is cured and sausages made are necessarily clean, cool, and airy for the purposes of trade. No women are employed in the yards where the animals are killed. The smell in the rooms where the women are working is extremely disagreeable, but not unwholesome. The floors in some of the rooms are wet, and the workers' clothes also, but the temperature is low and therefore there is not the same risk of cold in returning home as exists in the case of hot spinning rooms. At No. 659, boards slightly raised from the floor are provided. At No. 661 the women wear clogs and waterproof aprons provided by the firm. At No. 660, they have aprons and leggings similarly provided.

Miscellaneous

In Dublin and Cork the factories visited were well ventilated with strong currents of fresh air wherever workers are employed. The wages varied from 5*s* to 16*s* a week, the greater number earning 6*s* or 7*s* a week. The boxes were made by home workers, who supply paste, string, and firing and return boxes tied up. They get from 2¼*d* to 3*d* a gross. In one place two girls and a mother make 18*s* a week. In one place 2*d* is charged for 10 minutes late attendance, and after that the worker is shut out for half a day. No other fines were met with. The hours are from 8 a.m. to 7 p.m. and from 8 a.m. to 2 p.m. on Saturday with no overtime. At No. 663, the firm has refused an offer to have boxes made at a lower rate at an industrial school. No cases of necrosis[1] are reported.

1 Loss of tissue by disease or injury, usually associated with the symptoms of gangrene or pulmonary tuberculosis.

The amount of skill required in these industries is about the same as in the bacon curing factories. The girls earn from 2s 6d a week (learners) to £1 a week (skilled mixer in a sweet factory). The majority took about 1s a day with ordinary pay for overtime. Fines for late attendance are sometimes charged and are not complained of by the workers. Except in the case of confectioners before Christmas, there are no complaints of long hours. Overtime is generally paid at the ordinary rate. In all the places visited the ventilation and general arrangement for the workers' comfort were good. No sanitary accommodation was provided at one tobacco factory and one margarine factory, but the girls' homes in both cases were all close by. In nearly all cases meals are taken at home.

In No. 693, a meat preserving factory, the girls are allowed to eat what they like as they fill the cans, and their healthy appearance is remarkable. They are not allowed to carry food away with them. Women are not employed in bakeries except for cleaning.

Women are employed in paper mills in cutting rags, glazing and finishing, taking from 4s 6d to 10s a week. The employment is regular and healthy. No fines are imposed and the hours are not excessive. Finishers work very short hours, and rag cutters average seven hours a day.

Under the same head may be mentioned the work of gilding, stamping, bookbinding, &c., in printers' works and stationers' shops. Here the wages vary from 5s to 14s with occasional overwork paid at the usual rate. Hands are shut out for a quarter of a day in most shops if late. The workrooms are sometimes crowded and hot in spite of ventilation. Women of rather a rough class are employed in making paper bags. The beginners fold and past. The room where the bags are dried is at a high temperature. At No. 695, the girls take their meals at one end of the workroom, where they have a stove and cooking utensils. Their wages are from 2s 6d (learners) to nearly 8s a week in this factory. The girls made no complaint of fines or long hours, and looked healthy.

Women employed in boot factories take from 8s to 17s a week when working full time . . . Some of the hand sewers are on piece wages, and the machinists are paid by the week. In large boot factories, late attendance is punished with small fines, and damages are also fined. The hours are not long, and no overtime was reported. Sanitation is pretty good as the rooms are not overcrowded, work being slack. At No. 664 the sanitary arrangements were not good.

Some premises of rag merchants were visited in Dublin. In most cases the places were overcrowded, dirty, and ill ventilated. The employer at No. 673 refused information, and his rooms were unusually dirty. The wages run from 3s to 7s a week. The longest hours heard of were at No. 673, namely, 8 a.m. to 8 p.m. and on Saturday 8 a.m. to 7 p.m. Fines were not complained of.

Ropemaking in Belfast gives employment to a number of women who earn from 5s to 9s a week. Bonuses are paid as in the linen trade. At the place visited (No. 667) no fines are imposed, but the doors are locked at starting times. The arrangements here are excellent as regards meals, but the ventilation is bad, especially in the carding rooms . . .

In the jute mills the wages are as follows in the places visited:

Weavers, 3s to 24s a week
Preparers, 4s
Sewers, 6s to 8s, average 7s 6d; or 3d to 4d a dozen for outworkers

At No. 679 where 24s a week is taken by weavers, the work is continuous and for full time. At No. 635 a bonus of 6d a week is allowed on good production, and men and women are paid at the same rate. Fines are not excessive, and the sanitary conditions are very fair. There are no shuttle guards in use at No. 635, although accidents occur.

At a pottery in the north the girls earn 3s to 12s a week, employed as decorators, transferers, cleaners, and sorters. The doors are locked against latecomers until 10 a.m. The hours are from 8.30 to 6.30 in winter, and from 6.30 to 6 in summer. The sanitary conditions are fair.

Some large drapers employ outworkers in making tambour and run lace (Limerick) and an agent to collect the work and pay the workers. By one large firm 500 or 600 outworkers used to be employed in crocheting Irish Point. This was begun after the famine, but very few are now employed. There is no difficulty in getting new patterns taken up, and the children learn the work easily. The lace is now less in demand, and most of it is made in convents. The workers are paid by piece, a skilled worker, working 10 hours a day, earning 10s to 12s a week.

There is a lace school at Limerick and also a number of home workers organised by Mrs Vere O'Brien, who finds good designs for both the school and for these home workers. The laces made are tambour, run lace, and guipure. One home worker (No. 1,057) gave her usual hours as from 9 a.m. to 8 p.m. with intervals of four hours for meals, house work, and rest. She makes about 9s per week. In the school, orders are undertaken and the girls paid for what they do, but the primary object is to teach the industry. No. 1,057 gave an account of the four factories which used to exist in Limerick, giving employment to about 2,000 women. Their hours were from 6 a.m. to 7 p.m., with 2 hours off for meals, and they earned from 4s to 6s a week. The 'tryers' would make ¼ yard of lace, and so fix the payment for the workers. These 'tryers' received 5s a week set wage. The teachers received 5s or 6s a week set wage. The two teachers at the present lace school are paid 10s a week each. No. 1,057 states that a woman now 75 years of age was the first to learn how to make run lace. She was taught at an early age by some English ladies.

Donegal
One of the principal home industries in the north of Ireland is that of embroidering handkerchiefs and other linen, in the method know as 'sprig-

ging'. Several large firms in Belfast and elsewhere give employment to hundreds of families.

Mrs Hamilton, of Brownhall, County Donegal, gives a large amount of employment in Ballintree and the surrounding districts, and pays good wages. She herself designs the embroidery.

A sprigging and embroidery agent in Donegal, for several Belfast and Glasgow firms, gave the following information:

He has 700 families on his order book. At present employment is fairly good, and he has paid out £1,100 in six months, lately, for a Glasgow firm alone. A very good sewer can earn in full work 2s 6d a day, but the bulk of the work is at a low price, and many workers do not earn as much as 2d a day. He has distributed work since 1852, and until the failure of a large firm in Glasgow in 1857 the demand for work was very good. The Donegal trade became paralysed at that time, but in certain seasons even now there is a good deal of work to be done.

Another embroidery agent in Donegal acts for several firms. He says he gives employment to hundreds of people, many of whom, probably, work for other agents also. The work he distributes is worth about 2d to 9d a day; 1s a day can be made upon samples. Good workers are often unable to get any but the poorer paid work. A skilled worker brought into the shop, during the visit, a pinafore which she had embroidered; she was paid 2½d, and she stated that it would take from nine to ten hours to do. The agent agreed with this.

A third sprigging agent in Donegal says he pays £30 to £40 a week in wages. He employs 200 to 300 people, who can make from 3d to 8d a day.

A sprigging agent (a woman) for Belfast firms was seen at Ballintra. She has about 600 families on her books. She says there is a fair quantity of work now but it is badly paid. The general price earned is 3d a day; 8d a day is the highest. The work is paid at a rate of about one-third more in winter.

Another woman at Ballintra, also a sprigging agent for several Belfast firms, says she pays about £36 in wages in 10 days. The woman she employs earn from 5d to 8d a day.

A sprigger and embroiderer in Ballintra says she has fairly regular work, and earns from 6d to 8d a day.

Another important industry in Donegal is spinning and weaving woollen fabrics.

Mrs Ernest Hart employs a large number of women in the manufacture of homespuns and tweeds in Donegal and elsewhere. There are very few in the factory at Bunbeg, the larger number being home workers. In the factory there is one girl, a dyer, earning 10s a week; another, a burler, earning 12s a week. Some little girls used to be employed, but boys do the work now as the manager likes them better. In this factory all the looms are hand looms, except two power looms. Tweeds of a rougher sort are woven in the hand looms. Saxony and Bohemia tweed are made by the power looms. More power looms are much needed, so as to compete with Saxony, whence even Derry houses at present get their tweed; but while transit is so difficult and expensive it is impossible to put up more power looms. Mrs Hart thinks the hand loom is too heavy for women, but they could be employed to work power looms if more of these were set up. In the factory fines are imposed for spoiling the cloth, as some of the workers are very careless. The work in the factory is regular throughout the year. Mrs Hart states, in reference to home workers weaving rough tweeds, that at first all the wool was given out to the different workers from head-quarters, and when their task was done they brought it back and were paid. This worked well while on a small scale, but when the work grew and could not be so carefully overlooked the workers became careless, and this system had to be given up. Now they are left to get their own material and must bring in the web finished. They are paid at the following rates:

Spinners, 6*d* to 9*d* per lb
Carders, 2*d* per lb
Dyers, about 6*d* per lb

Women spinners make easily 9*d* per day, using only their spare time after domestic work. Dyers make 10*s* a week on an average.

A family makes easily two webs at £5 apiece in the whole year, the women doing the carding, spinning, and dyeing, and the men doing the weaving.

The home workers are widely distributed, some as far as the Bloody Foreland. There are none in the town of Donegal; some are in County Antrim.

A tweed merchant at Ardara says he employs about 250 women and girls in this district. The work is very irregular. Girls earn about 1*s* 6*d* a week, and women about 2*s*. This employer does not think the industry will develop till new looms are obtained, as the narrow width of the present ones prevents a large sale of the tweeds.

Another tweed merchant in Donegal acts as agent for various firms. He has several hundred names on his books, and employment is fairly regular. He cannot say how much is earned on an average. The trade has been established since 1842 . . .

Convent Industries
At many convents industries are carried on for the employment of women and girls living in the surrounding districts, or for those who reside within the precincts of the convent as penitents. The principal employment for penitents is laundry work. Amongst the industries started by sisters in various parts of Ireland are hand loom linen weaving, power loom tweed weaving with spinning, &c., hosiery, cooking, baking, dairy farming, poultry farming, embroidery, shirt making, and plain sewing and lace making. In the cases where the workers live in the convents no wages are given, as the maintenance is the recompense for the work done. In the cases where money wages are paid some education and other payment in kind is generally given, so that it is impossible to compare the amount paid with wages received by similar workers elsewhere.

In some convents laundry work is taught to the girls in the schools, and the pupils are either retained to work in the convent laundry at low wages, or places in England or elsewhere are found for them. Witnesses Nos. 1,286 and 1,287, members of an Irish trades council, stated that the prices charged by convents were so low as to force down the wages in ordinary laundries. After comparing the printed lists of prices charged by convents with those charged by several well-known laundries, and by some good shirtmakers who wash for customers (No. 1,309), this suspicion appeared to be unfounded. The prices charged by convents are generally higher, and in no cases we heard of lower than those of the other industries.

In the Magdalen Homes[1] the penitents are asked at stated intervals if they elect to remain in the home or to work elsewhere, and in the latter case efforts are made to find a suitable situation. One woman seen in one of these laundries came in 52 years ago. The workrooms visited were beautifully fitted up with all the latest appliances for washing and ironing. The floors were clean, the ventilation good, and the sleeping accommodation very comfortable and well arranged. A separate bed is allowed to each girl, and the dormitories are of ample size. The infirmaries are also carefully planned and tended. The training in laundry work or other occupations is systematically given by competent teachers. Plenty of custom from town and country, private families, hotels, barracks, &c., is obtained for the convent laundries.

An interesting experiment with hand looms has been made at Skibbereen, County Cork.

The weaving was started May 8th, 1889. At present there are 23 looms; they are all worked in one large, airy, and pleasant hall built for the purpose during the last three years. Five convents have taken up the work, and in all about 60 looms have now been set up. The girls taught are of the class which supply domestic servants to small shopkeepers. They are expected to continue in the weaving industry until they marry, and in several cases have then procured a loom for themselves and continued to weave at home for their families and also for the convent. In cases of emigration girls have taken looms to the colonies, with the intention of weaving linen for the family use.

The girls come at 9 a.m. and have some class work. They work till 6 p.m. in summer, with an interval of an hour for dinner (2 p.m. to 3 p.m.), and have some class work before leaving. In winter they take their dinner at the loom and leave at 4 p.m. The learners receive 1s a week. A good weaver gets from 10s to 12s a week for full factory hours. For the convent hours about 1s a day would be earned by a good weaver. Less experienced workers are receiving 2s 6d to 4s a week.

The goods produced include white and colored dress cambrics, handkerchiefs, towels, narrow sheeting, art linen for embroidery, and other similar fabrics.

1 See doc. 20.

At these factories no spinning is attempted and the fabrics are sent away to be bleached or dyed. A teacher has been employed from Belfast, but some of the nuns are now qualified to teach the newcomers.

At Foxford, County Mayo, a factory run by water power has been started. A loan has been received from the Congested Districts Board. It is well managed and the machinery good. There is a risk of the water power being stopped. About 50 workers, mainly women, and several children are employed. This number must be increased before a further loan can be obtained. Wages average 5s a week. The wool is prepared and dyed, the yarn spun, and the cloth woven and finished in this factory. First-rate blankets are made here.

Another convent is at Ballaghaderin, in County Mayo. The nuns started in 1892 stocking knitting, and now employ 90 workers at about 4s 6d a week working from 8.30 a.m. to 6.30 p.m. The workrooms are excellent, and steam power is used. Stocking knitting by machinery is also carried on at Foxford and other convents.

In Sligo a factory has recently been started under the control of the Sisters of Mercy. The success is pretty good, two new machines having been added since October 1892, and the number of working hours increased. These are now from 8 a.m. to 6 p.m. Learners receive nothing. Afterwards they receive for piecework 4s to 5s a week paid monthly. The nuns believe the work could be extended if they had capital for new machinery. They have refused work from Belfast because of the low prices offered.

In Sligo the domestic economy taught is more practical than in many convent schools and orders are taken for banquets, wedding cakes, &c. From the bakery in this convent, girls are sent to situations in bakeries where only women are employed.

Similar practical instruction is given at Sligo in dairy work, and the care of poultry and pigs, to such girls as are likely to need such knowledge. Gardening, butter-making, and laundry work are successfully taught at Foxford in the garden and out-buildings of the mill . . .

Employment of Married Women
In a previous report by Miss Abraham, the intention was expressed of collecting evidence as to the physical conditions affecting the employment of married women. Miss Abraham has taken evidence on this subject from medical officers practising in Belfast, and in some other districts where a large number of married women are employed, and from the women themselves.

Young married women at present employed in factories and mills are unwilling to admit injury to their own health, or to the health of their children. Older women state that their children have suffered in health from the careless nursing of those with whom they were 'put out'. They made no statement that their own health had suffered. These witnesses attribute most of the injury to the children to the use of cordials and sleeping draughts which are administered by the women who undertake their charge, and they believe from this point of view objection would be removed if satisfactory creches were established in every district. The medical officers hold a different opinion, and state that the health of both mothers and infants suffer from the employment of young married women. It is their experience that infants 'put out' are poorly and often injuriously fed, and that evil effects follow the separation of the mother and child, before it is weaned, for so long a period in the day. In some districts this separation seems unavoidable. A number of married women employ young girls to mind their infants and do house work while the mothers are engaged at the factory. In these cases the children less often suffer from the use of sleeping draughts, and the exposure to bad weather at an early hour in the morning is also avoided, but it is stated that owing to the youth of the girls who are employed to mind the children, accidents happen, which sometimes disable them for life.

The medical officers who have given evidence are of opinion that the present period of suspension from work after childbirth is too short, and two have suggested that the time be extended to three months. Such an extension would probably meet with opposition from the women themselves, many of whom are opposed to the enforced absence from work under the present law.

In a few factories the employment of married women is discouraged, but this is generally on the ground that their homes and home life suffer from their absence. In Belfast, Dr O'Neill, physician to the Royal Hospital, states that a large number of burns and scalds are caused by the absence of mothers from home. The children are left to get meals ready when they are too young to be even left alone. The matrons and nurses of the hospital give similar evidence, and state that the large majority of burns and scalds are brought to the hospital shortly after meal hours. . . . .

MATRONS IN IRISH HOSPITALS

Doc. 58: Anon., 'The lady superintendents of Irish hospitals', *Lady of the House* (Christmas 1902).

For much of the nineteenth century, nursing was generally undertaken by poor women, who had no formal training, in return for maintenance within an institution. Real changes in nursing care developed when nuns began to work in hospitals. St Vincent's hospital in Dublin was the first Catholic hospital in Ireland. It was founded in 1834 by the Sisters of Charity, who also ran the hospital. In the 1860s nuns gained access to work-house hospitals. By 1903 eighty-four workhouse hospitals were under the care of nuns.[1] The high public profile of nuns as nurses has tended to obscure the fact that by the end of the nineteenth century many lay women had also

1 See Luddy, *Philanthropy*, chapter two.

Mrs Kildare Tracey is a County Tipperary lady who qualified at the City of
Dublin Hospital when the nursing profession was new in Ireland, and was
among its earliest students. She was so fortunate as to be appointed superintendent of the City of Dublin Nursing Institution, in Upper Baggot Street,
after a year or two of staff work, in succession to Miss Fitzgerald of honoured
memory, whose sudden demise during the first epidemic of influenza was a
source of grief to a large social circle as well as a public loss. Although the
Nursing Institution in Upper Baggot Street is totally apart from any hospital,
it trains its probationers in several of them, and has a branch establishment at
Pau, in the South of France, so that the responsibility of its directoress is fully
as arduous – and we should say more widespread – as that of an hospital
superintendent. Mrs Tracey's personality is strongly marked by nervous
energy and administrative ability, and she is known to all classes of the
community throughout the length and breadth of Ireland.

The Misses Lyons are the daughters of a County Westmeath gentleman,
two of four sisters who are all lady superintendents. They trained at the Royal
Southern Hospital in Liverpool, and afterwards at the Hospital for Women
and Children at Cork. They are members of the Red Cross Order, and train
nurses for that society only.

Miss Lyons has directed the venerable Meath Hospital for eighteen years,
and Sister Bessie has served exactly the same term at the children's hospital,
Harcourt Street, both having been appointed as the first lady superintendents
of their respective schools. They are genial and accomplished ladies, with the
cordiality and happy manner of Irish country gentlewomen strongly marked in
their personality, and naively retained, even after so full a period of hospital life.

Miss Kelly has never left her native county throughout her professional
career. She trained at Dr Stevens' [hospital], and has now been for ten years
entire superintendent of that venerable house founded in Queen Anne's reign
by the truly 'Heavenly Twins', good Richard Stevens and his sister Grisel.
Two years after completing her studentship, Miss Kelly was chosen as nursing
instructress to the newly-organised nursing school at Jervis Street Hospital,
and was the first qualified lady nurse who taught modern practice under the
nuns. After two years of service, passed in the long, crowded wards there, she
was appointed to her present double post and so recalled to the house from
which she had, professionally, emanated.

Notwithstanding her double charge as matron and instructress at a
large hospital, Miss Kelly takes an active part as well as a keen interest in
matters connected with her profession at large. She is a Lady Consul for
the Royal British Nurses' Association, and is at present taking a prominent
part in the organisation of the Coronation Fund for Nurses.

Miss Hughes, Richmond District Asylum, Portrane, County Dublin, is
an Irishwoman of Scotch and Welsh parentage (an excellent combine!),

and took out her diploma at the Brownlow Hill Hospital in Liverpool, from whence she passed to Sir Patrick Dun's, and acted on Miss Huxley's nursing staff for three years. In 1887 she became lady superintendent of the Whitworth and Hardwicke Fever Hospitals, where she was Miss McDonnell's near neighbour, but in the following year entered on a course of nursing mental cases at St Anne's Heath, Virginia Water, from whence she returned to our Richmond District Asylum as chief nurse of the infirmary there, under Dr Conolly Norman's direction, and from which post she has been advanced during the present year to the onerous position of superintendent of the new asylum at Portrane. Miss Hughes had much experience of the nursing of paralysis during the earlier years of her professional career, and she holds the certificate of the Medico-Psychological Society.

Miss Bradshaw is a clever woman from the southern province. She graduated at the Adelaide under its first superintendent, Miss Poole; and on that lady's valued coadjutor, Miss Knight, matron of the hospital, being secured in a similar capacity for a leading hospital in Nottingham, she induced Miss Bradshaw to accompany her as assistant. After a term of seven years, during which Miss Bradshaw acted in several official departments, notably that of night superintendent, she left the large practice naturally consequent to life in a manufacturing and mining centre of the busy midlands for the more subdued and even tenor of administration required at our large Retreat for Chronics, if we may be permitted to so designate a local charity of which we are justly proud – namely, the Hospital for Incurables at Donnybrook; and there she has held the post of lady superintendent for four years.

WOMEN AND DOMESTIC SERVICE

Doc. 59a: *Report by Miss Collett on the Money Wages of Indoor Domestic Servants HC 1899 [C. 9346], xcii.*

Domestic service was a traditional area of employment for Irish women. The majority of domestic servants in the pre- and post-Famine periods were young, single women. Service was seen as a 'respectable' occupation for the lower classes. Room and board were generally provided. A portion of the wages earned often went in saving towards marriage, or in the support of the woman's family. Employers were expected to supervise and care for their servants, and to monitor their behaviour. Conditions for servants varied greatly and depended on the employer, and on the number of servants employed. Wages varied according to expertise.

Cook/housekeepers were generally the highest paid of the female servants. It seems likely that many Irish women engaged in domestic service due to the lack of other employment opportunities. In 1899 Miss Collett reported on the wages of female domestic service in Irish cities. The returns used to estimate average rates of pay for servants came from Belfast, Dublin, Cork, Limerick and the Limerick region.

Average wages [in pounds] of female domestic servants classified according to number of servants in household.

Household Employing	Dublin	Belfast	Cork & Limerick	Total Ireland
One servant	10.8	12.6	9.5	11.3
Two servants	13.5	13.9	11.1	13.3
Three servants	15.3	16.7	13.9	15.5
Four servants	16.6	17.1	14.7	15.9
Over four servants	19.8	19.7	17.4	18.7

Average rates of wages [in pounds] according to class of work:

Class of work	Age period	Ireland
Between maid	19	–
Scullerymaid	19	–
Kitchenmaid	20	11.3
Nurse-housemaid	21 & under 25	–
General	"	10.3
Housemaid	"	13.5
Nurse	25 & under 30	15.8
Parlourmaid	"	16.0
Laundrymaid	"	–
Cook	"	17.2
Lady's maid	30 & under 35	24.0
Cook-housekeeper	40 & upwards	–
Housekeeper	"	–

Doc. 59b: *Belfast Newsletter*, 8 January 1912.

Newspapers provided a prime source of information on employment opportunities, particularly for servants. It is interesting to note the references made to religion.

Situations Wanted
COOK (RC)[1] experienced, wishes an engagement; no objections country; understands dairy – Mrs Maxwell, 107 Donegall Street.

1 Roman Catholic.

HOUSEKEEPER, good cook, 5 years excellent character, wishes an engagement; good appearance – Mrs Maxwell, 107 Donegall Street.

COOK disengaged; hotel or private; good references – Mrs Robinson, 16 Lower Garfield Street; 'Phone 3204.

HOUSEKEEPER to one or two gentlemen; Protestant; good cook and well recommended – Mrs Robinson, 16 Lower Garfield Street; 'Phone 3204.

HOUSEMAID or Parlour-maid disengaged 1st February; young; Protestant; excellent references; Mrs Robinson, 16 Lower Garfield Street; 'Phone 3204.

GOOD COOK wishes engagement; excellent references; good at soups, entrees, &c; £24 – Mrs Rolston's Agency, 55 Arthur Street.

PARLOUR MAID wishes engagement; excellent servant; best references; can valet and carve; £22 – Mrs Rolston's Agency, 55 Arthur Street.

WAITRESS, thoroughly experienced in commercial and coffee room duties, requires position in good hotel; highly recommended – Miss Crozier, Arthur Place.

EDUCATED, highly recommended young Lady desires a position as Assistant Manageress or Cashier; would run tea rooms – Apply NS 612, this office.

LADY wishes post as Mother's Help where servant kept; young; capable; teach first lessons and music – Apply H W 751, this office.

LADY, educated, refined, desires post as Companion or Lady Help (servant kept); assist household duties; experience; reference – N E 646, this office.

RESPECTABLE, young General[1] (Protestant) wants situation to train as Housemaid or House-Parlour Maid – Mrs McCartney, General Agency, 29 Salisbury Street.

SITUATION wanted by young, experienced General Servant; good cook-laundress; highly recommended; Protestant – 7 Farnham Street, Ormead Road.

SCULLERY MAID or Kitchenmaid – Strong young Girl, well recommended, wishes situation as above; £17-£18; town or county – Miss Murray, 25 Atlantic Avenue.

WANTED, by respectable Girl, 4 days daily work; good reference – Address, D W 636, this office.

1 General servant.

DRESSMAKING – Joseph Johnson & Co, Ltd, Drapers, Leicester, England, have vacancies for experienced Bodice Hands and Sleeve Hands; high-class trade; permanent employment and liberal wages; live in or out – Apply to Mr Ritchie, 9 Brunswick Street, Belfast, on Monday, Tuesday or Wednesday (January 8th, 9th and 10th), between the hours of 12 and 4 p.m.

LADIES' Tailoring – C. McCullagh & Co, Castle Buildings, require a cutter of experience for ladies' coats and costumes.

LADY Baker wanted, new business, Bangor; competent, or amateur would be taught; assist sales; wear white uniform – Address, L B 647, this office.

PROVISION and Grocery Department (no drink) – Young Lady, good experience, to assist at above; smart appearance and address – State salary expected, send copies reference, Dawson's Maynooth . . .

WANTED, Companion Help to lady; musical; cheerful – State salary and give references to C H 628, this office.

WANTED General Servant for Bangor; good wages, given suitable girl – Apply immediately, G T 753, this ofice.

WANTED General Servant or Mother's Help for 15th; wages £15; well recommended; Protestant – Apply C F 857, this office . . .

WANTED English Nurse for two children; country town – Send copy of references and state wages expected to Nurse, 755, this office.

WANTED young General (Protestant) for 15th January; small family – Apply any evening between 6 and 8 o'clock, Montrose, Malone Road.

WANTED young Lady for Millinery and Sales; stylish trimmer, able to make up; Protestant – References, salary (outdoor), S M 863, this office.

WANTED young Lady Milliner, stylish trimmer, good stockkeeper, able serve in general draper; Protestant – References, age, salary, J. S. J., 623, this office.

WANTED young Lady for Grocery, hardware, and delph business, knowledge bookkeeping, country town – State age, religion, salary, J. J. S., 622, this office.

WANTED Lady Bookkeeper and Typist – Give references, state experience and salary expected. The Portadown Manufacturing Co, 17 Franklin Street, Belfast . . .

Trade Unionism

ORGANISING WOMEN WORKERS

Doc. 60a: *The Irish Worker,* 2 September 1911.

Women workers in Ireland in the nineteenth and early twentieth centuries were difficult to organise into unions. The Irish Women Workers' Union was established in 1911, with James Larkin (1876–1947) as president and his sister Delia(1878–1949) as secretary. The following document, written by Delia Larkin, details the meeting held in Dublin to inaugurate the union.

Great Meeting in the Antient Concert Rooms

On Thursday last, in response to our appeal, the Antient Concert Rooms was filled to its upmost capacity with women workers anxious to join the newly formed Women Workers' Union. By eight o'clock the hall and balcony were full, and those who came after had to be allowed on the stage, even then it was as much as we could do to find room for all.

The orderly manner in which the girls entered was astonishing, and might well be copied by the men. Throughout the whole proceedings there was the utmost enthusiasm and attention. Previous to the speeches many popular and National airs were played on the piano, and Cathal O'Byrne from Belfast delighted us with some of his sweetest songs.

In opening the meeting, the chairman, Mr Murphy, President Trades Council, said he was very pleased to preside at such a meeting . . . Countess Markievicz,[1] who was greeted with great applause, spoke as follows:

'Friends, I am very glad Mr Larkin asked me to come here and address you. Without organisation you can do nothing and the purpose of this meeting is to form you into an army of fighters. You will all, I hope, join this union, by doing so, you will be doing a good day's work not only for yourselves, but for Ireland. As you are all aware women have at present no vote, but a union, such as has now been formed will not alone enable you

---

1 Constance Markievicz (née Gore-Booth, 1868–1927), nationalist. She became an officer in the Irish Citizen Army and was active in the 1916 Rising. Was the first woman elected to Westminster in 1918 but did not take her seat. Was appointed Minister for Labour in the cabinet of the first Dáil Éireann.

to obtain better wages, but will also be a great means of helping you to get votes and thus make men of you all' (cheers and laughter) . . .

Mrs Sheehy Skeffington . . . said she felt proud to be on the platform at such an enormous and representative meeting. 'The men are organised and have succeeded to a great extent in obtaining justice. We, as women, have a good deal to learn from the men, who are experienced in the practice of trades unionism, and it is desirable that we should work together for the welfare of both sexes. The men and women should be united and work together.'

Mrs Sheehy Skeffington then dealt at some length with the question of the women's franchise which seemed to have the support of all present.

Mr Larkin, who was wildly cheered, spoke of the necessity for united action among all classes of women workers. He said:– 'Women are the basis of a nation's wealth. On them principally depends the efficiency and welfare of the race. Good or bad, the men are what the women made them. If the women are not healthy, the men will degenerate. If the women are ignorant, the men will be beasts. We cannot have healthy women while the present conditions remain unchanged. But health is not the only thing. We want good houses, good clothing and leisure. Every girl is entitled to be nicely dressed; yet a good many girls in Dublin tonight are compelled to clothe their bodies in filthy rags. When once you [the women] make up your minds to do a thing you will see it through. Women are more determined than the men. I have seen girls in Belfast wrench off a door and paste a bill on it saying, "We are on strike". This was in the middle of January, with snow on the ground, and many of the girls were barefooted.'

In conclusion he appealed to them to make the Women Workers' Union the success it should be . . .

Doc. 60b: *The Irish Citizen*, July 1918.

The following document tells of organising women into the IWWU in Waterford.

During the last month a branch of the Irish Women Workers' Union has been formed in Waterford by Mrs Callendar of Dublin, who spent three weeks as organiser in the city. In the case of several firms the whole staff of workers have joined the union, and one increase of wages has already been granted as a result of this organisation. The need for such a union among the women workers of Waterford is very great, and the thanks of all women is due to Mrs Callendar for her efforts in forming the branch and in investigating the conditions under which women, too poor and ignorant to help themselves, are suffering.

WOMEN ON STRIKE

Doc. 61: *The Irish Worker*, 15 June 1912.

Delia Larkin edited a women's column in The Irish Worker. *In the following extract she reports on a dispute that developed in a Dublin city laundry.*

In the last week's issue of *The Irish Worker*, attention was drawn to the workings of a certain laundry in the city. Since then a dispute has arisen, owing to the attitude taken up by the manager and manageress towards some of their workers. By the way, this laundry is called 'The Pembroke Laundry', is situated on the Mespil Road, and is managed by people named Mr and Mrs Sorohan. A fortnight ago 14 of the girls employed in this sweating den came along and became members of the IWWU. The manager and his wife, upon hearing this, stated that they would dismiss all those who had joined the union, and also anyone who would join it. They started their campaign last Friday, by dismissing one of the girls for leaving a machine heated, which they themselves, previous to this, had told her to leave heated, so that on her return she could start work immediately; but now when they find that this girl [*is*] a trades union member, these instructions of theirs had turned to negligence on the girl's part; and accordingly she is dismissed. On Saturday 3 more girls are dismissed, also members of the WWU.

. . . Some of the girls who are at present out on strike are receiving 4*s* per week for working from 8 a.m. to 7 p.m., one hour for dinner. 4*s* per week for a girl to feed and clothe herself. One of the girls who is receiving this magnificent wage has neither mother nor father. So how she manages to pay for lodgings, food and clothing is a mystery I am unable to solve. These girls certainly do not live in Baggot Street. It is necessary that every working man and woman should assist us in this fight. We are fighting for a principle and for the right of the working woman to combine – therefore

Girls!
Don't scab on your sisters.
Keep away from the Pembroke laundry.

LOUIE BENNETT ON WOMEN AND TRADE UNIONISM

Doc. 62: Louie Bennett, 'Women and trade unionism', *The Irish Citizen*, January 1918.

Louie Bennett (1870–1956), an active suffragist and pacifist, became the secretary of the Irish Women Workers' Union in 1917. Bennett wrote regularly for The Irish Citizen *and the following article recounts the success of the*

IWWU, and expresses her hope that the suffrage campaign will broaden its involvement in trade union issues.

The most notable development of the women's movement in Ireland during the past year has been the sudden growth of trades unionism among women workers. A year ago the members of the Irish Women Workers' Union numbered only a few hundreds: now they are over 2,000. The munition workers are strongly organised under the National Federation of Women Workers; tailoresses, shirt-makers and other workers with the needle are enrolling in great numbers in all the big towns in the Society of Tailors and Tailoresses. Women clerks are amongst the keenest and most active members of the Irish Clerical Union and the National Union of Clerks, although this time last year the women clerks of Dublin were in doubt whether they were not too nice for anything even resembling a union! The most interesting point in regard to this rapid organisation is the spirit in which the women have come into the movement; this spirit promises to atone for their tardiness in entering. They are keen and progressive; quick in their grasp of the fundamental principles of trades unionism, and loyal in their adherence to them. The stand of the women in the print trade made during the recent printers' strike was a surprise to many people – not least perhaps to the employers!

Do the women of other classes realise how significant and how far-reaching in effect this development amongst women workers will prove? Hitherto, these women have spent their idealism and loyalty mainly upon nationalism. Now their nationalism promises to express itself in a practical direction, and women will find the best means of serving Ireland through the power of the trades union. When they have lifted themselves out of the sweated conditions under which they work at present, we shall begin to feel their influence working in broader directions and stimulate the civic reforms which all classes desire but which only the workers themselves will ever effectually achieve.

Is it permissible to suggest that *The Irish Citizen* ought now to formulate a definite policy in accordance with the new ideas of the day. It is time that it extended its attention from the purely suffrage movement to broader aspects of feminism. The great merit of the paper since the war broke out has been its fidelity to the truth so clearly expounded by Mr Sheehy Skeffington, that feminism and militarism cannot work as partners. That truth is far as yet from general acceptance, and *The Irish Citizen* must still keep it in the foreground. But that truth in itself is but part of a greater truth:– that feminism and co-operative internationalism (the substitute for militarism) are dependent upon economic justice. When we have won economic justice for the worker of the nations, we shall be able to secure it as the basis of relations between nations, and thus, and thus only, make the world safe for democracy.

Why should not *The Irish Citizen* make itself the organ of economic justice for women? What better service could it render to the whole cause of feminism?

(*The Irish Citizen* has always been the organ of 'economic justice for women', and will, as in the past, be happy to receive and publish all matters relating to women's work. Should women trades unionists, therefore, see their way to sending us in reports of their activities we will be happy to publish them. Editor.)

WOMEN'S PAY IN 1918

Doc. 63: Florence Newman, 'Women's pay of to-day', *The Irish Citizen*, April 1918.

Women were usually paid less than men, even when they were doing the same work. Florence Newman questions the fairness of this. By 1918 the Great War had provided new job opportunities for women. Some, for example, found employment in munitions factories, while the civil service hired more women clerks. The war also brought rising prices. This affected women more than men since they were paid less. There were also shortages of basic foodstuffs.

The world of work today differs very much from that of a few years ago when women workers were held in abhorrence. Today the woman takes her place at the desk or in the workshop. There seems to be room for her everywhere. It has been proved that her work can be executed as satisfactorily and expeditely as any man's. The demand for women workers is increasing, but why, when their work has proved satisfactory and when their services are obtained to do the work of the men who are absent, are they not paid the same salary as these absent men? It is a fact that women are employed today to do men's work at a salary that is not even half that which was paid to them.

There are lots of women working today at a salary of one pound per week, yes, and less. These women are doing important work, work that cannot be left aside and work that requires the brains of the educated. Why then should there be a reduction in women's rate of pay? A woman cannot live any cheaper than a man, and why should she be compelled to drag out an existence and try to keep up her appearance and look her best on a starvation wage? Is it fair that her abilities should be made use of without giving her proper remuneration for them?

Take, for instance, the women government clerks. A few years ago it was an unheard of thing for a woman to enter the service of a government office. That has all been done away with and today the offices are employing hundreds of girls. The rate of wages paid in these offices vary very much, but there are girls who have received good educations and are now giving the result of these educations in doing the work, hitherto performed by men, who are in receipt of 25/-, more of £1 and, I am sorry to say, a great many at 15/- and 16/- per week. Can anyone say why this should be! Surely if work is properly executed and is worth the trouble of being executed proper remuneration should be given.

Under-pay for women is the order of the day and something must be done to put an end to it. Why should women not join together and refuse to give their services or take the place of men if they are not given a proper living wage.

Take the girl living in lodgings. What can she do on 20/– or 25/– per week? Who will board and lodge a working girl at less than 18/– or 20/–? No one. Food, etc., is altogether too dear and prices are too high and increasing to allow of anyone keeping any girl under that amount. Such a girl finds herself with 5/– or 7/– a week to clothe herself and meet her tram or train expenses. Unfortunately, there are too many cases where girls are trying to do it. These cases should be done away with, and a higher standard of wages should be fixed for women generally. It is to be hoped that one of the first benefits which will accrue from the women's votes will be a levelling up of women's rates of pay with those of men. It will be a benefit all round both to the man and the woman. Equal pay for equal work should be one of the causes the women should make their own.

VOL. I.—No. 1.　BELFAST, 15TH JANUARY, 1896.　PRICE TWOPENCE.

The Shan Van Vocht.

THERE is news from o'er the sea,
　　Says the Shan Van Vocht ;
There is news from o'er the sea,
　　Says the Shan Van Vocht ;
And this message o'er the sea,
From the land of liberty,
Brings the best of news for me,
　　Says the Shan Van Vocht.

Ere the dying of the year,
　　Says the Shan Van Vocht ;
From a land that's far but dear
　　To the Shan Van Vocht ;
In a voice that laughed at fear,
There rang forth defiance clear,
Let us send an answering cheer,
　　Says the Shan Van Vocht.

And a cloud is glooming now,
　　Says the Shan Van Vocht,
O'er our haughty tyrant's brow,
　　Says the Shan Van Vocht ;
Whilst like thunder bursts afar,
Where her sons and daughters are,
The din of dreadful war,
　　Says the Shan Van Vocht.

But there's light behind that cloud
　　For the Shan Van Vocht,
And that thunder roaring loud,
　　Says the Shan Van Vocht ;
Though it strikes the weakling dumb,
Shouts in tones of joy to some
That the dawn of Freedom's come
　　To the Shan Van Vocht.

But tell me who is she
　　Called the Shan Van Vocht ;
And if other name there be
　　For the Shan Van Vocht ;
Yea ! immortal is her fame,
She's the queen no foe could tame,
**For old Ireland is the name
　　Of the Shan Van Vocht.**

The Boy From Barnesmore.

(A STORY OF '67). BY IRIS OLKYRN.

THE train had stopped an unusually long time at
Strabane Station. Trains in Ireland are rarely in
a hurry ; indeed, when you come to think of it why
should they be, as some wit remarked "there is more time
to spare than there is of anything else in this distressful
country." And to-day there was every excuse for delay,
and plenty to divert my attention whilst we waited, for
that day had been the great spring hiring market in
Strabane, and the crowd upon the platform was an interesting and picturesque one.

Here were the wives of strong farmers in all the
flaunting bravery of their new spring bonnets, gorgeous
in scarlet and purple, and emerald green ribbons with
wondrous flowers, fresh from the milliners' hands ; whilst
in paper bags they carried the head-dresses in which
they had come to town that morning. Their crinoline
distended skirts, their gay fringed shawls, their loudly
creaking boots, were objects of wonder and envy to the
simply dressed country girls of Donegal, who had
entered into six months service with them that day, and
who had left homes among the mountain glens up by
Stranorlar and Glenties, and far away in Gweedore, to
do housework and field work on farms in Tyrone. I
could not help admiring the picturesque simplicity of
their plain kilted skirts of grey or dark blue
homespun ; the bright kerchiefs knotted simply over
their neatly braided locks as compared with the tawdry
grandeur of their newly found mistresses. The men were
shouting and talking excitedly, running this way and
that, and calling to their women folk to follow to the
seats they had secured in the carriages. Through the
swaying, surging crowd, with quiet sauntering step passed
two or three straight military looking men, easily recognised as members of the police force in plain clothes.
I thought nothing of their passing up and down and

Title page of the first issue of the *Shan Van Vocht*, the republican journal
edited by Alice Milligan (1866-1953) and Ethna Carbery (1866-1902).
(National Library of Ireland)

Part IV

POLITICS

Louie Bennett (1870-1956), pacifist, suffragist and trade unionist. (National Library of Ireland)

Hanna Sheehy Skeffington (1877-1946), founder of the Irish Women's Franchise League. (National Library of Ireland)

INTRODUCTION

THOUGH IRISH WOMEN were not granted the vote until 1918, they had always involved themselves in politics at local and national level in both an informal and formal way. Informal political activity took many guises. In public, women played a role in riots and disturbances at election times. In times of crisis, such as during periods of scarcity, they partook in food riots. In private, some women influenced the male members of their households to vote in particular ways, or to engage in various forms of political protest. Upper-class women in particular, had the opportunity, if they were interested, to discuss politics with their spouses, fathers, or brothers, some of whom would have been politically powerful. Through wealth and patronage many women had an opportunity to influence the political beliefs of men. But political activity was not confined to women of the middle and upper classes. As yet we do not know the extent to which women from the lower classes took part in agrarian secret societies, which proliferated in Ireland from the mid-eighteenth century, but there is enough evidence to suggest that such participation was far more common than many historians have assumed. Most agrarian outrages that occurred in pre-famine Ireland were carried out by groups or individuals with the explicit or implicit sanction of their local community. Women and men acted together in many of these outrages in an attempt to regulate economic and social relationships.[1] K. T. Hoppen[2] has shown that election mobs offered women, and indeed voteless men, an opportunity to influence formal politics. There is evidence, for example, that numbers of women negotiated their husbands' election bribes, and that they also organised and led mobs at election times. Women were also prominent in food riots which occurred throughout the first half of the nineteenth century. During the Great Famine, food riots and disturbances were particularly common.[3] Women's activities in these informal associations,

1 See the following articles all by James S. Donnelly Jr., 'The Rightboy movement 1785-8', *Studia Hibernica*, 17/18 (1977-8), pp 120-202; 'The Whiteboy movement 1761-5', *Irish Historical Studies*, 21 (1978), pp 20-54; 'Irish agrarian rebellion: the Whiteboys of 1769-76', *Proceedings of the Royal Irish Academy*, 83 (1983), pp 293-331.
2 K. Theodore Hoppen, *Elections, Politics and Society in Ireland 1832-85* (Oxford, 1984), pp 406-8.
3 James S. Donnelly Jr., *The Land and the People of Nineteenth-Century Cork* (London, 1975).

like those of men, were generally undertaken on economic grounds. It was within secret societies and through mob violence that the private concerns of families and communities confronted the public power of the law, landlords and the state.

Women are rarely acknowledged as having played an active role in the practical or theoretical formulations of nationalist organisations in the last century. References to women are generally made in symbolic terms only. But although the organisational pattern of men's and women's roles, in terms of participation and leadership, was not equal in groups such as the Young Irelanders or the Fenians, women still played an important role in creating a sense of national identity through their writings and their practical support for these organisations.[1] Women, for example, carried despatches between the local leaders of the Fenian movement in the 1860s.[2] In October of 1865 a group of women formed the Ladies' Committee to aid the families of imprisoned Fenians and that work continued until 1872 when a general amnesty was announced for the prisoners.[3]

Women's involvement in formal political activity developed very strongly in the nineteenth century. Some of the earliest activity is witnessed in the anti-slavery societies which Irish women, particularly Quaker women, organised from the 1830s. The political language of anti-slavery activists fashioned a rhetoric, based on gender difference, which was echoed in all other public organisations and societies established by women in the nineteenth century. Women in the anti-slavery societies looked particularly to other women to support their cause, believing that a universal bond of motherhood and feminine feeling united all women, whether free or in slavery.

The debates taking place in Ireland from the 1860s about women's education, employment, etc., were influenced by ideas infiltrating the country from England and America. These debates were affected by the changing cultural and economic values of post-famine Ireland. Informal committees of women were organised from the 1860s to campaign for changes in women's access to secondary and higher education, and to change the laws relating to the property of married women. It was not, however, until the formation of the Irish branch of the Ladies' National Association for the Repeal of the Contagious Diseases Acts in 1870 that an organised and extended campaign based on a perception of sexual and gender oppression operated on a national scale.

In 1864, parliament passed the first of three statutes which permitted the compulsory inspection of prostitutes for venereal diseases in certain military camps in England and Ireland. The three acts of 1864, 1866 and 1869 were introduced to control the spread of venereal disease amongst the soldiery,

1 See, for example, the women writers of *The Nation* and also MS 10,906, Women in the Young Ireland movement, NLI.
2 *The Gaelic American*, 24 March, 1906.
3 *The Irishman*, 28 October, 1865.

which by 1864 was deemed responsible for one out of every three sick cases in the army. In Ireland the 'subjected' districts were Cork, Cobh and the Curragh army camp in Kildare. Opposition to the acts arose for a number of reasons but in Ireland they centred on the belief that the Acts sanctioned vice and were an interference with the civil liberty of women. Some women in Ireland who opposed the Acts formed branches of the Ladies' National Association for the Repeal of the Contagious Diseases Acts, originally formed in England in 1869 by Josephine Butler. The methods used by the campaigners were typical of those strategies used by middle-class women in political campaigning: meetings, 'at homes', lobbying of MPs and other influential individuals, and the use of petitions and deputations. The campaign carried on until 1883, when the Acts were suspended and they were finally repealed in 1886. The majority, if not all, of the members of the Ladies' National Association in Ireland were Non-Conformists. Catholic women do not appear to have been involved in the campaign in Ireland. For 'respectable' women to speak openly on matters pertaining to sexual morality was to challenge the stereotype of the quiet, submissive and passive woman portrayed by the Victorians.

A number of activists in this campaign became involved in the suffrage issue, which began to be discussed seriously in Ireland in the early 1870s. By 1876, two suffrage societies had been established, one in Belfast organised by Isabella M.S. Tod, and another in Dublin initiated by Anna and Thomas Haslam. Those who joined these organisations again tended to be Protestant and Non-Conformist. The demand for suffrage was the principal means whereby women fought for political involvement on the same terms as men in the late nineteenth and early twentieth centuries. The majority of suffragists did not fight for universal suffrage, but wanted the vote, which was limited by property restrictions, on the same terms as men. It was not until the early years of the twentieth century, when militant suffragism forced itself on the public's attention, that suffrage became an important issue in Irish politics.

A sizeable majority of those women who organised around the suffrage issue in Ireland already had experience of campaigning as members of various philanthropic organisations. Anna Haslam and Isabella Tod, for example, had activist roots in philanthropy. That experience appears to have radicalised a number of women and led them to believe that the acquisition of the franchise was the most effective way of shaping society and having an impact on social legislation. Membership of these early suffrage groups tended to be small. In 1896, for example, the recorded membership of Haslam's Irish Women's Suffrage and Local Government Association was only forty three, and this reached a peak in 1911 with 647 members.[1] Campaigning consisted typically of drawing-room meetings, petitions to parliament and letters to newspapers. Haslam's group was relatively inactive from the mid-1880s to the mid-1890s. No public suffrage meetings were held, due, it was declared, 'to the present condition of

1   *Irish Women's Suffrage and Local Government Association, Annual Report, 1906.*

political controversy in Ireland, as well as other causes'.[1] Irish women also communicated with suffragists in England and America and formed friendships and alliances with activists in other countries.[2] Irish women, particularly those involved in the suffrage campaign, also lobbied the government for changes in the local franchise. In 1896 the government passed the Women's Poor Law Guardian (Ireland) Act, which enabled Irish women, with certain property qualifications, to vote and serve as Poor Law Guardians. In 1898 the Local Government (Ireland) Act, again with certain conditions, conferred the local government vote on Irish women. It is difficult to assess how influential Irish women were in bringing about these particular changes, since in both instances, the government was bringing Ireland into line with the situation prevailing in England. Women in England sat as Poor Law Guardians from 1875, and English women ratepayers had the municipal franchise from 1869.

The Ladies' Land League, established in 1880, was not formed to fight for the cause of women but provided women with a powerful political role in the land war. Anna Parnell's (1852–1911) view of the land issue was more radical than that of the male leaders of the Land league.[3] The Ladies' Land League lasted for nineteen months and was eventually forced to disband. Women's involvement in Irish nationalism became more diverse in the first decades of the twentieth century. The rhetoric of republicanism was strongly echoed in the newspaper the *Shan Van Vocht* (Poor Old Woman) published by Alice Milligan (1866–1953) and Anna Johnson (1866–1902). Maud Gonne (1866–1953) established Inghinidhe na hÉireann (Daughters of Ireland) in 1900, which had a specific cultural purpose and promoted the Irish language and Irish culture. In 1908 that organisation began to publish *Bean na hÉireann* (Woman of Ireland) which advocated militancy, feminism and separatism. Women were also involved in the cultural revival and played their part in the Gaelic League (1893) and literary revival.

The Home Rule struggle dominated Irish politics in the early years of the twentieth century. John Redmond, the leader of the Irish Parliamentary Party at Westminster, was personally hostile to the suffrage campaign, and was unwilling to declare support for any cause he saw as jeopardising the possibility of Home Rule. Attempts made to introduce women's suffrage bills in parliament in the years after 1910 failed. The Irish Party opposed a number of bills, particularly the Conciliation bill of 1912,[5] which had seemed likely

1 *Irish Women's Suffrage and Local Government Association, Annual Report, 1896.*
2 See Cliona Murphy, *The Women's Suffrage Movement and Irish Society in the Early Twentieth Century* (Brighton, 1989).
3 Anna Parnell, *Tale of A Great Sham* ed. Dana Hearne (Dublin, 1986).
4 Margaret Ward, *Unmanageable Revolutionaries: Women and Irish Nationalism* (London, 1983), pp 4–39.
5 After the general election of 1910 the Liberals no longer held a majority in parliament. Legislative success could not then be guaranteed through the support of one party. A committee, with representatives from all the political parties, was formed to approve bills. This was the conciliation committee. The bills proposed were named Conciliation bills, of which there were a number during these years.

to succeed. When the Home Rule Bill was finally passed in 1914 it did not include women's suffrage. From the first decade of the twentieth century Irish women also began to be more profoundly polarised by their unionist or nationalist sympathies. Isabella Tod, for example, had serious disagreements with suffragist colleagues in England and Ireland over the Home Rule issue. Tod established the first committee of women to fight against Gladstone's Home Rule bill of 1886, and from these small beginnings unionist women, determined to support the link with Britain, developed a powerful and active support group that has lasted to the present time. By the second decade of the twentieth century conditions in Ireland were complicated by the overt militarism which had arisen in nationalist and unionist camps. The formation and arming of the Ulster Volunteers in 1913, to act as a defence force against the imposition of Home Rule in the northern counties, led to the parallel formation of the Irish Volunteers in Dublin in November of the same year. The threat of civil war seemed very real. In 1914 Cumann na mBan (Women's Council) was established as an auxiliary to the Irish Volunteers. This group was not actively feminist but supported Irish freedom from British rule.

The early years of the twentieth century were years of intense political and cultural activity in Ireland, and in the midst of all the turmoil new suffrage organisations sprang up. These catered for particular regional, political or religious groups. For example, in 1909 an Irish branch of the Conservative and Unionist Women's Suffrage Association was established in Dublin, while in 1913 a branch of the Church League for Women's Suffrage for Anglican Women was formed. The most important of these new societies was the Irishwomen's Franchise League, established in 1908 by, amongst others, Margaret Cousins and Hanna Sheehy Skeffington. The group, influenced by the militant Women's Social and Political Union set up in England in 1903, supported militancy and through its campaigns helped place the suffrage issue very much in the public eye. The IWFL was non-party, and though it had links with the English women's suffrage movement, was determined to remain independent from it. Disagreements arose however between suffragists and women involved in nationalist organisations. Arguments arose over whether nationalist or suffrage issues should take precedence. Hanna Sheehy Skeffington, for example, saw women in nationalist organisations as playing a subordinate role. The outbreak of war in 1914 placed tremendous pressure on the various Irish suffrage organisations. Some suffragists threw themselves into war work, others remained pacifist, while more refused to support Britain and fought instead for a free Ireland.

The aftermath of the Easter rising of 1916, with its fifteen executions and mass internment, brought together many of the different strands of women's political activity in the south of Ireland. Cumann na mBan members became more interested in feminist issues, and nationalist women became more

1 See doc. 90.

243

involved in the trade union movement. Many suffragists became more sympathetic to nationalism after the executions of the leaders of the Rising. Thus, by 1918 Irishwomen had involved themselves in nationalist, unionist and labour politics on a grand scale. In 1917 the Representation of the People Act granted the parliamentary vote to women over thirty 'who were householders, the wives of householders, were possessed of a £5 occupation qualification or were graduates'. Women played a major role in the election of 1918, canvassing and propagandising for Sinn Féin. Constance Markievicz and Winifred Carney were selected as Sinn Féin candidates, with Markievicz being elected in St Patrick's constituency in Dublin. Markievicz was the first woman elected to Westminster, though she did not take her seat. The victory of Sinn Féin in the 1918 election culminated in the creation, on 21 January 1919, of the first Dáil in Dublin. That day also marked the beginning of the War of Independence. Irish political life was now overtaken by violence; men and women were to fight and die in the ensuing civil war. A new chapter in the history of Irish women had begun.

Informal Political Involvement

COMMENT ON WOMEN'S ACTIVITY

Women Take Part in Food Riots

Doc. 64.1a: *Cork Constitution,* 11 May 1847.

Food riots are associated particularly with the Great Famine. Men, women and children took part in these outbreaks, as the first extract reveals. Disturbances relating to food also arose in other times of want.

. . . On Wednesday as seven cart loads of flour, from the concern of Sir David Roche, at Carass, and four loads of Indian meal, from the mills of James D. Lyons, Esq., Croom, were being conveyed to Ballingarry under an escort of four police, a mob of about 500 men and women attacked the carriers near Kimacow, and despite the exertions of the constabulary in charge, carried off the entire of Sir David Roche's property; but on being told that the other carts were the medium of transmitting provisions for the use of the Relief Committee of Ballingarry, the marauders were content with relieving only one horse of its load.

Doc. 64.1b: *The Connaught Telegraph,* 17 January 1880.

The breadcart of Mr Thomas O'Donovan, J.P. . . . who has the contract of supplying the workhouse with bread, was attacked this morning shortly after eight o'clock on the way to the workhouse. The horse was stopped and the driver of the cart, a driver named Devaney, when trying to prevent the crowd from taking the bread which was in the cart had to run to save his life. An immense crowd of men, women and children, then ransacked the cart and carried away the contents to their respective homes. The driver of the cart got possession of it again, drove home, and reported the matter to his master; he was dispatched with a second load. This time the cart was allowed to pass without any molestation. Hundreds of the unemployed may be seen standing in groups at all the corners through the town. They present a shocking appearance.

The Castlepooke Murders

Doc. 64.2: *The Constitution or Cork Advertiser,* 28 March 1833.

The payment of tithes, primarily an economic grievance, was a particularly contentious issue in Ireland. Tithe payments supported the Protestant clergy in a country where most individuals were Catholics. Opposition to tithes had surfaced in agrarian disturbances from the 1760s, but by the 1830s this had developed into a full-scale 'tithe war'.[1] Women as well as men were involved in this agitation. The following reports, given as evidence in a trial, describe the murder of two tithe proctors in County Cork.

. . . Richard Lissen – I live in Doneraile. I knew the deceased. I last saw them alive on the 19th of September last, about a mile from Castlepooke at 12 o'clock in the day. Canning had a piece of paper in his hand in a potato field, and when I spoke to him he returned me no answer, but shook his head and beckoned at me. This was in Doneraile parish. I saw these men the same evening both dead in a stream of water nearer Castlepooke than when I first saw them. This was between four and five o'clock. They were laid in the water about twenty yards distant from each other, Cummins being higher up in the stream.

William Herbert, a boy of 10 years of age, having satisfied the Court that he knew the nature of an oath, said – My father is dead, and my mother lives in a house of Michael Haly's. I lived there last September, a day which, when I was cutting ferns in Hertnehy's field, I saw two men and three women hallooing a dog. I heard men near the castle shouting. The castle is on Frank Sullivan's land. There were about 10 or 11 near the castle. These men desired the women to strike two men with a stone and set a black dog on them. The two men ran down Haly's field, when the only persons near them were the women. They then ran down the boreen[2] to Haly's yard. There was a man ran down from John Linehan's house, and two men also came from the castle, and began to throw stones at them. I saw Mary Denneby, Ellen Duff, and another woman, who were throwing stones at them. The three men also struck them with stones. One of the men that was attacked went into Haly's haggard. This man had a white coat and a glazed hat on. He kneeled down to beg their pardon, and asked them to let him go home. When he was on his knees, I saw the same men and women, with some others, strike him with stones. I saw him leap over the ditch into the river; when he was rising he was knocked down again, and he fell into the river. I know David Heffy, who lives near me, and whom I know a long time. I saw him throw stones at the man who fell into the river. He was struck by other persons at the same time. He got up on the ditch three times and was knocked down again. Some

---

1 Tithes were a cause for resentment from the eighteenth century. From 1830–3 there was a great deal of violence throughout the country over the tithe issue which was resolved eventually in 1838 when tithe was incorporated into a rent charge payable to landlords.
2 Narrow dirt road.

more men then came from the castle and from Leonard Heffy's house, all of whom struck him. He was stretched on his back in the river, where he was struck. I saw two girls take him by the legs out of the water . . .

A Woman Accepts a Bribe for her Husband's Vote

Doc. 64.3: *Report from the Select Committee on the Newry Borough Election Petition HC 1833 (76), x.*

Although women did not have the vote in parliamentary elections in the nineteenth century, there were a number of roles they could play within the election process, as the following extracts reveal.

Evidence of Elizabeth Murtagh.
. . . He said, if my husband would give him his vote, I would get £22 an hour after my husband would poll for Lord Marcus Hill.
Did he say where the money was to come from?
He said that Mrs Black would have it for me an hour after he would poll.

A Woman Promises her Husband's Vote

Doc. 64.4: *Report from the Select Committee on the Londonderry Election Petition with the Minutes of Proceedings and Evidence HC 1833 (180), x.*

Evidence of Mrs Elizabeth Brown.
Did you promise your husband's vote for Mr Dawson to Mr Gillespie, at any time? Yes.

Women Intimidate Voters and Take Part in Election Riots

Doc. 64.5a: *Draft of letter from Lord Eglinton to Rt. Hon. J. H. Walpole, undated c. March–April 1852. Mayo Papers, MS 11031, NLI.*

The riots at Belfast, Limerick and Cork have been so serious that the demands from all parts for the protection of troops at the ensuing election have become so numerous that I am firmly convinced that an additional force of cavalry is absolutely necessary for the preservation of the public peace. We have already made every preparation in our power. All the cavalry at our disposal are now marching on their different parts. They have been apportioned troops to the different polling places and each will be able to attend two and some of them three elections but still there are many places where we know there will be voters left unprotected for there is an openly expressed determination on the part of the priests to carry their point by violence. In this they have succeeded in fact. The non-electors, the women and children, have been invited in the chapels to attend every polling place and mark the men who voted against their religion. Mobs of armed men have been going about at night dragging voters out of their beds and threatening them with instant death unless they promised to vote as they wished. . . .

Doc. 64.5b: Letter addressed to the Lord Lieutenant from magistrates at Stranorlar petty sessions, 16 August, 1852. Outrage Papers 1852, 7/1-7/434. NA.

Stranorlar Petty Sessions
16th August 1852

My Lord,

We consider it our duty to lay before your Excellency a statement of facts connected with the peace of this part of the country for your information and guidance. A short time before the election for this county a perfect stranger offered himself as a candidate on 'Tenant Right'[1] principles. He was at once adopted by the priest and all their powers were used to obtain support for him.

The Sunday before the election the priests of the three adjoining parishes desired their flocks to attend it, 'All who could walk or speak' and that votes for the 'enemy', meaning 'Hayes O'Connolly', were to be prevented going to vote by all means – the consequence was that at day break on the 27th ultimo enormous crowds of men, women and children assembled at different points on the road from Ballbofey to Lifford, and all voters supposed to be favourable to the old members were by force and violence prevented going to Lifford, and many respectable and unoffending persons were brutally beaten – Sir Edward Hayes and Mr Cockren (both magistrates) were shut up at Stranorlar for many hours with a party of freeholds, until liberated by a party of police. Mr Johnston Jr (with a party of Freeholders) was very roughly treated at Killygordan and obliged to fly in an opposite direction from Lifford. Mr Young (a magistrate) was most brutally assaulted at the same place, and obliged to return. On the night of that day large mobs visited the houses of very many voters and threatened them if they refused to vote for Campbell Johnston, and in many instances carried them away by force and compelled them to vote as they wished.

Since then, many persons who voted for Hayes O'Connolly have been violently assaulted at Ballybofey and such has been and is, the system of intimidation, and exclusive dealing adopted there, that the additional police which your Excellency has sent down there with a hope to be the means of preserving the peace of the district and also bringing to justice some of the guilty parties in the late outrages.

We remain your Excellency – faithful servants.

J. J. COLE [?]

JOHN CORCORAN

MR YOUNG.

1 Tenant Rights supporters wanted the implementation of the three 'Fs': free sale, fair rent and fixity of tenure.

Doc. 64.5c: Letter from Theo Kane to John Wynne, Esq., 15 July 1852, Outrage Papers, MS 1852/17/291, NA.

Limerick
July 15th 1852
7½, o c

Sir,

After sending my letter last evening to the Post Office – I regret to have to say that a riotous mob (principally composed of females) taking advantage of the temporary withdrawal of the military and police – attacked some houses – broke the windows and furniture and destroyed any property found in the shops and houses. The mobs were quickly dispersed by the magistrates aided by the military and police and quiet restored. This day the city is quiet and I see no reason to anticipate a renewal of the outrages of last evening.

I have the honour to be Sir
Your Obedient Servant
THEO KANE
Mayor

Doc. 64.5d: *The Tipperary Advocate*, 15 July 1865.

. . . In that yelling crowd of Langanites and O'Beirnites, all entangled and struggling in one heaving billow, young and old, lusty and infirm, male and female, were to be found shouting, whistling, groaning, dancing, foaming with irrepressible rage . . . here there was a fearful looking scene – well looking, well dressed girls, one a perfect Amazon, bared their arms, wound their shawls tightly around them, and rushed with the mêlée . . . That woman there, with the black chenille net and lilac muslin gown, is a perfect maniac . . . there is a little girl of sixteen, her features distorted and her whole frame quivering with frenzied agitation; now she beats the wooden planks and bites everything within her reach! . . .

Doc. 64.5e: *The Waterford Mail*, 18 September 1868.

. . . a number of women dressed in white, were mounted on cars, with green bushes in their hands, and they were guarded by a number of curious stragglers, amongst whom were several of the Catholic clergy . . . [procession attacked] . . . the roaring and screaming of women and children was shocking . . . there was a small black banner on which was inscribed 'Down with the moral assassin', this was in charge of a woman named Anne Moran or O'Brien, she acted the bravest of the brave. A mounted constable was directed to take the banner from her; she held her grip of it firmly and would not let go her hold. She was dragged under the horse's feet; she still held it, and would not let go . . .

Women Involved in a Political Demonstration

Doc. 64.6: *The Banner of Ulster*, 24 August 1869.

The following is taken from an account of a demonstration in Drogheda for the release of Fenian prisoners; about 10,000 individuals were said to be present.

[. . . [W]omen had their bonnets trimmed in green, or their hair bound in the national colour. From their necks flowed thin stripes of the green silk, in almost every instance some portion of their dress was rendered conspicuous by the introduction of the prevailing colour . . .]

Women Aid the Fenians

Doc. 64.7: Report from John Mallon to Dublin Metropolitan Police (DMP) 17 May 1878. Fenian Papers, File A585, NA.

With regard to the importation of rifles I have heard that they are frequently packed in the casks and cases containing American beef. This information I must take for its worth, and it relates principally to a Mrs Carroll of Mary Street, who deals in American beef and is the aunt of Peter Doyle . . .

Women and the Land War

Doc. 64.8: *Report from the Select Committee of the House of Lords on Irish Jury Laws* HL 1881 (117), viii.

[Evidence of Adam Mitchell, Sessional Crown Solicitor, King's County. There was a very bad case I prosecuted not long ago in Tullamore at the petty sessions, in which nine women were charged with violently beating a process server, taking the processes from him and throwing them into the canal. They battered his face. There were nine charged, and the magistrate convicted six out of the nine, and sentenced them to a month's imprisonment.]

Formal Political Involvement

LADIES' ANTI-SLAVERY SOCIETY

Doc. 65: *Annual Report of the Cork Ladies' Anti-Slavery Society for 1845* (Cork, 1845).

Irish women and men had been concerned with the issue of slavery from the eighteenth century. Anti-slavery societies were organised by women from at least the 1830s. One of the earliest societies formed was the Hibernian Ladies' Negroes' Friend Society. A Cork Ladies' Anti-Slavery Society was in existence from 1845 to 1847. These societies appear to have been organised by Quaker women. The primary objective was to raise the consciousness of the Irish people as to the horrors of slavery. Members corresponded with their English and American counterparts and sought support for their cause, primarily by appealing to other women.

The time for preparing articles for the 'TWELFTH BOSTON BAZAAR' is fast approaching. The friends of freedom will rejoice to hear that the fair held last Christmas in Boston was more productive and attractive than any former one.

Mrs Chapman, in a letter to one of our secretaries, writes thus, 'your beautiful consignments never fail to command great admiration and high prices' – further on she adds, 'all the things that came from Ireland, this year, (1844) sold with the utmost rapidity, all at good prices, and some at very high prices.'

From an account of the fair, published at full length in the American Anti-Slavery Standard, we extract the following:

The sense of what our cause owes to the friends in Great Britain and Ireland, in particular, has been officially expressed, as follows, in the recent quarterly meeting of the Boston Female Anti-Slavery Society:

Resolved – That the Boston Female Anti-Slavery Society takes this earliest opportunity to express to the abolitionists of Glasgow, Dublin, Edinburgh, London, Darlington, Tynemouth, Bristol, Tralee, Belfast, Limerick, Cork, Walthamstow, Woburn, Wrexham, and all the other beloved friends in Great Britain, who have aided the Eleventh Massachusetts Anti-Slavery Fair, the deep and grateful sense that we cherish, in common with all Anti-Slavery Americans, of the tender sympathy, the important pecuniary help, and the efficient

251

testimony which they have both now and always given to use in our advocacy of the cause.

The Fair was never before so productive, so attractive, and beautiful; and this we owe, in a large measure, to the taste, skill, and liberality of our British coadjutors.

. . . The question is often asked, 'how are the funds thus raised employed?' In the words of an American Anti-Slavery address, we would answer – 'The funds raised will be devoted, as heretofore, to the diffusion of Anti-Slavery Truth, and to sustaining and cheering onward such devoted persons as have given their lives to the glad yet severe service of arousing an unwilling nation to a sense of its moral responsibilities'.

Never have the American Abolitionists stood more in need of the combined and strenuous exertions of the friends of freedom – than at the present crisis. Texas, another Slave State of immense extent, has been added to the United States – thus increasing the preponderance in Congress of the slavery party, and also causing, what was feared, a considerable advance in the price of Slaves – thus giving an additional impulse and stimulus to the domestic Slave Trade – the horrors and atrocities of which no pen can fully describe . . .

WOMEN OF YOUNG IRELAND

Doc. 66: Women of Young Ireland, MS 10906, NLI.

The Young Irelanders launched the first issue of The Nation *in October 1842. They advocated physical force to secure independence from England, and organised an abortive rebellion at the height of the Famine in 1848. The Young Irelanders were also cultural nationalists. They were intellectual idealists who advocated self-reliance and self-respect for the Irish people. The following appeal to the women of Ireland appeared in the* United Irishman[1] *of 22 May 1848. It was written by Ellen Downing (1828–1869), who was a native of Cork. Her first poem appeared in* The Nation, *and she contributed about forty poems to that paper between 1845 and 1847. Downing later became a nun and joined the Presentation community in Cork but left due to ill-health. In 1860 she became the matron of the Cork Fever Hospital where she remained for a year. She appears to have suffered much ill-health and died in January 1869.*[2]

With desolation is the land made desolate because no one reflected in his heart . . . Long before, I have striven with my weak endeavours to work

1 The *United Irishman* was a republican newspaper established by the Young Irelander John Mitchell (1815–75) to advocate Irish separation from England.

2 For more information on Downing, see, Anon., 'More about Mary of *The Nation*', *The Irish Monthly* (1908).

for Ireland, because she is my country, and 'twas right to love and serve her. Won't you begin, too, and let us all work together? There is one thing which the least of us may do – support native manufacture – and, if all of us would write in this, it would be a great step towards Nationhood . . . [Do you love your country at all, and do you value your dress? If you cannot consent to wear a coarser dress for the sake of freedom and virtue, you don't deserve to be the wives and mothers of free men, and never will be, take my word for it, for 'no nation was ever great whose women were contemptible'] But that you will never be. You have not acted because you have not understood. For your country – your souls – your God – heart's soul will you do it? Some of us may work for charity, and others for freedom; but for heaven's sake, let each and all of us work. . . .

'EVA' OF *THE NATION*

Doc. 67: *Poems by 'Eva' of The Nation* (Dublin, 1909).

Mary Eva Kelly (18[?] – 1908) was born in Galway. Her first poem to appear in The Nation *was 'The Banshee'. She also contributed prose essays and ballads. She eventually emigrated to Australia with her husband Kevin Izod O'Doherty. They returned to Ireland in 1886, and O'Doherty became an MP for County Meath.[1] The following poems show how women, as mothers, could play their part in opposing British rule.*

The Patriot Mother

The darkest wrong your power can do
Can alter not the vow,
Which says my children ne'er shall see
That brand upon my brow.

The true man's words are borne aloft,
To shine among the stars;
We cherish them within our hearts
Despite of bolts and bars.
'Mid all our sorrow and our wrongs,
Our deep and burning shame,
The Brighter, purer for it all
Appears O'Donnell's[2] name!

---

1 See introduction to *Poems by 'Eva' of The Nation* (Dublin, 1909).
2 A peasant farmer who had refused to be sworn in evidence against the Young Irelander, Smith O'Brien in 1848.

The Patriot Mother

[*A Ballad of '98*]

'Come, tell us the names of the rebelly crew
Who lifted the pike on the Curragh with you;
Come, tell us their treason, and then you'll be free,
Or right quickly you'll swing from the high gallows tree.

'*Alanna! alanna!*[1] the shadow of shame
Has never yet fallen on one of your name,
And, oh, may the food from my bosom you drew
In your veins turn to poison if *you* turn untrue.

'The foul words, oh, let them not blacken your tongue,
That would prove to your friends and your country a wrong,
Or the curse of a mother, so bitter and dread,
With the wrath of the Lord – may they fall on your head!

'I have no one but you in the whole world wide,
Yet, false to your pledge, you'd ne'er stand at my side;
If a traitor you lived, you'd be farther away
From my heart, than if true you were wrapped in the clay.

'Oh, deeper and darker the mourning would be
For your falsehood so base, than your death, proud and free –
Dearer, far dearer, than ever to me,
My darling, you'll be on the brave gallows tree.

'Tis holy, *a ghra*,[2] from the bravest and best –
Go! go! from my heart, and be joined with the rest;
Alanna machree! O alanna machree![3]
Sure a "stag"[4] and a traitor you never will be.'

There's no look of a traitor upon the young brow
That's raised to the tempters to haughtily now;
No traitor e'er held up the firm head so high –
No traitor e'er showed such a proud, flashing eye.

1 My child, my child.
2 My love.
3 O child of my heart.
4 An informer.

The Contagious Diseases Acts allowed for the compulsory inspectio
for venereal diseases in certain army camps in England and Irei.
the Acts, a woman could be arrested by a policeman on suspicion of being a
prostitute and taken before a magistrate, who had the power to certify her as a
'common prostitute' and order her to be subjected to a medical examination. If
found to be suffering from a venereal disease she was forcibly detained in a Lock
hospital.[1] There was no similar check on men. The following notice refers to the
operation of these acts at the Curragh army camp in County Kildare.

War Office Circular Regarding the Medical Examination of Prostitutes

Doc. 68.1: Contagious Diseases Act, 1866 to 1869, notice issued
by the War Office, 18 September 1869.

CURRAGH DISTRICT

Periodical Examinations of the Common Women

1. All women subject to the provisions of the above Act are to be called upon to sign the Voluntary Submission Paper (vide 2nd Schedule, Form H).
2. Should any woman object to sign, she is to be informed of the penal consequences attending such refusal, and the advantages of a voluntary submission are to be pointed out to her.
3. Any such woman still refusing to submit herself is to be proceeded against under Section 4, Act of 1869, her name being first reported to the sub-inspector of constabulary at Kildare, and his sanction obtained.
4. A complete register is to be kept by the police of all women subject to the provisions of the Act.
5. Periodical examinations are made of such women at the time and place hereafter mentioned.
6. Such examinations being made by [a] visiting surgeon in the presence of a female attendant, and no other person, until further ordered.
Place of such examination: – Lock Hospital, Kildare.
Time of such examinations: – At 2 p.m. on Mondays.
One-third of the women weekly, and absentees from examinations at the next examination to that which they ought to have attended.
All new-comers into the district to be brought immediately under the operation of the Act.

By Order of the Secretary of State for War
War Office,
18th September, 1869

1 A Lock hospital was the name given to the medical institution which treated patients for venereal diseases. The word 'Lock' derives from the medieval 'Loke', a house for lepers.

Isabella Tod Opposes the Contagious Diseases Acts

Doc. 68.2: *Annual Report of the Ladies' National Association for the Repeal of the Contagious Diseases Acts, 1878* (London, 1878).

The introduction of the Contagious Diseases Acts heralded the beginning of the first feminist organisation in Ireland. Opposition to the Acts arose for a number of reasons. By some, the Acts were seen as an interference with civil liberties; by others, as the recognition and support of vice by the state. The Ladies' National Association was formed in England by Josephine Butler[1] in 1869 to campaign for the repeal of the Acts. The LNA opposed the Acts on various grounds, amongst which were the fact that they applied solely to women, and that they legitimated the prevalent double standard of sexual morality. By 1871 the LNA had branches in Belfast, Dublin and Cork. Isabella Tod and Anna Haslam were involved in the campaign from the beginning. The following extracts are taken from the annual reports published by the LNA. The first is from an address given by Isabella Tod to the annual meeting of the LNA held in Dublin in 1878. The second extract is taken from the 1882 annual report. In each annual report a section was given over to 'local reports' sent in by various branches of the association throughout Britain and Ireland. Tod and Haslam provided information on the extent of their work in Ireland. The Irish branches of the LNA survived until about 1884. The Contagious Diseases Acts were suspended in 1883, and repealed in 1886.

. . . [t]he unfortunate class of women against whom the Contagious Diseases Acts are directed are human beings like ourselves, the causes of whose fall are intelligible always, and generally most pitiable – not monsters of exceptional depravity, removed from all our sympathies. And yet I do think it is of more moment to remember, not so much the child that has been worse than murdered, or the girl whose best affections have been made the instrument of her ruin, as the hundreds and thousands of wretched and repulsive women, against whom society has sinned more deeply still. The ignorance, the hopeless poverty, the feebleness of mind and body inherited from debased parents, which simply leave these women without a chance of leading any other life than that of sin, are the fault not of one bad man, but of every man and woman in the community who is not stoutly fighting against their causes. This, therefore, is the especial call which our Ladies' National Association makes to every town and every circle – wash your hands clean from this stain – help us, first, to get rid of this legislation of despair – and in doing this work, and fighting this battle, help us on the one hand to uphold the same standard of Christian morality for men and women alike, and on the other to remove the evils, social and economic, which leave too many women ready for a prey. No doubt, it is not easy work to which we call you – you, Christian women, especially. I do not know whether we have been

---

1 Josephine Butler (1828–1906), became involved in the rescue of prostitutes in the 1850s. She formed, and led, the Ladies' National Association from 1869 to 1886.

hearing more than usual of the angry and contemptuous words which some people fling at every woman who comes forward actively to care for, or plead for, those whom society chooses to ignore. But it is at any rate necessary that we should clearly make up our minds as to what is our duty, and as to the reasons which make it right for us to know the facts – both as to the nature and working of the Contagious Diseases Acts, and as to the ends aimed at by the promoters, and the results – and to act upon that knowledge. Men and women are the two great halves of the human race, and are placed under the same law of God – the law of personal purity – a law which is alike enforced by all the discovered laws of moral and physical science. Violations of this law injure all society, for God has made of one blood all classes as well as races of men; and one cannot sin or suffer without all suffering, directly or indirectly. Simply as human beings, therefore, ladies who have sheltered and happy homes are bound to know whether any class of human beings is being dealt with oppressively, and, if so, to endeavour to prevent it. But they have a social duty in this case of oppression, because it is in their hands that the moral standard of the world is placed. It is quite a common-place of moralists, that it is the purity of women which is the salt of society. Yet when they go down to see the evils that are in the world, and seriously set themselves to cure them, they must be prepared to face an illogical and truly irreligious outcry at their doing so. Here we must not listen to man, but to God. We have not forgotten that our Lord Himself is the great exemplar of all Christians, men and women alike. We have to follow Him who 'went about doing good'. Moreover, we cannot help seeing that, to a very great extent, the triumph of the highest truth, in all social questions, depends upon the part which good women take in them. In nothing is this more true than in regard to the way in which society treats fallen women. Under the Contagious Diseases Acts it is women who suffer, women who are oppressed and degraded by the soul-crushing machinery of State regulation of vice – it is the poverty of women which is the very greatest of all the causes of their destruction – it is the inequality of the laws that affect women, and the still greater inequality of social judgments, that make that utter destruction possible. Is it any wonder that good women, who have the power and the will to act according to their consciences, feel it to be their most pressing duty to enquire into the causes of the misery of their weaker sisters – to set their whole heart to lessen or prevent them – and to stand between the victims and a still greater and fouler wrong than they have yet endured? We are not striving merely to get these inequitable and iniquitous laws repealed; we are aiming at the elevation of the tone of society on all these topics, as well as the purification of the statute-book. But it is not only the salvation of women which depends upon the fearless re-assertion of God's equal law of purity for both sexes. Who has a right to say that men are too pitiably weak to bear such a law? That they are incapable of responding to higher calls than those of self-indulgence? There are men who say it; and it is they who have

257

elaborated this and similar systems of State provision for vice – for safe and decorous and guaranteed vice – because they say that men must sin, and that a certain number of women, who have fallen out of the knowledge of society, may lawfully be seized and sacrificed for it.

Let no one imagine that we think less of this sin, this enormous sin, when committed by women, than our opponents do. On the contrary, it is our horror at the soul-destroying nature of the sin of unchastity, of its awful consequences both for time and eternity, which makes us seek the abolition of the Contagious Diseases Acts, and of all similar legislation; which is and must be based on the idea that vice is a necessity. These Acts are not only the offspring of sin, but of premeditated sin. Whatever were the motives of the ostensible movers in the matter, the men who devised such legislation meant to make it easy and safe to snatch at sensual pleasures, without caring at what cost to those who sinned with them.

Annual Report of the Ladies' National Association for the Repeal of the Contagious Diseases Acts

Doc. 68.3: *Annual Report of the Ladies' National Association for the Repeal of the Contagious Diseases Acts, 1882* (London, 1882).

Belfast – Our committee is thankful to find that a very great increase in interest in the subject of repeal has taken placed during the past year, not only in Belfast, but in many parts of Ulster where its influence is more or less felt. Early in the year the series of meetings which had been begun in the previous year was continued. Some were large and others small, but the object aimed at – namely, to carry information into every important division of the town and neighbourhood, and to arouse the active sympathies of every religious lady and philanthropic organisation – was to a considerable extent attained. The indirect results of this work have been of the most marked character.

During the sitting of the Select Committee of the House of Commons, our committee felt that it could give best help in regard to it by circulating the report of the conference in London, in October, 1881, and another summary in leaflet form – the evidence itself being by no means clear enough for popular use. But upon the close of that inquiry we have circulated a considerable mass of literature to enable the leaders of other good work to see their duty in regard to it. Having addressed to Mr Stansfeld two resolutions on the subject of the Select Committee's report, they received from him a most valuable letter, showing the spirit in which the work ought to be carried on by women, which they printed, and which was largely circulated in England and Scotland, as well as in Ireland.

In October we had the pleasure of a visit from Mrs Steward, of Ongar, – the first time in our thirteen years of vigorous life that any member of the LNA has visited us. We had fine meetings, which did the greatest possible good.

We have just adopted the plan of forming a list of associates – ladies who are interested in our work, but have not time, or live at too great a distance, to attend committees. This is chiefly with a view to register our scattered forces throughout Ulster, and we have already obtained some very influential names. – I.M.S. Tod.

Dublin – The Ladies' committee has met pretty regularly this year, and has tried to keep up the interest of friends here, by circulating papers, canvassing for signatures to petitions, and holding a few meetings. Fifty-three petitions were forwarded to the House of Commons, and seven to the House of Lords for the better protection of young girls, &c. In May, during the Friends' annual gathering, a meeting of women Friends was held, when Mrs Wigham read a very interesting paper giving a resumé of work in Great Britain and the Continent, during the past year. Mrs Richardson, of Plymouth, also delivered a very touching address on her experiences at Plymouth and neighbouring districts. She also attended the usual committee meeting, and delivered a similar address. In October, during the annual session of the Christian Convention, Mrs Steward, of Ongar, favoured us with her company, and addressed four meetings, viz., a drawing-room gathering at Mrs John Webb's, a mothers' meeting of poor women in Strand Street Institute, a little company at the Friends' Meeting House, Monkstown, and a meeting in the small hall, Christian Union Buildings, presided over by Mrs Richard Allen. It was a very favoured time, and Mrs Steward's addresses moved the hearts of many ladies, who, we trust, will help us more vigorously in the future. Petitions were signed at all these meetings and a good deal of literature distributed. A. Haslam.

The Ladies' Land League

A BRANCH OF THE LADIES' LAND LEAGUE IN ACTION

Doc. 69: Minute Book of the Maryborough[1] branch of the Ladies' Land League.
Lalor Papers, MS 2070, NLI.

⌈*The Ladies' Land League was formed in New York on 15 October 1880 to raise funds for the National Land League. Fanny Parnell (1848–82) and Anna Parnell (1852–1911) were the leading forces behind its foundation, and on 31 January 1881 helped to found the Ladies' Irish National Land League in Dublin. At this time the Land War was at its height and, realising that it was only a matter of time before they would be arrested, the leaders of the Land League, Michael Davitt, Charles Stewart Parnell and others, looked to the Ladies' Land League to take over their work, and to provide relief to evicted tenants.*⌉*The Ladies' Land League kept a register of evicted tenants, rents and valuations and the names of the landlords and their agents. They also engaged in propaganda and relief work.*⌋ *The executive of the LLL met once a week, and its reports were published in the* Freeman's Journal. *Numerous branches of the LLL were formed throughout the country. The following document reports the establishment of a branch of the LLL in County Offaly. Meetings of the LLL were frequently interrupted by the RIC.[2] In December 1881 Hannah Reynolds was imprisoned for her League activities and spent a month in Cork Gaol. A copy of her letter to Mrs A. M. Sullivan,[3] of the London branch of the LLL, shows her determination in her work. Thirteen members of the LLL were to be imprisoned before the League was disbanded in 1882.*

Maryborough, Queen's Co
16 February 1881

At a meeting of the ladies of Maryboro' held this day, the following resolutions were adopted unanimously.

1 Now called Portlaoise.
2 The Royal Irish Constabulary, the Irish police force.
3 Frances Sullivan was the Irish–American wife of Alexander Martin Sullivan (1830–84), an Irish MP. She was a founding member of the Ladies' Land League.

Proposed by Mrs J. T. Whelan. Seconded by Miss Burke. Resolved that we hereby form a branch of the Irish National Ladies' Land Relief League. That the following officers and committee be appointed.

President   Mrs Fitzpatrick Tenahill
Treasurer   Mrs Corcoran Maryboro'
Assistant do Miss Mary Lalor Tenahill
Committee Mrs Mary Doran, Mrs Nora Meehan, Mrs Mary Redington, Miss Mary Gowing, Miss Julia Condran, Miss Julia Gowing, Miss Bridget Burke, Miss M. A. Denis, Mrs Mary Tynan, Miss Johanna Walshe, Mrs M. Kelly, Mrs J. T. Phelan, Miss Duff, Mrs Bowes, Mrs Burton, Miss Bray, Mrs Aldriff, Miss Fitzpatrick.

Proposed by Mrs Tynan. Seconded by Miss Gowing. Resolved that the officers of the committee as at present constituted are hereby elected for a period of one year.

Proposed by Miss Lalor. Seconded by Mrs Redington. Resolved that we hereby put on record our sympathy with our brothers throughout Ireland in their struggle against the oppression and misgovernment of our country and we protest against the arrest of Mr Michael Davitt and against the Coercion Act[1] which the British government, with its usual policy, is forging for our country.

Proposed by Miss Duff. Seconded by Miss Dunne. Resolved that the following be appointed a council to carry out all details in connection with our Relief League Mrs Fitzpatrick, Mrs Corcoran, Miss Murphy, Miss Lalor, Mrs Doran, Mrs Meehan, Miss Walshe.

Proposed by Mrs Meehan. Seconded by Mrs Redington. Resolved that the council meet every second Wednesday and the committee meetings be held on the first Wednesday in every month.

After receiving subscriptions the meeting adjourned.

H. Fitzpatrick . . .

February 10th 1882

A meeting of the committee was held. Mrs Fitzpatrick, president, in the chair. Mrs Tynan, treas., Mrs Corcoran, vice-pres., Mrs N. Fitzpatrick, Mrs Aldritt, Mrs Kelly, Miss Dunne, Mrs Redington, Miss J. Gowing, Miss Whelan, Miss Condran, Mrs McDermot. Shortly after meeting began the head constable acting sergeant put in an appearance, after addressing some few important remarks to the president who answered them too much to the point to give them satisfaction they quietly withdrew – several new members were enrolled, cards filled and subs handed in –

Mannie Fitzpatrick.

---

1 The Protection of Person and Property Act of 1881, was known as the Coercion Act, and it gave the authorities power to arrest on suspicion.

1881 – number of members in branch February 16th.
117 to 27th February
105 to 25th March 1881
103 to 11th May 1881
108 to 24th December 1881

City Gaol
Cork
Cell No. 48

To Mrs A. M. Sullivan.

Dear Madam,

Will you kindly present to the Central Committee of the Ladies' Land League of London my grateful thanks and warm appreciation of the highly flattering resolution passed by them in my favour at their meeting on the 3rd inst.

When the government has graciously provided for all the ladies in Ireland by giving them quarters in Her Majesty's Hotels throughout the country – then on our sisters in England and elsewhere will devolve the entire duty to carry on the great and Christian work of Charity for which our league was formed. May the staff daily increase a hundredfold is the sincere wish of yours truly.

HANNAH M. REYNOLDS

ARCHBISHOP MCCABE OPPOSES THE LADIES' LAND LEAGUE[1]

Doc. 70: *Freeman's Journal,* 12 March 1881.

The formation of the Ladies' Land League provoked serious opposition. Amongst its clerical opponents was Archbishop McCabe who issued a pastoral letter, read at Mass in all the churches of the archdiocese of Dublin, condemning the Ladies' Land League. The pastoral caused outrage and members of the League quickly wrote letters in their defence to local and national newspapers. McCabe's pastoral evoked an ideal image of Irish womanhood, similar to that found in prescriptive literature of the period. The pastoral letter not only caused outrage amongst the members of the League, but also roused other clerics, particularly Archbishop Croke of Cashel,[2] to come to the League's defence.

---

1 Edward McCabe (1816–85) was Archbishop of Dublin from 1879.
2 Thomas William Croke (1824–1902), was Archbishop of Cashel from 1875.

. . . [t]he daughters of our Catholic people, be they matrons or virgins, are called forth, under the flimsy pretext of charity, to take their stand in the noisy streets of life. The pretext of charity is merely assumed. . . . They are asked to forget the modesty of their sex and the high dignity of their womanhood by leaders who seem reckless of consequences, and who by that recklessness have brought misery on many families. God grant that they may not have brought defeat on the cause which they appeared to advocate.

. . . Very Rev. dear fathers, set your face against this dishonouring attempt, and do not tolerate in your societies the women who so far disavows her birthright of modesty as to parade herself before the public gaze in a character so unworthy as a Child of Mary.[1] This attempt at degrading the women of Ireland comes very appropriately from men who have drawn the country into the present terribly deplorable condition. . .

THE *ENGLISHWOMAN'S REVIEW* APPROVES ACTION AGAINST THE LADIES' LAND LEAGUE

Doc. 71: *Englishwoman's Review*, 14 January 1882.

In October 1881, the government banned the Land League and imprisoned its leaders. From October women were in control of the Land League movement. The Englishwoman's Review *of January 1882 provided details of the repressive measures to be taken by the police. The authorities used the concept of 'good behaviour', or being 'bound to the peace', as an excuse to imprison women. To this end they invoked an ancient statute dating from the time of Edward III who had reigned in the fourteenth century. This statute allowed anyone suspected of bad behaviour to be asked to give bail; if they refused they could be sent to prison. It is clear from the report attached to the police circular that the EWR, the feminist journal of the period, was not sympathetic to the LLL.*

Royal Irish Constabulary Office, Dublin Castle

1. The Inspector-General is advised that the proclamation of his Excellency the Lord Lieutenant, dated the 20th of October, 1881, and which declared the Land League to be an unlawful and a criminal association, included female as well as male persons, and that the promotion of the objects and purposes of that association on any pretext by females, whether under the name of Ladies' Land League or any other designation, is unlawful and criminal.

---

1 The Children of Mary was a Society organised by nuns in Catholic schools. Girls were encouraged to emulate Mary, the Mother of God.

2. When the constabulary have reason to believe that a meeting of females for any such object or purpose is intended to be held in any house, they shall warn the owner or occupier of such house that he will act criminally and at his peril in permitting his house to be used for such unlawful and criminal purpose; and they shall also warn every person who they have reason to believe is about to attend or take part in any such meeting; and he or she will act criminally and at his or her peril in doing so.

3. In other cases when the constabulary find any females, either collectively or individually, actually engaged in promoting any such objects or purpose, they are forthwith to take the offender or offenders before a magistrate and apply that she or they may be bound with solvent sureties to good behaviour or to the peace (as the case may be), or in default committed to prison: and the constabulary are to report any repetition of the offence, in order that the more stringent measures of the law may, if necessary, be enforced against the offender in addition to the estreat of the reognizances.[1]

4. Females who take part in or incite to any unlawful assembly are forthwith to be made amenable and prosecuted in the ordinary way.

The police authorities in Dublin have at last discovered that, when the Land League was proclaimed illegal, the proclamation included the Ladies' Land League as well as the one over which Mr Parnell presided. How there could be any doubt on this question surpasses all understanding. When the Protection Act was before parliament efforts were made to exclude women from its provisions. The government repeatedly and positively refused to make any such exemption. They could not have taken any other course without making themselves and the law ridiculous. It has been our decided opinion, expressed again and again, that it was absurd to summarily suppress the Land League as an illegal association, and to allow the Ladies' Land League, with the same objects, to hold meetings, and even individual members to interfere with the action of the police. When the *United Ireland*[2] newspaper was seized last Friday several ladies of the Ladies' Land League appeared on the scene and openly challenged the legality of the authorities. They avowedly directed the newspaper, and supplied the money to keep it going. They were in communication with the treasurer of the League in Paris, and telegraphed to him for instructions. It is not denied that since the Land League was suppressed the Ladies' Land League have been carrying on all the operations. The law in criminal acts can make no distinction between men and women. There ought never to have been any doubt or hesitation respecting the course the police authorities ought to pursue under such circumstances.

The circular now issued ought not to have been necessary. If women choose to engage in an illegal confederacy for the non-payment of rents,

1 A copy of the court record of a fine for use in a prosecution.
2 *United Ireland* was a weekly newspaper founded in 1881 and under the direct control of Charles Stewart Parnell.

or to deprive any persons of their property, they have no right whatever to expect immunity. They must accept the full responsibility for their acts, and cannot justly plead any privilege of sex. The notion is absurd. Why, indeed, should they not, like their husbands and brothers, be prepared to incur the consequences such illegal proceedings involve? The suppression of the Land League while allowing the Ladies' Land League to exist, was a half-measure. It has had the common result of such half-measures. The snake was scotched, not killed. It has revived into vigorous life, eager to bite the hand which, through mistaken indulgence, sought to protect it as an act of gallantry. It is much to be regretted that there should be any occasion for such repressive measures: but since they are necessary they ought to be systematically and resolutely carried out.

JENNIE WYSE POWER DESCRIBES THE ACTIVITIES OF THE LADIES' LAND LEAGUE

Doc. 72: *Sinn Féin,* 16 October 1909.

One of the women who became prominent in the LLL was Jennie O'Toole (1858–1941), who later became Jennie Wyse Power. Wyse Power went on to become involved in the suffrage campaign. She became the first president of Cumann na mBan,[1] and was active in the 1916 Rising. Following the establishment of the independent Irish state, she was appointed to the first senate. In 1909 she gave a lecture on the Land League, and outlined the role of the Ladies' Land League during the Land War.

. . . It occurred to the leaders that the way to arrange for the continuity of their task was to start a Ladies' Irish National Land League. Accordingly, on the 4th February, 1881, we find published an appeal to their countrywomen signed by Miss Anna Parnell, Clare Stritch, Nanie Lynch, and Harriet Byrne, calling for help in the impending crisis. Branches were formed rapidly, and the women at head-quarters set about the work that was before them. It is useless to conceal the fact that between the men and women's League there was not complete unity of method or administrative work. In Miss Parnell's recently published 'History of the Land League' she shows minutely how the differences arose, and how the policy of 'No rent at the point of the bayonet' was only a farce as a fighting strategy, seeing that the enormous costs entailed by this procedure had to be paid out of the funds collected.[2] A more serious

1 See below p 314.
2 Anna Parnell deemed that the Land League's policy of 'rent at the point of a bayonet' demanded a general resistance to the payment of rent. She also realised the the Land League had no intention of pursuing this policy. She later stated that if she had been fully aware of the Land League's intentions she would not have become involved in the Land League. See Anna Parnell, *Tale of a Great Sham*, ed. Dana Hearne (Dublin, 1986).

consequence was the demoralising influence this policy of make-believe fight had when the time came to proclaim 'No Rent'.

During the interval, the Ladies' Land League, as well as the Land League, had their hands full, as evictions, seizures of crops and cattle and arrests were the order of each day. The police went to evictions with fixed bayonet and ball-cartridge, and frequently were soon returning in a state of intoxication, having beaten women and children with the butt end of their rifles. In order that these ruffians could not be identified they were brought from different localities. . . . On the 18th October the Irish National Land League held its last meeting, with Father Cantwell, Adm., of Thurles in the chair. . . . Then follows the period that men became panic-stricken and fled to England or the continent. The entire staff of the Land League were under arrest and the country was practically in a state of war. Thousands of tenants were under eviction notices, hundreds of men were in prison without trial, and the only remaining shield between the oppressor and the oppressed was the women of the country who had joined the Land League. Looking back upon that period one wonders how those women undertook and carried out the enormous and responsible work that lay before them. It became necessary for them to direct the movements of the male organisers who travelled quietly through the country to see that the enormous sums of money necessary for the upkeep and housing of the evicted tenants, the sustenance of close on one thousand men in the jails, and for many other necessary works of importance and political necessity, reached the proper quarter regularly. To understand the difficulties of this undertaking one practically needs to have lived and worked through the strenuous period I chronicle.

But an instance of my own personal experience will best serve to illustrate the difficulties that had to be encountered in order to carry on the work of providing for those about to be evicted. It so happened that I found myself in the country that is my native place in November of this year, and where a whole estate were being evicted for non-payment of rent on principle. Fifty families were to be sheltered and looked after. The little village of Hacketstown, on the borders of Wicklow and Carlow, was the centre of operations. For the purpose of being close to the scene, I stayed in a licensed premises, whose proprietor was a member of the local League, the ordinary hotel of the village being under a boycott[1] – for what reason I never could make out. The evening before the expected evictions I went abroad to see what could be done to house the families about to be evicted, and took on myself to hire and repair a large disused house, sufficient to shelter three families. When I returned to my lodgings I found that a detachment of soldiers were quartered in the house, and that the ladies in Dublin had sent down Miss Helen Taylor, a sympathetic Englishwoman of advanced years, and Miss Cantwell, of Dublin, whose age was fifteen

---

1 This means that the local community refused to have any dealings with this business. Named after Capt. C. Boycott, land-agent, who had refused to reduce rents after a bad harvest. The Irish Land League encouraged the tenants to have no dealings or communication with him.

years. When we were making plans for the morrow's work the local constabulary men entered and insisted on having our names and addresses, and warned us against unlawful assembly and illegal practices. Next morning we were out with the tenants before the eviction began, and in all cases were prevented by the police when possible from speaking to those about to be cast out of their homes. It required young hearts and stout wills to outwit these officers of law and order, so as to be able to reach the houses – ditch-climbing became an accomplishment – without which one was [of] little use. Unless you were able to get to the house before the police and soldiery, all chance of keeping the tenant (by gentle persuasion) in the combination was over. On the second day, the law officers made up their minds to prevent us speaking with the tenants before eviction, and it then became necessary to surround us individually with red coats. In the midst of all this the arms and ammunition of the detachment of soldiers were stolen, and we were all practically under arrest in the little licensed house, being only allowed egress under an escort. On the second day after the disappearance of the arms the sergeant asked to see me alone, and offered me his hand and heart if I only told him where his guns were. I lost that chance, not knowing their whereabouts. But some days after they were found concealed under the rafters of a church two miles away, where they might have remained till this day but for an informer. This incident increased our difficulties ten-fold, and to this day I can never understand how the work we set before ourselves was ever carried out.

The attack on the Ladies' Land League

On the 16th December, the Inspector General of the RIC thought he would send out a circular – of which practically no notice was taken by the women – but arrests of their members throughout the country began. Miss Reynolds was seized and imprisoned. Her arrest caused widespread alarm amongst the friends of the Ladies' Land League, and it acted as a danger signal to those at head-quarters, who by this time were forced to toil through the greater part of the 24 hours, in order to cope with the work, which kept on increasing. For already there had been added to our ordinary and extra-ordinary cares, the conduct of the Land League organ – United Ireland, brought under the ban by the Liberal government. Mr William O'Brien,[1] its editor, was in jail with all the other members of the staff. The difficulty of printing and circulating the paper was enormous, and it was found necessary to have the paper printed in a different centre weekly. Beginning in Liverpool, and moving along, as far as Paris. After a few weeks of this, we started to print and circulate it from its own office at 32 Lower Abbey Street, and while the DMP[2] were watching and seizing all suspicious-looking matter on the quays, we were taking away the illegal production, concealed in our clothing, and

1 William O'Brien (1852–1928), editor of the newspaper United Ireland, MP from 1883–1918.
2 Dublin Metropolitan Police.

267

distributing it all over Ireland from our private addresses. When the editor of the *Freeman's Journal* heard that we intended to continue printing the paper he wrote: 'I hear the LLL [Ladies' Land League] are going to take over *United Ireland* but it is absurd to think that a handful of girls can defy the government.' However, as events proved, we defied them. Mr Forster[1] followed up the imprisonment of Miss Reynolds by arrests in Kerry, Limerick, Athlone, and other places, but our movement was only stirred to new vigour, and in the early days of 1882, he determined to have two more of us, and issued the usual proclamation stating that we were 'unlawful females' and that after that date, if we were found assembling for any purpose whatsoever, we were to take the consequences. I remember well the night that we read this proclamation in the evening papers, and heard the newsboys cry out: 'The Ladies' Land League proclaimed – the whole discovery now found out.' Our answer to that proclamation was a direction to all our branches to meet the following Sunday at a certain hour and let Mr Forster do what he could. Most loyally was that direction obeyed. Not one of our numerous branches faltered, and the RIC was helpless. In almost every village in Ireland we had branches, so it will be understood how difficult it would have been to arrest so many women at one stroke. This finished the career of Mr Forster as a politician; he became the laughing-stock of Europe, and our work went on as if no proclamation had appeared. . . .

---

1 William Edward Forster (1818–86), Chief Secretary for Ireland from 1880 to 1882.

The Suffrage Issue

THOMAS HASLAM ARGUES FOR WOMEN'S SUFFRAGE

Doc. 73: *The Women's Advocate*, 1 April 1874.

The Quaker couple, Thomas and Anna Haslam, worked together to fight for women's suffrage in Ireland. Thomas published a series of pamphlets in April, May and July 1874 promoting suffrage. It seems that The Women's Advocate *was the first attempt at creating a forum for debate on the subject. It was not until the advent of* The Irish Citizen *in 1912 that a newspaper was devoted entirely to debating issues relating to feminism and suffrage.*

It is a reproach to our metropolis that the claims of women to a more positive legal status have not received a cordial recognition from our press. Those claims are manifestly just in themselves; no valid argument has been produced against them; they are the claims of the weaker sex upon the stronger; and they appeal with especial force to the generous sentiments which are supposed to be inherent in our national character. There must surely be some cogent reason for this reluctance to support a cause which has so many weighty arguments upon its side. We are not aware of any ground for such reluctance, except, perhaps, the defective taste in which the rights of women have been sometimes championed by imprudent advocates. Now, granting that some over-zealous partisans have transgressed good taste in their platform utterances, is that a reason why our countrywomen should be defrauded of their just rights? We put this query frankly to every candid Irishman; is it right that women should be denied all participation in the blessing of self-government, because a few enthusiasts in the United States have been too emphatic in the assertion of their equality with men? This appears to be the substance of the issue between us. The moral right of properly-qualified women to some share in the enactment of the laws which they are required to obey, as well as in the imposition of the taxes of which they have to pay their full quota, is so clear that no plausible objection has ever been raised against it. If we were not led astray either by self-interest, or by prejudice, we could not hesitate for an instant as to the justice of their claim.

No doubt we hear it said that women degraded themselves by stepping out of their natural sphere of unobtrusive modesty, and claiming political privileges. Allow us to ask you – are you in earnest in this objection? Or is it only offered as an excuse for your neglect of duty? If you are sincere in the expression of this opinion; if you are grieved to see so many of our best and noblest women 'unsex themselves' – as you affect to call it – what have you done to prevent the necessity for their so demeaning themselves? Why have you not come forward, and insisted on their enfranchisement, before they were constrained to enter into the field of controversy on their own behalf? Is this in accordance with your conceptions of true chivalry? Do you seriously believe that so many of our accomplished women – not a few of them brought up in the lap of luxury, and holding an honoured placed among the brightest ornaments of our country, – have willingly subjected themselves to all this obloquy for the sake of any personal gain that will ever accrue to them for the privilege of dropping their voting-paper once every four or five years into the ballot-box? If you can give a moment's credence to so base a thought you certainly do not know them. They move in a sphere of exalted motive into which your coarser nature permits you not to enter. These ladies have been drawn – may we not say *dragged*, – from the privacy of their firesides by an overpowering sense of duty, not merely to themselves, or their own sex, but even to the very men who scoff at their 'want of delicacy'. And it is a cowardly thing for any man to ridicule them for the public action which has thus been forced upon them against their inclination by *his* neglect of duty. It is your indifference to their just claims that has constrained them to face the opprobrium which they foresaw would greet them, and which is often as painful to them as martyrdom would be to you. They are acting under a supreme sense of public obligation; and they may not shrink from the consequences however hard to bear.

We ask you, if you have any true chivalry of feeling, to come forward manfully, and assist them in their uphill battle. They assert their inalienable right to a voice in the enactment of the laws by which this great Empire is governed. They ask to be released from the vexatious restrictions which the unwisdom of our forefathers has placed upon the free development of their powers. They claim an equitable share of our educational appliances, so that ignorance may no longer disqualify them for the performance of their varied duties. They ask to be treated as reasonable beings, who are personally responsible for the talents which have been confided to their care. They feel that in the regeneration of the world they have a work to do which men are unable to perform. They do not despise their home duties; on the contrary, they wish to become more capable wives and mothers than their stunted education has ever yet permitted them to be; but none the less do they desire to take an earnest part in the stirring movements which are going on around them. They want in fine to be true women in the highest meaning of the words – thoroughly fitted to discharge the trusts which God has laid upon their shoulders, and which no restrictive legislation can annul. And they look to you for honest fellowship in the attainment of these aims. It is not a selfish battle they are fighting. Our whole future race will be blessed by everything which raises them in knowledge, in intelligence, in self-help, in capacity of every kind. This is the scope of their aspirations; and nothing less will satisfy them. Will you not assist them in their generous struggle?

THE HISTORY OF THE IRISHWOMEN'S SUFFRAGE AND LOCAL GOVERNMENT ASSOCIATION

Doc. 74: *Reports of the Irishwomen's Suffrage and Local Government Association from 1896–1918* (Dublin, 1918).

The first suffrage society in Ireland had been formed in Belfast in 1872 by Isabella Tod. That society was called the North of Ireland's Women's Suffrage Committee. Anna Haslam formed the Dublin Women's Suffrage Association in February 1876. This was the best-known of Irish suffrage groups. After changing its name on a number of occasions, it finally became the Irish-women's Suffrage and Local Government Association in 1901. In 1918 the association published an account of its history from 1896 to 1918.

The Irishwomen's Suffrage and Local Government Association was founded in February, 1876, as the Dublin Women's Suffrage Association. The Minute book states that the preliminary meeting was held in the Leinster Hall, Molesworth Street. The work of the founder of the association, Mrs Haslam, had commenced ten years earlier, in 1866, when she was one of the 1,499 women who signed the first suffrage petition ever sent to the House of Commons. Among the signatories were 25 Irishwomen. Suffrage meetings had also been held at intervals, notably one attended by Mrs Fawcett, in 1870. On the platform were, amongst others, Prof. Fawcett, MP, the Provost of Trinity College, Dr Ingram, F.T.C.D., Dr Mahaffy, F.T.C.D., Sir John Gray, MP, and Sir William and Lady Wilde. The meeting aroused much interest and was fully reported in the Dublin press. Meetings had also been held in 1873 in Belfast and Dublin, at which the chief speaker was Miss Tod, of Belfast. Much propaganda had also been carried on by distribution of suffrage literature, especially *The Women's Advocate*, edited by Mr Haslam, and by frequent letters in the press. The formation of the society had followed immediately on the very successful meeting held in the Exhibition Palace, at which a deputation of English suffragists were present, including Miss Becker and Miss Ashworth. An executive committee was appointed, and Mrs Haslam and Miss McDowell consented to act as hon. secretaries.

The first work of the society was the collection of signatures in favour of the Women's Disabilities Bill, and at the second meeting of the committee in April, 138 signatures had been collected. The total number of Irish signatures finally amounted to 3,741. The women to be enfranchised by this bill would have been in the proportion of one to seven of the electorate through the country. A leaflet giving details of the bill was largely circulated by the society. Meetings were carried on with great activity, Miss Tod frequently speaking at them. In July, 1877, Miss Wigham, of Edinburgh, said 'though the work is uphill, and the opposition at present envenomed, eventually victory is certain'. Forty-one years later the speaker's words were fulfilled, and during these long years the Irish Women's Suffrage Society, under the devoted guidance of Mrs Haslam, has steadily kept the cause of women's emancipation in the forefront.

The society has always cooperated actively with the London Women's Suffrage Society, and has been represented whenever possible at its meetings. The first time on May 9th, 1879, and also at the great meetings held in Manchester and London in support of the Suffrage Bill of 1885. The earlier propaganda by the distribution of literature was carried out continuously, the *Women's Suffrage Journal*[1] was sent to ten reading rooms in Dublin, and later to all the Free Libraries. The Trade Union Congress met in Dublin in 1880, during which a successful meeting was held, Jesse Craigan being the chief speaker, the first instance in Ireland of the effort to enlist the sympathies of labour. Another important meeting was held during the Social Science Congress in 1881, with Lady Harberton as principal speaker.

The general policy of the society, from 1881 to 1894, may be summarised as follows: when any suffrage resolution or measure was before the House of Commons, letters were sent to all Irish members of parliament urging them to support the measure, letters were also sent to the Irish press, explaining the bearing of the particular measure, and asking all in sympathy with it to communicate with their local parliamentary representatives. This was done, for instance, in 1881 and 1884; in the latter year, voting lists were published, giving the result, and urging householders to write to their representatives on the matter. Special memorials were sent to the Chief Secretary, and Mr Gladstone, then prime minister, with regard to the suffrage measure introduced by Mr Woodall in 1885. Irish members were again circularised in 1890 and 1892 in favour of bills and resolutions in the House of Commons during those years. After the general election of 1895 letters were sent to successful candidates, and in 1896 the same course was followed with regard to the bill before the House that year. The method of petitions initiated in 1866 was continued. One such petition has already been mentioned, and when the new House of Commons met after the general election of 1880, a new petition was handed in, for which the Women's Suffrage Society had worked hard. In 1886, 27 petitions were sent to the House, and in 1890, 17. These letters and petitions

1 The *Women's Suffrage Journal* was established in 1870 and published monthly from London.

dealt with the Parliamentary Enfranchisement of Women, but the society also worked energetically for the Women Poor Law Guardians Bill, and the Municipal Franchise Bill . . .

THE BEGINNINGS OF MILITANT SUFFRAGISM IN IRELAND

Doc. 75a: James H. Cousins and Margaret Cousins, *We Two Together* (Madras, 1950).

Membership of the IWSLGA was predominantly Protestant and non-conformist. Their methods of promoting suffrage relied on organising petitions, drawing room-meetings and lobbying MPs. In 1908 the Irish Women's Franchise League was formed by Hanna Sheehy Skeffington and Margaret Cousins. They admired the work of the Pankhursts' Women's Social and Political Union.[1] The members of the IWFL were also very involved in Irish nationalism and the cultural revival. The IWFL wished to bring the issue of suffrage to a much wider audience, and felt that Haslam's IWSLGA was too 'genteel' to make any significant impact on Irish society. In the following extract Margaret Cousins relates the origins of the League.

While we were entirely in sympathy with the British women in their spirited frontal attack on their government (then Conservative under Bonar Law) their policy of opposing at by-elections any candidate who did not promise to support a bill for woman suffrage had no parallel in Ireland. Our work was to see that votes for women was incorporated in the Home Rule bill for which Ireland was fighting. Besides, we had no desire to work under English women leaders: we could lead ourselves. So a group of us went on November 6 to the dear old leader of the constitutional suffragists, Mrs Anna Haslam, to inform her that we younger women were ready to start a new women's suffrage society on militant lines. She regretted what she felt to be a duplication of effort. She was also congenitally a person of peace, non-violent, law-abiding to the finger-tips. But she sensed the time spirit, and we parted as friends, agreeing to differ our means, though united in aim and ideals.

On November 11 the new society, which was named 'The Irish Women's Franchise League' was founded. I became treasurer, Hannah Skeffington its secretary, Mrs Charles Oldham its president, all honorary; and in the latter's house the militant women's league in Ireland was made public on November 17. Both Jim and I spoke at that meeting. It was a milestone for united lives, an occasion which brought us personally a blessing, and eventually gave the franchise to the women of Ireland even before the British women got it.

1 Mrs Emmeline Pankhurst (1857–1928), with her daughters Christabel (1880–1958) and Sylvia (1882–1960), formed the militant Women's Social and Political Union in England in 1903.

The aim of the Irish Women's Franchise League was to win the parliamentary vote for the women of Ireland on the same terms as men then had it, or as it might be given to them; our policy was to educate by all forms of propaganda the men, women and children of Ireland to understand and support the members of the League in their demand for votes for women, and obtain pledges from every Irish member of parliament to vote for Women Suffrage Bills introduced in the British House of Parliament, and to include women suffrage in any Irish Home Office bill. The forms of propaganda of the Irish Women's Franchise League were to be both constitutional and non-constitutional, as dictated by political circumstances. Its own constitution consisted of a headquarters in Dublin, manned by a committee, president, secretary and treasurer, and voluntary organisers who should tour the country and form branches of the League with an annual branch subscription to the central funds. Only women could be members. The League would co-operate where possible with the suffrage societies of Great Britain and other countries, especially with the militant suffrage organisations.

Within a fortnight of its foundation the Irish Women's Franchise League got an opportunity of high-light publicity. Miss Mary Gawthorpe, one of the recently imprisoned London suffragettes, was invited to speak on women suffrage by the Solicitor's Apprentices Debating Society at the Four Courts. Tom Kettle[1] was to be the second speaker. When our committee sat on the evening before this highly advertised meeting, to draw up our first month's programme, word came that Mr Kettle would not attend the meeting, and the Irish Women's Franchise League was invited to send one of its members as substitute for him. There and then they unanimously decided that I should be the substitute for the brilliant young politician. I was scared to death; but I agreed to do my best, though I had very little time to prepare. There were a thousand people present. Miss Gawthorpe's ability as a speaker was immense. It was my first big test as a speaker. But I survived it.

We became quite attached to our Headquarters Office and Committee Room in the Antient Concert Rooms building. There we planned speakers for meetings. From its door issued poster parades and special processions. There our large green, orange and white flag hung out; and the weekly contents poster of 'Votes for Women' and later of our own weekly paper *The Irish Citizen*. It was not an impressive building, but its location was central. It became the hub of our activity. Starting with a dozen enthusiasts, we grew to about fifty women whose hearts were in the movement, and who could be relied on to take the share in every kind of propaganda. We were a very mixed lot, a cross-section of all the classes, political parties, religious groups and avocations open to women in those days (1908–1914). The cause broke down all social barriers. For each of us the cause was a whole-time job, without pay, demanding all kinds of sacrifice, forcing us to do things for which we had no training, pushing us into dreaded and undesired publicity; bringing a ridicule, scorn,

---

1 Thomas Kettle (1880–1916), nationalist MP.

misrepresentation, but also times of affluence, of a sense of great blessing, an expansion of capacities, the happiness of great friendships, a widening of contacts with our kind of all degrees, a greater understanding of the difficulties of social living, an enlarged experience of the inequalities of opportunity imposed on women, an increasing sense of protest against the injustices under which women lived, most of all the women of the working classes.

Some of our members embroidered our green silk flag with 'Irish Women's Franchise League' and 'Votes for Women'. I remember rehearsing open-air speaking in a field behind our house, with only one ass as my audience. Later I found it easier to speak out of doors than in halls. Experience had taught the English suffragettes the convenience, economy, mobility and reliability of speaking from four-wheeled lorries without horses. We adopted the same technique. The lorry made a strong, raised, steady, dignified platform. We always had two women speakers (one seated while the other spoke) and one man. We did not ask people to come to us. We had the lorry placed where the people themselves were accustomed to gather, and they never failed to come and listen and ask questions at the end of the hour.

In rousing and educating opinion in country towns our experiences were very varied. Usually we set off two by two on tours. There were difficulties in securing places for meetings, difficulties in finding hotel accommodation or a press which would, urgently, print our notices of the meeting. Very rarely did we find a local man or woman who would preside. The policy of the English suffragettes in opposing politicians of any and every party which opposed votes for women had roused the ire of the press, which in Ireland then was the mouthpiece of one or other political party or sub-party. At first the suffragettes had been misunderstood, then ridiculed, misrepresented, later tolerated; but when they showed their power to influence by-elections, and even turned the typical male-man, Winston Churchill, out of Manchester, and when they made all sorts of difficulties for Government, the press gave them no mercy, and built up a legend of them as 'wild women', 'hooligans', 'unsexed females', and the like. Being fed by such falsehoods, it was no wonder that ample newspaper readers in small Irish country towns shrank from the coming into their midst of the unknown quantity, the Irish suffragette.

We never knew how a meeting would go. At Castlebar, in County Mayo, a band of irresponsible men tried to ruin our meeting by singing songs to drown our voices. But after regaling us with 'Put me on an island where the girls are few', there was a moment's quiet, and Meg Connery asked them if they would really like such an island. They were so pleased with her repartee and her plucky spirit that they quieted down and became quite sensible. At another country meeting rowdies brought flour with them and threw it towards us on the platform. Commotion ensued among the audience. We could not make ourselves heard. One of the elders of the town chided them with, 'Can you not give the young girls a chance to speak?' We won them round; but we found 'apple-pie beds' laid out for us in the hotel. . . .

Doc. 75b: *Annual Report of the Irish Women's Franchise League for 1913* (Dublin, 1913).

Your committee has met forty times since its election, and is pleased to present a record of increased activity in many directions, of many new and important ventures. Though our cause has suffered reverses in the House of Commons through the treachery of the politicians, in Ireland it has been well to the fore. The special feature of 1913 has been the initiation by the League of a strenuous policy of heckling. Members of Parliament have thus for the first time in Ireland been reminded in their constituencies of the claims of Irish-women. The militant spirit is as strong as ever; several new recruits have passed through the ordeal of imprisonment in Ireland, and have asserted (and won) at the risk of their lives the principle of political treatment for political offences. Our League has also foiled the attempt of the government to enforce the Cat and Mouse Act[1] in this country, and the magnificent public spirit aroused by this attempt has strongly reinforced the ranks of militancy in Ireland, while many recent events have immensely strengthened our hold upon the popular mind in Ireland. The working classes particularly have shown themselves friendly, and have rallied to our support whenever called upon.

The great event of the year, as far as Irishwomen are concerned, was the concession by the Ulster Unionist Council of votes to Ulster women under a scheme of Provisional Government.[2] The concession, though hypothetical, may have far-reaching results. Irishwomen of all parties are determined to press it, should occasion arise for a 'settlement by consent' or 'concession' of the Ulster problem . . . At Cahirciveen in September, at the opening of the Irish Party's autumn campaign, another member made her presence felt at a large open air meeting addressed by Mr Redmond.[3] In Limerick, on October 12th, Mr Dillon[4] and his colleagues were interviewed by Mrs Connery and Mrs Sheehy Skeffington and two Limerick members, while Mr Redmond was subsequently heckled during his speech by Mrs Connery. On this occasion Mr Redmond had churlishly refused the request of local constitutional suffragists for an interview. On October 20th Miss Cahalan[5] and Miss Houston heckled Mr Dillon and others at Navan, and the majority of the audience was manifestly on their side. On October 24th Mr T. W. Russell, MP, was subjected at Rathmines Town Hall to a fusillade of questions by Mrs Palmer, Mrs Hoskin, and others, and later on 24th November, at a meeting held in the Gresham

---

1 The Prisoners' (Temporary Discharge for Ill Health) Bill 1913, was popularly known as the Cat and Mouse Act. It allowed for the temporary release of hunger-strikers when their health was endangered. Once fit they could be returned to jail.

2 Opposition by northern unionists to Home Rule led Edward Carson in September 1911 to state that if Home Rule became a reality a provisional government would take over the governence of Ulster. Women would be granted the vote in this provisonal state.

3 John Redmond (1856–1918), MP, was leader of the Irish Parliamentary Party.

4 John Dillon (1851–1927), MP and member of the Irish Parliamentary Party.

5 Cissie Cahalan (1876–1948), trade unionist.

Hotel, Mr Russell's carefully rounded periods about liberty and liberalism were punctured by many well-timed reminders. On October 26th, at an open-air meeting in Carlow, Mr Dillon was effectively heckled by Mrs Emerson and Miss Kilbride. This was the only occasion on which the crowd indulged in violence, owing chiefly to deliberate incitement from the platform. On November 5th the various speakers at a big demonstration in Cavan were subjected to severe heckling, the crowd hugely enjoying the apt retorts of the women, and, two days later, at University College, Dublin, on the occasion of a speech by Mr Dillon on the 'Healing Power of Freedom', his oration was once more appropriately interrupted at various points. When Mr Bonar Law addressed a large unionist demonstration on November 28th at the Theatre Royal, Dublin, despite extreme precautions to ensure immunity from suffragist interruptions by excluding all but a few party women, the unionist leader was reminded of his duty to women. Mr Bonar Law had refused the request of various suffragist bodies (including that of the Unionist Association) for an interview.

MEG CONNERY ON IRISH MILITANTS, THE WAR, AND RELIEF WORK

Doc. 76: *The Irish Citizen*, 19 September 1914.

The outbreak of war in August 1914 caused many suffragists to reasssess their position and their attitude to the state. Many chose to suspend their suffrage activities and contribute to the war effort. In this extract Meg Connery justifies the stance of non-involvement in the war effort taken by the Irish Women's Franchise League.

Whatever else may be said of the war we must admit at once that it has proved a tremendous testing time for individuals and organisations no less than for nations. We rejoice that once again the IWFL[1] has proved the soundness of its metal by the way in which it has stood this fiery ordeal and resisted the manifold efforts made to seduce it from the cause of its true allegiance. Our position is simple, and scarcely needs explaining. We have adopted the only attitude consistent with womanly dignity and self-respect, based on our conception of what are the true and real interests of the nation in this crisis.

We are never without a crisis of one sort or another. Men take care to keep us plentifully supplied with them in order to divert our attention from our own wrongs and grievous disabilities as a sex. Are we weather vanes, then, that we turn about with every breeze that blows or are we serious human beings with a serious purpose in life? The present state of affairs will furnish

1 Irish Women's Franchise League.

the answer to each of us. A few months ago we were in this country faced with a crisis which touched us far more nearly – we were faced with a civil war.[1] We did not on that occasion haul down our flag, suspend our activities, range ourselves on the side of the respective combatants whose cause we personally favoured. We refused to split our forces on that rock; we still more emphatically refuse to split them on this one.

In the autumn of last year there was wide-spread suffering and want in Dublin. Gaunt famine stalked through our streets.[2] Thousands of people were thrown out of employment, thousands of men, women and children were hungry and cold and ragged and homeless. There was urgent need for relief works. The health and well being of the nation was threatened through famine and disease, yet we did not witness any wild stampede of women to grapple with this national problem. Individuals amongst us were free then as now to give what aid we could to lessen the general distress, but we recognised clearly that relief works, however praiseworthy and necessary, were outside the scope of our organisation.

Our movement was founded with the definite aim of securing the political freedom of women. To this work we have pledged ourselves, and to no other. Nothing has occurred within the last few weeks to justify us in turning aside from our life's propose. The European war has done nothing to alter our condition of slavery. It has only served to make us realise more deeply and poignantly than ever the utter helplessness and defenselessness of our position as political outcasts in attempting to stem the tide of masculine aggression and brute force.

We stand now where women all down the ages have stood – without the pale of citizenship and human fellowship with man – a state of things so intolerable, so morally indefensible, so disastrous to our national well being and so gross an offence against the spirit of liberty that we dare not at this juncture turn aside from our great crusade against the forces of evil lest the principles, and ideals, on which alone true nationhood are founded be wholly swept away and the nation itself destroyed.

There is a profound truth behind the old saying that 'a rolling stone gathers no moss'. The need of the moment for women is to concentrate. We have always held the view that success in this women's war against male dominance and chattel slavery depends on the tenacity of purpose, the

1 With the introduction of the third Home Rule Bill in 1912 unionist fears were heightened. Their opposition to Home Rule led to the formation of the Ulster Volunteers in early 1913. They were now prepared to defend the north by force of arms. In November 1913 the Irish National Volunteers was established in Dublin to exert pressure of the British government to implement Home Rule. Both groups quickly armed themselves. The growing tension was somewhat dissipated by the government forcing Redmond, in 1914, to agree that individual Ulster counties could opt out of Home Rule for a six-year period.

2 In 1913 the success of the Irish Transport and General Workers Union alarmed employers. Some employers began sacking members of the ITGWU and replacing them with non-union men. Strikes ensued and over 400 employers locked out all members of the ITGWU. Many thousands of men were left unemployed, with families going hungry.

singleness of aim and unswerving devotion to principle of the women engaged in it. It must be 'fought to a finish'. We are neither going to bury the hatchet nor yet to resurrect the domestic mop (true emblem of our enslaved condition)! What possible affinity can there be between women struggling for freedom and the forces responsible for precipitating the present horrible catastrophe? Let those who have plunged the nation into war be made to shoulder the full responsibility for their deed. This is the duty of the state. If the state must drive men forth like 'dumb driven cattle' to be slaughtered, let it at least have sufficient humanity to make provision against want for the homes it has desolated, for the widows and the orphans its policy has made. For groups of private individuals to attempt to cope with a condition of distress so far-reaching and complex is on a level with the labours of the historic lady who strove to keep out the tide with a broom.

We are opposed to this war, as we are opposed to all war, because we are profoundly convinced that war is in itself an unmitigated evil and the greatest existing menace to true human progress. It is anti-Christian and anti-social, and is only calculated to foster the lowest and most bestial passions of mankind. Further, it is our conviction that feminism and militarism are natural born enemies and cannot flourish on the same soil. As the spirit of militarism (based on brute force) grows and triumphs so must decay the spirit of comradeship, human co-operation, and sympathy for which our women's movement stands. Let us consider the calibre of those individuals who are behind the war and satisfy ourselves if they are deserving of the confidence or respect of women. There is Lord Kitchener[1] – the ruthless despot, the notorious woman hater. There is Mr Asquith,[2] 'a grey old wolf and a lean', the fanatical Joigot who has stubbornly blocked the way of woman's emancipation for years, under whose government and sanction suffragists have been subjected to every conceivable form of insult, personal injury, calumny, mob violence and prison torture. There is the whole tribe of harpies who follow in their team and there is the corrupt press which is their mouthpiece. Behold, then, the new saviours of humanity, the champions of freedom and civilization! Ah, do we not know them of old, and shall we not refuse to be beguiled from the path of honour and righteousness by the false doctrine of these political mountebank![3]

Let us clear our minds of the cobwebs of sentimental humbug and cant and consider well under what banner we shall serve. All the old, evil problems of a corrupt and decaying civilisation are with us today, even as they were yesterday. Woman slavery, the double moral standard, the sweating and exploitation of women, the violation of children, vice, intemperance, political corruption, and loathsome disease – these are the real dangers which threaten

1 Horatio Herbert Kitchener (1850–1916), British soldier. Secretary of State for War 1914.
2 Herbert Henry Asquith (1852–1928), British Liberal statesman and Prime Minister (1910–18).
3 Swindler.

the nation's life. How often and how vainly have we appealed to the people to come to our aid and help us in the struggle to save the nation from destruction; but men refused to leave their work or their play or their political squabbles to listen to our cry. Now that the nations are at war, blinded with fury and mad unreasoning rage against one another, these things and every other rank and poisonous weed will flourish exceedingly and take on a new lease of life because some who might have protested against wrong and roused the public conscience have proved false to their trust and abandoned their posts to pursue some worthless will-o'-the-wisp. This nightmare of horror shall pass, but the grim realities and tragedies of life will remain; and we shall continue to cry out against them, even though we stood alone in a world gone suddenly mad. Already a new generation of women come thronging behind us. We must not lay down our arms now and pass on to them only a heritage of failure and defeat. To us they look for guidance and inspiration. We must not fail them we dare not fail them!

OPPOSITION TO WOMEN'S SUFFRAGE

Doc. 77: David Barry, 'Female suffrage from a Catholic standpoint', *Irish Ecclesiastical Record*, 27 (September 1909).

There were many in Ireland who opposed the granting of women's suffrage. Opposition was especially strong amongst the Catholic hierarchy. David Barry STL claimed that the Catholic church was the true emancipator of women and the granting of the suffrage was unnecessary. He believed very much in the image of the 'ideal' woman who was morally and spiritually superior to man.

The Catholic church has done so much to emancipate woman, to raise her status, and to dignify and ennoble her position, that it must be of some interest to ascertain what judgment is to be passed on the present movement for female suffrage in the light of Catholic principles.

Before the advent of Christianity, the position of woman was little better than that of a slave; she could be discarded as a wife, and deprived of the custody of her children at the mere whim of her husband, and her arbitrary degradation was a matter of everyday occurrence. But the Catholic church, by emphasizing the sublime function of one woman as Mother of God, by the number of women placed on the calendar of her saints, and by the vigilance and care that she lavished on the female communities that devoted themselves to God, under her auspices, became responsible for the present honourable, and even privileged position that is accorded to woman in all civilized societies. And above all, by the rigidity of her marriage laws, and the noble stand she, alone of all the churches, has maintained on the subject of divorce, she has elevated woman from being the handmaid, and even the mere chattel of her husband, to the dignity of his helper and partner in the domestic society.

The Catholic church was the pioneer, and is still, and will be ever the mainstay of the rights of woman, and the question arises: do Catholic ideals or Catholic principles lend any support to the theory that woman has a right to exert her energies in a wider sphere of action than has hitherto been within her competence? Besides having her recognized position in the life of the family, and in the guidance of its destinies, has she a right, in addition, to exercise a judgment on, and to practically concern herself with municipal and state affairs? Is it her province to be conversant with questions of policy, other than purely domestic ones, to make up her mind on them, and to translate her opinion into action, by casting her vote for the candidate that is opposed, it may be, to her father or husband?

Because women do not, as a rule, work for their livelihood, they are generally exempt from the obligation of providing for themselves by the exertions of father, or brother, or husband. Consequently, if legislation is made by these, and is sufficiently favourable to their interests, there does not seem to be much reason why women should interfere in it. On Catholic principles, at any rate, it is not explicitly defined that woman has the right to a living wage, or the duty of supporting herself at all. She is supposed to be shielded by her male relatives from most of the hardships and disabilities of citizenhood. As a wife, the efficient discharge of her duties under the Fourth Commandment renders it impossible for her to make her own way in the community, and hence there is no reason why she should have any direct part in the polity of the state.

The virtue of distributive justice has no direct concern with her; for, as a rule, her household duties will not permit her to aspire to the salaried posts of the state that are its greatest rewards to deserving citizens; neither is she amenable to taxation nor, generally speaking, to any peculiarly vexatious legislation. Most laws affect her only directly through her husband or father, and it is enough that she can influence their enactment indirectly through them.

Separate representation is made necessary, as we have seen, by the conflict of opposing interests; and it is a mistake to assume that the interests of a woman are indifferent to the male members of her family, and still more to assume that her interests and theirs are incompatible or in antagonism. But if, in a particular instance, the duty of supporting herself or her family devolves on a female, it must be acknowledged that her claim to vote is not in any way weakened by these considerations.

Again, it seems plain enough that allowing to women the right of suffrage is incompatible with the high Catholic ideal of the unity of domestic life. Following the doctrine of Christ and St Paul, the Church teaches that husband and wife become indissolubly one. Their personalities become, to a certain extent, merged in each other; while the wife has her well-recognised sphere of influence and authority in the domestic circle, the final word, even in that circle, rests with the husband, for he is the head of his wife, as Christ is of the church. And if in the little world of home politics the husband is supreme, how much more in the relations of the household with the great outside world?

It is no doubt the duty and privilege of a wife to advise and suggest to her husband how he is to comport himself, even in regard to extraneous matters, but she has only a consultative and not a definitive voice. When a wife forgets her place, trenches on his rights, and does not defer to the authority of her husband in the home, peace is destroyed, children are disedified, and the solidarity of the domestic kingdom is threatened. But how much would these evils be intensified if the bickering and contention became public, if they appeared on opposing platforms and denounced each other, as would be a natural enough sequel of acknowledging the equal right of both to interfere in public affairs?

Is it probable that a husband and wife that were in rival political camps during the day would call a truce in the evening, and unite in training their children, and cherishing them, and each other? Is it probable that their home would have much of the peace and harmony of the model home of Nazareth? It would surely be subversive of the unity of family life, and the acme of disedification to their children, if the two chief members of the household spoke on public matter with a divergent or discordant voice.

Even those who do not hold the high and rigid ideal of the unity of the family that the Catholic church clings to, must recognize some authority in the family, as in every other society. Is this authority the conjoint privilege of husband and wife? If so, which of them is to yield, if a difference of opinion arises? Surely the most uncompromising suffragette must admit that the wife ought to give way in such a case. That is to say, every one will admit that the wife's domestic authority is subordinate to that of her husband. But is she to be accorded an autonomy in outside affairs that is denied her in the home? Her authority is subject to her husband's in domestic matters – her special sphere; is it to be considered co-ordinate with his in regulating the affairs of the state?

Furthermore, there is an argument that applies universally, even in the case of those women who are not subject to the care and protection of a husband, and even, I do not hesitate to say, where the matters to be decided on would come specially within their cognisance, and where their judgement would, therefore, be more reliable than that of men. It is this, that in the noise and turmoil of party politics, or in the narrow, but rancorous arena of local factions, it must needs fare ill with what may be called the passive virtues of humility, patience, meekness, forbearance, and self-repression.

These are looked on by the church as the special prerogative and endowment of the female soul, and priests see conspicuous examples of them in the everyday exercise of their ministry. They not only constitute the difference between the virago and the gentlewoman, but they assimilate the soul to that of the Blessed Virgin and the great female saints. But these virtues would

other societies. They are also on sale at the new office, with which we begin our second year. We hope to continue our monthly evening meetings and discussions on subjects concerning women's interests, and to make the office in the day time a meeting place for our own members and our friends in the other suffrage leagues, who have all shown friendly and sympathetic interest in our beginnings.

Looking back over the past year we are greatly encouraged by what has been accomplished. Looking forward we see far more to be done, for when this calamitous war is over we must be prepared for our responsibility and claim our right to help in reconstructing dislocated social conditions.

LUCY KINGSTON QUESTIONS THE EFFECT OF ENFRANCHISEMENT ON WOMEN

Doc. 79: L.O. Kingston, 'The Irishwoman's outlook', *The Englishwoman*, 37 (January–March 1918).

The Representation of the People Act of January 1918 granted the vote to Irish and British women of thirty years of age and over. In 1922, under the provisions of the Irish Free State Constitution, all Irish citizens over the age of twenty-one were enfranchised. What were women to do with the vote? Below, Lucy Kingston, suffragist and pacifist, discusses the effect enfranchisement will have on women, and the possible impact of women voters on Irish politics.

Surmise and curiosity gather thickly round the possible effects which enfranchisement will have upon women. Various theories propel themselves into print from time to time tinged with the colour of the minds that evolve them, and ranging from deepest shades of Humphry-Wardian[1] gloom to rainbow hues of utopian hope.

Prophecy is indeed at this juncture hazardous, and to attempt it in Ireland, even though writing as an Irishwoman, and from an Irish suffrage Society, it savours of presumption. Nevertheless I venture to assume the prophetic mantle, with a wary eye on the future, which has a knack of springing the unforeseen upon us, and making even seemingly smooth paths bristle with unsuspected dangers.

In order to appreciate the possible effects of enfranchisement in Ireland, it is first necessary to clear our minds of cant and prejudice. It is not to be expected, however much the will may try to drive the reason, that enthusiasm, joy, and gratitude will break forth, and that the daughters of Erin (over thirty) from Portrush to Cape Clear will sing a unanimous paean of thanksgiving. The fight for women's suffrage has been a struggling, sporadic, and not at any time

1 Mrs Humphry-Ward (neé Mary Augusta Arnold 1851–1920) was an English novelist. She was a leading figure in the intellectual life of her day.

very popular thing; the joy in victory will, therefore, have proportionately these limitations. For various reasons the cause of women's suffrage in Ireland, though carried on with great courage by a few, never became a vital movement, partly owing to the fact that much of the best public spirit of Ireland's womanhood has been absorbed by the Home Rule question, to which precedence was given rather than to franchise reform.

The news of the passing of the Representation of the People Bill will fall quietly upon the women of Ireland, but at least one good result may be looked for without undue optimism. Anything that tends towards unification in Ireland carries with it the germ of hope, and enfranchisement, irrespective of class, creed, or party, should give women a common bond, one with another, and in doing so help to break down old prejudices and political or religious barriers. In suffrage circles this bond will be strongly felt, but much spade work will still be necessary. It may seem paradoxical to say so, but the movement, while bringing Irishwomen into closer touch with one another individually, has tended to separate them collectively. Irish political conditions – exceptionally thorny, as everyone will admit – have not only given rise to the formation of more societies than are essential to the strength of the suffrage cause, but have in all too many instances drawn a sharp line of cleavage between them. Once enfranchised, however – and leaving the 'national question' on one side, as we hope a satisfactory solution of its many problems will by then have been arrived at – there should, in my opinion, be only one strongly marked line of cleavage (the question of party politics is dealt with later) between the reorganised suffrage societies. Some will devote themselves without a break to further agitation for a complete measure of enfranchisement, whilst others will prefer to turn their attention to social reform and educative work, making the demand for full enfranchisement subsidiary to the opportunities afforded by what they have already gained.

It is unlikely, however, that any Irish society, however moderate and conservative, will really accept with complete satisfaction the terms of the present Act, with its penalisation of youth; but in many cases the suffrage societies will not remain purely suffrage in their aim, and there will be more than ever a tendency to branch off into social work. It has been interesting to notice the rapid growth of this tendency for some time past. It has been especially apparent since the war has put a premium upon concrete activity, and a handicap upon the seemingly less practical work of political agitation; work whose delayed result taxed the patience of sympathisers, who preferred ameliorative and local practical work which presented a tangible issue, and which had a bearing on the life around. With the outsider, and the critic of suffrage activities, there is this same inclination to regard the social worker as the real agent of amelioration and progress. Everywhere one finds that there is a great deal more sympathy with and respect for the reformer who is 'doing something' that one can see and understand, than with the purely political worker – and this describes very largely the attitude of men towards the suffrage movement here. It may be partly owing to the fact that if one did undertake political work in Ireland it was expected that it should have some national bearing: 'Seek ye first the granting of Home Rule, and all these things shall be added unto you', having always been in effect the advice of the typical nationalist Irishman to the women of Ireland.

The effect of the enfranchisement of Irishwomen upon the political parties in Ireland may be measured by the effect which this reform is likely to have on the fortunes of the parties themselves. The women's suffrage clause, *per se*, did not excite very greatly either antagonism or support.

When the Ulster parliamentary party pressed for the exclusion of Ireland, it did so with a single eye to the chance of forcing redistribution of seats into the bill. It stood to gain by redistribution of seats; for, as Sir John Lonsdale pointed out, there was such an anomaly in the old distribution that East Belfast, with nearly twenty thousand inhabitants, sent one representative to the House; while Galway, Newry, Kilkenny Borough, and Waterford, with a combined electorate of two thousand four hundred less than east Belfast, sent between them six members. Such anomalies as this stood a fair chance of being redressed by redistribution, and fully explain the efforts of the unionist to combat the bill unless the clause were carried.

The issue was similarly involved as regards nationalist Ireland. Although antagonism to woman suffrage seems to have been inextricably melted into Mr John Redmond's system by some malign fairy, yet we must read the signs of the political times without prejudice, and acknowledge that woman, as such, weighed lightly in the balance of his opposition to the bill. A heavier and possibly more concrete danger threatened him; for the extended franchise would open political roads to numbers of young men (and possibly to numbers of thirty-year old young women), whose opinions, if freely expressed at the polls, might threaten the prestige, if not the actual existence, of the great political party of which Mr Redmond is leader.

Perhaps Sinn Féin stands to gain more than any other party by the enfranchisement of women, although it is true that, owing to the youth of the women who subscribe to republican principles in Ireland (it is considered that the vast majority have not yet arrived, or will not for some time arrive, at the voting age), this statement is open to question. But whether this be the case or not, it is certain that Sinn Féin has emphasised the value of the vote as nothing else has done in this country. Before its existence as a party (if, indeed, it can be called a party), the issue between unionist and nationalist candidates at elections was more or less a foregone conclusion, depending upon, and being largely decided by geographical boundaries. The coming of Sinn Féin (Mr William O'Brien's meteoric flights across the political horizon scarcely disturbed the old regime, as he did not oppose unionist candidates), and the presence of a third party at the polls, generated a keenness and excitement which needs no illustration, for the elections which have taken place since 1916 are proof enough in themselves. It therefore happens that the existence of Sinn Féin would strengthen the effect of the women's vote upon the three great parties in Ireland, and would render every vote of more vital importance to the candidate.

The moral effect of 'the woman-element in politics' has been very much discussed, and there is in certain circles a great deal of hope, but unfortunately no evidence whatever to prove, that women will rise superior to party interests, and devote themselves to educative work, and to social ameliora-tion. It is, or course, true that woman does not live by party legislation alone; but it is to be feared, nevertheless, that 'the woman-element in politics' will be inextricably bound up with party feeling. How can it be otherwise seeing that in the present state of evolution of Irish sympathies and ambitions, the non-party woman would be regarded exactly as the non-party man is – a person without honour in his own country: without honour or recognition or appreciation. In estimating the duration of the present predominance of party feeling in Ireland, it is impossible, however, to forget that this rests largely upon the result of the Irish convention; but if this body should conclude its deliberations without definite result or satisfaction to the country which waits upon it, party feeling can only be more bitter and pronounced than before, and all attempts to allay it be useless.

Women as well as men in these unhappy circumstances will fail to realise that they are members of a great body politic, but rather will remember that they are members of a party political, and it must be frankly admitted that in the average case their vote will be registered as thoughtlessly and with as narrow a vision as that of men has been in the past.

Nevertheless, there are many signs that in other directions than party politics a spirit of fellowship is growing up amongst Irishwomen which will empower and encourage them to stand by one another, and may, under the new conditions, result in more loyal support by women of women candidates for municipal and Poor Law and other elections. If the support be guar-anteed, there will be no dearth of candidates for positions such as these, and the enfranchisement of women here will give a considerable impetus to the woman who has leisure and opportunity and inclination to qualify for public work.

In the main, one may sum up the whole state of mind of the educated, thinking Irishwoman by saying that it is less of a triumph in a victory which is to bring about great results, and more of a natural feeling of pride in the (partial) recognition of the fact that the stigma hitherto placed upon her as a citizen was an injustice and a mistake.

This is what the passing of the Representation of the People Bill really means to the woman who it most concerns.

Local Franchises

WINNING THE MUNICIPAL FRANCHISE FOR BELFAST WOMEN

Doc. 80: *Northern Whig*, 23 July 1887.

The suffrage issue was not the only formal political concern of Irish women. Irish suffragists had long been concerned with the municipal franchise, which had been granted to women in England in 1869. In Belfast, women householders gained the vote in 1887 as the result of a local Act concerned with drainage plans for the city.[1] During the progress of the bill through parliament, Isabella Tod organised a group to press the claims of Irish women to the municipal franchise. In this letter to the Northern Whig, *Tod explains how her group succeeded in having women inserted into the bill.*

I have waited until the Belfast Municipal Bill received the royal assent before drawing the attention of the women householders and ratepayers of the town to the new rights and duties which it places in their hands. Ever since the admission of women to the municipal franchise in the corporate towns of England, by a clause in the Municipal Act of 1869, the friends of women's suffrage here have been on the watch to raise a similar claim, and especially so since the same right was granted to Scotchwomen in 1882. But in the hurry and rush of recent years it had been found very difficult to get any independent action taken on behalf of the Irishwomen. When however, in the early spring of this year, Sir James Corry brought in a bill to assimilate the municipal to the parliamentary franchise in Irish boroughs, the long sought opportunity presented itself. The North of Ireland's Women's Suffrage Committee laid the question fully before a number of leading MPs and others and received much support. Sir J. P. Corry consented to alter the phrase descriptive of the qualified voter from 'man' to 'person' in accordance with the English precedent. The history of

1 Belfast Corporation wanted to undertake a major drainage project in the city. The scheme would affect every rate payer and it was argued that the franchise should be extended to all rate payers so that they could have some say in how the corporation spent its funds. See Virginia Crossman, *Local Government in Nineteenth-Century Ireland* (Belfast, 1994), pp 83–4.

the bill, in matters unconnected with the claims of women, has been peculiar, and more than once it has seemed on the point of being ship-wrecked. In consequence of some of these difficulties its operation is limited to Belfast alone. Although we should gladly have seen this undoubted right bestowed upon women in all Irish boroughs at once, yet at least we have the satisfaction of knowing that it will hence forth be impossible to deal with municipal affairs in these boroughs without at the same time acknowledging and securing the rights of women who are householders as well as those of men. At the moment when the bill was passing from the House of Commons to the House of Lords it was suggested by Miss Becker,[1] whose knowledge of such matters in England is more complete than that of anyone else, that to prevent any chance of the new Act being construed with an older Act which is unfavourable to women, it would be well to have an explanatory clause added to it, to show that the word 'person' was intended to include women, as in the English Consolidating Act of 1882. Upon stating the case to Lord Erne, who had charge of the bill in the Upper House, he at once accepted the explanatory clause and moved it as an amendment.

For the first time in Ireland women in our town possess the most important of local franchises.[2] We hope, and from the experiences of our friends in Great Britain, we have good reason to hope, that they will care less for mere party politics than men do, and more for the great social and moral questions which ought to be the end for which party politics are only the means. . . . They will now have a share in choosing the policy of the town and the men who are to carry it out, they can influence efficiently all matters concerning the peace and good order of the streets, the progress of sanitary reform, the cause of temperance, and other questions in which they have a vital interest. . . .

WOMEN AS POOR LAW GUARDIANS

Along with campaigning for the municipal franchise, Irish suffragists also pressed a claim for women to act as Poor Law Guardians. English women were first elected as PLGs in 1875. Many women held that a long tradition in philanthropy prepared them for the work of a guardian. The very fact that they were women, and thus deemed by society to have particular moral and spiritual qualities, was also to their advantage. Emily Dickson argued

1 Lydia Becker (1827–90) was a leading figure in the British women's suffrage movement. She edited the *Women's Suffrage Journal.*
2 4,756 women were qualified to vote in Belfast in 1890, by 1895 this had increased to about 6,200, roughly 17 percent of those entitled to the municipal vote in the city. See Crossman, *Local Government*, p 84.

in 1895 that women were ideal candidates to sit on Poor Law boards because of their domestic capabilities.

The Advantages that Women can Bring as Poor Law Guardians

Doc. 81.1: Emily Winifred Dickson, 'The need for women as Poor Law Guardians', *Dublin Journal of Medical Science*, 99 (April 1895).

. . . Among some of the duties which Boards of Guardians have to perform, and in which surely they would find a woman's knowledge of service, are the following:

(1) Engagement of officials, the majority of whom – matron, nurses, and servants – are women.
(2) Superintending the quality of the material and the making of clothes for the women and children.
(3) Inspection of the supplies sent in, to see that they fulfil the contract requirements, and inspection of the food, to see that it is properly cooked and served.
(4) Inspection of the infants and children, to see that they are well fed and cared for.
(5) Inspection of beds, bed linen, and towels. All these matters a woman is accustomed to see to as a matter of routine in her own house, and she is trained to notice them, and if they are badly done to have them set right. It is no question of special professional training, it is a question of using the training and habits of home in a wider field and on a larger scale; the essentials are the same. It is often said that women are unbusinesslike, and this might be urged as an objection to their undertaking the more extensive work of a Guardian, but business habits are largely a matter of training, and most women who have to organise and manage their households have a very fair idea of business in their own line at least, though they may not understand stocks and shares. They are also often more economical than men, because they are accustomed to deal with smaller sums of money. Besides, it is not proposed that any Board should be entirely feminine – I believe in the co-operation of men and women here as elsewhere; what I wish to urge is the very great need for one or two women on each Board to assist and give advice in matters concerning the women and children and domestic affairs. And as I believe that nearly four-fifths of the paupers are women and children, this does not seem a very unreasonable proposal. . . .

Women can Become Poor Law Guardians

Doc. 81.2: Anon., 'Women as Poor Law Guardians in Ireland', *Englishwoman's Review*, 15 October 1896.

Irish women were finally granted the right to act as Poor Law Guardians in 1896. The Englishwoman's Review *commented on the passage of the Act, and noted the efforts Irish women were undertaking to ensure the election of women candidates. In 1897 there were thirteen women acting as Poor Law Guardians around the country. By 1898 that number had increased to twenty-two, and by 1899 over eighty women had been elected. Although this represented a tiny minority among more than 8,000 Guardians, women now had direct access to an important sphere of local government.*

The following is the text of the Act to enable women to be elected as Poor Law Guardians in Ireland, which received the Royal assent on March 31 [1896]:

(59 Vict.) An Act to enable women to be elected, and act as Poor Law Guardians in Ireland (Ch.5).

1. No person otherwise qualified to be elected and to be a Guardian for a poor law union in Ireland, shall be disqualified by sex or marriage for being elected or being such Guardian, anything contained in any Act to the contrary notwithstanding.
2. This Act may be cited as the Poor Law Guardians (Ireland) (Women) Act, 1896.

The date of the passage of the Act did not admit of advantage being taken of it at the election for Guardians in March, but it has set much active preparation on foot in view of the elections next year.

In Dublin the Women's Suffrage Society had long felt that the election of women as Poor Law Guardians would work together for good with their own movement by strengthening the sympathies of the public in women's share in public duties. They have consequently taken this movement also within their sphere of action, and since the Act was passed have been in communication with ladies in various parts of Ireland, as well as in Dublin, with a view to having candidates ready before the next election.

Mrs Haslam, the hon. secretary, has also exerted herself successfully in organising visits by ladies to several of the workhouses in and around Dublin, thus helping much to prepare the way for their hereafter coming forward in the more responsible position of candidates for election. She has also received letters evincing great sympathy with her endeavours from ladies in many places, and nowhere with more hearty response than from Tralee. A public meeting was held in that town in July, at which the principal speakers were Miss Rowan, of the Primrose League,[1] and Mrs E. Harrington, wife of the nationalist ex-MP; in fact, men and women of all political and religious parties met on common ground, and unanimously agreed on the value of women

---

1 The Primrose League was set up in 1883 to promote conservative principles.

taking their share in the work of the Poor Law. In Belfast a meeting was held at the residence of Miss Tod, on September 23, and a public meeting is in course of preparation.

Meantime, a by-election, caused by the retirement of Mr J. G. V. Porter, at Lisbellaw (Co. Fermanagh), has given opportunity for a lady to come forward, and Miss Martin, who is well known in the district, and who takes great interest in the promotion of home industries, was elected early in September, the first woman Guardian in Ireland.

IRISH WOMEN ARE GIVEN THE LOCAL GOVERNMENT FRANCHISE

Doc. 82: Anna Haslam, 'Irishwomen and the Local Government Act', *Englishwoman's Review*, 15 October 1898.

In this extract Haslam examines the position of women in local government.

The last two years have been eventful ones in the political history of the women of Ireland. Down to 1896, with some trifling exceptions that I need not particularise, there was not a single public franchise that we enjoyed except that of voting in the election of Poor Law Guardians, and that was so commonly carried out upon exclusively party lines, and with so little regard to the welfare of our destitute poor, that we were fairly excusable for taking little interest in it. But backward as Ireland has heretofore been in so many respects, she has never lacked capable women equal to the efficient discharge of whatever public duties lay open to them; and when Mr W. Johnson's Poor Law Guardians Bill was passed in 1896, thirteen ladies of the very highest character immediately responded to the call. During the present year the number has increased to seventeen; and had it not been for the unscrupulous tactics adopted by opponents in two or three unions would probably have reached twenty. In one or two of the elections, moreover, those ladies were returned triumphantly at the head of the poll. But, what is even more encouraging from a general point of view, as illustrating the preparedness of many of our female ratepayers for the duties now for the first time imposed upon them, in one of our Dublin elections there is good reason to believe that not only did several hundred women vote for the lady candidate, but in a large number of cases they rose above all sectarian prejudices, and gave her their votes, though she belongs to a different church to themselves, simply because she is well known for her deeds of mercy to the poor, and can be absolutely trusted to do her duty by them.

Of the manner in which our lady Guardians have already performed their work it would be perhaps premature to speak; but I may without invidiousness be permitted to mention that at the opening meeting of the recently elected Board in the Rathdown Union, the chairman, Lord Powerscourt, publicly testified that the presence of Mrs Lawrenson and Miss Burton upon the Board during the previous year 'had been of great advantage to the management, and that their fellow Guardians owed a debt of gratitude for the help which they had given'. So far as I know, the result has been very similar in most if not all the other Unions.

The number of our Poor Law Unions is 159 and, in the greater majority of these, there are as yet no ladies prepared to offer themselves as candidates; but our Intermediate education system, and our Royal University – whatever their shortcomings – are doing their work, and eligible candidates will be found to offer themselves in increasing numbers every year. It is now becoming generally recognised in Ireland that there is scarcely a department in our Poor Law administration in which the help of experienced women is not urgently needed – more urgently, if possible, than even in England; in many of our remoter Unions the dietary is wretchedly bad, the nursing is worse, and the training of the unhappy children for the practical work of life is of the most rudimentary character.

The passing of the Local Government Act has effected some momentous changes in relation to our lady Guardians; and the acceptance by the government of the dual-member amendment has averted a most serious peril. Women will still have a reasonable prospect of being elected second upon the list where they would have no chance of being returned head of the poll. But, more important still, the addition of the residential qualification, effected largely through the exertions of the Women's Local Government Society, has thrown open the offices of Guardian and District Councillor to numbers of eligible women, married and single, who would otherwise be excluded from both. Indeed, from the point of view both of electors and elected, the passing of the Act is the most signal political revolution that has taken place in the history of Irishwomen. We have, in round numbers, somewhere about one hundred thousand women ratepayers who are now invested with powers they never possessed before – which most of them indeed never even dreamed of possessing – and a very considerable proportion of these are certain to exercise the franchises now conferred upon them . . . [T]he duties of District Councillors are so much less familiar than those of the Poor Law Guardians that many capable women will no doubt for some time be deterred from facing them; but this is a difficulty which a very few years' experience will suffice to remove.

Some persons have expressed regret that the County Councils, as well as the District Councils, have not been thrown open to our women; but there are certainly very few at present who would be willing to undertake that office; nor are its duties at all so well calculated to enlist their sympathies, or draw out their special gifts. And on the whole it is certainly better that Ireland should not precede Great Britain in the extension of these franchises. . . .

So far as the County Councils are concerned, a very short enabling Act will now suffice for both countries; and it will be the fault of our English friends if they do not before long succeed in passing it.

For Parish Councils, Ireland is certainly unprepared; their establishment would be not only premature but probably mischievous. And the same remark applies to the much more important question of the School Board system. For obvious reasons a generation will probably elapse before our people will be anxious to adopt it; at all events, until they are, its compulsory obtrusion upon us could only result in the stirring up of acrimonious controversies, which would gravely retard the healing process at present visibly going on around us.

To myself personally the Local Government Act is interesting far more as a political educator than from the specific benefits that may in other directions spring from it. For the great majority of our countrywomen in all our rural districts their political education commences with the present year. So far, our women's suffrage agitation has never penetrated much beyond the outskirts of Dublin, Belfast, and one or two other towns. Even in Cork no suffrage association has ever been permanently established; and the same is true of Limerick, Waterford, Galway, Dundalk, Drogheda, Londonderry and other similar places. In some of these important centres the very nucleus of such an association has not heretofore existed; women saw no practical good in agitating for a reform which never seemed likely to be realised; they accordingly threw their energies into the charitable work that lay nearest to their hand, and the results of which would be visible in their own life-time. The next few years – with these periodical district elections brought home to their doors, and with the women in ever-increasing numbers sitting side by side with men upon their respective councils – will revolutionise their ideas, and make them, not only desire the parliamentary vote, but willing to take some little trouble in order to obtain it. The immediate duty of women suffragists in Ireland is the establishment of active working committees in all these local centres, and to this indispensable work the Dublin committee are now more especially addressing themselves.

IRISH WOMEN IN LOCAL GOVERNMENT

Doc. 83: Mrs Maurice Dockrell, 'Irishwomen in local government', in Lady Aberdeen, (ed.), *Women in Politics: The International Congress of Women, 1899* (London, 1900).

Mrs Maurice Dockrell spoke in 1899 at an International Congress of Women. She was an elected Urban District Councillor in Dublin, and a Protestant. She notes the particular qualities desired of women in public roles.

By the provisions of the Local Government Act of 1898, following closely upon the passage of the Women's Poor Law Guardians Act of 1896, a large field of useful public work has been opened up for Irishwomen. This work ranges itself under the head of the three classes – electors, Poor Law Guardians and District Councillors.

That Irishwomen have not been slow to avail themselves of the privileges rather grudgingly granted by the new Act is shown by the fact that not fewer than 100,000 women are qualified to become local government electors, and 85 have been elected to the rural councils and Poor Law Boards, and four – of which I am one – are sitting as Urban District Councillors. To properly appreciate the difficulties these women have to contend with, you must try to recollect the position of affairs in the sister country.

Ireland is in a transition state. The governing power in local affairs has passed from the unionist to the nationalists, from Protestants to Catholics, from the educated, cultured, leisured classes to the traders, small farmers, and, in many cases, even to the labourers; but the women who have been elected nearly all belong to the highly-educated class, and some of them are unionists and Protestants. From this hasty sketch it will be seen that the women who enter public life require a great deal of tact, patience, and what I must call a level-headed devotion to the public good; but I believe that this feminine element, particularly when allied with a certain masculinity of intellect and administrative ability, is destined to become a very potent factor in public life. The Irish are a gallant, chivalrous race, to whom anything feminine powerfully appeals. My own individual experience fully bears out this optimistic view. I am a unionist and a Protestant, about two-thirds of the members of my council are nationalists and Catholics, yet I was unanimously elected to be deputy vice-chairman, and I have been placed upon several committees, including being made chairman of the Dwellings for the Very Poor. I have always received the utmost courtesy and consideration, and when any purely feminine question comes up, my opinion generally carries some weight. But then I have to confess that I am quite old-fashioned in some respects. I still believe in husbands and babies and frocks. I seem to be a connecting link between the old type of woman who thought men must be always right and the new type who think they are always wrong.

In conclusion, may I be permitted to say a few hopeful words as to the future of my own dear country. I do not believe Ireland is going to destruction because the nationalists are in the majority. I hold that the possession of power will steady them. They will gain the courage of responsibility, and will weed out or restrain the more uncontrollable members of their party. And I think it is upon us women especially [that] devolves the task of reconciling the opposing forces, softening asperities, and cementing all classes, so that peace and harmony shall reign in our land, and that truth and justice, religion and piety, may be established among us for all generations.

The National Question

WHY MUST WE STRIVE FOR FREEDOM

Doc. 84: *Shan Van Vocht*, 4 August 1896.

A large number of Irish women, many of them suffragists, were involved in the Irish nationalist movement. In January 1896, Alice Milligan (1866–1953) and Anna Johnson (1866–1911) began to publish the Shan Van Vocht (Poor Old Woman) from Belfast. The paper took as its motto the following phrase from a '98 ballad:

'Yes, Ireland shall be free/ From the centre to the sea/ And hurrah for liberty,/ Says the Shan Van Vocht.' The paper contained stories, poems, and accounts of the progress of the Irish language. It also provided one of the earliest platforms for the views of James Connolly. Milligan and Johnson believed that through the pages of the magazine, and through Milligan's advocacy of the Irish language, they were '. . . not working merely for the preservation of a language but for the existence of a distinct nationality'. The paper ceased publication in April 1899.

An answer to this momentous question [why must we strive for freedom?] should be in the hearts of all of us, as a deep and unshakable conviction, ready for utterance in response to the questioning of the credulous and despairing who love Ireland and would fain serve her, but who are not assured of the necessity of this strife for freedom, as the best, nay, the only honourable and loyal way for Ireland's sons to uplift her. Freedom must be with us more than a matter of political opinion, more than an exalting sentiment, more even than an ardent desire. We must, as I have said, be convinced of its absolute necessity, and make its attainment the aim and goal of our hopes, the inspiring motive of all our best work.

Without that inward conviction, we may have enthusiasm; we may have patriotism; our enthusiasm however will not be steadfast but will come to us in sudden and uncertain gusts, and we will find ourselves incapable of persistent, untiring, and hopeful effort. Our patriotism will at times sink to a lower level and we will find ourselves easily content to accept for our country the prospect of a less noble destiny. Our love for Ireland may still endure, and we may desire for her the best things possible, yet be persuaded to believe that amongst these best things freedom must not be longer dreamed of. The hope of seeing Ireland a nation once again that illumined the youthful heart of Davis,[1] and that has shone through the prison bars on many a patriot, will seem to us to have been a mocking flame, a phantom will o'wisp that lured them to useless and vain pursuit, and led them at last to destruction.

We are often urged by so called wise and practicable people, who claim to be the truest patriots, that we are wronging and harming our country rather than serving her by our foolish talk of freedom; we are keeping her in unrest and misery, bringing upon her people poverty and famine and persecution, and driving them to prison and to death, all to no end. We are told that we can be just as patriotic and do far more service to Ireland by abandoning the pursuit of the unattainable and settling down to accomplish some real practical benefit. Why should we not accept for Ireland the place and destiny to which the dispensation of Providence has guided her. She is linked with the mightiest empire in the world, and is called upon to share in governing it; through that alliance with England she can extend her commerce, and find a scope for the valour of her sons in wars of conquest and defence. She need not abandon her national characteristics, but can develop her genius in the domain of literature and music, as Scotland has done. Her fertile hills and plains tilled by a peaceful and contented race will support a greater population in ease and comfort.

The transformation of Ireland to such an Elysium[2] would be immediate if only those voices could be silenced which are for ever disturbing her peace, but flattering her with unreal hope, and recounting to her the dream of freedom.

How shall we reject for our country this offer of prosperity, happiness, and power, the 'peace with honour' which, at the end of a long-contended strife, is offered to us by an antagonist who has learned to respect us. We talk of past wrongs, but the desire of revenge would not be sufficient warrant for us to continue the strife and cast aside all thoughts of a truce. What then is to be our guiding motive. Why must we strive for freedom. It is because we believe that our nation has a high and noble destiny to fulfil, a part to play in the advancement of the human race along the upward path of progress. She cannot barter that birthright and heritage of hope for any mere material good, nor consent to sink her individual nationality, as part of an empire whose run was extended over her island by force and injustice. She has a higher aim than to enrich the literature of England or share her tyrant sway. Ireland has a message for the world through her literature, a message that cannot be uttered

1 Thomas Davis (1814–45), co-founder of *The Nation* newspaper and unofficial leader of the Young Irelanders.
2 Heaven.

by the voice of a slave in willing bondage. Let us be faithful in believing it – the liberation of Ireland will be for the welfare of all the world, and with the day-start of her freedom a bright and happier era will dawn.

A WOMAN'S ROLE IN PROMOTING THE IRISH LANGUAGE

Doc. 85: Mary Butler, *Some Suggestions as to how Irishwomen may help the Irish Language Movement* (Gaelic League Pamphlet No. 6, Dublin, 1901).

The Gaelic League was established in 1893 with the specific aim of reviving the use of the Irish language. Part of the cultural revival of the late nineteenth and early twentieth centuries, it was the only cultural society that allowed membership on equal terms to men and women. Mary E. Butler (1874–1920), was a writer who edited a woman's page in the Irish Weekly Independent *between 1899 and 1903. She was a member of the executive of the Gaelic League, and an active member of Sinn Féin.[1] She made the following suggestions specifically to encourage women to support the language movement.*

1. Realise what it means to be an Irishwoman and make others realise what it means by being Irish in fact as well as in name.
2. Make the home atmosphere Irish.
3. Make the social atmosphere Irish.
4. Speak Irish if you know it, especially in the home circle, and if you have no knowledge of the language, set about acquiring it at once. If you only know a little speak that little.
5. Insist on children learning to speak, read and write Irish.
6. Insist on school authorities giving pupils the benefit of a thoroughly Irish education.
7. Use Irish at the family prayers.
8. Give Irish names to children.
9. Visit Irish speaking districts. If Irish people who are students of the language go among their Irish-speaking fellow country people in the right spirit and instill the right principles in them, they will be conferring a benefit on the people, and the people will in return confer a benefit on them by imparting their native knowledge of the spoken language to them.
10. Encourage Irish music and song.
11. Support Irish publications and literature.

1 Sinn Féin developed from the National Council organised by Arthur Griffith (1871–1922). The purpose of the National Council was to protest against the royal visit. It promoted cultural and economic nationalism and looked for Irish autonomy with an attachment to the English crown. Mary Butler provided the name Sinn Féin for the organisation.

12. Employ Irish-speaking servants whenever possible.
13. Join the Gaelic League, and induce others to do so.
14. Spread the light among your acquaintances.
15. Consistently support everything Irish and consistently withhold your support from everything un-Irish.

INGHINIDHE NA HÉIREANN

Doc. 86: *United Irishman*, 13 October 1900.

The following document recounts the first meeting of Inghinidhe na hÉireann.

Central Branch Inghinidhe Bhrighidhe.

The above society held its inaugural meeting at 32 Lower Abbey Street on Thursday, the President, Miss Maud Gonne, in the chair.

The following ladies were elected members – Mrs James F. Egan, Mrs J. Wyse Power, Mrs W. O'Leary, Mrs O'Beirne, Mrs Sullivan, Mrs O'Malley, Miss Anna Johnson (Belfast), Miss Alice Furlong, Miss Harriet Rose-Byrne, Miss Bebe Nally (Claremorris), Miss O'Kennedy, Miss Kileen, Miss Attie O'Brien, Miss Rooney, Miss Hacket, Miss White, Miss Whelan, Miss Devlin, Miss Meagher, Miss M. Meagher, Miss Morgan, Miss Perolz, Miss Quinn, Miss M. Quinn, Miss Moran, Miss Murray, Miss Fanning, Miss M. Moran, and each selected a Gaelic name by which she will be known in the association in future.

The objects of the society are:–
   I. To encourage the study of Gaelic, of Irish literature, history, music, and art, especially amongst the young, by the organising and teaching of classes for the above subjects.
  II. To support and popularise Irish manufactures.
 III. To discourage the reading and circulation of low English literature, the singing of English songs, the attending of vulgar English entertainments at theatres and music halls, and to combat in every way English influence, which is doing so much injury to the artistic taste and refinement of the Irish people.
  IV. To form a fund called the National Purposes Fund for the furtherance of the above objects.

The rules were submitted to the meeting and adopted as follows:–
   I. The Inghinidhe na hÉireann, remembering that they are all workers in the same holy cause, pledge themselves to mutual help and support, and to stand loyally by one another.
  II. Each member must adopt a Gaelic name by which she shall be known in the association.

III. Each member shall pledge herself to aid in extending and popularising Gaelic as a spoken tongue, and to advance the Irish language movement by every means in her power.

IV. Each member shall pledge herself to support Irish manufactures by using as far as possible Irish made goods in her household and dress.

Membership – to be eligible, the proposed member must be of Irish birth or descent, and must accept the principle of independent nationality for Ireland, candidates must be proposed and seconded by two members of the association – a week to elapse between nomination and election. Election by ballot.

Affiliations

Irish women's clubs in the provinces or in any part of the world, if they adopt the rules and accept the objects of the association, may affiliate on payment of 5s yearly to the Central branch.

A programme was then drawn up, which provided amongst other things, for classes for children over nine years old . . . for the teaching of Gaelic, Irish history, and Irish songs. These classes are free to all children, and the society hopes they will be well attended throughout the winter . . .

NATIONALISM VERSUS SUFFRAGISM

Doc. 87: Hanna Sheehy Skeffington, 'Sinn Féin and Irishwomen', *Bean na hÉireann,* November 1909; reply: *Bean na hÉireann,* December 1909.

Bean na hÉireann *first appeared in November 1908. It was established by women involved in Inghinidhe na hÉireann. Its editor was Helena Molony (1884–1967), an actress in the Abbey Theatre who later became involved in the Irish Women Workers' Union, and in 1937 became president of the Irish Trades Union Council. The women of Inghinidhe na hÉireann were more concerned with nationalism than with the suffrage issue, and supported the use of physical violence to attain Irish freedom. Hanna Sheehy Skeffington criticised the Inghinidhe's stance on suffragism. In November 1909 Skeffington, in an article for the paper called 'Sinn Féin and Irish Women', argued that Irish women could not rely on Irish men to provide them with the vote on achieving independence. Independence alone, she stated, could not alter deep-rooted attitudes about gender roles. The second document is a reply to Skeffington's piece and appeared in the paper in December 1909. It was signed anonymously 'Sinn Féiner'. It disagreed fundamentally with Skeffington's stance and urged Irish women to join the nationalist movement as the only way forward for Ireland, and for women. The competition between advocates of nationalism and suffragism for the attention of women was a divisive feature in Irish society in the first two decades of the twentieth century.*

We all, unionists and nationalist alike, live overmuch on our past in Ireland. . . . This tendency is nowhere more aptly illustrated than with regard to the position of Irishwomen in the Ireland of to-day. Nowhere in the pitiful tangle of present-day life does the actual more sadly belie the far-off past. It is barren comfort for us Irishwomen to know that in ancient Ireland women occupied a prouder, freer position than they now hold even in the most advanced modern states, that all professions, including that of arms, were freely open to their ambitions . . .

Is the degradation of the average Irishwoman the less real, her education sacrificed to give her brothers ampler opportunities of having a good time loitering through their examinations in the capital, her marriage a matter of sordid bargaining, broken maybe because an over-insistent prospective father-in-law demands a cow or a pig too much. . . . Whatever its uses, the bride's portion belongs irrevocably to the husband's family . . .

I have chosen but a few salient examples to illustrate the disabilities Irishwomen suffer today. The result of Anglicization? This is but partly true; much of the evil is, however, inherent in latter-day Irish life. Nor will the evil disappear, as we are assured, when Ireland comes to her own again, whenever that may be. For until the women of Ireland are free, the men will not achieve emancipation. It is for Irishwomen, therefore, to work out their own 'Sinn Féin' on their own lines, for with the broader, non-party aspect of Sinn Féin – namely, the reformation from within, outwards all nationalists have always been in agreement. . . .

In the Gaelic movement, in the industrial revival and in the Sinn Féin organization she has undoubtedly made her power felt. So much the better for the movement . . . The Gaelic League must make its final appeal to the young, unless those to whom the very beginning are entrusted take up Irish it will surely perish. So too with the industrial revival – it is the woman who looks after the domestic budget, her voice can make or mar Irish indus-trialism. Therefore, it is primarily in her capacity as mother and housekeeper, not as individual citizen, that these movements have of necessity recognised her importance . . . That is why, doubtless, many worthy Gaelic Leaguers get restive at the thought of women having places on the executive body, that is why, too, in spite of theoretical equality, some Sinn Féiners have not yet rounded Cape Turk where women are concerned. One of the leaders afforded an interesting object-lesson to his women colleagues in the move-ment by founding university scholarships from which girls were expressly excluded. Irishwomen may be excused, therefore, if they distrust all parties in Ireland, for what I have said of the Sinn Féin organisation applies with far greater force to the parliamentarian movement which, since the extinction of the Ladies' Land League in the eighties, has steadily ignored Irishwomen, hitherto indeed with impunity. It is for Irishwomen of every political party to adopt the principle of Sinn Féin in the true sense of the word, and to refuse any longer to be the camp-follower and parasites of public life, dependent on caprice and expediency for recognition. It is for Irishwomen to set about working out their political salvation. Until the parliamentarian and the Sinn Féin women alike possess the vote, the keystone of citizenship, she will count but little with either party, for it is through the medium of the vote alone that either party can achieve any measure of success. This is a fact of which we parliamentarians have long been aware to our cost, but which Sinn Féin women have yet to learn.

A Chara.

Mrs Sheehy Skeffington sums up a very interesting and able article on 'Sinn Féin and Irishwomen' by saying that 'until the parliamentarian and Sinn Féin women alike possess the vote, the keystone of citizenship, she will count but little with either party, for it is through the *medium of the vote alone that either party can achieve any measure of success.*'

This from a Sinn Féin and a separatist point of view strikes me as being a very curious and inaccurate statement; probably Mrs Skeffington belongs to that section of Irish who do not desire separation, but who merely wish to see Ireland growing more prosperous, quiet, and resigned under British rule, who can contemplate with serenity the national spirit gradually absorbed into imperial jingoism, and Ireland becoming a servile and contented west British province.

If this be so she is quite logical when she advises Irishwomen to organise for the purpose of joining in the Englishwomen's agitation for a vote. . . .

I would ask Mrs Skeffington to regard the question from a broader standpoint, not from the standpoint of a woman scrambling for her mess of pottage, and willing to join with her country's conquerors and worst enemies to gain her end, but from the point of view of an Irish nationalist. A woman who knows the truth, knows that in an independent Ireland alone can the men and women who compose the Irish nation ever hope to find justice and liberty, peace and prosperity. The suffrage for the English parliament granted to Irishwomen would not make them free as it would Englishwomen. Do our nationalist men consider themselves free while Ireland lies in chains? It would only mean another chain linking yet another section of the Irish to England. Another confusion of Irish with English ideas. A connection established along which the thoughts and interests of the newly-awakened women of Ireland are to be carried away to Westminster.

The situation should be plain enough, and there are but two roads for Irishwomen to walk on. The one leads them to fight to redress the wrongs that are ours under English rule, and the other is to fight till we make an end of English rule in Ireland.

Into this struggle all the driving force that Ireland is capable of needs to be put – the struggle for the freedom of Ireland – her women with her men. . . .

The nation must almost be reborn before we can free ourselves, and there is work for every one of Ireland's children to do for Ireland and against England. The women with the men, and if the women of Ireland throw themselves into the national struggle, who is to stop them from taking their rightful place in their nation on the day that she wins her freedom?

How, on the contrary, will an agitation of Irishwomen to gain the English franchise help the cause of independence? Freedom to Ireland must be made to mean also freedom to women; prosperity to Ireland, prosperity to Irishwomen. . . .

Hitch your wagon to a star. Do not work for the right to share in the government of that nation that holds Ireland enslaved, but work to procure for our sex the right of free citizenship in an independent Ireland.

A SINN FÉINER

THE HISTORY OF CUMANN NA MBAN

Doc. 88: *An Phoblacht,* 8 April, 15 April 1933.

The following document is taken from a lecture given by the president of Cumann na mBan, Eithne Ní Chumhaill (Eithne Coyle) in 1933.

. . . The unperishable spirit of freedom which lay dormant owing to centuries of oppression and the despondency caused by the Fenian failure of 1867 was once more revived. The national revival was largely due to the publication of a stirring and fearless little organ known by the appropriate name of *An Sean Bhean Bhocht*,[1] which was edited by two illustrious Irishwomen from the north of Ireland, Eithne Carbery McManus and Alice Milligan. This little paper voiced the gospel of nationality fearlessly and unmistakably in the latter part of the 19th century. . . .

Gaelic Classes
The Irish language, which was thrown in the rubbish heap for years owing to England's tactics and the anglicised system of education in this country was taken up. Gaelic classes were formed and our people took pride once more in our native tongue. Irish games and ancient pastimes of Cuchulainn[2] and the Red Branch Knights were revived. Home manufactures, native Irish dancing were encouraged, and trusanna [excursions] to places of historic interest which were almost forgotten by the people was one of the many activities of these clubs.

Later the Leinster Literary Society was formed and William Rooney,[3] an ardent advocate of Ireland's rights, eventually succeeded in capturing

1 The *Shan Van Vocht*, see document 87 above.
2 A mythical celtic hero.
3 William Rooney (1872–1901), poet and founder of the *United Irishman*.

the elements of national thought in that group, and he at once formed the Celtic Literary Society. This society consisted of people of advanced ideas and high intellectual minds who used all their efforts in educating the masses of the people and in getting them ready for their national emancipation. The will to be free made itself daily manifest and in order to meet the growing demand for freedom the Irish representatives in the British House of Commons introduced a wobbly Home Rule Bill which was favourably received by the more liberal elements in that assembly.

Carson's Guns

The unionists in the north-east corner of Ireland, ably assisted by British money and influence, prepared to oppose by force of arms the passing of this little measure of freedom. Sir Edward Carson, later rewarded by the title of Lord Carson, for perpetuating the union and helping England in her old policy of dividing and conquering the people of Ireland, succeeded in landing thousands upon thousands of arms and ammunition in secret at Larne. These guns were to be freely used against their Catholic countrymen, if and when Home Rule was to be passed for Ireland.

The southern Gaels, inspired by the spirit of the men of 1798, 1803, '48 and '67,[1] realised the danger of allowing an armed and undisciplined mob to be let loose on unarmed and helpless citizens, determined to meet force with force. Consequently, a private meeting was arranged for Wynn's Hotel, in Abbey Street, on November 13th, 1913. This meeting was addressed by P. H. Pearse,[2] Bulmer Hobson,[3] Eoin McNeill,[4] L. Kettle and the late Dr Michael Davitt. A discussion arose regarding the menace in the north and it was there and then decided to organise a body of men who were to become known as the Irish Volunteers.

In 1913, a few ladies decided to hold a meeting in Wynn's Hotel for the purpose of discussing the possibility of forming an organisation for women, who would work in conjunction with the recently formed Irish Volunteers and who would be pledged to help that body in any action which they would decide on for breaking the connection with England.

In the following May at a representative meeting which was held in the Pillar Room in the Mansion House, Cumann na mBan was launched. The first branch of the organisation which was formed was the Ard Chraobh. These women held their first meetings in Brunswick Street, in fact they met there continually till after the Rising in 1916.

1 Referring to the rebellion of 1798, Robert Emmet's rebellion of 1803, the Young Ireland rising in 1848 and the Fenian rising in 1867.
2 Patrick Henry Pearse (1879–1916), executed for his role in the 1916 rising.
3 Bulmer Hobson (1883–1969) organised the Howth gun-running, also member of the Gaelic League.
4 Eoin McNeill (1867–1945), first vice-president of the Gaelic League and editor of its newspaper *An Claidheamh Soluis*.

The Inghinidhe na hÉireann Club was in existence for over twenty years previous to the formation of Cumann na mBan,[1] and its members, really the pioneers of our organisation, did magnificent work at an unpopular period when to hold an Irish outlook or to protest nationalism was not only 'unladylike' but 'disreputable'. These women were mainly responsible for the loyal reception which was given to our noble king and queen, George and Mary of England, when they honoured this distressed country of ours by their royal presence on July 8th, 1911.

George's Picture

Amongst the other Punch and Judy side shows which were organised by the Castle hacks and time-servers in this country was a large illuminated photograph of his Majesty which was displayed at the foot of Grafton Street for the edification of the mere Irish. It is evident that his Majesty's beauty did not appeal to the members of Inghinidhe na hÉireann for it is recorded that a monstrous outrage was committed by one bold disloyal lassie who seized a fat comfortable brick and smashed poor George's photograph. This disloyal subject was, of course, lodged in Mountjoy Jail for the safety of the realm.

It is worth quoting William Rooney's remarks on the women of Ireland during this period. 'The women', he says, 'who succeeded in gathering together 30,000 children to signify their contempt for the Queen of England and her satellites will, I am sure, do much more.' 'You know', he continued, 'how much the women with Irish hearts who will recognise their duty of sacrifice and glory in the cause they love, who have men's courage and men's determination to do the right thing when the time comes. I think that Inghinidhe na hÉireann will go far in creating such a generation of Irish women.'

Shortly after the formation of Ard Chraobh [the Inghinidhe] branch became affiliated with Cumann na mBan, sub-branches formed in Blackhall Street and then the Fairview Branch was formed. The formation of four branches provided an organised group of women for each Volunteer battalion. The country soon followed and branches sprang up in Killarney, Cork, Limerick, Tralee, Dingle, Enniscorthy and Wexford town.

In 1914 the Redmondite party became alarmed at the rapid growth of the militant organisation over which they had no control. They, therefore, decided to seek representation on the Volunteer Council, in order to curb the growing militant spirit and to induce the Irish Volunteers to abandon their efforts in seeking to overthrow the might of England by force of arms and to seek concessions from the robber instead.

. . . John Redmond, the leader of that party in the British House of Commons, in a speech . . . declared that the Irish Volunteers would fight and die for England in the fields of Flanders and Gallipoli. Well indeed might the men and women of our race blush with shame, when hearing from this

1 Inghinidhe na hÉireann was, in fact, founded 14 years before Cumann na mBan. See doc. 89.

man who was in a responsible position at the time, that our Volunteers were willing to help England in her campaign of blood lust and greed.

This outrageous statement which was made without the sanction of the Volunteers, aroused the fiercest indignation in their ranks and the controlling council of that body broke into two camps. . . .

Cumann na mBan during this time . . . holding to the constitution and agreeing with the men who issued the Manifesto repudiating Redmond and his nominees on the Elective Council. Owing to the steadfast attitude of our organisation, we lost some members but adherence to principle always brings its rewards and hundreds of recruits flooded to our ranks. A scheme of activities was drawn up about this time which embraced – 1. First Aid. Lectures. 2. Home Nursing. 3. Signalling and Arms. 4. The use, care, cleaning, loading of rifles and revolvers was taught. 5. A rifle practice in the Father Matthew Hall in Fairview and at the Inghinidhe Hall in Camden Street was keenly taken up by some of our members. 6. Physical drill was practised at each branch meeting because Cumann na mBan realised that discipline was one of the most essential things in the organisation. 7. Irish classes were held and our members were requested to acquire a knowledge of their own language. Punctuality was insisted upon, and misfortune overtook anyone who dared to turn up one minute after the hour fixed for parade.

Work with Volunteers

In 1915 the Volunteers were an efficient body. Route marches, army manoeuvres, sham battles were fought and members of Cumann na mBan were specially selected to accompany the Volunteers on these activities.

An Aemdheabht Mhor at St Enda's, Rathfarnham, was the first proud occasion on which our members wore their distinctive uniform. They were congratulated on their smart appearance by some of the men who later led the fight for freedom and whose names will be for ever immortalised in the history of our country. Some of the British soldiers' wives pelted mud and stones at the girls when they saw them appearing in their green uniforms and called them by the undignified name of 'grass-hoppers'.

On Easter Sunday, 1916, Cumann na mBan, like the Volunteers, were mobilised, but owing to John MacNeill's[1] peculiar action in cancelling the mobilisation orders, some of our members could not be got in time for the general order which the executive issued to all members of the organisation in Dublin, but many of them found their way back to the firing line when the fighting started.

Some of the girls who were mobilised for the central areas, O'Connell Street, the Four Courts and Church Street, met in Dominick Street on Easter Sunday, but owing to some misunderstanding, Comdt. Ned Daly, afterwards executed, advised the girls to disband.

1 Eoin McNeill, see note 4, p 305.

Later in the day, two of the members got in touch with Pearse, Connolly and Clarke in the GPO and a hurried mobilisation was sent out. Most of the girls turned up and took up positions in the fighting areas, and they fully responded to the faith which the men of Easter Week placed in them, and well may we in Cumann na mBan today be proud of our old members who participated in the glorious epoch, and who risked their lives in order to help the soldiers of Easter Week to break the chains of slavery.

Easter Week

Their work was hard and heavy, sleep and rest impossible, food irregular and insufficient. They nursed and tended the wounded, carried dispatches, arms and ammunition, night and day, through showers of shrapnel, picking their way through broken walls and burning houses, caring less for their own safety than for the war equipment and dispatches they carried for the Volunteers.

On the Friday of Easter Week the different positions occupied by the Volunteers and by our members were becoming hourly unsafe and untenable, the buildings around were one mass of red flame which lit up the countryside for miles outside the city. It was eventually decided by the men that some of the women should leave the buildings. This decision brought tears to the eyes of many of the girls who were willing to share the fate of the men.

The Commander-in-Chief, P. H. Pearse, seeing their sorrow and grief, spoke to them in that high-souled and idealistic tone which characterised this soldier of Ireland and raised him above his fellow men during his life service to the cause of Cait Ní Dhuibhir.[1] He briefly thanked them for their great help during the week and said that when the history of that fight would be written the foremost page in the annals should be given to the women of Dublin who had taken their place in the fight for the establishment of an Irish republic. He told them that by their presence they had inspired the men of the Irish Volunteers with hope and courage and without that inspiration they could not hold out so long against such overwhelming odds.

Pearse's Work

He reminded them of the heroism of the women of Limerick in Sarsfield's days, of Ann Devlin in Emmet's time, of the great devotion of the wife of Tone, but said that such heroism, wonderful though it was, paled before the devotion to duty of the women of Cumann na mBan. Pearse, concluding his address, begged of the God of Justice to bless, guard and protect the women of Cumann na mBan to carry on the fight until Ireland would be free. He then shook hands with each girl in turn and it was with heavy hearts they turned away from that sad, pale, aesthetic face, always gazing on that far-away vision of a free Ireland. They knew that they would never again see this man except in a better land to ours.

---

1 The figure of Cáit Ní Dhuibhir was a symbolic representation of Ireland.

[Extract continued in *An Phoblacht*, 15 April 1933]
Two of the members of branch who were appointed members of the staff of
Comdt. James Connolly in Liberty Hall the night before the Rising,
remained with the men until the final evacuation. One girl, who served in the
Citizen Army during the fight, was badly wounded and had to be removed to
hospital, while the other members of the organisation who occupied other
buildings with the Volunteers surrendered with the men. Many of them were
arrested and taken to Kilmainham Jail for ten days where they listened to the
merciless daily volley which sent their comrades in the Irish Volunteers before
a higher and more just tribunal than that of General Maxwell. . . .

THE EASTER RISING 1916

*The rising which began in Dublin on Easter Sunday 1916 brought about
great changes in Irish politics. About sixty women from Cumann na mBan
acted as nurses and cooks during the week-long rebellion. Women who had
formed part of the Irish Citizen Army acted as an ambulance corps, and
also took an active part in the fighting. Helena Molony and Constance
Markievicz, for example, were armed. Not everyone was sympathetic to the
rebels. The following accounts of the rising offer very different perspectives.*

A Personal Experience of the Dublin Rebellion

Doc. 89.1: Nora Tynan O'Mahony 'A personal experience of the Dublin rebellion', *The
Englishwoman*, 31 (July–September 1916).

*Tynan O'Mahony's son was a cadet in Portobello Barracks. Her major
concern was about his safety.*

. . . On our way home that Monday evening we learnt from friends that a
great 'Sinn Féin' rising had taken place in the city, that already the Post
Office, St Stephen's Green, the bridges over the canals, Jacob's Biscuit
Factory, and many public buildings were in the hands of the insurgents; that a
great many soldiers and civilians had been shot down in the streets. . . .

Meanwhile stories were rife on all sides of the performances of the Sinn
Féin party, who were said to have blown up Milltown Bridge and a great part
of the Great Southern and Western Railway line, to have taken Dublin Castle,
the Four Courts, and the south Dublin Union, and to have cut the city off
from communication with the outside world by telephone or telegraph. Not
an evening paper was be had, and it was said that the insurgents had all the
newspaper offices of Dublin, save one, in their possession. . . .

Before leaving, my friends and I had gone as far as Portobello Bridge, to see the damage done there to a corner house, a publican's, which had been one of the first places the Sinn Féiners had chosen as a stronghold. From this commanding position they had on Monday shot several soldiers, who happened to be walking in the line of fire. An officer and some men with a machine gun, however, had soon put the insurgents to flight. Every window was riddled with bullets, which made only a small hole and hardly cracked the surrounding glass. The windows were rudely barricaded with beds and other furniture, while in the shop and lower part of the building, now in the hands of the military, shattered glass and empty wine cases told of the havoc which had been wrought. . . .

Wednesday passed, with all sorts of reports flying about, most of them thoroughly unreliable, as to what was happening in the city. Still there was no doubt but that matters were decidedly serious. At first it had seemed so decidedly impossible to realise that such a thing could happen, 'all in a slap', without a moment's warning, as it were. It was useless to go to the city, for one could not pass any of the bridges save at the serious risk of one's life.

The Sinn Féiners were entrenched in Stephen's Green, where they had made barricades of motor-cars commandeered from passers-by; they had also commandeered the bread and milk from the bakers' and dairymen's carts, giving their drivers in each case a written receipt for the amount, which they said would be paid for by the leaders of the 'Irish Republic'. They had taken the horses out of the dairymen's carts, of which they made barricades in the streets leading to their principal strongholds, firing from behind them at the military or any civilians who tried to pass. Many horses were lying dead in the city, especially in the vicinity of Stephen's Green. The Sinn Féiners had laid in stores of provisions in the Green; they had also a staff of trained nurses and stretcher-bearers ready for emergencies.

Reports came constantly of people being shot down, in some cases accidental no doubt, the victims being children. It was not safe for any man to be seen out in khaki; and a poor wounded officer, home on a few days' leave from the front, was, on the first day of the outbreak, shot through the brain, just a few seconds after he had laughed at a friend's warning entreaty to take cover in a neighbouring house. The house of a judge, a personal friend of my husband's, was taken by the Sinn Féiners on account of its commanding position and its owners held as hostages in the basement. This was in almost the immediate vicinity of Beggars' Bush Barracks, and as I was told that there was a great deal of shooting in the neighbourhood, where also the insurgents held possession of the railway line, my uneasiness began to grow.

On Thursday morning two kind friends volunteered to try to get to the barracks in search of information – no easy task seeing that the thoroughfares were nearly all stopped, no tramcars or hired vehicles were running, and even a motor-car, supposing one lucky enough to be able to get sufficient petrol to run it, was in constant and eminent danger of being commandeered by one or other party. There was nothing to do but walk, and this they did, for a considerable portion of the way, with bullets whizzing on every side of them, and pools of blood staining the roads as they passed. To get near to the barracks was no easy matter, for all the approaches to it were being fired on by the Sinn Féiners from houses in a commanding position. Finally they reached the gates; the visitors were successful in seeing my son, who looked well and happy as only a boy ardent for adventure could be. My ambassador was besieged before he left the barracks with many messages from husbands and fathers – members of the veteran and other civilian corps temporarily imprisoned willy nilly, to worried wives and families at home, anxiously waiting for news, and not knowing whether their beloved ones were living or dead. A company of these GRs, many of them men well on in years, had been fired on by the Sinn Fé.iners on the Monday afternoon, while returning quietly to barracks; seven of them were shot down, two being killed, while two more died of wounds within a few days.

My cadet was quite content in barracks, and it would have been madness to bring him out into the dangers of the streets.

My friends that day, during their journey across the southern suburbs, had been held up for more than an hour at one point by the passing of many thousands of soldiers, just disembarked at Kingstown; some of whom, as it happened, were fated to march a little later with sad and fatal results right into the fire of the insurgents. These soldiers and marines met with an enthusiastic reception; ladies handed them fruit and cigarettes, running back into the shops for further supplies as the first ones were exhausted.

Friday, the fifth day of the rising, was in many respects the most sombre and nerve-straining of the week. All night long we had listened to the roar of the guns; from a tiny hill just opposite our hall door, which gave a full view of the city's environments, we had watched until a late hour the strong fires and huge flames that leaped from where Sackville Street was burning.

All the week motor-cars had been flying and racing past our gates to and from the city; generally carrying people who would be the last one would expect to find in vehicles of the kind – frowsy, ill-dressed, suspicious-looking characters. By the middle of the week it was apparent, however, that many people were fleeing with their families from the threatened city. People with set faces raced by in motor-cars all day and late into the night. Again, motors came from the opposite direction down-country. These, I was told, were mostly making for Kingstown and the non-existent mail-boat, with the hope, sure to be disappointed, of flying from Ireland for good. . . .

For days no baker came to our own and neighbouring villages; people had scrambled for the favour of a single loaf on the last occasion on which he did come, and finally were glad to travel any number of miles in search of a loaf or a stone of flour or potatoes. Flour was now from 2s 6d to 5s per stone, according to the district; in the Dublin suburbs potatoes were 2s 6d a stone, while even at the farmhouses the unprecedented price of £1 per sack was being charged. One farmer in our neighbourhood, who had been unable to take his potatoes out of the ground all winter, now reaped a rich harvest of profit. People came to him from all parts in such numbers, with carts for potatoes, that he was obliged to lock his gates against them, and only admit a couple of carts at a time. . . .

None of the people about us are active Sinn Féiners – that is, as regards fighting, though it is abundantly evident that in nineteen cases out of twenty they are in full sympathy with the insurgents. On the second evening of my sixteen-year-old son's absence, some of the amiable youths of the neighbourhood were heard to declare that 'they hope he was in hell', for no other reason than that he wore the khaki and belonged to a schools' Cadet Corps. Even such of them as were not sympathisers at least with the movement were afraid to declare their opinions.

On that dreadful Friday, when the city burned and cannon thundered all day, I said resentfully to a man employed working in my garden, as the dismal reverberations rolled out again and again: 'What fine work the Sinn Féiners are doing for their city and county now!' At that moment a voice cried loudly across the hedge, like that of a Parisian communist, 'Liberty!' 'Lunacy!' I answered back, and ran to see who it might be; but the speaker had skulked off cautiously out of sight.

Late that same evening another friend came to my door in distress. He was the editor of a Dublin weekly paper, who had gone to Cork for Easter on a few days' leave, and did not learn till the middle of the week how serious things were in Dublin. Owing to the cutting of the telegraph wires and the complete stoppage of all mails, the people of Cork and other distant centres did not know for some days what had actually happened, but were under the impression that this stoppage of all news had been brought about by a breakdown on the GS and W Railway line[1] . . .

That was the worst night of the firing, which had continued all day and incessantly on through the night and the earlier hours of Saturday. At eight o'clock Mass in the village church that Saturday morning there was a great feeling of tension and strain. All through the Holy Sacrifice the boom of the guns went on constantly. The little church held a great many strangers, refugees seeking for safety; and nearly everybody who attended Mass that morning went also to Holy Communion.

Soon after noon the firing began to die away; the quiet and silence of the atmosphere felt strange now to ears for days accustomed to the boom and turmoil of war. A few nights ago we had seen the lights of an aeroplane, flying probably from Dublin to the Curragh; indeed a week or two before the outbreak we had been greatly puzzled by the appearance one night of two similar lights, which apparently flew up and down the coastline between Kingstown and Dublin city.

Later on the Saturday evening we could still hear firing, but only intermittently. It was apparent, even at this distance from the city, that the back

1 Great Southern and Western Railway line.

of the rebellion was by this time pretty well broken. Early on the Sunday morning we saw posted up near the gates of both the Protestant and Catholic churches the following war communique:

> The county Inspector of constabulary at Howth has been directed to give the widest and most immediate publicity to the following document signed by the leaders of the Rebels.
>
> The document runs:
>
> In order to prevent further slaughter of unarmed people, and in the hope of saving the lives of our fellows, now surrounded and hopelessly outnumbered, Members of the Provisional Government present at Headquarters have agreed to an unconditional surrender, and the Commanders of our Unit of the Republican forces will order their followers to lay down their arms. (signed) P. H. Pearse
>
> Dated this 29th April, 1916

These notices seemed to have a disheartening effect on the village Sinn Féin sympathisers, who earlier in the week had been decidedly cock-a-hoop. Still, their spirits rose as the firing continued more or less through the day, though nothing like as ominous as on Thursday and Friday; they were loath to believe that all was up yet with the insurgent, who they believed to have a further surprise up their sleeves for the government.

Shots were still heard on the Monday, especially about six and seven o'clock in the evening, and even on Tuesday there was some individual sniping on the part of Sinn Féiners hidden in different houses in the city and suburbs. . . .

Odd stories were told of the looting in the city, Clery's great emporium and several different boot-shops having been amongst the chief and earliest victims. It was said that the military could not get the crowd to move on out of danger, so intent was it on securing the spoils of war; old women sat on the kerbstone refusing to budge until they should have secured the match of one boot that they tried on from somebody else similarly engaged. Fish-women and fruit-sellers carried baskets or trundled perambulators in front of them, the upper part of their persons being clad in magnificent silk dresses and chic hats, while they showed stockings full of holes, and underskirts ragged and mud-stained. Valuable brooches and other pieces of jewellery looted from a shop nearby were being offered for sale at a penny or three-pence a piece. We heard later that the priests were taking steps to secure that much of the looted stuff should be given back to the owner, but with what success I know not. . . .

From the Monday on things gradually quietened down, though even through the middle of this, the second week, occasional sniping and firing still went on. Then came the news that the leaders of the Sinn Feiners had been shot – first, P H Pearse, Connolly, and MacDonagh, and later Major John MacBride, Plunkett, and the rest, while a large number, including Countess Markievicz, were sent to penal servitude, and others for internment in England.

A Woman Recounts her Experience in the Easter Rising

Doc. 89.2: Anon., 'A Dublin woman's story of the rebellion',
The Gaelic American, 18 November 1916.

On Easter Monday, April 24, the various branches of Cumann na mBan in Dublin were mobilized in different quarters of the city and instructed to await further orders. The Colmcille branch of which I was a member – assembled at the Fianna Hall, Merchants' Quay, thirty members being present, but as the day wore on and no orders arrived some of them tried to make their way home.

About 6 p.m. the secretary requested me to accompany her to the Four Courts which had been in possession of the Volunteers[1] since early that morning – to ascertain if any orders had been received for us by Captain Fahy, who was in charge there. He had received none, but advised us to get in touch with the Executive on the north side of the city. This we did, and found they had been disbanded for the night, but we were instructed to hold ourselves in readiness [for the] next day. We went home after arranging means of communication with each other, but I found my home occupied by the Volunteers so [I] secured shelter for the night at a friend's house.

On Tuesday morning several members of our branch met again, but as no orders had yet arrived we decided to do whatever came to hand. So we did what seemed most urgent at the time by bringing all the ammunition we could lay hands on – many of the boys had it stored in their homes – down to the barricades in Brunswick and North King Streets, which were the nearest posts occupied by our men.

At Father Mathew Hall

On Wednesday morning, however, on learning from Captain – (who is still detained at Frongoch Camp)[2] that there were wounded men in the Father Mathew Hall in Church Street and that help was needed there, my cousin and I offered our services for hospital work, which were accepted, and we remained at that post until after the surrender on the following Sunday.

On arrival we found twenty men, some slightly, others seriously wounded, and seven members of Cumann na mBan attending to them. One portion of the hall was set apart as a hospital and in another section were held the soldiers captured in the Linenhall barracks. Besides these there were several spies and police touts detained. Here also was located the commissariat, provisions from which were distributed raw to those at any distance, which we cooked for the men stationed at the barricades near us. No food, however, was given out except on a signed order from the officer in charge . . .

1 The Irish National Volunteers, see note 1, p 278.
2 The internment camp in Wales where many Irish men were confined after the Easter Rising.

Negotiating the Surrender

The men in Brunswick refused to surrender, as they had been winning all along, and would not believe the bad news till they had seen the terms of surrender in Pearse's own handwriting. Father — and one of the Volunteers negotiated for a truce while removing the wounded and at the enemy head-quarters the Volunteer was taken in charge by two of the enemy who had him covered with their rifles. They threatened to shoot him if his comrades fired a shot. He told them to 'shoot away' and was held for two hours. Then enemy officers asked Father — 'What security have we that those fellows will keep their promise' and was informed that he (Father —) would vouch for their honour as Irishmen.

The wounded were then removed to the hospital, the Volunteers returned to their posts, and some of us girls went to the caretakers' apartments in the rear, where we had our first real sleep for the week. Curiously enough, we found it difficult to sleep at first, as we had grown so accustomed to the sound of firing that we missed it that day. Next morning (Sunday) Father — came to take us to Mass and told us afterwards to make our way home through the crowd. Two of us returned to the hall instead, and cooked breakfast for ourselves and the Red Cross men who still remained there. We also cleared away and burned anything we thought incriminating, such as orders, despatches, etc., signed by the leaders, which had been left behind in the confusion of surrender. . . .

The Fighting Very Heavy

Fighting in this area was not very heavy till Friday afternoon, when the enemy employed armoured motors to rush the barricades. These vehicles were covered with steel, with loopholes in the sides for rifle fire, and mounted two machine guns each. There was also an aperture in front for the driver to watch through. Each car held six soldiers besides the driver. It was impossible to pierce the steel casing except with heavy-calibrated Mauser bullets or hand grenades. All Friday night the fighting was heavy and at close quarters – as the motors had broken through the barricades in the afternoon – and firing was incessant. . . .

. . . John Hurley also died that night, but there was no hope for him from the first. His skull was fractured by a piece of shell and his right arm broken in three places. He was unable to speak and carried no means of identification, and though we had spoken to him several times during the earlier part of the week no one knew his name, and it was not till some days later we learned his name and that he came from Cork city.

Devoted Work of the Priests

That night the fighting outside was so desperate that we were in momentary expectation that the soldiers would succeed in their efforts to break into the hall. Two of the priests heard our confessions about 11 o'clock, and at 12.30

we all received Communion. Father — spoke to us and said: 'The situation at present is very grave, and we all know that if the English break in here there will be no mercy shown to anyone. I want you all, therefore, to offer your lives to God as a willing sacrifice for Ireland. If it is so needed.'

He went on to say that he and another priest would stay with us to the end and we all felt the end was near.

About 1 o'clock, however, we heard singing, faint at first, but growing louder and clearer, and as we listened there in the dark of night, over all the tumult of the fight, we heard the voices of our boys at the barricades singing 'The Soldier's Chorus',[1] and what a change seemed to come over us all. The effect was electrifying and though we did not understand its meaning, we all felt greatly relieved. None of us were afraid to die, but the strain and nervous tension of waiting there for death was terrible. We knew that if the military came in it would mean death and worse than death for us, but the thought of seeing the wounded butchered before our very eyes was maddening. We had seen the fiendish conduct of the English troops that day, and knew what to expect.

A Gallant Bayonet Charge

After some time a Boy Scout came in and informed us that our boys had charged with the bayonet and recovered the ground lost earlier and had driven the enemy back to his own barricades. Then some of the girls sobbed while others laughed hysterically, and many of the wounded sat up and sang 'The Watch on the Rhine' in a half-frantic outburst of enthusiasm. After a while some of the girls retired to sleep and the night passed quietly. We had not had more than two hours rest out of twenty four at first, but at this time we had had none for forty-eight hours. We lay down with only a rug to cover us, but could not sleep owing to the nervous strain. In fact, we did not seem to require sleep at all.

At 5 next morning we prepared breakfast for the boys at the barricades, who were exhausted by their all-night fight. Accompanied by Captain Lynch, another girl and I carried breakfast to the nearest barricade. We had served rations to five volunteers at this point when shooting commenced again and two of the boys we had just left were struck down. A few moments delay would have cost us our lives, as we were kneeling, and bullets were flying in all directions.

---

1 Became the Irish national anthem.

Doc. 90a: Letter from the Rt. Hon. Sir J. G. Maxwell, Commander in Chief, Ireland, to the Secretary, War Office, 10 May 1916. WO141/19 Public Record Office, Kew.

The administration attempted to deal with the Rising by imprisoning individuals they considered to be members of Sinn Féin, or sympathisers of the Rising. A number of women were interned for their suspected activities.

Sir,

On the conclusion of the fighting which took place in the Dublin area, I found that about seventy women had either surrendered with the rebels or had been arrested by the police.

The majority of these belonged to the Sinn Féin ambulance society, an association which did not entirely confine itself to Red Cross work; it was in fact the women's brigade of the Irish Volunteers and was highly seditious in its activities.

I ordered the investigation of these cases to take place without delay, and on the 8th May sixty-two of the prisoners were released after being cautioned as to their future behaviour.

This was reported to you in my cipher telegram, No. 14329P of the 11th May.

As regards the remainder, the reports which I had received disclosed the fact that the allegation that they were merely Red Cross workers could not be sustained. They were also persons who were known to the police before the rising, and who, had they been male prisoners, I would have at least recommended for internment.

In view of their sex, however, I considered that it would be desirable that they should be granted their liberty, but, at the same time, I could not consent to allow them to be at large in this country while the present unsettled state of affairs continues.

I therefore came to the conclusion that the best solution of the difficulty was to serve them with removal orders under Regulation 4 of the Defence of the Realm Regulation, requiring them to reside in England.

Orders were accordingly signed by me forthwith, but considerable delay in giving effect to these orders has been raised by the prisoners raising difficulties in regard to selecting their places of residence, and, subsequently, owing to the instructions I received in War Office telegram 4190 dated 23/5/16, saying that the Prime Minister did not desire these deportations to be carried out.

I now enclose relevant extracts from the files of these women showing the reasons which influenced me in not permitting them to go free with the other prisoners, and in placing on them the restriction that they should reside for the present in England and not in this country.

It would be very desirable that an early decision should be come to on this matter, as the continued detention of these persons without legal sanction cannot be justified, and it will undoubtedly give rise to discontent.

Doc. 90b: Letter from General Sir J. G. Maxwell to the Secretary, the War Office, 15 June 1916. WO 141/20 Public Record Office, Kew.

Sir,

In continuation of my letter of 30 May referring to the case of the twelve women prisoners, I have the honour to inform you that this matter was, by the Prime Minister's direction, fully discussed with the Home Secretary yesterday morning. As a result of this discussion, it has been decided to release the following:–

B. Ffrench Mullen[1]

Eibhlin Gifford

Mary Ryan

Kathleen Brown

and

Annie Higgins,

and orders have accordingly been issued to this effect.

The Countess Plunkett is being sent to Oxford under a deportation order made under Regulation 14. Dr Kathleen Lynn[2] is being sent to Bath under a similar order.

The remainder namely:–

Winifred Carney[3]

Maura Perolz[4]

Helena Moloney

Breida Foley

and

Ellen Ryan

are to be interned at Aylesbury under Regulation 14B of the Defence of the Realm Regulations.

I accordingly submit herewith in duplicate a recommendation signed by me, as a competent Military Authority. As soon as you have received information from the Home Office that they are prepared to receive these women, I will issue orders for their being sent to Aylesbury in charge of female wardresses and escorted by plain clothes policemen. It is desirable

1 Madeleine ffrench Mullen (1880–1940) was a member of Inghinidhe na hÉireann and Cumann na mBan.

2 Kathleen Florence Lynn (1874–1955) took her medical degree in 1899 from the RUI. She was a member of the Irish Citizen Army.

3 Winifred Carney (1888–1943), trade unionist and member of Cumann na mBan. She stood, unsuccessfully, as a Sinn Féin candidate for Belfast in the 1918 election.

4 Maura Perolz was a member of Inghinidhe na hÉireann.

that these prisoners should be removed from Ireland with the least possible delay.

I have the honour to be,
Sir,
Your obedient servant,
J. G. MAXWELL
General
Commanding-in-Chief the Forces in Ireland

CUMANN NA MBAN ADVISES VOTERS IN 1918

Doc. 91: The Present Duty of Irishwomen (issued by the executive of Cumann na mBan, Dublin, *c.* 1918).

Responsibility for the Easter Rising was falsely attributed by the government to Sinn Féin. With the execution of the leaders of the rebellion, and the intern-ment of hundreds of sympathisers, the fortunes of Sinn Féin rose dramatically. The 1918 election was a landslide victory for the party. The women of Cumann na mBan had actively campaigned for women to use their newly acquired vote to further the Irish cause.

Irishwomen, your country calls to you to do your share in restoring her to her rightful place among the nations. No great sacrifice is asked of you. You have merely to secure the votes, to which you are entitled, and use them on behalf of the SF[1] candidates at the next general election. How can that benefit Ireland? you ask. It will benefit her because of these things:

The Sinn Féin Party stands for an Ireland developing all her resources industrial and agricultural, and able to provide well paid employment for all Irishmen and Irishwomen.

An Ireland collecting her own taxes, and spending them in the country which produced them, for the development of that country.

An Ireland free from the bad of England's war debt.

A prosperous Ireland – prosperous as Denmark, Holland, Norway and Sweden are prosperous.

An educated and enlightened Ireland.

An independent Ireland . . .

1 Sinn Féin.

Other Political Movements

WOMEN AND SOCIALISM IN IRELAND

Doc. 92: James Connolly, *The Reconquest of Ireland* (Dublin, 1915).

Many women suffragists had strong links with the labour movement. Hanna Sheehy Skeffington, for example, was a member of a socialist party. Louie Bennett became a leading trade unionist. James Connolly (1868–1916) founded the Irish Socialist Republican Party in 1896. He organised the Irish Transport and General Worker's Union in Ulster, and established the Irish Citizen Army in 1914. Connolly was a strong feminist who supported the suffrage cause and the cause of women workers. In his book The Reconquest of Ireland, *Connolly included an analysis of the situation of women in Ireland.*

. . . It will be observed by the thoughtful reader that the development in Ireland of what is known as the woman's movement has synchronised with the appearance of women upon the industrial field, and that the acuteness and fierceness of the woman's war has kept even pace with the spread amongst educated women of a knowledge of the sordid and cruel nature of the lot of their suffering sisters of the wage-earning class.

We might say that the development of what, for want of the better name is known as sex-consciousness, has waited for the spread amongst the most favoured women of a deep feeling of social consciousness, what we have elsewhere in this work described as a civic conscience. The awakening amongst women of a realisation of the fact that modern society was founded upon force and injustice, that the highest honours of society have no relation to the merits of the recipients, and that acute human sympathies were rather hindrances than helps in the world was a phenomenon due to the spread of industrialism and to the merciless struggle for existence which it imposes.

Upon women, as the weaker physical vessel, and as the most untrained recruit, that struggle was inevitably the most cruel; it is a matter for deep thankfulness that the more intellectual women broke out into revolt against the anomaly of being compelled to bear all the worst burdens of the struggle and yet be denied even the few political rights enjoyed by the male portion of their fellow-sufferers.

Had the boon of political equality been granted as readily as political wisdom should have dictated, much of the revolutionary value of woman's enfranchisement would probably have been lost. But the delay, the politicians' breach of faith with the women, a breach of which all parties were equally culpable, the long continued struggle, the ever spreading wave of martyrdom of the militant women of Great Britain and Ireland, and the spread amongst the active spirits of the labour movement of an appreciation of the genuineness of the woman's longings for freedom, as of their courage in fighting for it, produced an almost incalculable effect for good upon the relations between the two movements.

In Ireland the woman's cause is felt by all labour men and women as their cause; the labour cause has no more earnest and whole-hearted supporters than the militant women. Rebellion even in thought produced a mental atmosphere of its own; the mental atmosphere the woman's rebellion produced opened their eyes and trained their minds to an understanding of the effects upon their sex of a social system in which the weakest must inevitably go to the wall, and when a further study of the capitalist system taught them that the term 'the weakest' means in practice the most scrupulous, the gentlest, the most humane, the most loving and compassionate, the most honourable, and the most sympathetic then the militant women could not fail to see that capitalism penalised in human beings just those characteristics of which woman supposed themselves to be the most complete embodiment. Thus the spread of industrialism makes for the awakening of a social consciousness, awakes in women a feeling of self pity as the greatest sufferer under social and political injustice; the divine wrath aroused when that self pity is met with a sneer and justice is denied leads women to revolt, and revolt places women in comradeship and equality with all the finer souls whose life is given to warfare upon established iniquities.

The worker is the slave of capitalist society, the female worker is the slave of that slave. In Ireland that female worker has hitherto exhibited in her martyrdom an almost damnable patience. She has toiled on the farms from her earliest childhood, attaining usually to the age of ripe woman-hood without ever being vouchsafed the right to claim as her own a single penny of the money earned by her labour, and knowing that all her toil and privation would not earn her that right to the farm which would go without question to the most worthless member of the family if that member chanced to be the eldest son.

The daughters of the Irish peasantry have been the cheapest slaves in existence – slaves to their own family who were in turn slaves to all the social parasites of a landlord and gombeen[1] ridden community. The peasant in

1 A money lender.

whom centuries of servitude and hunger had bred a fierce craving for money usually regarded his daughters as beings sent by God to lighten his burden through life, and too often the same point of view was as fiercely insisted upon by the clergymen of all denominations. Never did the ideas seem to enter the Irish peasant's mind, or be taught by his religious teachers, that each generation should pay to its successors the debt it owes to its forerunners; that thus by spending itself for the benefit of its children the human race ensures the progressive development of all. The Irish peasant in too many cases treated his daughters in much the same manner as he regarded a plough or a spade – as tools with which to work the farm. The whole mental outlook, the entire moral atmosphere of the countryside, enforced this point of view. In every chapel, church or meeting-house the insistence was even upon duties – duties to those in superior station, duties to the church, duties to the parents. Never were the ears of the young polluted by any reference to 'rights' and growing up in this atmosphere the women of Ireland accepted their position of social inferiority. That in spite of this they have ever proven valuable assets in every progressive movement in Ireland is evidence of the great value their co-operation will be when to their self-sacrificing acceptance of duty they begin to unite its necessary counterpoise, a high-minded assertion of rights . . .

The militant women who, without abandoning their fidelity to duty, are yet teaching their sisters to assert their rights, are re-establishing a sane and perfect balance that makes more possible a well ordered Irish nation. . . .

None so fitted to break the chains as they who wear them, none so well equipped to decide what is a fetter. In its march towards freedom the working class of Ireland must cheer on the effects of those women who feeling on their souls and bodies the fetters of the ages have arisen to strike them off, and cheer all the louder if in its hatred of thralldom and passion for freedom the women's army forges ahead of the militant army of labour.

IRISH WOMEN OPPOSE HOME RULE

Doc. 93a: Anon., 'Irish women and Home Rule', *Englishwoman's Review*, 16 October 1893.

Gladstone introduced his first Home Rule Bill for Ireland in 1886. Isabella Tod immediately organised a women's committee to oppose the bill. By 1888 she had linked up with the British based Women's Liberal Unionist Association. The following document from 1893, the year of Gladstone's second Home Rule Bill, is a memorial to Queen Victoria outlining some of the reasons for women's opposition to Home Rule.

. . . On August 12th, a memorial addressed to the Queen, signed by upwards of 103,000 women, exclusively Irish, was deposited at the House.

The memorial, which had been started under the superintendence of the ladies' committee of the Irish Unionist Alliance, ran as follows:

'To her Most Gracious Majesty, Victoria, Queen of the United Kingdom of Great Britain and Ireland. May it please your Majesty, we, the undersigned women of Ireland, of all creeds and classes representing those of your Majesty's subjects who continue loyal to the constitution of Great Britain and Ireland, do hereby approach your Majesty to express our sorrow and consternation at the possibility of the severance of this country from the government of Great Britain by the establishment of a separate parliament, as contemplated in the "Government of Ireland Bill", now before the House of Commons.

We believe that this bill, if passed into law, would endanger the true liberties of the Irish people, and prove oppressive and unjust to your Majesty's loyal subjects in Ireland, so that a number of whom, throughout every part of the country, are expressing by every means in their power their sense of the evils, social and financial, which its proposals involve. Those of your Majesty's memorialists who reside in Ulster, where the principal manufactures of this country are carried on, thereby providing a large amount of employment for women as well as men, and creating a condition of more than average comfort, dread the removal of the trade and capital which have caused this prosperity, being convinced that such will be the inevitable consequence of legislative separation from Great Britain.

We believe that throughout the whole country distress and insecurity would take the place of the peace, safety and increasing prosperity which we have hitherto enjoyed under a united parliament, and we view with the profoundest anxiety any attempt, direct or indirect, to sever us from your beloved Majesty's rule and government, upon which every subject has hitherto relied for protection, and under which all now enjoy the blessings of civil and religious liberty.

That it may please Almighty God long to continue the beneficent reign of your Most Gracious Majesty over this United Kingdom of Great Britain and Ireland is the fervent prayer of your Most Gracious Majesty's humble and devoted subjects.' . . .

Doc. 93b: *Londonderry Sentinel,* 21 March 1893.

The following letter, which appeared in the Londonderry Sentinel *in 1893, makes clear how proficient women were at orchestrating a political campaign.*

Dear Sir,

Will you kindly allow us space in your paper to ask the wives and daughters of the clergy of all denominations in Ireland, and any other ladies who can do so, to help us in trying to make some of the reasons against Home Rule more plain to our sisters, the wives of the clergy of all denominations in England, Scotland and Wales? What we want is to get as many Irish ladies as possible to make and post six or more copies of a short letter. We would send them the letter to be copied, and pamphlets or papers to be enclosed. It is thought that private letters thus written and sent will be more likely to be read than printed circulars.

ELEANOR ALEXANDER, Church of Ireland
BLANCHE BELL, Congregational
DOROTHEA A. BOYTON, Church of Ireland
AGNES M. CARGIN, Presbyterian
S. E. COWAN, Church of Ireland
H. G. HAYES, Church of Ireland
G. E. KNOX, Church of Ireland
M. J. LOWE, Presbyterian
S. E. PERCY, Church of Ireland
LIZZIE QUARRY, Methodist
F. ROSS, Presbyterian
META RODGERS, Presbyterian
T. A. STUART, Presbyterian
ANNA MARY STEVENSON, Church of Ireland
DOROTHEA SMYLY, Church of Ireland

PS – Any ladies who will kindly undertake this will please send name and address, enclosing three penny stamps, to hon. secretary, Mrs Stevenson, The Vicarage, Clooney, Londonderry, and state how many copies of the letter they will make, when they will be furnished with the necessary number of addresses.

Doc. 93c: Anon., 'Women and the Irish question', *Englishwoman's Review*, 15 April 1893.

Women organised a number of demonstrations against Home Rule in 1893. These were not confined to the northern counties. In order to influence British politicians more effectually, Irish women also travelled to England and organised meetings there.

. . . [A] meeting with a large and representative attendance of ladies of Coleraine and district, was held in the Town Hall, Coleraine, Mrs O'Hara presiding. The following resolutions were passed with enthusiasm, and a committee formed:

That we, the women of Coleraine and neighbourhood, in public meeting assembled, declare that we are faithful, loyal and devoted subjects of Queen Victoria, and claim it as our birthright to live under the British constitution, to which we are ardently attached and to be subject only to such laws as are passed by the imperial parliament.

That we record our solemn protest against the 'Bill for the Better Government of Ireland', introduced into parliament by Mr Gladstone; we believe that the passing of this measure into law would inflict incalculable injury on our country, and would be certain to lead to bloodshed and the other miseries of civil war; we pledge ourselves to do all in our power to influence the voters of the United Kingdom, by informing them of the true nature of the present agitation, and to resist by every means in our power the separation of ourselves and our families from the United Kingdom of Great Britain and Ireland, to which it has been hitherto our privilege and happiness to belong.

Girls' Friendly Society (Ireland)[1] – A special meeting of the Girls' Friendly Society for Ireland, held at 4 Molesworth Street, Dublin, towards the end of March, unanimously resolved:

That we, the central council of the Girls' Friendly Society in Ireland, recognising that the members of the GFS are distributed throughout the whole of Ireland, feel called upon strongly to protest against the passing of the Home Rule Bill. We believe that its operation would endanger the liberty of the subject and the free exercise of religion; that it would be fatal to the progress of Ireland and to her growing industries, and would therefore add to the hardships of the poor. And while we feel deeply the benefits of close association, as subjects of our gracious Queen, with our sisters in England, Scotland and Wales, we believe that the proposed bill would tend to the separation of Ireland from Great Britain, and would be the cause of future trouble and inevitable weakness to the British Empire.

Demonstration in Donegal – On March 27th, the women of Donegal held a demonstration in the Town Hall, Donegal. Many of them belonged to the farmer population, and had walked five miles rather than miss the opportunity to enter their protest; numbers also came in on vehicles from a circuit of twenty miles round, and in their resolution recorded their unchangeable loyalty to the Queen, their anxiety at the prospect unfolded by Mr Gladstone's Bill, and their determination to oppose it to the utmost of their power.

Irish women's petition against Home Rule. The petition against Home Rule from the ladies of Londonderry and the north west contains 20,000 signatures and measures 350 yards. Lady Londonderry has telegraphed to the Mayoress of Londonderry that she will undertake to convey the petition in her own carriage to Westminster on the day on which the second reading of the Home Rule Bill is moved, and personally deliver the monster document into the hands of Mr John Ross, QC for presentation to the House of Commons. It is wound on a stout pole, and will require two men to carry it.

Irish women in the south – The activity of women in the south cannot be so readily chronicled, as their work is not separate from that of the men, but women have worked energetically to promote the great demonstration against the Home Rule Bill held in Waterford, and in procuring to the large petition sent from Co. Cork.

1 The Girls' Friendly Society was a Protestant organisation which looked after the welfare of young women. It was founded in England in 1874 and the first branch was established in Ireland in 1877.

Several ladies belonging to the southern provinces have volunteered their services to come over and spread information in England. Some are already at work. . . . .

More demonstrations against the bill – A great assemblage of the women of Belfast in St George's Hall, on April 7th. The lady mayoress (Lady Dixon) was in the chair, and a resolution unanimously passed that 'we view with abhorrence the bill now before parliament for setting up a petty and dangerous separate legislature in Ireland, and pledge ourselves to use every wise, fair, and honourable method to resist Home Rule to the utmost of our power.' Mrs King-Kerr, who moved this resolution, said that the men of Ulster had declared against Home Rule, and the women would stand by them in whatever trouble or difficulty the future might have in store. It was found necessary to hold an overflow meeting in the Central Hall, Rosemary Street, at which Mrs Arnold-Forster and other ladies delivered addresses.

On the same day the unionist women in Monaghan held a large meeting, Lady Constance Leslie presiding, when resolutions in support of the union were unanimously adopted.

Doc. 93d: *Belfast Newsletter*, 19 January 1912.

The threat of Home Rule continued to hang over the Irish political scene in the first years of the twentieth century. On the 23 January 1911, the Ulster Women's Unionist Council was established to resist Home Rule for Ulster. Between 1911 and 1913 the UWUC organised numerous demonstrations in opposition to Home Rule.

Ulster Women and Home Rule
Great Demonstration in Belfast

A demonstration under the auspices of the Ulster Women's Unionist Council was held last night in the Ulster Hall, and in point of attendance and enthusiasm it was one of the most successful gatherings ever held inside that building. . . . The scene was certainly a remarkable one, and afforded proof, if such were necessary, of the zeal and earnestness of the loyal women in the cause of unionism. Indeed a feature of the present campaign is the active part being taken by women in defence of civil and religious liberties. . . . .

The Duchess of Abercorn proceeding said she need not tell them what a great pleasure she felt and she might add honour in being asked to preside at the great meeting that evening – a meeting of the unionist women of Ulster. They were assembled there for one purpose, and for one only, namely, to protest with one voice against the action of the present government in trying to force Home Rule upon Ireland and the people of Ireland (*applause*). They were well aware that women were able to do a great amount of good with gentleness, tact and quiet influence when they were well organised and worked well together. Might she say also that they could do a great amount of harm (*laughter*). But they were there that night to do good in the way of protesting in the strongest and most emphatic manner against the evil results which would accrue in the event of Home Rule being carried. She would like to hear all their united voices say it would not be carried, that it would never be carried (*applause*) – and that was the moment when they could, with one voice, protest to the people in England and Scotland that as far as they were all concerned there would never be Home Rule in this country (*applause*). They would hear some excellent speeches that evening from many ladies and it was a cause for pride and joy that they had such strong support from those who had already for the year past devoted time, energy, health and money to help the poor in Ireland with their cottage industries, their Protestant orphan societies in each county, and the many other charitable acts and institutions that they had organised and supported (*hear, hear*). Let them think of the result of Home Rule in this country, with consequent increased taxation. Orphanages, homes and cottage industries and infirmaries would all have to disappear from want of subscriptions and support, leaving misery and poverty behind them. . . . . As to infirmaries their admirable staff of thoroughly trained nurses would be done away with, and would be replaced by nuns who had little or no training, and who were not allowed by their religion and spiritual advisers to have the proper experience required for infirmaries for nursing the sick poor. And that was only one item in connection with the many charities which would cease to exist if Home Rule came, 'which', added the Duchess, 'it must and shall not'. . . . . She only ventured to touch on all that had been done for the poor of Ireland, and all that continued to be done, and all that must naturally cease to be done in the event of Home Rule coming upon them. . . . .

IRISH WOMEN AND THE CO-OPERATIVE MOVEMENT

Doc. 94: Ellice Pilkington, 'The United Irishwomen: their work', *The United Irishwomen* (Dublin, 1911).

Nationalist, unionist, suffrage and cultural organisations co-existed in the first decades of the twentieth century, and claimed the attention of Irish men and women. Sir Horace Plunkett, the pioneer of the co-operative movement in Ireland, founded the United Irishwomen in 1910, with Mrs Ellice Pilkington as the first organiser. The organisation encouraged the development of rural society, and expected women to serve their local communities.

. . . Mrs Harold Lett,[1] . . . started a branch of United Irishwomen at Bree, in County Wexford, on June 15th, 1910. Mrs Lett – herself a practical

1 Anita Lett (1872–1940), rural organiser.

farmer, farming her own land, vice-President of the County Wexford Farmers' Association, in close touch with the needs of farmers' wives and labourers' wives, and having her own interests bound up with theirs – formed a woman's committee, on which the county families, the farmers' wives and the labourers' wives were represented under the presidency of Lady Power. Rules were drawn up, and the branch set to work to brighten the social life of the district by bringing the people together in the parish hall, to which it was soon able to subscribe, and by setting the women to work at those practical details of their life to which, hitherto, they had not devoted enough attention. A successful Flower Show was held at Bree on August 20th, which provided funds for working expenses. Finding that her initial effort had been successful, Mrs Lett called a meeting at the Plunkett House of all the women, who had become interested, to discuss the desirability of forming an all-Ireland society. A committee was formed in order to draw up rules, and these rules were based on those that had worked so well at Bree. A resolution was passed at this meeting to the effect that where societies dealing with the objects of the United Irishwomen were already in existence, they should be made use of, as far as possible, so as to avoid conflict or overlapping. After this it still remained for us to find out if the people we wanted to help wanted to be helped, and, above all, if they wanted to be helped by us. We asked to be allowed to send representatives to the Aannual meeting of the Irish Agricultural Organisation Society, and were invited to do so, and also to read a paper there stating our aims and objects.

We stated our case very simply, saying that we were of [the] opinion that men could not make full use of their legislative and social oganisation without our co-operation any more than we can attain our ends without their assistance. We promised to help them if they would help us by encouraging us to start branches of our women's union close to their co-operative societies. A vote of assent was given to our proposal, and we started at once to fulfil our part of the bargain. On the following day we met at the Plunkett House, and established a provisional committee, electing Mrs Lett as president. This committee was empowered to undertake the organisation of branches.

Now, it may be as well to consider what our qualifications were for undertaking such work. We had no experience beyond that which is gained in the ordinary every day life of women. We had no special training for doing what we intended to do, and we, none of us, aspired to reform society or preach any gospel but that of domestic economy, good comradeship and truth.

The very first day we appeared in public we were attacked on account of our want of training as nurses. The attack was, perhaps, justified because the training of most of us only amounted to this – some of us were mothers, some of us had devoted our lives to the nursing of aged relatives, some of us had seen men die in hospitals during war, and others were beginning lives in which they would be likely to meet with similar experiences. Whatever our lack of skill might be, we all knew what we intended to do, and were determined to do it, and therefore we never doubted but that we should find the way, and secure the willing services of those who possessed the training that we lacked.

A certain number of ladies resident in or near Dublin undertook to do research work and to procure information which they proposed to summarise for the use of organisers. This work has proved most valuable.

On December 3rd I started for Dungloe, Co. Donegal, with a diminutive personal equipment, but with the best substitute that good fellowship could give me – an organiser's bag and map lent by the secretary of the Irish Agricultural Organisation Society, a thermos bottle and a passport in the old tongue given voluntarily by the president of the Gaelic League. A herald in telegraphic form was despatched before me by Father Finlay.

On arrival I found an independent capable community, a flourishing co-operative society with a manager who not only knew his work, but held the confidence of his people, a knitting industry in the hands of the women and girls, and all around them great possibilities for cottage gardening, dairying, and jam-making; a village hall for social meetings, a fine healthy race of men and women, bilingual, capable of enjoying intellectual pursuit, and not ashamed to use their hands. And yet there was a silent sorrow here, for the curse of emigration was upon them. The young women and girls were slipping off one by one to the land of promise on the other side of the broad Atlantic, and only some of them came home again to listen mournfully to the sad sobbing of the sea on a dreary shore. The women did not speak to me of this, but the men did.

A meeting was held in the newly-opened village hall, where I gave the message the United Irishwomen had sent me to deliver. The proposal to start a branch of United Irishwomen was welcomed enthusiastically, and the men promised to safeguard the interests of the sister society and free the women from the oppression of the 'truck' system.[1] Members were elected to act on a committee, and within a week the officers of this committee were appointed. I left on December the 5th with these encouraging words in my ears: 'A good honest movement like this is sure to succeed.' There is now at Dungloe a busy branch of United Irishwomen with over two hundred members; two instructresses under the home improvement scheme are at work (subjects – house-hold economy, home dairying, cottage gardening); the village hall is a centre for meetings of all kinds. . . .

On 6th December, Mrs Lett formed a second branch of the United Irishwomen in County Wexford, at Davidstown. On the 7th and 8th I visited Oylegate and Glenbrien, and also Bree, where I was sent by the executive committee to thank the women of Bree for the pioneer work they had done, and to study the methods of their branch.

The executive committee held several meetings in Dublin, and a great deal of individual work was done by members of the society in connection with organisation.

1 See doc. 48.3 and p 187 n 2.

In January and February I visited Wicklow and Wexford, and inaugurated branches at Oylegate, Glenbrien, and Coolgreany. County Wexford is admirably suited to, and quite ready for, branches of United Irishwomen in consequence of the progressive character of the people, their spirit of enterprise and their practical ability to create societies of their own, for their own purposes, and to avail themselves of every facility put at their disposal by the Department of Agriculture and the Irish Agricultural Organisation Society.

On 8th February Mrs Stopford, who volunteered to act as hostess for the United Irishwomen, presided over their first social gathering; Mr H. F. Norman gave an address on women's part in co-operative work, which gave rise to much interesting discussion.

On 10th February, I started on a tour through Waterford, Tipperary, Cork and Clare, the results of which the future will show. At Kilkee I found a people with great advantages at their disposal, but needing the stimulus of the United Irishwomen to induce them to make use of them. The hospitality of the people, from the parish priest to my hostess at the hotel, was unbounded. The problems of education, domestic economy, and public health, which they will have to work upon, are such as to interest any body of capable women, to say nothing of the sturdy little group of patriots I left behind me in the Kilkee branch.

General Select Bibilography

Akenson, D. H., *The Irish Education Experiment: The National System of Education in the Nineteenth Century* (London, 1970).

Barnes, Jane, *Irish Industrial Schools, 1868–1908* (Dublin, 1989).

Boyce, D. G., *Nineteenth-Century Ireland: The Search for Stability* (Dublin, 1990).

Burke, Helen, *The People and the Poor Law in Nineteenth-Century Ireland* (Dublin, 1987).

Connolly, Seán, *Religion and Society in Nineteenth-Century Ireland* (Dublin, 1985).

Daly, Mary E., *A Social and Economic History of Ireland since 1800* (Dublin, 1981).

Daly, Mary E., *The Famine in Ireland* (Dublin, 1986).

Foster, R. F., *Modern Ireland 1600–1972* (London, 1988).

Graham, B. J. and L. Proudfoot, (eds.), *An Historical Geography of Ireland* (London, 1993).

Hoppen, K. T., *Ireland Since 1800: Conflict and Conformity* (London, 1989).

Lyons, F. S. L., *Ireland Since the Famine* (London, 1971; new edition 1973).

McCartney, Donal, *The Dawning of Democracy: Ireland 1800–1870* (Dublin, 1987).

Ó Gráda, Cormac, *The Great Irish Famine* (London, 1989).

Ó Tuathaigh, Gearóid, *Ireland before the Famine* (Dublin, 1972).

Women's History in Ireland: A Select Bibliography

General Works

Beale, Jenny, *Women in Ireland: Voices of Change* (Dublin, 1986).

Bitel, Lisa M., '"Do not marry the fat short one": The early Irish wisdom on women', *Journal of Women's History*, 6/7, 4/1, (Winter/Spring 1995), pp 137–59.

Brady, Anne M., *Women in Ireland: An Annotated Bibliography* (Connecticut, 1988).

Cosgrove, Art (ed.), *Marriage in Ireland* (Dublin, 1985).

Crowe, Caitriona, 'Some sources in the National Archives for women's history', *Saothar*, 19 (1994), pp 109–14.

Cullen, Mary, 'Women, history and identity', *Maynooth Review* (May 1980), pp 67–79.

——, 'Invisible women and their contribution to historical studies', *Stair: Journal of the Irish History Teachers' Association* (1982), pp 2–6.

——, 'Women's history in Ireland', in Karen Offen, Ruth Roach Pierson, Jane Rendall, (eds.), *Writing Women's History: International Perspectives* (London, 1991), pp 429–41.

——, 'History women and history men: the politics of women's history', *History Ireland*, 2, 2 (Summer 1994), pp 31–6.

Curtin, Chris, Pauline Jackson and Barbara O'Connor, (eds.), *Gender in Irish Society* (Galway, 1987).

Dewar, Bernadine, (ed.), *Living at the Time of the Siege of Limerick* (Limerick, 1991).

Donovan, Katie, A. Norman Jeffares and Brendan Kennelly, (eds), *Ireland's Women: Writings Past and Present* (Dublin, 1994).

Doughan, David and Denise Sanchez, *Feminist Periodicals 1855–1984: An Annotated Critical Bibliography of British, Irish, Commonwealth and International Titles* (Brighton, 1987).

Evason, Eileen, *Against the Grain: The Contemporary Women's Movement in Northern Ireland* (Dublin, 1991).

Fitzpatrick, David, 'Review article: women, gender and the writing of Irish history', *Irish Historical Studies*, 27, 107 (May 1991) pp 267–73.

Gallagher, S. F., (ed.), *Women in Irish Legend, Life and Literature* (Buckinghamshire, 1983).

Hill, Myrtle and Vivienne Pollock, *Image and Experience: Photographs of Irishwomen 1880–1920* (Belfast, 1993).

Kelly, A. A., 'Irish women travel writers: an overview', *Linen Hall Review* 10, 1 (1993), pp 4–8.

Loftus, Belinda, *Mirrors: William III and Mother Ireland* (Dublin, 1990).

Luddy, Maria and Cliona Murphy, 'Cherchez la femme: the elusive woman in Irish history', in Maria Luddy and Cliona Murphy, (eds.), *Women Surviving: Studies in Irish Women's History in the 19th and 20th Centuries* (Dublin, 1990), pp 1–14.

Luddy, Maria, 'An agenda for Irish women's history, 1800–1900', *Irish Historical Studies*, 28, 109 (May 1992), pp 19–37.

MacCurtain, Margaret and Donncha Ó Corráin, *Women in Irish Society: The Historical Dimension* (Dublin, 1978).

MacCurtain, Margaret and Mary O'Dowd, 'An agenda for Irishwomen's history, 1500–1900, Part 1', *Irish Historical Studies*, 28, 109 (May 1992), pp 1–19.

Meaney, Gerardine, *Sex and Nation: Women in Irish Culture and Politics* (Dublin, 1991).

Montgomery, Pamela and Celia Davies, *Women's Lives in Northern Ireland Today* (Coleraine, 1990).

Mullin, Molly, 'Representations of history, Irish feminism and the politics of difference', *Feminist Studies*, 17, 1, (1991), pp 29–50.

Murphy, Cliona, 'Women's history, feminist history or gender history', *The Irish Review*, 12 (Spring/Summer 1992), pp 21–6.

Ní Chuilleanáin, Eiléan, (ed.), *Irish Women: Image and Achievement* (Dublin, 1985).

O'Connor, Anne, *Child Murderess and Dead Child Traditions: A Comparative Study* (Helsinki, 1991).

Public Record Office of Northern Ireland, *Guide to Sources for Women's History* (Belfast, 1993).

Sawyer, Roger, *'We Are But Women', Women in Ireland's History* (London, 1993).

Scott, Liz Steiner, (ed.), *Personally Speaking: Women's Thoughts on Women's Issues* (Dublin, 1985).

Smyth, Ailbhe, (ed.), *Women's Studies International Forum, Special Issue: Feminism in Ireland*, 11, 4 (1988).

Ward, Margaret, *The Missing Sex: Putting Women into Irish History* (Dublin, 1991).

Education

Breathnach, Eibhlín, 'Women and higher education in Ireland, 1879–1910', *The Crane Bag*, 4 (1980), pp 47–54.

———, 'Charting new waters: women's experience in higher education, 1879–1908', in Mary Cullen, (ed.), *Girls Don't Do Honours: Irishwomen in Education in the Nineteenth and Twentieth Centuries* (Dublin, 1987), pp 55–76.

Butler, Sr Katherine, 'A sister and her school, Dublin 1830', *Dublin Historical Record*, 16, 2 (1988), pp 55–69.

Coombes, James, 'Catherine O'Donovan 1788–1858, educational pioneer', *Seanchas Chairbe*, 1 (December 1982).

Coonerty, Paula, 'The Presentation order and the National school system in Limerick, 1837–1870', *North Munster Antiquarian Journal*, 30 (1988), pp 29–34.

Cunningham, Bernadette, 'Women and Gaelic literature, 1500–1800', in Mary O'Dowd, and Margaret MacCurtain, (eds.), *Women in Early Modern Ireland* (Edinburgh, 1991), pp 147–59.

Jordan, Alison, 'Opening the gates of learning in Belfast: the Belfast Ladies' Institute, 1867–97', in Janice Holmes and Diane Urquhart, (eds.), *Coming into the Light: The Work, Politics and Religion of Women in Ulster 1840–1940* (Belfast, 1994), pp 33–57.

MacCurtain, Margaret, 'Women, education and learning in early modern Ireland', in O'Dowd and MacCurtain, *Women*, pp 160–78.

O'Connor, Anne V. and Susan Parkes, *Gladly Learn and Gladly Teach: A History of Alexandra College and School, Dublin, 1866–1916* (Dublin, 1983).

O'Connor, Anne V., 'Influences affecting girls' secondary education in Ireland, 1860–1910', *Archivium Hibernicum*, 141 (1986), pp 83–98.

———, 'The revolution in girls' secondary education in Ireland, 1860–1910', in Cullen, *Girls*, pp 31–54.

O'Flynn, Gráinne, 'Our Age of Innocence', in Cullen, *Girls*, pp 79–99.

Walsh, Lorcan, 'Images of women in nineteenth-century school books', *Irish Educational Studies*, 4, 1 (1984), pp 73–84.

Social and Economic

Appleby, John, 'Women and piracy in Ireland: from Gráinne O'Malley to Anne Bonny', in O'Dowd and MacCurtain, *Women*, pp 53–68.

Ballard, Linda, '"Just whatever they had handy". Aspects of childbirth and early child care in Northern Ireland, prior to 1948', *Ulster Folklife*, 31 (1985), pp 59–72.

———, 'Irish lace: tradition or commodity?', *Folklife: Journal of Ethnological Studies*, 31 (1992–93), pp 43–56.

Bolger, Pat, (ed.), *And See Her Beauty Shining There: The Story of the Irish Countrywomen* (Dublin, 1986).

Bourke, Joanna, 'Women and poultry in Ireland', *Irish Historical Studies*, 25, 99 (May 1987), pp 293–310.

———, 'The health caravan: female labour and domestic education in rural Ireland 1890–1914', *Éire/Ireland*, 24 (Winter 1989), pp 21–38.

———, 'Dairywomen and affectionate wives: women in the Irish dairy industry, 1890–1914', *Agricultural History Review*, 38, 11 (1991), pp 149–64.

———, 'Working women: the domestic labour market in rural Ireland, 1890–1914', *The Journal of Interdisciplinary History*, 21, 3 (Winter 1991), pp 479–99.

———, 'The best of all Home Rulers: the economic power of women in Ireland, 1800–1914', *Irish Economic and Social History*, 18 (1991), pp 34–47.

———, *Husbandry to Housewifery: Women, Economic Change and Housework in Ireland 1890–1914* (Oxford, 1993).

Boyle, Emily, *The Irish Flowerers* (Belfast, 1971).

———, 'The linen strike of 1872', *Saothar*, 2 (1976), pp 12–21.

Brophy, Imelda, 'Women in the workforce', in David Dickson, (ed.), *The Gorgeous Mask: Dublin 1700–1850* (Dublin, 1987), pp 51–63.

Carbery, Mary, *The Farm by Lough Gur* (Cork, 1986, reprint).

Casway, Jerrold, 'Irishwomen overseas, 1500–1800', in O'Dowd and MacCurtain, *Women*, pp 112–32.

Clarkson, Leslie and Margaret Crawford, 'Life and death: widows in Carrick-on-Suir, 1799', in O'Dowd and MacCurtain, *Women*, pp 236–54.

Clarkson, Leslie, 'Love, labour and life: women in Carrick-on-Suir in the late eighteenth century', *Irish Economic and Social History*, 20 (1993), pp 18–34.

Cohen, Marilyn, 'Survival strategies in female headed households: linen workers in Tullyish, County Down, 1901', *Journal of Family History*, 17, 3 (1992), pp 308–18.

Collins, Brenda, 'Sewing and social structure: the flowerers of Scotland and Ireland', in Rosalind Mitchison and Peter Roebuck, (eds.), *Economy and Society in Scotland and Ireland 1500–1939* (Edinburgh, 1988), pp 42–54.

———, 'The organisation of sewing outwork in late nineteenth-century Ulster', in Maxine Berg, (ed.), *Markets and Manufacture in Early Industrial Europe* (London, 1991), pp 139–56.

Connolly, Seán, 'Family, love and marriage: some evidence from the early eighteenth century', in O'Dowd and MacCurtain, *Women*, pp 276–90.

Conway, Sheelagh, *The Faraway Hills are Green: Voices of Irish Women in Canada* (Toronto, 1992).

Crawford, W. H., 'Women in the domestic linen industry', in O'Dowd and MacCurtain, *Women*, pp 255–64.

Cullen, Mary, 'Breadwinners and providers: women in the household economy of labouring families, 1835–6', in Luddy and Murphy, *Women Surviving*, pp 85–116.

Cullen, Nuala, 'Women and the preparation of food in eighteenth-century Ireland', in O'Dowd and MacCurtain, *Women*, pp 265–74.

Daly, Mary E., 'Women in the Irish workforce from pre-industrial to modern times', *Saothar*, 7 (1981), pp 74–82.

———, 'Women and trade unions', in Donal Nevin, (ed.), *Trade Union Century* (Dublin, 1994), pp 106–16.

Dickson, David, 'No Scythians here: women and marriage in seventeenth century Ireland', in O'Dowd and MacCurtain, *Women*, pp 223–35.

Diner, Hasia, *Erin's Daughters in America* (London, 1983).

Eagar, Clare, 'Unequal opportunity: women, employment and protective legislation, 1919–1937', *Retrospect* (1988), pp 11–15.

Fitzpatrick, David, 'A share of the honeycomb: education, emigration and Irishwomen', *Continuity and Change*, 1, 2 (1988), pp 217–234.

———, 'The modernisation of the Irish female', in P. O'Flanagan, et al, (eds.), *Rural Ireland: Modernisation and Change 1600–1900* (Cork, 1987), pp 162–80.

———, 'Divorce and separation in modern Irish history', *Past and Present*, 114 (February 1987), pp 173–96.

Gillespie, Raymond, 'Women and crime in seventeenth-century Ireland', in O'Dowd and MacCurtain, *Women*, pp 43–53.

Gordon Bowe, Nicola, 'Two early twentieth-century Irish arts and crafts workshops in context: An Tur Gloine and the Dun Emer Guild and Industries', *Journal of Design History*, 2 (1989), pp 193–206.

———, 'Women and the arts and crafts revival in Ireland, *c*. 1886–1930', *Irish Women Artists from the Eighteenth Century to the Present Day* (Dublin, 1987), pp 22–27.

Gray, Jane, 'Gender and plebian culture in Ulster', *Journal of Interdisciplinary History*, 24, 2 (Autumn 1993), pp 251–70.

Guinnane, Timothy, 'Re-thinking the western European marriage pattern: the decision to marry in Ireland at the turn of the twentieth century', *Journal of Family History*, 16, 1 (1991), pp 47–64.

Hearn, Mona, 'Life for domestic servants in Dublin: 1880–1920', in Luddy and Murphy, *Women Surviving*, pp 148–179.

———, *Below Stairs: Domestic Service Remembered in Dublin and Beyond, 1880–1922* (Dublin, 1993).

Hynes, Christine, 'A polite struggle, the Dublin seamstresses' campaign, 1869–1872', *Saothar*, 18 (1993), pp 35–40.

Irvine, Jimmy, (ed.), *Mary Cumming's Letters Home to Lisburn from America, 1811–1815* (Coleraine, 1982).

Irwin, Leonora, 'Women convicts from Dublin', in Bob Reece, (ed.), *Irish Convicts: The Origins of Convicts Transported to Australia* (Dublin, 1989), pp 161–91.

Jackson, Pauline, 'Women in nineteenth-century Irish emigration', *International Migration Review*, 18, 4 (1984), pp 1004–20.

Jones, Greta, 'Marie Stopes in Ireland – the mother's clinic in Belfast, 1936–47', *Social History of Medicine*, 5, 2 (August 1992), pp 255–76.

Jones, Mary, *These Obstreperous Lassies: A History of the Irish Women Workers' Union* (Dublin, 1988).

Kelly, James, 'Infanticide in eighteenth-century Ireland', *Irish Economic and Social History*, 19 (1992), pp 5–26.

Kinane, Vincent, 'A galley of pie: women in the Irish book trades', *Linen Hall Review* (December 1991), pp 10–13.

King, Carla, 'A separate economic class?: The Irish Women Workers' Union', *Saothar*, 14, (1989), pp 67–70.

Langan-Egan, Maureen, *Women in Mayo: An Historical Perspective* (Westport, 1991).

— —, 'Some insights on women in Mayo, 1851–1881', *North Mayo Historical Journal*, 11, 5 (1992), pp 44–7

Lennon, Mary, Máire McAdam and Joanne O'Brien, *Across the Water: Irish Women's Lives in Britain* (London, 1988).

Lewis, Gifford, *The Yeats Sisters and the Cuala* (Dublin, 1994).

Luddy, Maria, 'Women and charitable organisations in nineteenth-century Ireland', *Women's Studies International Forum*, 11, 4 (1988), pp 301–5.

———, 'Prostitution and rescue work in nineteenth-century Ireland', in Luddy and Murphy, *Women Surviving*, pp 51–84.

———, 'An outcast community: the "Wrens" of the Curragh', *Women's History Review*, 1, 3 (1992), pp 341–55.

———, 'Irish women and the Contagious Diseases Acts', *History Ireland*, 1, 1 (Spring 1993), pp 32–4.

————, 'Women and work in Clonmel: the evidence of the 1881 census', *Tipperary Historical Journal*, (1993), pp 95–101.

————, *Women and Philanthropy in Nineteenth-Century Ireland* (Cambridge, 1995).

MacDonald, Charlotte, *A Woman of Good Character* (Wellington, 1990).

Maguire, W. A., 'The Verner rape trial, 1813: Jane Barnes –v– the Belfast establishment', *Ulster Local Studies*, 15, 1 (1993), pp 47–57.

Malcolm, Elizabeth, 'Women and madness in Ireland: 1600–1850', in O'Dowd and MacCurtain, *Women*, pp 318–34.

Malcomson, A.P.W., *The Pursuit of the Heiress: Aristocratic Marriage in Ireland, 1750–1820* (Antrim, 1982).

McCaffrey, Patricia, 'Jacob's women workers during the 1913 lockout', *Saothar*, 16 (1991), pp 118–29.

McLoughlin, Dympna 'Workhouses and Irish female paupers', in Luddy and Murphy, *Women Surviving*, pp 117–47.

————, 'Women and sexuality in nineteenth-century Ireland', *The Irish Journal of Psychology*, 15, 2&3 (1994), pp 266–75.

Messenger, Betty, *Picking up the Linen Threads: Life in Ulster's Mills* (Belfast, 1988).

Mooney, Brenda, 'Women convicts from Wexford and Waterford', in Reece, *Irish Convicts*, pp 115–27.

Moser, Peter, 'Rural economy and female emigration in the west of Ireland, 1936–1956', *UCG Women's Studies Centre Review*, 2 (1993), pp 41–51.

Murphy Lawless, Jo, 'The silencing of women in childbirth or let's hear it for Bartholomew and the boys', *Women's Studies International Forum*, 11, 4 (1988), pp 293–98.

————, 'Images of "poor women" in the writing of Irish men midwives', in O'Dowd and MacCurtain, *Women*, pp 291–303.

Murphy, Maureen, 'Charlotte Grace O'Brien and the Mission of Our Lady of the Rosary for the Protection of Irish Immigrant Girls', *Mid-America: An Historical Review*, 74, 3, (October, 1992), pp 253–70.

National Gallery of Ireland/Douglas Hyde Gallery, *Irish Women Artists from the Eighteenth Century to the Present Day* (Dublin, 1987).

Neill, Margaret, 'Homeworkers in Ulster, 1850–1911', in Holmes and Urquhart, *Into the Light*, pp 2–32.

Neville, Grace, '"She never then after that forgot him": Irishwomen and emigration to the United States in Irish Folklore', *Mid-America: An Historical Review*, 74, 3, (October, 1992), pp 271–89.

Nicholls, Kenneth, 'Irishwomen and property in the sixteenth century', in O'Dowd and MacCurtain, *Women*, pp 17–31.

Nolan, Janet, *Ourselves Alone: Women's Emigration from Ireland 1885–1920* (Lexington, 1989).

O'Carroll, Íde, *Models for Movers: Irishwomen's Emigration to America* (Dublin, 1990).

O'Connor, Anne, 'Images of the evil women in Irish folklore: a preliminary survey', *Women's Studies International Forum*, 11, 4 (1987), pp 281–85.

———, 'Women in Irish folklore: the testimony regarding illegitimacy, abortion and infanticide', in O'Dowd and MacCurtain, *Women*, pp 304–17.

O'Leary, Eoin, 'The Irish National Teachers' Organisation and the marriage bar for women National teachers, 1933–1958', *Saothar*, 12 (1987), pp 47–52.

Pollock, Vivienne, 'Co. Down herring girls and the herring curing industry', *Folklife*, 29 (1990–91), pp 29–43.

Preston, Margaret H., 'Lay women and philanthropy in Dublin 1860–1880', *Éire/Ireland*, 28, 4 (1993), pp 74–85.

Pyle, Jean Larson, *The State and Women in Economy* (Albany, 1990).

Rhodes, R. M., *Women and the Family in Post-Famine Ireland* (Connecticut, 1991).

Robinson, Portia, 'From Colleen to Matilda, Irish convict women transported to New South Wales', in Kieron, Colm, (ed.), *Australia and Ireland Bicentennial Essays* (Dublin, 1986), pp 96–111.

———, *The Women of Botany Bay* (Melbourne, 1988).

Rudd, Joy, 'Invisible exports – the emigration of women this century', *Women's Studies International Forum*, 11, 4 (1988), pp 307–11.

Scanlon, Pauline, *The Irish Nurse: A Study of Nursing in Ireland: History and Education 1718–1981* (Manorhamilton, 1991).

Simms, Katherine, 'Women in Gaelic society during the age of transition', in O'Dowd and MacCurtain, *Women*, pp 32–42.

———, 'The legal position of Irishwomen in the later middle ages' *The Irish Jurist* (1975), pp 96–111.

Tweedy, Hilda, *A Link in the Chain: The Story of the Irish Housewives' Association 1942–1992* (Dublin, 1992).

Wall, Rita, *Leading Lives: Irish Women in Britain* (Dublin, 1991).

Women's Committee of the National Union of Public Employees, *Women's Voices: An Oral History of Northern Irish Women's Health (1900–1990)* (Dublin, 1992).

Politics

Anton, Brigitte, 'Women of *The Nation*', *History Ireland*, 1, 3 (1993), pp 34–7.

———, 'Northern voices: Ulsterwomen in the Young Ireland movement', in Holmes and Urquhart, *Into the Light*, pp 60–92.

Bunting, Anne, 'The American Molly Childers and the Irish Question', *Éire/Ireland*, 23, 2 (1988), pp 88–103.

Candy, Catherine, 'Relating feminisms, nationalisms and imperialisms: Ireland, India and Margaret Cousins's sexual politics', *Women's History Review*, 3, 4, (1994), pp 581–94.

Carroll, Clare, 'Representations of women in some early modern English tracts on the colonization of Ireland', *Albion*, 25, 3 (Fall 1993), pp 379–93.

Claffey, Úna, *The Women who Won: Women of the 27th Dáil* (Dublin, 1993).

Clancy, Mary, 'Aspects of women's contribution to the Oireachtas debate in the Irish Free State, 1922–1937', in Luddy and Murphy, *Women Surviving*, pp 206–32.

Côté, Jane, 'Writing women out of history: Fanny and Anna Parnell and the Irish Ladies' Land League', *Études Irlandaises*, 17, 2 (December 1992), 123–34.

Coulter, Carol, *The Hidden Tradition: Feminism, Women and Nationalism in Ireland* (Cork, 1993).

Cullen, Mary, 'How radical was Irish feminism between 1860 and 1920?', in P. J. Corish, (ed.), *Radicals, Rebels and Establishments, Historical Studies 15* (Belfast, 1985) pp 185–201.

Curtin, Nancy, 'Women and eighteenth-century Irish republicanism', in O'Dowd and MacCurtain, *Women*, pp 133–44.

Daly, Mary E., 'Women in the Irish Free State 1922–1939: the interaction between economics and ideology', *Journal of Women's History*, 6/7, 4/1, (Winter/Spring 1995), pp 99–116.

Did Your Granny have a Hammer? A History of the Irish Suffrage Movement, 1876–1992 (Dublin, 1985).

Doan, James, 'Gaelic women's responses to the Elizabethan settlement of Ireland', *Donegal Annual*, 41(1988), pp 20–27.

Dunne, Tom, *Maria Edgeworth and the Colonial Mind* (Cork, 1984).

Fairweather, Eileen, Róisín McDonough and Melanie McFadyean, *Only the Rivers Run Free: Northern Ireland, The Women's War* (London, 1984).

Gardiner, Frances, 'Political interest and participation of Irish women 1922–1992: the unfinished revolution', *Canadian Journal of Irish Studies*, 18, 1 (July 1992), pp 15–40.

Harp, Richard, 'The *Shan Van Vocht* (Belfast, 1896–1899) and Irish nationalism', *Éire/Ireland*, 24 (1989), pp 42–52.

Hazelkorn, Ellen, 'The social and political views of Louie Bennett, 1870–1956', *Saothar*, 13 (1988), pp 32–44.

Hearne, Dana, 'Rewriting history: Anna Parnell's "Tale of a Great Sham"', in S. F. Gallagher, (ed.), *Women in Irish Legend, Life and Literature* (Gerrard's Cross, 1983).

———, (ed.), *Anna Parnell's Tale of a Great Sham* (Dublin, 1986).

———, '*The Irish Citizen*, 1914–1916: nationalism, feminism, militarism', *Canadian Journal of Irish Studies*, 18, 1 (July 1992), pp 1–15.

Innes, C. L., *Women and Nation in Irish Literature and Society, 1880–1935* (London, 1993).

———, 'A voice directing the affairs of Ireland': *L'Irlande libre, The Shan Van Vocht* and *Bean na hÉireann*', in P. Hyland and N. Samnells, (eds.), *Irish Writing: Exile and Subversion* (London, 1991), pp 146–58.

Kingham, Nancy, *United we Stood: The Official History of the Ulster Women's Unionist Council, 1911–1974* (Belfast, 1975).

Lawrenson Swanton, Daisy, *The Lives of Sarah Anne Lawrenson and Lucy Olive Kingston, Emerging from the Shadow* (Dublin, 1994).

Markievicz, Constance, *Prison Letters of Countess Markievicz* (London, 1986, reprint).

McDonnell, Kathleen Keyes, *There Is a Bridge at Bandon* (Cork, 1972).

McKillen, Beth, 'Irish feminism and national separatism 1914–1923', *Éire/ Ireland*, 18, 3, (1982), pp 52–67, continued in *ibid*, 18, 4 (1982), pp 72–90.

McGuire, Maria, *To Take Arms: A Year in the Provisional IRA* (London, 1973).

Murphy, Cliona, *The Women's Suffrage Movement and Irish Society in the Early Twentieth Century* (Brighton, 1989).

———, 'The tune of the stars and stripes: the American influence on the Irish suffrage movement', in Luddy and Murphy, *Women Surviving*, pp 180–205.

———, 'Suffragists and nationalism in early twentieth-century Ireland', *History of European Ideas*, 16, 4 (1993), pp 1009–15.

O'Dowd, Mary, 'Women and war in Ireland in the 1640s', in O'Dowd and MacCurtain, *Women*, pp 91–111.

O'Neill, Máire, 'The Ladies' Land League', *Dublin Historical Record*, 25, 4 (1982), pp 122–33.

———, 'The Dublin women's suffrage society and its successors', *Dublin Historical Record*, 37 (December 1984–September 1985), pp 126–40.

———, 'The struggle of Irish women for the vote', *Breifne*, 8, 3 (1993), pp 338–53.

O'Reilly, Emily, *Candidate: The Truth Behind the Presidential Election* (Dublin, 1991).

Owens, Rosemary Cullen, '"Votes for ladies, votes for women", organised labour and the suffrage movement, 1876–1922', *Saothar*, 9 (1983), pp 34–47.

———, *Smashing Times: The History of the Irish Suffrage Movement, 1890–1922* (Dublin, 1984).

———, 'Votes for women', *Labour History News*, 9 (Summer 1993), pp 15–19.

Ryan, Louise, '*The Irish Citizen*, 1912–1920', *Saothar*, 17 (1992), pp 105–11.

———, 'Women without votes: the political strategies of the Irish suffrage movement', *Irish Political Studies*, 9 (1994), pp 119–39.

Scannell, Yvonne, 'The constitution and the role of women', Brian Farrell, (ed.), *De Valera's Constitution and Ours* (Dublin, 1988), pp 123–36.

Schwind, Mona L., 'Nurse to all rebellions: Grace O'Malley and sixteenth-century Connacht', *Éire/Ireland* 13, 1 (1977), pp 40–61.

Shannon, Elizabeth, *I Am of Ireland: Women of the North Speak Out* (London, 1989).

Sheehan, Aideen, 'Cumann na mBan policies and activities', in David Fitz-patrick, (ed.), *Revolution? Ireland 1917–1923* (Dublin, 1990), pp 88–97.

Sheehy Skeffington, Andrée D., and Rosemary Owens (ed.), *Votes for Women: Irish Women's Struggle for the Vote* (Dublin, 1975).

TeBrake, Janet K, 'Irish peasant women in revolt: the Land League years', *Irish Historical Studies*, 27, 109 (May 1992), pp 63–80.

Urquhart, Diane, '"The female of the species is more deadlier than the male"? the Ulster Women's Unionist Council, 1911–40', in Holmes and Urquhart, *Into the Light*, pp 93–123.

Valiulis, Maryann Gialanella, 'Defining their role in the new state, Irishwomen's protest against the Jury's Act of 1927', *Canadian Journal of Irish Studies*, 18, 1 (July 1992), pp 43–60.

———, '"Free women in a free nation": feminist nationalist expectations of independence', in Brian Farrell, (ed.), *The Creation of the Dáil* (Dublin, 1994), pp 75–90.

———, 'Power, gender and identity in the Irish Free State', *Journal of Women's History*, 6/7, 4/1, (Winter/Spring 1995), pp 117–36.

van Voris, Jacqueline, 'Daniel O'Connell and women's rights, one letter', *Éire/Ireland*, 17 (Autumn 1982), pp 33–39.

Walsh, Oonagh, 'Testimony from imprisoned women', in Fitzpatrick, *Revolution?*, pp 69–85.

Ward, Margaret, 'Marginality and militancy: Cumann na mBan, 1914–1936', in Austin Morgan and Bob Purdie, (eds.), *Ireland: Divided Nation, Divided Class* (London, 1980).

———, 'The Ladies' Land League', *Irish History Workshop*, 1 (1981), pp 27–35.

———, 'Suffrage first above all else! an account of the Irish suffrage movement', *Feminist Review*, 10 (1982), pp 22–36.

———, *Unmanageable Revolutionaries: Women in Irish Nationalism* (Dingle, 1983).

———, 'The women's movement in Northern Ireland: twenty years on', in S. Hutton and P. Stewart, (eds.), *Ireland's Histories* (London, 1991), pp 149–62.

Biography, Autobiography and Memoirs

Baker, Ruth, 'The innocent eye: Meta Mayne Reid, 1905–1990', *Linen Hall Review* (December 1991), pp 17–19.

Byrne, E. Costigan, 'Sydney, Lady Morgan', *Dublin Historical Record*, 38, 2 (1985), pp 61–73.

Callaghan, Mary Rose, *Kitty O'Shea: A Life of Katherine Parnell* (London, 1989).

Campbell, Mary, *Lady Morgan: The Life and Times of Sydney Owenson* (London, 1988).

Casway, Jerrold, 'Ross O'Dogherty: a Gaelic woman', *Seanchas Ard-mhacha*, 10, 1 (1980–1), pp 42–62.

Chambers, Anne, 'Granuaile: a most famous feminine sea captain', *Etudes Irlandaises*, 6 (1981), pp 101–7.

———, *As Wicked A Woman: Eleanor Countess of Desmond* (Dublin, 1986).

Clarke, Kathleen, *Revolutionary Woman: An Autobiography* (Dublin, 1991).

Collins, Timothy, 'Some Irish women scientists', *UCG Women's Studies Centre Review*, 1 (1992), pp 39–53.

Colum, Mary, *Life and the Dream* (London, 1947).

Condon, Jim, 'Elizabeth, Lady Thurles', in William Corbett, and William Nolan, (eds.), *Thurles, The Cathedral Town* (Dublin, 1989), pp 41–45.

Coxhead, Elizabeth, *Daughters of Erin* (Gerrard's Cross, 1979).

Culloty, A. T., *Nora Herlihy: Irish Credit Union Pioneer* (Dublin, 1990).

Day, Angélique, (ed.), *Letters from Georgian Ireland: The Correspondence of Mary Delaney, 1731–68* (Belfast, 1991).

Devlin, Bernadette, *The Price of My Soul* (London, 1969).

Devlin, Polly, *All of Us There* (London, 1983).

Donnelly, Mowena, 'Susanna Marie Brooks, her family, the Brookes and Lough Eske Castle', *Donegal Annual*, 41 (1989), pp 89–93.

Eagar, Irene French, *The Nun of Kenmare* (Cork, 1970).

Elizabeth Grant of Rothiemurchus, *The Highland Lady in Ireland: Journals 1840–50* (Edinburgh, 1991).

Elizabeth K, Countess of Fingall, *Seventy Years Young* (Dublin, 1992 reprint).

Fallon, Charlotte, H., *Soul of Fire: A Biography of Mary MacSwiney* (Cork, 1986).

Fitzgerald, Brian, *Emily Duchess of Leinster 1731–1814* (London, 1949).

———, *Lady Louisa Connolly 1743–1821* (London, 1950).

Ford, Connie M., *Aleen Cust, Veterinary Surgeon* (Bristol, 1990).

Forristal, Desmond, *Edel Quinn 1907–1944* (Dublin, 1994).

———, *The First Loreto Sister: Mother Teresa Ball 1794–1861* (Dublin, 1994).

Gildea, Rev. Denis, *Mother Mary Arsenius of Foxford* (Dublin, 1936).

Hages, Alan, 'The real Maud Gonne', *UCG Women's Studies Centre Review*, 1 (1992), pp 55–68.

Haverty, Anne, *Constance Markievicz, An Independent Life* (London, 1988).

Heron, Marianne, *Sheila Conroy: Fighting Spirit* (Dublin, 1993).

Hughes, Vera, *The Strange Story of Sarah Kelly* (Naas, 1988).

Hussey, Gemma, *At the Cutting Edge: Cabinet Diaries, 1982–1987* (Dublin, 1990).

Johnston, Sheila Turner, *Alice: The Life of Alice Milligan* (Omagh, 1994).

Jordan, Alison, *Margaret Byers* (Belfast, 1991).

Kohfeldt, Mary Lou, *Lady Gregory: The Woman Behind the Irish Renaissance* (London, 1984).

Lankford, Siobhán, *The Hope and the Sadness: Personal Recollections of Troubled Times in Cork* (Cork, 1980).

Levenson, Leah and Jerry Naderstad, *Hanna Sheehy Skeffington: A Pioneering Irish Feminist* (Syracuse, 1988).

Levine, June, *Sisters: The Personal Story of an Irish Feminist* (Dublin, 1982).

Lewis, Gifford, *Eva Gore Booth and Esther Roper: A Biography* (London, 1988).

————, (ed.), *The Selected Letters of Somerville and Ross* (London, 1989).

Linklater, Andro, *An Unhusbanded Life: Charlotte Despard, Suffragette, Socialist and Sinn Féiner* (London, 1980).

Luddy, Maria, (ed.), *The Diary of Mary Mathew* (Tipperary, 1991).

MacNéill, Máire, *Máire Rua: Lady of Leamaneh* (Clare, 1990).

Marreco, Anne, *The Rebel Countess: The Life and Times of Constance Markiewicz* (London, 1967).

MacBride, Maud Gonne, *A Servant of the Queen* (Suffolk, 1983 reprint).

McDowell, R. B., *Alice Stopford Green: A Passionate Historian* (Dublin, 1967).

McL. Côté, Jane, *Fanny and Anna Parnell: Ireland's Patriot Sisters* (Dublin, 1991).

Melville, Joy, *Mother of Oscar: The Life of Francesca Wilde* (London, 1994).

————, *Mother of Oscar: The Life of Francesca Wilde* (London, 1994).

Meehan, Helen, 'Ethna Carbey – Anna Johnston McManus', *Donegal Annual*, 45 (1993), pp 55–65.

Metscher, Pricilla, 'Mary Ann McCracken: a critical Ulsterwoman in the context of her times', *Études Irlandaises*, 14, 2 (1989), pp 143–58.

Missing Pieces: Women in Irish History (Dublin, 1983).

More Missing Pieces: Her Story of Irish History (Dublin, 1985).

Mulvihill, Margaret, *Charlotte Despard: A Biography* (London, 1989).

Ní Chinnéide, Máiréad, *Máire de Buitléir: Bean Athbheochana* (Baile Átha Cliath, 1993).

Ní Ghacháin, Máiréad, *(eag.), Lúise Gabhánach Ní Dhufaigh agus Scoil Bhríde* (Baile Átha Cliath, 1993).

Ó'Cléirigh, Nellie, 'Lady Aberdeen and the Irish connection', *Dublin Historical Record*, 39 (December 1985–September 1986), pp 28–32.

O'Neill, Marie, *From Parnell to de Valera: The Life of Senator Jennie Wyse Power* (Dublin, 1991).

O'Sullivan, Michael, *Mary Robinson; The Life and Times of an Irish Liberal* (Dublin, 1993).

Retrospections of Dorothea Herbert 1770–1806 (Dublin, 1988).

Rose, Marilyn Gaddis, *Katherine Tynan* (London, 1974).

Sheán, Bridhid Mhic, *Glimpses of Erin: Alice Milligan: Poet, Protestant, Patriot* (Belfast, 1994).

Smith, Bríd, 'Cissy Cahalan', *Labour History News*, 8 (Autumn 1992), pp 14–17.

Ten Dublin Women (Dublin, 1991).

Thomson, David and McGusty, Moyra, *The Irish Journals of Elizabeth Smith, 1840–1850* (Oxford, 1980).

Tillyard, Stella, *Aristocrats, Caroline, Emily, Louisa, and Sarah Lennox 1740–1832* (London, 1994).

Van Morris, Jacqueline, *Constance de Markievicz and the Cause of Ireland* (Amherst, 1967).

Ward, Margaret, *Maud Gonne: Ireland's Joan of Arc* (London, 1990).

Religion

Bitel, Lisa M., 'Women's monastic enclosures in early Ireland', *Journal of Medieval History*, 12 (March, 1986) pp 15–36.

Bolster, Sr. Angela M., (ed.), *Catherine McAuley in Her Own Words* (Dublin, 1981).

———, *Mercy in Cork, 1837–1987* (Cork, 1987).

———, (ed.), *The Correspondence of Catherine McAuley 1827–1841* (Cork, 1989).

Clear, Caitriona, *Nuns in Nineteenth-Century Ireland* (Dublin, 1987).

———, 'Walls within walls: nuns in nineteenth-century Ireland', in Chris Curtin et al, *Gender in Irish Society*, pp 134–51.

———, The limits of female autonomy: nuns in nineteenth-century Ireland', in Luddy and Murphy, *Women Surviving*, pp 15–50.

Condren, Mary, *The Serpent and the Goddess: Women, Religion, and Power in Celtic Ireland* (San Francisco, 1989).

Corish, Patrick J., 'Women and religious practice', in O'Dowd and MacCurtain, *Women*, pp 212–20.

Ebel Brozyna, Andrea, '"The cursed cup hath cast her down": constructions of female piety in Ulster evangelical temperance literature, 1863–1914', in Holmes and Urquhart, *Into the Light*, pp 154–78.

Fahey, Tony, 'Nuns in the Catholic church in Ireland in the nineteenth century', in Cullen, *Girls*, pp 7–30.

Hempton, David and Myrtle Hill, 'Women and Protestant minorities in eighteenth-century Ireland', in O'Dowd and MacCurtain, *Women*, pp 197–211.

Holmes, Janice, 'The "world turned upside down": women in the Ulster revival of 1859', in Holmes and Urquhart, *Into the Light*, pp 126–53.

Hoy, Suellen and Margaret MacCurtain, *From Dublin to New Orleans: The Journey of Nora and Alice* (Dublin, 1994).

Hoy, Suellen, 'The journey out: the recruitment and emigrationof Irish religious women to the United States, 1812–1914, *Journal of Women's History*, 6/7, 4/1, (Winter/Spring 1995), pp 64–98.

Hurley, Frank, 'Kinsale nuns in the Crimea: 1854–56', *Kinsale Historical Journal* (1986), pp 31–6.

Kenneally, James J, 'Sexism, the church, Irish women', *Éire/Ireland* (Autumn 1986), pp 3–16.

Kelly, Sr. M. St Dominic, *The Sligo Ursulines: The First Forty Years, 1826–1876* (Sligo, 1987).

Kilroy, Phil, 'Women and the reformation in seventeenth century Ireland', in O'Dowd and MacCurtain, *Women*, pp 179–96.

Luddy, Maria, 'Presentation convents in County Tipperary, 1803–1900', *Tipperary Historical Journal* (1992), pp 84–95.

Mahon, Evelyn, 'Women's rights and Catholicism in Ireland', *New Left Review* (1987), pp 53–77.

MacCurtain, Margaret, 'Towards an appraisal of the religious image of women', *The Crane Bag*, 4, 1 (1980), pp 26–30.

——, 'Fullness of life: defining female spirituality in twentieth century Ireland', in Luddy and Murphy, *Women Surviving*, pp 233–63.

——, 'Late in the field': Catholic sisters in twentieth-century Ireland and the new religious history', *Journal of Women's History*, 6/7, 4/, (Winter/Spring 1995), pp 49–63.

O'Connell, Marie, 'The genesis of convent foundations and their institutions in Ulster, 1840–1920', in Holmes and Urquhart, *Into the Light*, pp 179–206.

O'Dowd, Liam, 'Church, state and women: the aftermath of partition', in Curtin, *Gender in Irish Society*, pp 3–36.

Peckham, Mary L., 'Re-emergence and early development of women's religious orders in Ireland, 1770–1850', *Women's History Working Papers*, 3 (University of Wisconsin, Madison, 1990).

Sullivan, Mary C., 'Catherine McAuley's theological and literary debt to Alonso Rodriguez: the "spirit of the institute" parallels', *Recusant History*, 20, 1 (May 1990), pp 81–105.

Subject Index

347

General Index

Christian Brothers, 68, 119
Church League for Women's Suffrage for Anglican Women, 243, 283
Claidheamh Soluis, 305n
Clare, County, 26–7, 37, 38, 166–7, 330
Clarke, Thomas, 308
Clonfert, Co. Galway, 167
Clonmel, Co. Tipperary, 164, 169
    Clonmel Boarding School for Girls, 103–4
Clontuskert, Co. Galway, 167
Cloughjordan, Co. Tipperary, 40
Cobbe, Frances Power (1822–1904), 41–2, 46–7
Cobh, Co. Cork, 163, 240
Coleraine, Co. Derry, 324
Colum, Mary (1885–1957), 113, 115, 146
Congested Districts Board, 223
Connery, Meg, 275, 276, 277
Connolly, James (1868–1916), 297, 308, 309, 313, 320
Conservative and Unionist Women's Suffrage Association, 243, 283
Coolgreany, Co. Wexford, 330
Coote, Sir Charles, 161
Cork
    city, 19, 77, 89, 164, 179, 240, 247, 283, 295, 306, 315
        Cork Fever Hospital, 252
        Cork Gaol, 260
        English Market, 169
        Glanmire Industrial School, 132–3
        Hospital for Women and Children, 225
        Munster Civil Service College, 118
        Queen's College, 141
        Seminary for Young Persons Designed to be Governesses, 121–2
        Ursuline Convent, 106
    county, 37, 325, 330
Cork Ladies' Anti-Slavery Society, 251
Cork Ladies' Relief Society for the South of Ireland, 53–4

County Wexford Farmers' Association, 328
Cousins, James H. (1873–1956), 20–21, 273
Cousins, Margaret *see* Gillespie, Margaret
Coyle, Eithne, 304
Crimean Home, 185
Croke, Archbishop Thomas William (1824–1902), 262
Cumann na mBan, 243, 265, 304, 305, 306, 307–9, 314–16, 317, 318, 319
Curragh army camp, Co. Kildare, 199–202, 240, 255
Cusack, Margaret Anna (1832–99), 15–17

D'Alton, Catherine, 42–4
Daly, Edward, 307
Daly, Lilian, 142
Davidson, Margaret, 75
Davidstown, Co. Wexford, 329
Davis, Thomas (1814–1845), 298
Davitt, Michael, 260, 261, 305
Deane, Margaret E., 139
Derry (Londonderry), 158, 295, 324
    infirmary, 39
    Magee College, 139
    Strand House, 139
Devlin, Ann, 308
Dickson, Emily, 290–1
Dillon, John (1851–1927), 276, 277
Dingle, Co. Kerry, 306
Dockrell, Mrs Maurice, 295
Donaghmore, Co. Cork, 169
Donegal
    town, 158, 219–20, 221, 325
    county, 158, 209, 219–20
Doneraile, Co. Cork, 246
Downing, Ellen (1828–1869), 252
Drogheda, Co. Louth, 250, 295
    Dominican Convent School, 113
Drysdale, George (1825–1904), 32
Dublin, 74, 147, 230, 232, 244, 262, 271, 278, 295, 308, 312, 313, 329
    Abbey Theatre, 301
    Alexandra College, 90, 136, 137, 138, 151

Molony, Helena (1884–1967), 301, 309, 318
Monaghan
  Sisters of St Louis Convent School, 113
  Sparke's Lake Reformatory, 125–32
Morgan, Lady *see* Owenson, Sydney
Morony, Maria, 38–9
Morris, Elizabeth, 103
Moycullen, Co. Galway, 167
Mulally, Teresa (1728–1803), 89
Mullen, Madeleine Ffrench (1880–1940), 318
Mulvany, Isabella, 112, 138
Murphy, Mary, 12–13
Murray, Daniel, Archbishop of Dublin, 93, 94, 105

Naas Hospital, Co. Kildare, 201
Nagle, Nano (1718–1784), 89
Nation, The, 252, 253, 298n
National Association for the Promotion of Social Science, 181
National Board of Education, 68, 89, 94, 98, 100, 102, 119, 147, 149
National Federation of Women Workers, 233
National Union of Clerks, 233
National Union for Improving the Education of Women, 108–9
National Union for the Technical Education of Women, 102
National University of Ireland, 283
Navan, Co. Meath, 276
Newman, Florence, 234
Newmarket-on-Fergus, Co. Clare, 166
Newry, Co. Down, 15
Nun of Kenmare *see* Cusack, Margaret Anna

O'Brien, Kate (1897–1974), 145
O'Brien, William (1852–1928), 267, 287
O'Callaghan, Andrew (school inspector), 100
O'Connell, Daniel (1775–1847), 30–1
O'Connell, Mary (1778–1836), 30–1
O'Doherty, Kevin Izod, 253

Oldham, Alice (1850–1907), 136
Oldham, Mrs Charles, 273
O'Mahony, Nora Tynan (1865–1954), 17–19, 309–13
Orme, Eliza, 209
Owens, Catherine, 19–20
Owenson, Sydney (?1776–1859), 22, 47
Oylegate, Co. Wexford, 329, 330

Pankhurst, Christabel (1880–1958), 273
Pankhurst, Emmeline (1857–1928), 273
Pankhurst, Sylvia (1882–1960), 273
Parkes, Bessie Rayner (1829–1925), 205
Parnell, Anna (1852–1911), 242, 265
Parnell, Charles Stewart, 260, 264, 264n
Pearse, Patrick Henry (1879–1916), 305, 308, 313, 315
Pentrill, Mrs Frank (pseud. of Mrs Carew Rafferty), 45–6
Perolz, Maura, 300, 318
Pilkington, Ellice, 327
Plunkett, Joseph Mary, 313
Poor Clares, 15
Poor Servants of the Mother of God, 57
Portrane, Co. Dublin
  Richmond District Asylum, 225, 226
Potts, Sarah Jane, 73
Power, Jennie Wyse, née O'Toole (1858–1941), 265, 300
Primrose League, 292

Rathcoole, Co. Dublin, 170
Redmond, John (1856–1918), 242, 278, 287, 306–7
Reynolds, Hannah, 260, 262, 267, 268
Rooney, William (1872–1901), 304, 306
Roscrea, Co. Tipperary, 165
Royal British Nurses' Association, 225
Royal Commission on Labour, 174, 209
Royal Holloway College, London, 139